Marketing
Strategy

mi.ie

mi.ie

Marketing Strategy

Jim Blythe

 **Education**

THE McGRAW-HILL COMPANIES

London ● Boston ● Burr Ridge, IL ● Dubuque, IA ● Madison, WI ● New York
San Francisco ● St. Louis ● Bangkok ● Bogotá ● Caracas ● Kuala Lumpur ● Lisbon
Madrid ● Mexico City ● Milan ● Montreal ● New Delhi ● Santiago ● Seoul
Singapore ● Sydney ● Taipei ● Toronto

Marketing Strategy
Jim Blythe
ISBN 0077098420

 **Education**

Published by McGraw-Hill Education
Shoppenhangers Road
Maidenhead
Berkshire
SL6 2QL
Telephone: 44 (0) 1628 502 500
Fax: 44 (0) 1628 770 224
Website: www.mcgraw-hill.co.uk

British Library Cataloguing in Publication Data
A catalogue record for this book is available from the British Library

Library of Congress Cataloguing in Publication Data
The Library of Congress data for this book has been applied for from the Library of Congress

Acquisitions Editor: Tracey Alcock
Associate Development Editor: Catriona Watson
Editorial Assistant: Nicola Wimpory
Senior Marketing Manager: Petra Skytte
Production Editor: Eleanor Hayes
New Media Developer: Doug Greenwood

Produced for McGraw-Hill by Bibliocraft Ltd, Dundee
Cover design by Senate Design
Text design by Claire Brodmann
Printed and bound in Spain by Mateu Cromo

Brief Table of Contents

Detailed Table of Contents

Case Study List

Preface

Marketing has, for most of its history, been regarded as a tactical tool used to meet corporate objectives. It is only relatively recently, as firms have become more customer-focused, that marketing has been elevated to the status of a strategic philosophy in its own right.

In practice, of course, many firms still regard marketing as a function, subservient to the overall corporate mission. Many firms still only pay lip service to the idea of customer focus, relegating the customers to second or third place in the organization's hierarchy of stakeholders. Many strategy textbooks scarcely mention the customers, being much more concerned with competitors: many marketing textbooks scarcely mention the strategic overview which managers need to have if they are to chart a course through the 21st century business environment.

One of the difficulties inherent in strategic thinking is that there are no certainties. The business environment is changing rapidly (and perhaps always has done, though we like to pretend that change is a particularly 21st century phenomenon), and therefore the forward planning that is basic to traditional strategic thinking is all but impossible to achieve. This book tries to lay down a way of thinking, rather than a blueprint for success. Through the use of examples drawn from a wide range of industries, and through the use of challenging questions, it is an attempt to equip the managers of tomorrow with the mental tools needed to run modern organizations.

This book is written from the viewpoint of a former company director, now an academic. In the course of writing it, I have been helped considerably by a lot of people. I would like to thank Haydn Blackey, Robin Croft, and my other colleagues at Glamorgan Business School for their practical help and advice. I would like to thank Catriona Watson at McGraw-Hill and Tim Page for keeping the faith, and of course my wife Sue for listening to me complain about my workload.

Earlier on, I used the phrase "chart a course". Charting a course implies a steady progress, like that of a ship following lines on a chart. In fact, modern management is much more like white-water rafting, where rocks may suddenly appear, spray obscures the view, waves and eddies threaten to swamp the canoe, and everybody on board is screaming at once. I hope this book will help the reader to keep hold of the paddle – and enjoy the ride!

Additional material for lecturers and students including case studies, Power Point slides website links, and notes can be found at the following address:

www.mcgraw-hill.co.uk/textbooks/blythe

Guided Tour

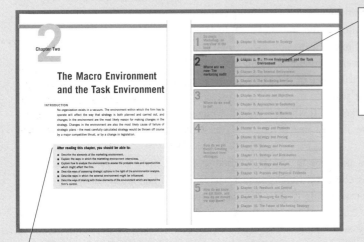

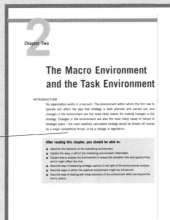

Map
A map can be found at the beginning of each Part and Chapter opener. This feature aims to help the reader navigate through the text, relating each chapter to others in the text, as well as the wider context of Marketing Strategy

Introduction
Each chapter opens with an introduction that sets the scene and introduces the reader to the issues that will be addressed in the chapter

Learning Objectives
Each chapter begins with learning objectives that identify the key concepts that you should understand and be able to apply when you have completed the chapter

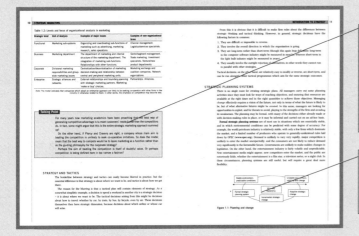

Talking Points
These boxes are integrated throughout each chapter and provide topics of discussion for lectures and seminars. They encourage students to reflect on, criticise and assess what they have learnt in the chapter

Figures/Tables
Each chapter includes a number of figures and tables to illustrate and summarise important concepts

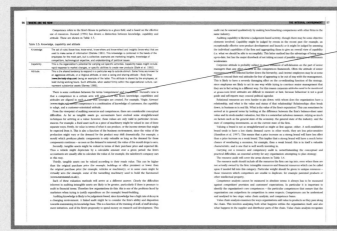

Web links
References to companies made throughout the text are supported by the company's website. These are highlighted in the text and encourage the reader to explore Marketing Strategy topics further through the use of the Internet

End of Chapter Case Study/ Questions
Each chapter ends with a case study that aims to illustrate the main themes of the chapter, allowing you to visualise marketing strategy in practice. Questions are found at the end of each case study to test your understanding of the case

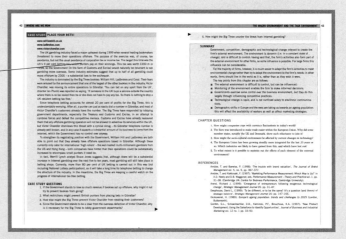

Summary
This section briefly reviews and reinforces the main issues covered in each chapter to ensure that you have acquired a solid understanding of the key topics

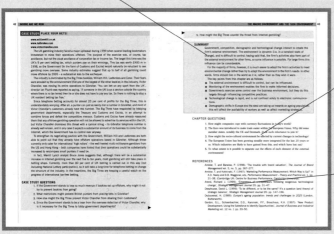

Chapter Questions
These short questions enable you to test your understanding of the main topics and issues discussed in the chapter

References
Each chapter ends with a full listing of the books and other sources referred to in the chapter, providing you with an opportunity to undertake further study and research into topics of interest

Acknowledgements

Our thanks go to the following reviewers for their comments at various stages in the text's development:

Declan Bannon, *Paisley University*
Geraldine Cohen, *Brunel University*
Nigel Culkin, *University of Hertfordshire*
Fiona Davies, *University of Cardiff*
Robert Duke, *University of Leeds*
Jenny Evans, *University of Hertfordshire*
Michael Flynn, *University of Gloucestershire*
Jeanne Hill, *University of Central Lancashire*
Steve Mitchell, *University of Gloucestershire*
D. O'Reilley, *Bradford University*
Bill Riley, *University of Central England*
Malcolm Sullivan, *Coventry University*
Roger Willets, *University of Northampton*
For permission to reproduce material in this book, we would like to thank the following:

1. The Marketing Audit on p. 19, Kotler, Armstrong, Saunders and Wong, (2001) *Principles of Marketing*, 3rd European Edition, p.100 © Pearson Education Limited 2001, reprinted by permission of Pearson Education Limited.
2. Figure 6.4 on p. 124, Parasuraman A., Zeithaml V.A, and Berry, L.L (1985) 'A conceptual model of service quality and its implications for future research' Reprinted with permission from *Journal of Marketing*, published by the American Marketing Association, Fall 1985 Issue 49, p 41-50.
3. Table 6.5 on p. 119, from Relationship Marketing by Christopher, Ballantyne and Payne. Reprinted with permission of Elsevier Science.
4. Figure 16.1 on p. 277, 'Generic Perspectives on strategy' in Richard Whittington; (2001) *What is Strategy - and does it matter?* Thomson Publishing Services has been reprinted with permission from Thomson Publishing Services, North Way, Andover, Hants, SP10 5BE.
5. Figure 16.2 on p. 279, 'Contexts for Strategy' in Richard Whittington; (2001) *What is Strategy - and does it matter?* Thomson Publishing Services p. 120 has been reprinted with permission from Thomson Publishing Services, North Way, Andover, Hants, SP10 5BE.
6. Table 6.2 on p. 111, Case study -- 'Internet Auctions' on p. 180-8, Case Study -- 'Lastminute.com' on p. 203-4, Case study -- 'Chapters Bookstore' on p. 215-6 all from Blythe, J. (2000) *Essentials of Marketing*, 2nd Edition © Pearson Education Limited 2000, reprinted with permission of Pearson Education Limited.

We have endeavoured to clear all permissions for material reproduced in this book. However, if you are aware of any outstanding permissions, please do not hesitate to contact us.

Dedication

To Sue, with love, and to Columbus, who knew exactly where he was going, ended up somewhere different, and still persuaded everybody the voyage was a great success.

Jim Blythe

Strategic Marketing

an overview of the book

This book is intended to provide a comprehensive view of current thinking on marketing strategy. The book is divided according to the stages in formulating and implementing strategy, beginning with an analysis of where the firm is now, moving through deciding where the firm should be going, and ending with an explanation of techniques for maintaining competitive position.

Strategy is discussed at four levels: the enterprise level, the corporate level, the business level, and the functional level. Each chapter contains discussion topics (called Talking Points) in which controversies are raised – these should be taken as questions for discussion, not as established fact.

The diagram overleaf shows the structure of the book.

Chapter 1 gives an overview of what strategy is about, and contrasts strategic decision-making with tactical decision-making.

Chapter One

Introduction to Strategy

INTRODUCTION

Strategy is not necessarily easy to define, and the precise nature of marketing strategy is a subject which is still (perhaps surprisingly) open to debate. The point at which marketing strategy leaves off and corporate strategy begins, and the point at which strategy leaves off and tactics begin, are equally vague and subject to argument. Because of the rapidly-changing nature of business life, strategy cannot be reduced to a set of simple rules and formulae which can be followed like a route map: strategic planning is a creative process, although some signposts and analysis tools can be applied which will help somewhat.

The richness of thinking about strategy, and about marketing strategy in particular, should not be seen as a barrier, but rather as a resource from which creative ideas can flow.

After reading this chapter, you should be able to:

- Explain some of the current thinking about the nature of strategy.
- Describe some of the theories explaining the relationship between marketing strategy and corporate strategy.
- Identify ways of distinguishing between strategy and tactics.
- Show how a customer orientation affects strategy.
- Explain the nature of the planning system.
- Explain the difference between top-down and bottom-up planning.
- Describe what should be contained in the marketing plan.

1	Strategic Marketing: an overview of the book	▶ Chapter 1: Introduction to Strategy
2	Where are we now: The marketing audit	▶ Chapter 2: The Macro Environment and the Task Environment ▶ Chapter 3: The Internal Environment ▶ Chapter 4: The Marketing Interface
3	Where do we want to be?	▶ Chapter 5: Missions and Objectives ▶ Chapter 6: Approaches to Customers ▶ Chapter 7: Approaches to Markets
4	How do we get there?: Creating functional-level strategies	▶ Chapter 8: Strategy and Products ▶ Chapter 9: Strategy and Pricing ▶ Chapter 10: Strategy and Promotion ▶ Chapter 11: Strategy and Distribution ▶ Chapter 12: Strategy and People ▶ Chapter 13: Process and Physical Evidence
5	How do we know we got there, and how do we ensure we stay there?	▶ Chapter 14: Feedback and Control ▶ Chapter 15: Managing the Process ▶ Chapter 16: The Future of Marketing Strategy

DEFINING STRATEGY

Unfortunately there is considerable disagreement among academics and practitioners about what strategy actually is. Although academics write about it, and practitioners do it, there is no real consensus about a definition of what it is (and, by extension, what it is not). Here are some examples:

'Strategies are means to ends, and these ends concern the purpose and objectives of the organization. They are the things that businesses do, the paths they follow, and the decisions they take, in order to reach certain points and levels of success.' (Thompson 1997).

'The positioning and relating of the firm/organization to its environment in a way which will assure its continued success and make it secure from surprises.' (Ansoff 1984).

'Strategy is making trade-offs in competing. The essence of strategy is choosing what not to do. Without trade-offs, there would be no need for choice and thus no need for strategy.' (Porter 1998).

Similarly, attempts have been made to distinguish between strategy and tactics by describing the features of either or both. Here are some examples.

Steiner and Miner (1977):

1. Importance. Strategic decisions are significantly more important than tactical ones.
2. Level at which conducted. Strategic decisions are usually made by top management.
3. Time horizon. Strategies are long-term; tactics are short-term.
4. Regularity. The formulation of strategy is continuous and irregular; tactics are periodic and fixed time, for example annual budget/plan.
5. Nature of problem. Strategic problems are usually unstructured and unique and so involve considerable risk and uncertainty. Tactical problems are more structured and repetitive and the risks easier to assess.
6. Information needed. Strategies require large amounts of external information, much of which relates to the future and is subjective. Tactical decisions depend much more on internally generated accounting or market research information.
7. Detail. Strategy broad; tactics narrow and specific.
8. Ease of evaluation. Strategic decisions are much more difficult to make.

Weitz and Wensley (1984) said:

'Strategic decisions at the corporate level are concerned with acquisition, investments, and diversification. At the business or SBU (strategic business unit) level, strategic decisions focus on how to compete in an industry or product market. . . . . . . Strategic decisions at the business level are concerned with selecting target market segments and determining the range of products to offer.'

The divergence of opinion about what strategy is is only the beginning: there is also considerable debate about almost all the key issues in strategy. For this reason, it is not feasible to present strategy as a series of steps which can be followed in order to achieve a strategic objective – any attempt to do so is likely to leave out substantial areas of current strategic thinking.

Talking Point

Point 6 of Steiner and Miner's list says that strategic decisions are based on external information, much of which is subjective, whereas tactics rely on objective market research. If strategic decisions are more important than tactical ones (point 1), and are taken by senior management (point 2), then presumably decisions based on market research are less important than those taken by senior management, based on subjective information.

This, of course, conflicts with the marketing concept, which implies that all decision-making begins by looking at the customers' needs. So how is this apparent conflict to be resolved? Could it be that strategy is subjective, and tactics objective? Could it be that the marketing concept does not apply to strategic decision-making?

Or could it simply be that marketing (and strategy) sometimes rely on subjective, creative impulses?

Of course, some of the conflicts which appear in the literature are a result of differing angles on the problem rather than fundamental conceptual difficulties. Some authors are writing about strategy at the highest level of the organization, others are writing about strategic activities which take place at lower levels. Although strategic decisions are usually taken at the highest levels, decisions which affect strategic outcomes are taken at all levels of the organization. Some authors advocate that organizations recognize this, and devolve some strategic decision-making downwards.

This makes the study of strategy somewhat complex. One approach might be to study the theories first, then see how to apply them to particular areas of strategic decision-making; the other would be to begin with the decision-making areas and study how the theories apply to those areas. The main advantage of the latter approach is that it enables the student to see how theories relate to each other when applied in the real world. The former approach would tend to imply that the theories are always mutually exclusive or conflicting, which is clearly not always the case.

In fact, theoreticians are often offering up differing theories because they are examining different parts of what is a highly complex structure.

THE PURPOSE OF STRATEGIC PLANNING

The purpose of strategic planning is to work towards the organization's objectives. For most organizations, this translates into gaining some form of competitive advantage. For some organizations, this is linked to profitability; for others it may be linked to growth in market share, to increasing shareholder value, to achieving stability in an unstable market, to developing a particular reputation within an industry, or to any one of a large number of possible objectives.

Given the rapid changes that most organizations are experiencing at present, planning may seem like a futile exercise, but an organization with no strategic plan rapidly finds itself lacking in direction. The key issue in strategic planning is to give the organization a co-ordinating framework within which managers can apply tactical decision-making. The days when senior management could hand down instructions which would be obeyed to the letter are gone: junior managers, and even front-line employees such as receptionists, salespeople and delivery drivers are often empowered to make on-the-spot decisions in order to fine-tune customer care. Some of these decisions may have strategic consequences in the longer term, but this does not make them strategic decisions. The overall strategic plan is what gives the organization its direction, and enables such grass-roots tactical decisions to be made in the light of an overall plan.

THE NATURE OF STRATEGY

Strategy has three dimensions: process, content and context (Pettigrew and Whipp 1991). The process element is concerned with the ways in which strategy comes about: it is about the how, why and when of strategy. The content of strategy is concerned with the 'what' of strategy: what is, or should be, the strategy for the company and its subdivision?

The context of strategy is about the 'where' of it: the environment in which the strategy takes place and must succeed. This includes the internal environment of the organization.

These three dimensions constitute different perspectives on strategy, rather than different components – in other words, each dimension cannot be considered in isolation.

Strategy Process has often been portrayed as a linear progression through analysis, formulation and implementation. In the analysis stage, the environment is examined in terms of threats and opportunities; strategic options are identified in the formulation stage; and in the implementation stage the formulation is put to the test of being applied in practice. There is an underlying assumption that the process is rational – that the planners are working to a set of decision-making rules, and that the process is one of careful consideration. In fact, this is often not the case – much strategic thinking is intuitive or even emotional, and good strategic thinking is certainly creative, and therefore unlikely to be linear. Secondly, the process is often messy, with planners re-examining the formulation in the light of experience obtained from the implementation, and even going back to the analysis stage if experience throws up new evidence. This is, of course, a sensible approach. Strategies are therefore formed incrementally in an iterative process, subject to change in the light of experience. Thirdly, strategy is unlikely to be comprehensive, in other words it will not necessarily cover all the aspects of the organization's activities.

Strategy Content is likely to differ widely between organizations, and writers on strategy tend to agree that each strategy is unique. Three fundamental levels of strategy exist within organizations: the functional level, which is about the strategic decisions being made by the different departments within the organization; the business level, which seeks to integrate the functional strategies within a profit centre or strategic business unit; and the corporate level, which seeks to integrate strategies from all SBUs. In some cases there will be a higher level, perhaps an industry level, where organizations group together to achieve a common overall goal. Examples of this type of industry-level strategy might be trade organizations which seek to improve the status of industries.

One of the conceptual difficulties involved in considering marketing strategy is that it may be considered by some organizations to be a functional-level issue. This view is seriously out-of-date, but still seems to be common in practice: many firms claim to be customer-centred, but in fact only pay lip service to the marketing concept. For other, more customer-orientated firms, the marketing strategy actually is the corporate strategy. From a PR viewpoint at least, the industry-level strategy may very well consist almost entirely of marketing objectives. In the case of customer-orientated firms, the marketing strategy may be the corporate strategy, then there may be a business-level group of strategies based around SBUs, with (below them) the advertising strategy, the PR strategy, the pricing strategy, the product portfolio strategy, and so forth.

Strategy Context is concerned with the environment within which the strategy has to be implemented. It comprises the internal environment (the organizational structure and culture, the attitudes of staff, and so forth); the industry environment (levels of competition, structure of the industry, power relationships between suppliers and intermediaries); and the international environment (levels of foreign competition, opportunities for internationalization, restrictions on supplies of raw materials or sales of finished products).

Organizations exist to fulfil a purpose: strategy is intended as a guide towards reaching that purpose. The purposes of organizations vary greatly, even in the business world: although it is commonly supposed that businesses exist in order to make profits, it is quite clear that many company directors see making profits as being a survival tactic to ensure that the firm keeps going in order to meet other objectives. For other members of the organization, for example the employees, the organization may exist in order to provide jobs, or to serve the public: most company mission statements refer to almost anything other than making a profit. This means that the organizational context of the strategy may be more complex than at first supposed – and this is even more likely to be the case when dealing with not-for-profit organizations. The conflict between meeting the interests of shareholders (who are likely to be interested in profits and capital growth) and meeting the interests of other stakeholders (staff, customers, suppliers etc.) is one which is a subject of much debate – and it is even debatable whether such a conflict exists at all, if a long-term view is taken.

Hax (1990) identified six dimensions of strategy, as shown in Table 1.1.

Table 1.1: Six dimensions of strategy

Dimension	Explanation
Strategy as a coherent, unifying, and integrative pattern of decision.	Strategy is the major force which provides a comprehensive blueprint for the organization's efforts, and which allows each function to integrate with the others.
Strategy as a means of establishing an organization's purpose in terms of its long-term objectives.	Long-term objectives need to be defined, and this is often contained within the firm's mission statement.
Strategy as a definition of the firm's competitive domain.	This is about defining what business the firm is really in. For example, is it a bus company, or is it in the transportation business? Is it an oil company, or is it in the energy business? These definitions are important for defining the firm's competitive position.
Strategy as a response to external opportunities and threats, and to internal strengths and weaknesses.	The well-known SWOT analysis is often the basis for decision-making about survival issues.
Strategy as a logical system for differentiating management tasks at corporate, business, and functional levels.	The overall strategy allows managers to understand their own part of the process: at the corporate level, to look at tasks which require the fullest scope; at the functional level to develop appropriate competences; and at the business level to enhance competitive position.
Strategy as a definition of the economic and non-economic contribution the firm intends to make to its stakeholders.	Stakeholders refers to everyone who is directly or indirectly affected by the firm's actions. For most organizations, taking care of stakeholders is essential to survival.

Note: Ultimately, the organization's strategy is what holds it together and gives it its continuity.

MARKETING STRATEGY AND CORPORATE STRATEGY

If marketing strategy is seen as a functional area, concerned only with the 4 Ps (or 7 Ps) of marketing: product, price, place, promotion, people, process and physical evidence (Booms and Bitner 1981), corporate strategy would stand above marketing strategy in the hierarchy, so that the overall corporate strategy would inform, if not dictate, the marketing strategy or strategies. In a truly customer-orientated firm, the corporate strategy and the marketing strategy are indistinguishable since the company's whole approach is dictated by the marketplace.

Marketing strategists tend to agree that marketing should represent the guiding philosophy of the organization rather than being confined to a functional role (Webster 1992, McKinsey 1993). Piercy and Cravens (1999) go so far as to say that the marketing organization is not only concerned with the management of the interface between the organization and its environment, but deals with intra-organizational relationships as well as inter-organizational alliances. In the Piercy and Cravens model, marketing strategy and corporate strategy are presumably indistinguishable.

In this model, the marketing strategy is the overall guide for the functional strategies, so that the finance strategy, the production strategy, the personnel strategy, and the functional marketing strategies are all dictated by the market. This might mean, for example, that the firm judges its success by the loyalty of its customers, by its brand image, or by its market share rather than by its profitability or turnover. It may mean that the personnel department recruits people who are themselves customer-orientated. It may mean that the production department takes its lead from the market researchers rather than the scientific researchers.

The fundamental basis of marketing is that organizations exist to satisfy the needs of the people on whom they depend for their survival, which usually means the customers and consumers of the products, but of course might also mean employees, shareholders, and government departments. Only in this way can the organization encourage the exchanges between itself and those on whom it depends, and thus survive and grow. In strategic terms, this means that need-satisfying objectives will take precedence over other objectives, since they are instrumental in achieving the most basic objective of all, which is the survival of the organization.

Marketing management comprises the following elements:

1. Identifying needs among those on whom the organization depends.
2. Developing methods of meeting those needs – products or activities which do so.
3. Promoting those products to customers in order to demonstrate how their needs will be met.
4. Handling the exchange processes which result.
5. Monitoring the overall process to ensure that changes in customer needs or competitive activity have not made the solutions inappropriate.

The marketing strategy will encompass all of these elements, and give the process coherence.

Piercy and Cravens (1999) offer a model which illustrates the level and focus of organizational analysis in marketing. This is shown in Table 1.2

Table 1.2: Levels and focus of organizational analysis in marketing

Strategic level	Unit of Analysis	Examples of major issues	Examples of new organizational forms
Functional	Marketing sub-systems	Organizing and coordinating sub-functions of marketing such as advertising, marketing research, sales operations.	Channel management. Logistics/services specialists.
Business	Marketing department	The department of marketing and internal structure of the marketing department. The integration of marketing sub-functions. Relationships with other functions.	Sector/segment management. Trade marketing. Investment specialists. Venture/new product departments.
Corporate	Divisional marketing responsibilities and group-wide marketing issues	Centralization/decentralization of marketing decision-making and relationship between central and peripheral marketing units.	Marketing exchange and coalition companies. Network organizations.
Enterprise	Strategic alliances and networks.	External relationships and boundary-spanning with strategic marketing partners. Marketing 'make or buy' choices.	Partnerships. Alliances.

Note: The model indicates that companies which adopt an enterprise approach are likely to be seeking co-operation with other firms in the industry or otherwise related to them: in other words, the emphasis on competition may become less.

Talking Point

For many years now marketing academics have been preaching that the best way of generating competitive advantage is to meet customers' needs better than the competitors do. In fact, some might argue that this is the entire strategic marketing approach summed up!

On the other hand, if Piercy and Cravens are right, a company whose main aim is beating the competition is unlikely to seek co-operative initiatives. So does the model mean that the best way to compete would be to leave marketing as a function rather than as the guiding philosophy for the corporate strategy?

Perhaps the aim of beating the competition is itself of doubtful value. Or perhaps competition is being defined here in too narrow a fashion?

STRATEGY AND TACTICS

The borderline between strategy and tactics can easily become blurred in practice, but the essential difference is that strategy is about where we want to be, and tactics is about how we get there.

The reason for the blurring is that a tactical plan will contain elements of strategy. As a somewhat simplistic example, a decision to spend a weekend in another city is a strategic decision – it is about where we want to be. The tactical decisions arising from this might be decisions about how to travel: whether by car, by train, by bus, by bicycle, even by air. These decisions themselves then have strategic dimension, because decisions about which airline or whose car will arise.

From this it is obvious that it is difficult to make firm rules about the differences between strategic thinking and tactical thinking. However, in general, strategic decisions have the following factors in common:

1. They are difficult or impossible to reverse.
2. They involve the overall direction in which the organization is going.
3. They are long-term rather than short-term (though this again begs definition: long-term in the computer software industry might be measured in months, whereas short-term in the light bulb industry might be measured in years).
4. They usually involve the outright rejection of alternatives, in other words they cannot run in parallel with other strategies.

Tactical decisions, on the other hand, are relatively easy to modify or reverse, are short-term, and can be run alongside other tactical programmes which aim for the same strategic outcomes.

STRATEGIC PLANNING SYSTEMS

There is no single route for creating strategic plans. All managers carry out some planning activities since they must look for ways of reaching objectives, and ensuring that resources are available at the right times and in the right quantities to achieve those objectives. Managing change effectively requires a vision of the future, not only in terms of what the future is likely to be, but of what alternative futures might be created. In this sense, managers are looking for opportunities to exploit, and for threats to avoid, playing to the strengths of the firm and avoiding its weaknesses. The planning may be formal, with many of the decisions either already made or with decision-making rules in place, or it may be informal and carried out on an ad-hoc basis.

Formal strategic planning systems are of most use in situations which are essentially stable, and in which environmental conditions can be predicted with some degree of accuracy. For example, the world petroleum industry is relatively stable, with only a few firms which dominate the market, and a limited number of producers who operate to generally-understood rules laid down by OPEC (**www.opec.org**). Demand is unlikely to vary very rapidly, major competition is unlikely to enter the market unexpectedly, and the consumers are not likely to reduce demand very significantly in the foreseeable future. Governments are unlikely to make sudden changes in legislation. On the other hand, the entertainment industry is fairly volatile and unpredictable. New entertainment media might appear, new competitors enter the market, and the public are notoriously fickle, whether the entertainment is a film star, a television series, or a night club. In these circumstances, planning systems are still useful, but will require a great deal more flexibility.

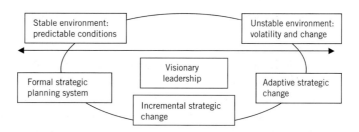

Figure 1.1: Planning and change

In this context, **visionary leadership** has a place. The visionary leader, who has a clear idea of where the organization should be going, often has a firm grasp of the products, services and approaches that customers and other stakeholders will find acceptable. Examples of such visionary leaders include Sir Richard Branson, head of Virgin (**www.virgin.net**), Anita Roddick of Body Shop (**www.the-body-shop.com**) and Alan Sugar of Amstrad (**www.amstrad.com**). In each case these leaders have a vision of where the organization should be going, and have been able to adapt the strategy as necessary to lead the firm onwards. It should be said that such leaders are rare, and also that, even when they do exist, the vision sometimes does not match up to the needs of the stakeholders.

Some organizations will be characterised by **adaptive strategic change**, in which managers throughout the organization are encouraged to look for opportunities and threats and to innovate at the business level. The rationale for this is that those at the grass roots of the organization are likely to be nearer to the customers and to the problems, and therefore are in a better position to formulate rapid responses. This type of strategic planning favours firms in unstable or rapidly-changing environments, since adaptation will happen much faster. Chaos theory (Stacey 1993) implies that intentional strategies are too inflexible for dealing with an inherently chaotic world, and therefore reliance on a tightly-structured plan will lead to stagnation. Adopting an adaptive approach involves extensive decentralization, empowerment and accountability of managers throughout the organization, and the adoption of a more organismic organization structure, in which responsibility and power devolve onto those most able to deal with the current problem facing the organization. In this scenario, strategies emerge from the day-to-day running of the organization, not from a prepared position.

Incremental strategic change is a halfway house between the fully-planned system and the adaptive system. The strategic leadership provides the overall direction, but strategies can emerge from within the decentralized system of the organization. Managers need to meet regularly, both formally and informally, to discuss progress and changing trends: they will plan new courses of action, and then try them out in small stages to see whether they are effective or not. For this system to work, managers must communicate freely with each other and operate on a team basis: they also need to learn from their own and each others' mistakes. This implies that the organization must be tolerant of mistakes, which of course is not always the case. According to Mintzberg (1989), managers need to have access to a quantity of appropriate information in order to formulate strategy, and the implementers of strategy must have sufficient power to be able to make the necessary changes in the organization.

The systems described above are not mutually exclusive, and in fact it is not unusual to find more than one system operating within the same organization. Much depends on the individual management style of the people involved: a junior manager with a strong personality may well choose to ignore or pervert a strategic plan which seems unrealistic, so that the planned strategy actually becomes adaptive. Equally, circumstances may dictate a switch in strategic planning style – a change in the environment may force a company to establish a formal plan for dealing with a crisis, or equally may destroy an existing formal plan and cause a switch to an incremental approach. Whatever happens, it is useful to remember that strategic planning does not happen in isolation: no battle plan survives first contact with the enemy, and no strategic plan is ever set in concrete. Therefore the plan needs to be monitored in action, and systems need to be in place to revise the plan as necessary when deviations occur or when circumstances so dictate. In other words, planning is not a linear process: it is cyclical, as shown in Fig 1.2.

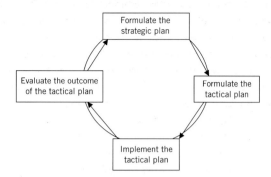

Figure 1.2: The cyclical nature of planning

THE WRITTEN DOCUMENT

At some point in the strategic planning process it will become necessary to commit the strategy to paper. Broadly, there are three categories of written statement: the vision statement, the mission statement, and the objectives statement. An individual organization may not have a written statement in all of these categories: commonly, organizations only have a mission statement.

A **vision statement** describes what the company is to become in the long-term future. The essential elements focus on those values to which the organization is committed, and often sets appropriate standards of conduct for employees. Sony's (**www.sony.com**) vision statement, for example, states the following: 'Sony is a trail blazer, always a seeker of the unknown. Sony will never follow old trails, yet to be trod. Through this progress Sony wants to serve mankind.'

A **mission statement** contains the reason for the organization's existence. It states what the organization seeks to achieve. Ackoff (1986) suggests that a mission statement should have the following five characteristics:

1. It will contain a formulation of objectives that enable progress towards them to be measured.
2. It differentiates the company from its competitors.
3. It defines the business(es) that the company wants to be in, not necessarily is in.
4. It is relevant to all the stakeholders in the firm, not just the shareholders and managers.
5. It is exciting and inspiring.

Mission statements should reflect corporate values: the statement should clarify the purpose of the organization. For example, a company's purpose might be to maximize earnings for the shareholders (although use of the word 'maximize' is not helpful in setting an objective). On the other hand, a University's mission statement might include a statement to the effect that it exists in order to develop and disseminate knowledge.

Mission statements should help in creating competitive advantage by ensuring that managers (and indeed other employees) throughout the organization are 'singing from the same songsheet'. The hidden benefit of the mission statement is that it forces the organization's senior managers (and others) to give consideration to the issues contained in it – it is very easy to assume that the organization's reason for existing is obvious, when in fact it is not obvious to all those involved. Additionally, it is by no means unusual for there to be disagreement about what the organization's purpose ought to be, even when senior managers have laid down clearly what its purpose is.

The **objectives statement** is a statement of the immediate long and medium-term objectives of the organization usually linked to specific timescales. An objective must be measurable, otherwise it is merely an aim or a reason for behaving in a particular way and thus belongs in a vision statement or a mission statement rather than in an objectives statement. The objectives statement gives a set of clear, measurable outcomes to judge performance by: the objectives might be open as in British Airways' (**www.british-airways.com**) objective to 'enhance the value of shareholders' investments by achieving steady and remunerative growth' or they may be closed, as in Kirin Breweries' (**www.kirin.com**) objective to 'increase sales of non-beer products to 60 per cent of total revenue during the 1990s'.

The objective statement is the most likely document to be changed over time, as new objectives become apparent, as old objectives are achieved, and as the environment throws up new opportunities and threats. The mission statement may need to be adapted periodically also, but the overall vision of what the organization is about should rarely, if ever, change. Even such major international companies as Boot's Chemists (**www.boots-plc.com**) have managed to maintain the original vision of the founder, Jesse Boot, in seeking to provide cheap self-medication for the general public.

CASE STUDY: IBM, TOM WATSON, AND THE VISION

www.ibm.com

In 1914 a new chief executive was appointed to run the ailing Computer Tabulating Recording Company: this man was Thomas J. Watson. Watson changed the name of the company to International Business Machines, a rather more exciting name, and began to institute his vision about what the ideal company should be. Watson introduced a vision which was, at the time, revolutionary, and which still inspires a degree of awe almost 90 years later. The principles under which Watson formed the company were:

1. The individual must be respected.
2. The customer must be given the best possible service.
3. Excellence and superior performance must be pursued.

These were always referred to as the Three Basic Beliefs, and indeed the company ran with a cult-like zeal for more than 70 years – IBMers were encouraged to socialise with each other, not with the outside world, they were bombarded with slogans such as 'Time lost is time gone forever', 'There is no such thing as standing still', and of course the famous 'Think!'.

He is quoted as saying: 'I want the IBM salesman to be looked up to. Admired. I want their wives and children to be proud of them. I don't want their mothers to feel that they have to apologise for them when asked what their sons are doing.'

For Watson, individuals make a difference. From the beginning, IBM has had a policy of promoting from within, and of using extreme reluctance to fire anyone. Non-performers are occasionally fired of course, but Watson preferred to move them to other departments or retrain them, believing that every IBM staff member has some talent which can be put to use. There are no titles on the doors of IBM executives, no separate executive toilets, and no reserved parking areas for senior managers. During the Depression of the 1930s no IBM staff were laid off at any time.

IBM's respectful approach even extends to competitors. While it is acceptable for IBM people to talk about the quality of their own products, there is to be no 'knocking' of the competition, and no boasting about the size of the company or the number of technical people available to help solve customers' problems.

Further visionary strictures laid down by Watson were:

▶

▶ 1. IBM would provide the best service in the world, of ANY company, not just its competitors.
2. Complaints must be responded to promptly, and preferably solved, within 24 hours.
3. Each new IBM product must be superior to the one it replaces.
4. Each manager must receive 40 hours a year of training, minimum.

The vision has been carried down through the company. Al Williams, a former IBM president, said 'It is not bigness we seek, it is greatness. Bigness is imposing. Greatness is enduring.'

The end result of this visionary approach to business is that IBM is one of the world's largest and most successful corporations, with the power to engender intense loyalty among its staff: stories about IBM loyalty are legion. There is the story of the Second World War bomber commander, who had been drafted from his job at IBM, who ordered the planes not to bomb IBM plants in Germany. There is the story of the IBMer, at a meeting far from his home, who happened to mention to Watson that his wife was ill, to which Watson replied 'Well, what are you doing here, then? Get home!' Watson paid the man's fare home and sent flowers to his wife.

On the other side of the coin, Watson imposed strict rules of behaviour. He required employees to be well-groomed, he encouraged marriage (on the grounds that married men would work more diligently in order to support their families), he discouraged smoking and banned alcohol altogether. IBM tends to hire young people, fresh from university, so they can be indoctrinated into the IBM Way. Some observers have compared joining IBM to entering a monastery, or signing up for the Army. IBM is a complete way of life – yet one that has provided extremely well for its employees. IBMers are confident that they are working for the world's best corporation: if the growth and success rate of the company are anything to go by, they may well be right.

CASE STUDY QUESTIONS

1. Why is there no mention of profitability in Watson's Three Beliefs?
2. What factors in IBM's philosophy might be responsible for generating such strong staff loyalty?
3. What personnel problems might arise in IBM's pursuit of cult status?
4. What are the marketing advantages of IBM's approach?
5. IBM went through a series of setbacks and retrenchments in the 1980s and 1990s. What might account for this?

SUMMARY

Strategy is a complex concept, with a definition which is open to debate and often misunderstood. The key elements are that it is concerned with the overall character and direction of the organization, rather than with the detail of how to maintain that character and arrive at a destination.

The key points from this chapter are as follows:

- Strategy consists of process, context and content.
- Strategy is about where the organization is going: tactics is about how to get there.
- Planning systems may be formal, visionary, adaptive, or incremental – they do not all have to comprise a formal or indeed structured planning system.
- The written plan may have a vision statement (about the character of the organization), a mission statement (about the direction in which the firm is going) and an objectives statement (containing specific, measurable outcomes). The plan might not contain all of these elements.

CHAPTER QUESTIONS

1. How might a company maintain the continuity of the founder's vision after the founder retires or dies?

2. Consider the music business. Which type of strategic planning system might work best, and why?

3. In a truly customer-orientated company corporate strategy and marketing strategy are identical. Why is this?

4. Why is it difficult to distinguish between strategy and tactics?

5. How does a strategic plan enable an organization to co-ordinate its efforts?

REFERENCES

Ackoff, R.L. (1986): *Management in Small Doses* (London: John Wiley).

Ansoff, H. Igor (1984): *Implementing Strategic Management* (Prentice Hall).

Booms, B.H. and Bitner, M.J. (1981): 'Marketing strategies and organization structures for service firms', in *Marketing of Services*, J. Donnelly and W.R. George, eds. (Chicago II: American Marketing Association).

Hax, A.C. (1990): 'Redefining the Concept of Strategy and the Strategy Formation Process', *Planning Review*, May/June pp. 34–40.

'Marketing's Mid-Life Crisis', *The McKinsey Quarterly*, 1993.

Mintzberg, H. (1989): *Mintzberg on Management* (New York: Free Press).

Pettigrew, A. and Whipp, R. (1991): *Managing Change for Competitive Success* (Oxford: Basil Blackwell).

Piercy, N. and Cravens, D.W. (1999): 'Marketing organization and management', in *Encyclopaedia of Marketing* pp. 186–207. (London: International Thomson Business Press).

Porter, M.E. (1998): *The Competitive Advantage of Nations* (London: Macmillan).

Stacey, R.D. (1993): 'Strategy as order emerging from chaos', *Long Range Planning* vol. 26 no. 1, pp. 10–17.

Steiner, G. and Miner, J. (1977): *Management Policy and Strategy: Text, Readings and Cases* (New York: Macmillan).

Thompson, John L. (1997): *Strategic Management: Awareness and Change* (London: Thomson).

Webster, E. (1992): 'The changing role of marketing in the corporation', *Journal of Marketing*, October.

Weitz, B.A. and Wensley, R. (1984): *Strategic Marketing* (Boston, MA: New-Publishing).

Where are we now

The marketing audit

In order to find a route to where we want to be, we first need to know where we are now. The tool for doing this is the marketing audit, shown in the diagram which follows. Following the marketing audit gives planners a clear idea of which issues need to be addressed: it is a useful practical exercise in identifying weaknesses, but also in identifying the strengths and resources which the firm has at its disposal.

The following three chapters are devoted to different aspects of the marketing audit, and provide a fuller explanation of the advantages, disadvantages and difficulties of auditing the firm's current position.

The Marketing Audit

Main Areas	Sub-sections	Issues to be addressed
MARKETING ENVIRONMENT AUDIT		
Macro-Environment	Economic-Demographic	Inflation, materials supply and shortages, unemployment, credit availability, forecast trends in population structure.
	Technological	Changes in product and process technology, generic substitutes to replace products.
	Political-legal	Proposed laws, national and local government actions.
	Cultural	Attitude changes in the population as a whole, changes in lifestyles and values.
	Ecological	Cost and availability of natural resources, public concerns about pollution and conservation.
Task Environment	Markets	Market size, growth, geographical distribution, profits, changes in market segment sizes and opportunities.
	Customers	Attitudes towards the company and competitors, decision-making processes, evolving needs and wants.
	Competitors	Objectives and strategies of competitors, identifying competitors, trends in future competition.
	Distribution and dealers	Main trade channels, efficiency levels of trade channels.
	Suppliers	Availability of key resources, trends in patterns of selling.
	Facilitators and marketing firms	Cost and availability of transport, finance, and warehousing; effectiveness of advertising (and other) agencies.
	Publics	Opportunity areas, effectiveness of PR activities.
MARKETING STRATEGY AUDIT	Business mission	Clear focus, attainability.
	Marketing objectives and goals	Corporate and marketing objectives clearly stated, appropriateness of marketing objectives.
	Strategy	Core marketing strategy, budgetting of resources, allocation of resources.
MARKETING ORGANIZATION AUDIT	Formal structure	Seniority of marketing management, structure of responsibilities.
	Functional efficiency	Communications systems, product management systems, training of personnel.
	Interface efficiency	Connections between marketing and other business functions.
MARKETING SYSTEMS AUDIT	Marketing information system	Accuracy and sufficiency of information, generation and use of market research.
	Marketing planning system	Effectiveness, forecasting, setting of targets.
	Marketing control system	Control procedures, periodic analysis of profitability and costs.
	New product development system	Gathering and screening of ideas, business analysis, pre-launch product and market testing.
MARKETING PRODUCTIVITY AUDIT	Profitability analysis	Profitability of each product, market, territory and distribution channel. Entry and exit of segments.
	Cost-effective analysis	Costs and benefits of marketing activities.
MARKETING FUNCTION AUDITS		
	Products	Product portfolio: what to keep, what to drop, what to add, what to improve.
	Price	Pricing objectives, policies and strategies. Customer attitudes. Price promotions.
	Distribution	Adequacy of market coverage. Effectiveness of channel members. Switching channels.
	Advertising, sales promotion, PR	Suitability of objectives. Effectiveness of execution format. Method of determining the budget. Media selection. Staffing levels and abilities.
	Sales force	Adequate size to achieve objectives. Territory organization. Remuneration methods and levels. Morale. Setting quotas and targets.

Source: Kotler, Armstrong, Saunders and Wong, (2001) *Principles of Marketing*, 3rd European Edition, p.100 © Pearson Education Limited 2001, reprinted by permission of Pearson Education Limited.

Establishing the starting-point for the planning process is not necessarily easy. The marketing audit appears to be a simple matter of ticking boxes, but in fact it requires a considerable degree of judgement, of objectivity, and of honesty on the part of those collecting and supplying the information.

For example, functional managers may be reluctant to admit to problems within their departments, fearing that their own status might be at risk. Information may be biased, or it may be designed to cover up shortcomings on the part of staff, or it may be intended to provoke a response from senior management which will be beneficial to the person supplying the information. Since the supply of information is, in many cases, subject to judgement on the part of the managers, there is really no way of ensuring its authenticity.

Having said that, there is no doubt that managers need to start somewhere. Problems can be minimised by triangulation, in other words by obtaining the necessary information from several sources and cross-referencing it in order to 'tune out' any discrepancies. This will not, of course, remove all sources of bias, but should improve objectivity. The bottom line, as always, is that management is not an exact science.

Chapter Two

The Macro Environment and the Task Environment

INTRODUCTION

No organization exists in a vacuum. The environment within which the firm has to operate will affect the way that strategy is both planned and carried out, and changes in the environment are the most likely reason for making changes in the strategy. Changes in the environment are also the most likely cause of failure of strategic plans – the most carefully calculated strategy would be thrown off course by a major competitive thrust, or by a change in legislation.

After reading this chapter, you should be able to:

- Describe the elements of the marketing environment.
- Explain the ways in which the marketing environment interrelates.
- Explain how to analyse the environment to assess the probable risks and opportunities which might affect the firm.
- Describe ways of assessing strategic options in the light of the environmental analysis.
- Describe ways in which the external environment might be influenced.
- Describe ways of dealing with those elements of the environment which are beyond the firm's control.

STRUCTURE OF THE EXTERNAL ENVIRONMENT

The external environment within which the organization operates is composed of a large number of elements. These can be conveniently grouped as shown in Fig 2.1.

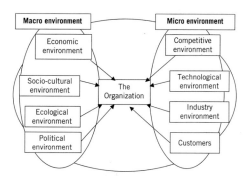

Figure 2.1: Elements of the external environment

ECONOMIC ENVIRONMENT

Most national economies follow the boom-and-bust cycle: every seven or eight years the economy goes into recession, which means that production of goods and services shrinks and unemployment rises. During periods of recession consumers will reduce purchases of major capital items such as houses, cars, fitted kitchens and washing machines: equally, businesses will postpone purchases of major equipment, and will not be looking to expand. The management of demand in the economy has become very much a government responsibility during the last 70 years or so, since the great Depression of the 1930s.

Like most elements of the external environment, the macro economy is extremely difficult for organizations to influence, let alone control. National governments seem to be unable to control the boom-and-bust cycle, and only the very largest of firms are able to influence government economic policy. At present, the main instrument of economic control which governments use is the level of interest rates. Interest rates control the economy in two ways: firstly, raising the rates encourages money dealers to buy the currency in order to take advantage of the higher interest rates. This in turn raises the value of the national currency because demand for it increases; this reduces the costs of imports, and increases the cost of exports, which causes the national economy to slow down and also reduces inflationary pressures. This is shown in Fig 2.2.

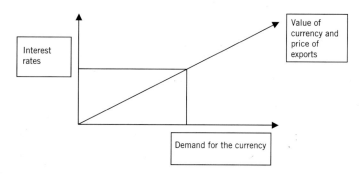

Figure 2.2: Effects of a rise in interest rates

Secondly, a rise in interest rates makes individuals and businesses reluctant to borrow money, and also raises the cost of servicing loans, which removes spending power from the economy and thus reduces inflationary pressure. A cut in interest rates has the reverse effects: exports become more competitively priced, imports become more expensive, the national economy is boosted and unemployment falls. Unfortunately, this also feeds inflation and raises the cost of raw materials. Managing the economy is therefore a fine balancing act between ensuring that the currency retains its value, and ensuring that the country retains enough economic stability to maintain the standard of living of its population.

The impact of economic changes can be assessed in many ways. The Treasury provides forecasts periodically: these are based on their own econometric models. Some universities and business schools also publish information and forecasts, but since these are usually based on different models they may well offer different predictions. Banks, City institutions and the financial press also make predictions, and spokespeople from various institutions are often quoted on TV or in newspapers. Two problems arise here: the first is that predicting the future is always difficult because there are too many factors to take into account, and secondly the effects of economic change will differ according to the company's individual circumstances. For example, a company with a major emphasis on exporting will be adversely affected by a rise in the value of the pound since this will make the products less competitive in overseas markets. On the other hand, a company which sells mainly in the home market but which imports raw materials, would gain greatly from a rise in the pound as this will make its raw materials cheaper.

Micro economics deals with exchanges at the individual level, and is intimately linked with marketing. The macro economic climate will dictate how much money people are able and willing to spend, but micro economics also includes factors such as level of competition, and opportunity costs. Economists have contributed the concepts of supply and demand (whereby prices tend to rise if demand exceeds supply and falls if supply exceeds demand), the concept of marginal utility (whereby the extra use the customer is able to gain from purchasing further units tends to reduce) and the concept of indifference (the degree to which one product can substitute for another). Although micro economics do not explain all aspects of buyer behaviour, since social and psychological factors are also involved, the contribution is considerable.

CUSTOMER ANALYSIS

The rational approach favoured by economists assumes that customers, whether they are end consumers or industrial buyers, follow a reasoned and logical process when buying. Although this may be true in some cases, especially for those products which are purchased infrequently, psychological and social elements also influence buyer decision-making. Although these elements are beyond the scope of this book, they may form part of the basis for analysing the customer base. Segmentation is the key to analysing customers: being able to group customers with similar needs enables the marketing strategist to decide which customers are likely to be the most productive to target. There is more on segmentation in Chapter Six.

Analysing the customer base is a process of asking who they are, what do they buy, where do they buy it, how do they buy it, when do they buy it, and (perhaps most importantly) why do they buy? This process needs to be carried out for the customers of the firm itself, and also for competitors' customers wherever possible. This type of analysis is basic to marketing thinking, but it needs to be carried out within the framework of what the business is able to achieve: in other words, the firm's capability to deliver customer satisfaction must form part of the equation.

Creating a customer-led or customer-centred business ethos is not as simple as it might at first appear. This is because it is generally much easier to focus on the needs of the organization (and even the personal aspirations of the managers) than it is to anticipate and meet customer needs. Measuring corporate success in terms of customers seems to be even more problematical: most firms report their successes in financial terms rather than in customer-based terms. For example, annual reports will emphasize such issues as return on capital employed, profit on turnover, stockturn rate and so forth. A truly customer-centred firm might be expected to judge its success on customer retention, return on advertising investment measured in terms of new customers recruited, and the rate at which the customer base is replaced (customer churn rate) (Ambler and Kokkinaki 1997). These measures are rarely reported, although some City analysts now pay attention to them, since they are proving to be better predictors of a company's future prospects, both in profitability and in long-term survival.

The move from financial to non-financial measures of success has advanced considerably throughout the 1990s: such measures as customer satisfaction, customer loyalty, and brand equity have received considerable academic attention. Calculating the lifetime value of customers is a half-way measure, since it is a way of reporting a non-financial issue in financial terms (Wyner 1996). Brand equity has been moved from its former position, expressed on the balance sheet as the global 'goodwill' of a firm, to a position in which there has been a change in the UK's financial reporting regulations to accommodate it (Ambler and Barwise 1998).

TALKING POINT

Most firms talk about being customer-centred, but how deep is that commitment likely to be? After all, each firm is made up of people who have bills to pay and careers to build: not to mention that businesses are financed by shareholders and banks who also expect to get a return. Presumably a business which is really customer-centred will put the customers' interests ahead of everybody else, and will quickly find that it has no employees and no financial backing!

Or perhaps the situation is a little more complex than that. Do businesses merely say that they are putting customers first in order to lull the customers into a false sense of security? Or perhaps they actually put shareholders first, but see customer satisfaction as the instrument for achieving profitability? Perhaps there is a delicate balancing-act going on, with the managers acting as a clearing-house for pressures generated by the various stakeholders, with each stakeholder being told what he or she wants to hear?

In practice there is no doubt that money is an important measure of success for firms, but it is not the final purpose, or reason for the existence, of most firms, at least not if the mission statements and vision statements of most organizations are to be believed.

COMPETITION

One of the most important elements in the micro environment is the existence and nature of competition. Competitors are organizations which seek to meet our customers' needs better than we can: the assumption is that, if they succeed in this aim, they will eventually take our customers away and destroy the support for the business.

Taking this broad view of competition means that some competitors may not actually be in the same industry. For example, cinemas compete with pubs and television companies as well as with other cinemas: each organization provides entertainment, which is the basic consumer need being met. Organizations often do not realize that such competition can take away their customers until it is too late. A prime example of this is the way that the Internet has made inroads into the entertainment industry, not just in terms of delivering music, video and the printed word in a more convenient format than the traditional routes, but also in the way that surfing the Net has become a popular pastime, especially among younger consumers.

Table 2.1: Competitive structures

Type of competitive structure	Economic Assumptions	Examples
Perfect competition	There is a large number of suppliers, no one of which is powerful enough to influence the supply level overall. Products are homogeneous. There are few barriers to market entry. Suppliers and consumers have full knowledge of the market.	Examples of perfect competition are rare: few marketers would be dealing with such markets. A typical example is international money markets.
Monopolistic competition	One major supplier has used a differentiated marketing approach to obtain a large share of the market, but other competitors can still enter the market.	McDonald's (**www.mcdonalds.com**) dominate the world's hamburger market, but other firms can still enter.
Oligopoly	A few companies control the market almost entirely. This tends to happen when there are high barriers to entry; often the possible market share which could be captured by a new entrant will not justify the capital cost of entry. Oligopolies are often investigated by government monopoly regulators, who exist to ensure that large firms do not abuse their power.	Commercial aircraft manufacture. The detergent industry. Oil extraction and refining.
Monopoly	A single firm has a product with no close substitutes. This situation is as rare as perfect competition; few examples are permitted by government regulators, and are usually 'natural monopolies' which would clearly not be efficient if effort were duplicated.	Rail networks in most countries, utilities such as water supply, postal services.

There are four basic competitive structures, as show in Table 2.1.

Michael Porter's Five Forces model offers a model for competitor analysis (Porter 1990). The five forces are:

1. The bargaining power of suppliers. If suppliers have strong bargaining power, competitive pressure will be greater.

2. The bargaining power of customers. Customers with strong bargaining power will be more demanding and will set one supplier against another: this will make competition fiercer.

3. The threat of new entrants. Preventing new firms from entering the market will mean that existing firms will need to maintain a competitive edge.

4. The threat of substitute products and services. If there are close substitutes for the products on offer, competitive pressure will be greater. This is a danger which is often not recognized by firms: classic examples include the film industry, which did not recognize television as competition until it was far too late, and more recently the failure of postal services to recognize competition from e-mail.

5. The rivalry among current competitors. In some industries, suppliers have a 'live and let live' philosophy which reduces competition. This is particularly the case in oligopolistic markets. If, on the other hand, rivalry is strong, each firm will be trying to grab a bigger market share and competition will be stronger as a result.

Predicting the behaviour of competitors can be difficult. Each is likely to be trying to offer something different (although there will undoubtedly be some followers and me-toos) but because the competitive environment is dynamic, and firms are understandably secretive about their plans, the exact form of such differentiation will be subject to frequent change. Planners also often forget that any attempt to challenge a competitor, particularly a market leader, is likely to lead to retaliation – strategists therefore need to plan one or two moves ahead. Industry analysis seeks to examine the industry as a whole and assess the relative positions of the companies within it.

The threat of new entrants is mitigated considerably by the existence of barriers to entry. Low entry barriers mean that competitors can easily enter the market: high entry barriers usually mean that few will attempt entry, and those that do will meet with a rapid response from the established firms in the industry. Examples of barriers to entry are these:

1. Economies of scale. If the industry is such that production can only be carried out economically if it is undertaken on a large scale, it is difficult for new firms to enter because they would need to obtain a substantial market share in order to be competitive against established firms. This is obviously the case for such industries as petroleum refining, but it is also true even when there is not a large requirement for start-up capital: e-commerce companies (e-tailers and dot.com firms) have sometimes found to their cost that, although the start-up costs are minimal, the cost of establishing a presence in the market is prohibitive.

2. Product differentiation. A key issue in creating a barrier to entry is that of product differentiation. New entrants to the market need to find some differentiating feature or benefit of their products in order to distinguish them from existing products: these benefits must be perceived as advantageous by customers in the market, or no business will result. Establishing a presence may well require substantial investment in promotion in order to publicize and explain the features and benefits – this may also provide a financial barrier to entry.

3. Capital requirements. The european detergent market is dominated by Procter & Gamble (**www.pg.com**) and Unilever (**www.unilever.com**): this is because of the capital cost of the plant needed to manufacture detergents. It is extremely difficult for new firms to enter the market because the market share such a new entrant might obtain would be unlikely to be sufficient to repay the capital cost of starting up. Procter & Gamble was only able to enter the market in the first place because of its domination of the american market, which allowed the firm to support an expansion into Europe. This is one of the forces which leads to globalization: firms are able to expand into overseas markets by using profits from their existing markets to support the new venture.

4. Switching costs. These are the costs incurred by a customer when switching from one supplier to another. This is particularly relevant in industrial markets, where a buyer may have established a good relationship with a supplier, and may be reluctant to take the risk of switching to a new, untried supplier. There may be other costs in terms of establishing new procedures, perhaps retraining staff, changing delivery and materials handling systems, and so forth. Switching costs have been reduced in the computer industry by adopting industry standards: hardware and software producers have collaborated to

ensure that all software will run on all machines, and all peripheral equipment is compatible with all machines.

5. Access to distribution channels. Often the distribution channels are under the control of one or other member (not necessarily the manufacturer). This makes it difficult or impossible for a newcomer to obtain distribution for products. Even if there is no restrictive agreement in place, there may be a switching cost incurred for some or all of the channel members.

6. Cost advantages independent of scale. Sometimes firms within an industry will have access to raw materials, or perhaps own patents, which give them a cost advantage over entrants. Such advantages have nothing to do with the scale of the operation.

For firms entering a new industry, an additional barrier is likely to be the threat of retaliation by firms already within the industry: such retaliation may take the form of price cutting, restricting access to distribution or raw materials, or the establishment of new products which pre-empt the entrant. To assess possible retaliation, the entrant should examine the past behaviour of the established firms, the level of commitment existing firms have to the market (in other words the amount they have to lose by allowing a competitor in), and the rate of growth of the industry. In a fast-growing industry, existing firms are likely to feel less threatened by competitors, on the basis that there will be more than enough business to go round, and it might not be possible to service the whole market anyway.

The bargaining power of suppliers, if it is high, can squeeze industry profits. The power of suppliers is determined by the following factors:

1. Concentration among suppliers. If there are few suppliers, the buyers have very little scope for bargaining: the suppliers in such circumstances can operate oligopolistically, setting prices either through collusion (which is illegal in most countries) or by tacit agreement not to compete on price (which is extremely common). In such circumstances the prices will always be higher than they would otherwise have been: strangely, profits are not necessarily higher. The lack of a need to compete often makes managements complacent and inefficient.

2. The degree to which suppliers' products can substitute for each other. A buyer might be forced to use a particular supplier simply because other suppliers cannot meet the same product specification.

3. Vertical integration. This is the degree to which the supply chain is, or can be, bought or controlled by one of its members. A vertically-integrated industry such as oil refining, where the same company controls the entire supply chain from extraction through refining to the garage forecourt, does not allow much chance for independent companies to enter the market.

4. The importance of the buyer to the supplier. Buyers who are much larger than suppliers will have the power in the relationship: where suppliers are much larger, the buyers can only exercise power by grouping together in some way.

5. Switching costs. If the buyers' switching costs are high, the suppliers occupy a powerful position.

The bargaining power of buyers is the reciprocal of the bargaining power of suppliers: competitive action by buyers will depress industry profits, but co-operation (or even vertical integration) with buyers can be mutually beneficial.

The bargaining power of retailers has led to the huge growth in own-label brands: some retailers, notably Tesco's (**www.tesco.com**) have several competing own-label brands aimed at different market segments. Bargaining power of travel agencies eventually led the tour operators to merge with, or acquire, their own agencies.

Bargaining power is determined by the following factors:

1. The concentration and size of the buyer. Large supermarket chains have strong buying power since they usually control a very substantial share of the market.
2. Buyers' involvement in the purchase. If the purchase must be of a specific quality, or be supplied at a specific price, the buyer's power becomes less and the supplier's power becomes greater.
3. The degree of product standardization. In a highly-standardized market such as that for PCs the buyer has a great deal of power since one product can substitute for another. In a market such as antiques, the buyer has rather less power – each product is probably unique.
4. Switching costs. Again, it may be expensive or difficult in some industries for buyers to switch supplier easily.
5. The possibilities for vertical integration. Vertical integration not so much reduces power in the relationship, but rather removes it from the equation altogether.

The threat of close substitutes entering the market is an ever-present one for most companies. The presence of substitutes affects the elasticity of demand for products: the fewer substitutes, the less elastic the demand. Predicting the entry of close substitutes, and even recognizing them when they enter the market, can be much harder than one might expect: for example, the entry of home video recorders might have been seen as creating even further competition for pubs, clubs and other entertainment venues. In fact there is some evidence to indicate that these organizations have benefited from home VCRs because people have been able to move their favourite programmes or movies to times which do not interfere with going out for the evening.

Competitive rivalry (or what Porter calls 'jockeying for position') may take the form of price competition, promotional competition, or product differentiation. In some cases, rival firms may have considerable co-dependency due to links with suppliers, distributors, and even the public: in some cases it is necessary to consider the reputation of the industry as a whole. This means that any competitive action will need to be considered in the light of possible retaliation. The intensity of competition will depend on the following factors:

1. The degree of concentration in the industry, in other words the number of competitors. The fewer firms in an industry, the greater the likelihood of oligopolistic or monopolistic competition.
2. The rate of growth of the industry. Rapidly-growing industries are subject to less competitive pressure, because firms can easily increase the size of their markets without having to seek growth by grabbing market share from competitors. When there is enough business to go round, there is little pressure to compete.
3. The degree of differentiation. If the product is homogeneous (for example, petrol) firms either have to become oligopolistic, or they have to compete on price. Oil companies periodically enter price wars, but quickly return to the 'status quo' under which prices remain close. Supermarkets conduct a virtual price war, in which each claims to offer lower prices, but in fact (apart from a few loss leaders) the overall price level remains similar across the board.

4. Cost structures. If fixed costs are high (for example because the industry is capital intensive or because it uses a large amount of real estate) profits are dependent on maintaining a high volume of sales. The breakeven point is higher, and therefore firms become price-sensitive when it might appear that they would otherwise be operating at less than full capacity. An example of this is the airline industry, which has high costs in terms of leasing or buying aircraft, and therefore cannot afford to have 'planes standing idle or flying half-full.

5. Investment structures. If the industry is one in which new investment has to be made in sizeable blocks (for example, the major hotel industry), an increase in supply will almost certainly impact very unfavourably on other firms in the industry until demand catches up. For example, if there are three major hotels in a town and a fourth one opens up, each of the existing three might expect to experience a 25 per cent drop in occupancy levels (even if the market is shared equally). This means that, given the capital intensive nature of the business, those hotels might well be forced into a loss-making position until the market increases sufficiently to restore their occupancy levels.

6. Competitive information. This is the extent to which firms are aware of their competitors' strategies. If business is conducted in a transparent manner, firms are able to take account of each others' activities. This will almost certainly lead to oligopolistic or monopolistic competition, and (depending on how the information is exchanged) may be illegal in most countries. Monopoly regulators generally take a dim view of companies exchanging information and making agreements to fix the market.

7. Strategic objectives of competitors. Sometimes different firms in the same industry may have aims which do not conflict with other firms. For example, one firm may be concerned with winning a mass market, whereas another may be interested in the exclusive or luxury end of the market. Ford (**www.ford.com**) does not compete strongly with Rolls Royce, for example, nor does Cartier (**www.cartier.com**) compete with H. Samuel (**www.hsamuel.co.uk**). In fact, such firms may find that their main competition comes from outside the industry: Harley-Davidson (**www.harley-davidson.com**) does not regard Honda (**www.honda.co.uk**) as serious competition in the motorcycle market, but it does regard home-improvement companies and swimming-pool manufacturers as competition. The reason is that the average Harley rider is a male in his mid-50s, reliving his lost youth: his wife, meanwhile, would rather spend the money on a new kitchen or double-glazing.

8. Cost of leaving the industry. In some cases, the downside of leaving an industry can be very high. Capital equipment valued at millions on the firm's books may have virtually zero second-hand value, for example. This makes it impossible for a firm to leave the industry without also leaving behind its assets, and thus going bankrupt. The steel industry or the mining industry might be examples – once a steel mill closes, it is unlikely to re-open.

The result of the jockeying for position described by Porter is that firms will, eventually, fall into one of the following positions:

1. Market leader. This is the firm which has the bulk of the market, and which sets the general price level and tone of the industry. For such a firm, the emphasis will be on maintaining its position, while at the same time avoiding the attentions of the monopoly regulators.

2. Market follower. This is a firm which has a respectable share of the market, but which is content to avoid a direct conflict with the market leader.

3. Market challenger. This is a firm which intends to overthrow the market leader one day. Typical strategies for market challengers would be strong differentiation, or sometimes cost leadership.

4. Cost leader. Cost leadership is not necessarily incompatible with any of the other positions, nor does it necessarily imply the lowest prices: costs and prices do not bear any relationship to each other, since the former is determined by the firm's situation and the latter is (ultimately) determined by what customers are prepared to pay.

Competitive advantage is usually considered to be at the core of strategic thinking. The reason that business strategists borrow so much terminology from the military strategists is that business has traditionally been thought of as a battle for supremacy between competing organizations.

According to Porter (1985), there are two basic strategic choices, depending on what the company is seeking to achieve. In the first instance, companies may compete by achieving a lower cost base than their competitors. This in turn can be turned into increased market share through lower prices, or increased profitability allowing the firm to increase its promotional spend or expand its production capacity. In the second instance, companies may seek to differentiate their products by offering added value in an area which the customers regard as important. Provided that the cost of adding the value is less than the premium the consumers are prepared to pay for it, the firm will again increase profitability and/or market share.

From a marketing viewpoint, there are three generic strategies, as follows:

■ Cost leadership. Here the company achieves the lowest cost base. Examples are EasyJet (**www.easyjet.com**) (the cheap airline) and Lidl (**www.lidl.de**) (the Germany-based low-cost supermarket).

■ Differentiation. The company offers a wide range of different brands each of which appeals to a different market segment. Examples are Nestlé (**www.nestle.com**), which offers a range of several hundred different food brands, and Ford, which offers a range of vehicles for different uses and different markets.

■ Focus strategy. Here the company focuses on one small segment or a very limited range of segments. Within this, the company might seek low costs or differentiation. Examples are Sock Shop (**www.sockshop-group.co.uk**), Knickerbox (**clayton.merseyworld.com/ knicker**), and McDonald's.

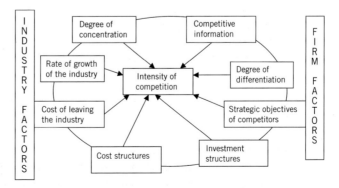

Figure 2.3: Competitive intensity factors

To obtain maximum advantage from cost leadership the firm must be *the* cost leader: there is only room for one firm in this position. Competition for market leadership is likely to be based on price, which may in turn squeeze profit margins – in a price war it is the firm with the deepest pockets which wins since profits quickly become losses in those circumstances. However, cost leadership does not necessarily equate to low prices. Some firms prefer to invest the extra profits in establishing their brands, and since low-price products are often perceived as being of low quality, cutting prices may actually be counter-productive in terms of establishing the brand. Low cost companies may also be able to provide well for employees and shareholders: cost cutting is not always to be equated with penny-pinching or with low profit margins. Some firms achieve low costs by extensive automation, for example, or by introducing more efficient working practices. An example of this is the Toyota (**www.toyota.com**) car manufacturing company, whose ability to maximize use of capital equipment and to operate a zero-defect policy on the production line mean that its costs are far below those of equivalent european or US manufacturers.

Differentiation strategies involve developing a wide range of products to suit different market segments: inevitably this will lead to a higher cost base, since economies of scale in production will be lost and a greater capital investment in equipment will be needed. This means that a differentiation strategy and a cost-leadership strategy are mutually exclusive in most cases, but exceptions do exist. Differentiation creates superior performance by offering a unique, or at least very different, solution for each group of customers.

Focus strategy involves concentrating on one small group of customers. A focus strategy may combine well with a cost leadership strategy, but is mutually exclusive of a differentiation strategy. Firms following a focus strategy usually do so either because they have limited resources, or because the largest segments of the market are already tied up by firms operating a differentiation or cost-leadership strategy.

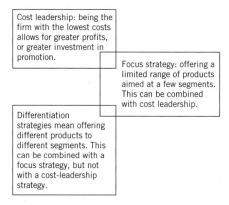

Figure 2.4: Generic strategies

Fig 2.4 shows the relationship between the different generic strategies.

The problem with this type of thinking is that it ignores the development of co-operative strategies, and the build-up of strategic alliances. These developments have become much more commonplace in recent years, particularly as customers have come to expect a degree of standardization within some industries.

For example, 30 years ago the controls of cars were far from standardized. Although most cars had the accelerator, brake and clutch in a right-to-left configuration, gear positions varied between models, and some cars even had the gear lever mounted on the steering-column.

Headlamp dip switches might be on stalks, on the dashboard, or even on the floor as a foot switch. During the intervening period, consumer preferences and pressures have led manufacturers to standardize control layouts, since this removes a barrier to purchase: motorists do not have to learn to drive again whenever they get into a new car. Car hire firms have also played a role in this: from their viewpoint, allowing a driver to set off in a car with unfamiliar controls is not a good idea.

Another example is the computer industry. In order to sell peripherals and software, the hardware and operating systems must be standardized. Development and production costs are clearly dramatically lower for everybody if all the components are mutually exchangeable. By conforming, firms demonstrate legitimacy: by differentiating, firms reduce competition. This principle applies to most industries, from kitchen appliances to nuclear reactors.

Striking a balance between similarity and differentiation is therefore an exercise in examining the structure of the entire industry and its relationship with the customers, and balancing the pressures accordingly (Deephouse 1999). The evidence from research is that moderate amounts of strategic similarity will increase legitimacy, especially for market followers, and this in turn will improve performance overall. In either direction there are likely to be diminishing returns, so that increasing differentiation can lead to a lowering of performance. This is shown diagrammatically in Fig 2.5.

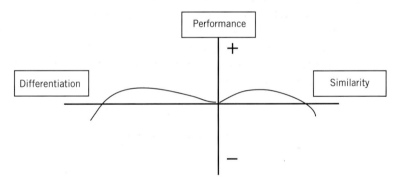

Figure 2.5: Performance trade-offs between differentiation and similarity

As the firm becomes more differentiated, performance will at first improve: this would be equally true if the firm becomes more similar to other firms. After a while, however, the advantages of differentiation begin to reduce as the firm moves further away from the mainstream of the industry. Equally, if the firm decides on a strategy of increasing similarity, eventually performance will reduce as competition becomes stronger.

From a planning viewpoint this theory is somewhat difficult to use in practice, since it is difficult to be sure exactly where the firm is on the continuum between similarity and difference.

The second development which tends to negate Porter's view of competition is that of increasing co-operation, particularly at international level. Co-operation is sometimes approached with caution by major firms because of the possibility that the partner firm may be using a 'Trojan horse' strategy, in which the partnership only lasts long enough for the incoming firm to learn about the market, and how to out-compete the incumbent partner. In fact, research evidence shows that this is not as common as is often feared (Hennart et al. 1999). Co-operation with competitors may, in the long run, be far more effective in increasing performance than would be expensive attempts to fight over what may well be a diminishing group of customers.

TALKING POINT

Marketers often extol the virtues of being different from competitors, of having a unique selling proposition, and of adding value to the product. For example, airlines originally offered frequent flyer programmes to encourage loyalty, but now any frequent flyer will join the programme of whichever airline he or she happens to be flying with. Ever-improving in-flight meals, seating, check-in procedures and so forth have been matched by other airlines, leaving few ways in which to differentiate. This has left the market wide open to basic, no-frills airlines such as EasyJet, which consistently shows a profit and flies at 82% capacity even in times of recession. (In the same week in 2001 in which Swissair (**www.swissair.com**) was grounded due to an inability to pay for fuel for its fleet, EasyJet reported a 27% increase in passenger bookings.) Does this mean that marketers got it wrong? Do customers really prefer not to be confused by all the extra frills? Should they perhaps all move closer to the EasyJet system? Or should they each go for a different niche instead of trying to fit several different market segments onto one aircraft?

Co-operation may be a desirable strategy in some industries, but regulatory problems may arise if it is carried out between firms operating within a single country, due to monopoly regulations.

POLITICAL AND LEGAL ENVIRONMENT

The political and legal environment affects firms in the following ways:

1. Government policies affect the way the economy is run. In particular, governments see it as part of their role to manage demand in the economy so as to control inflation and maximize employment.
2. Equally, the economy dictates government policy.
3. Different political parties apply different emphases to regulating business. In general, right of centre governments (Conservative, Republican, or Christian Democrat) tend to reduce regulation on businesses and favour employer interests, whereas left of centre governments (Labour, Democrat, or Socialist) tend to increase legislation and favour employee interests.
4. Case law, which is decided by judges, often changes the rules or introduces new pitfalls for firms without actually being ratified by governments.
5. Taxation law can make big differences to the way business is conducted. Some business methods attract bigger tax liabilities than others – it is sometimes worthwhile to run the business in an inherently less efficient way because tax breaks more than compensate for the lost profits.

Small and medium sized firms are unlikely to be able to exercise much direct influence over government policy: larger firms and trade organizations are able to influence decision-making by lobbying politicians and by making representations through the civil service. Politicians can be influenced, however. On a practical level they need to act in ways that curry favour with the electorate in order to be re-elected, but on a more personal level the majority of politicians actually want to improve the lives of the people of their countries – most are not as self-centred as the media might have us believe. This means that they are open to ideas which might make business function more efficiently, or which might make life easier for staff or customers.

The legal situation is often complex: company law changes through legislation, but more importantly is changed by courts as they decide particular cases. Sometimes laws can be interpreted in ways which open up or close loopholes, or which create new liabilities for companies and their directors. Sometimes practices which have been commonplace are ruled to be unacceptable, or new practices need to be adopted to avoid pitfalls. Firms have virtually no control over this: the independence of the judiciary is one of the cornerstones of justice in most western countries.

Government legislation will affect industries in a global way, but it is probably the case that governments affect individual businesses most by having an effect on the five forces which determine the competitive environment. During the 1980s most governments in the industrialized world went through a period of deregulating private industry and privatizing publicly-owned industry. The welter of regulation which had built up around businesses since the end of the Second World War was largely swept away, and the remainder streamlined. At the same time, governments seized on the idea of selling off nationalized industries and state assets as a way of raising funds without raising taxation. This was a key factor in defeating the hyper-inflation of the 1970s and restoring national economies to reasonable health.

Reducing restrictions and regulations in the airline industry created an aggressive competitive environment for firms. When the US airline industry was deregulated in 1976 the result was (at first) a burgeoning of cheap airlines and extremely low-cost airfares: at one point it was perfectly feasible to live in San Francisco and commute daily by air to Los Angeles, 600 miles away. The $7 air fare was simply not a factor. By the late 70s, the situation had settled down to the point where six major airlines controlled the long-haul routes, with smaller airlines acting as feeders to regional hubs. This meant that, for example, a journey from Baltimore to Portland, Oregon, might involve flying a short distance to New Jersey or New York, flying coast-to-coast from New York to San Francisco, then flying another short hop to Portland. This arrangement was efficient, but (not surprisingly) led to oligopolistic competition. Meanwhile, the transcontinental bus companies disappeared altogether and even the rail system has to be kept alive with massive subsidies.

The lessons of the US experience were not lost on EU regulators, and deregulation has been carried out with rather less abandon. EU countries have the power to implement 'open skies' agreements (the UK has such agreements with Ireland and the Netherlands), but there is no general 'open-skies' arrangement. Cheap carriers must still obtain route approval from the national governments of member states as well as approval from airports and air traffic control, but governments are under pressure not to withhold such permissions except on safety grounds. Airlines are also prevented from using monopoly power to exclude other airlines from airport facilities: even in cases where the airline also owns the airport, it is not allowed to use this power to the detriment of competitors.

TECHNOLOGICAL ENVIRONMENT

The type of technology available within the industry will dictate the competitive environment because creative use of new technology is what often gives firms their competitive advantage. This does not necessarily mean the use of electronic information technology, although there has been a great emphasis on this area in recent years. For example, Toyota's creative use of heavy engineering technology to re-tool stamp mills overnight (rather than the months needed by its American competitors) enabled the firm to make much more effective and flexible use of its capital equipment. This meant that the firm could respond much more quickly to changes in demand for different models of vehicle, simply by re-tooling to manufacture more of a particular body shape, and also reduce dramatically the number of stamp mills needed to form body parts.

Technological breakthroughs can create new industries almost overnight: the invention of the mountain bike is a case in point. Increasing use of these bicycles has resulted in a resurgence of cycling both as a recreation and as a means of transport: consequently, services for selling and maintaining mountain bikes have grown up, and also routes through mountainous areas have become popular for the sport. Sales of helmets, cycling clothing, and accessories have also rocketed, and at the same time other forms of transport have been affected adversely, even if only to a small extent.

TALKING POINT

Theory on the adoption of innovative products by consumers shows that there is a considerable cost (and risk) attached to buying 'the latest model'. Since there is also a large cost attached to being an innovative firm, particularly in terms of retooling and R&D costs, might it not be better for all concerned if innovation was suppressed?

And yet we find each new scientific breakthrough greeted with cries of delight from all sides. Is this because firms are always seeking an innovative edge in order to differentiate themselves? In the light of the research quoted earlier, which shows that co-operation and similarity might also improve performance, even the rush to differentiate might be a false move!

Because technology has such a large effect on industries, most large corporations fund research and development departments in order to stay ahead of their competitors (Roberts 1999). For some firms – 3M (**www.3m.com**) and Sony (**www.sony.com**) being prime examples – maintaining a technological lead is a part of the company's mission. Both firms take pride in being at the forefront of technology, and gear the entire firm's efforts towards achieving this end. At the other end of the scale, many small firms owe their existence to technological breakthroughs. Research shows that some large firms do not apply new technology even when they have the capability to do so, preferring to leave the new market to the smaller new entrants (Arend 1999).

SOCIO-CULTURAL ENVIRONMENT

The social and cultural environment of the country encapsulates demands and tastes of consumers, fashions in thought and behaviour, and trends in demography. These issues clearly affect consumption behaviour, but they also affect employees' attitudes and behaviour. This is an important consideration when setting up subsidiaries in other countries: firms should not assume that cultural conditions which apply in the home country will also apply in the new country, even in circumstances where the language is the same. For example, the cultural differences between Britain and the US are marked, and business practice differs greatly between the two countries. The same applies to Portugal and Brazil, or to Spain and Argentina.

The socio-cultural environment changes as a result of business activities, especially through the entertainment media. Changes in British culture since the Second World War have come about in part through the prevalence of American films and TV programmes: fashions in thought, behaviour, clothing, and language all reflect this. Words such as elevator, T-shirt, truck, and even radio were not in common use 40 years ago, and baseball caps were unheard of. Even chewing-gum was a rarity before the Second World War.

Demographics is the study of the composition of the population. It encompasses areas such as the age structure of the population, their occupations and incomes, sizes of family, birth rate, death rate, and marital status. Throughout western Europe, the birthrate has been steadily falling for the last 20 years or so, and has long since passed the point at which births do not replace deaths (deJouvenal 1989). If it were not for immigration, the population of Europe would be shrinking: the average British family has only 1.8 children, compared with 2.4 in the 1960s. Additionally, people are marrying later and having children later – not to mention that many couples live together without marrying, which was extremely rare even 30 years ago.

A further major demographic change has been the increasing longevity of the population: as life expectancy has increased, western Europe and the United States have an increasingly aged population. Not all of these elderly or retired people are poor: many have substantial capital assets derived from home ownership, and many also have substantial pensions and investment income. This has meant that new industries have grown up around servicing the needs of an elderly, well-off group of people. There are many other examples of demographic changes which have affected businesses.

Changes in the structure of the population are relatively easy to forecast since (for example) knowing how many five-year-olds there are now provides a fairly accurate estimate of how many ten-year-olds there will be in five years' time. Income levels can be predicted, but often give an inaccurate picture of spending behaviour. Someone may decide to spend large amounts of money on foreign travel, but buy the cheapest food; a car enthusiast might be relatively poor, but own an expensive car. Categorizing people according to their socio-economic status can be seriously misleading – not everyone earning over £50,000 a year will live in a large house, and not everyone earning less than £10,000 a year will holiday at home.

ECOLOGICAL ENVIRONMENT

Public interest in the ecology has increased rapidly since the early 1980s, but industrial and business interest in the topic goes back a lot further. Industrialists have long realised that maintaining supplies of raw materials, and avoiding law suits from people who have been adversely affected by pollution or noise, are subjects which require attention. Interestingly, some examples of environmentally-friendly practices (for example, deposits on bottles to ensure their return for cleaning and refilling) were discontinued as a result of public apathy during the 1970s.

In most cases the ecological environment impinges on companies as a result of pressure from environmental groups: in this sense, the ecological environment is part of the socio-cultural fabric. Health and safety issues will impinge on companies as a result of government legislation.

Green marketing has become an important area of interest. As part of the societal marketing philosophy, green marketing holds that maintaining an environmentally-friendly approach to business activities is essential if the business is to remain sustainable in the long run. For example, a business which fails to recycle will find that supplies of raw materials will eventually run out; and a business which continues to pollute its local environment will eventually find that legislation will penalize it. The problem from the viewpoint of the environmentalists is that, for many firms, the cost of polluting is an external one, in other words it is paid by other people.

From a strategic viewpoint, assessing the impact on the environment can be considered from two angles. The first is the incremental approach, in which any environmentally-sensitive improvement to a product is considered to be valid, and improves the 'environment-friendly' credentials of the product. The second approach is the 'cradle to grave' or 'life cycle inventory' approach, which considers the total environmental impact of the product from its raw-material stage through to its disposal. Table 2.2 shows a life cycle inventory which was commissioned by Procter & Gamble to compare the impact of cloth nappies against the impact of disposables.

Table 2.2: Cloth versus disposable nappies

	Cloth	Disposable
Raw material consumption (pounds weight)	3.6	25.3
Water consumption (gallons)	144	23.6
Energy consumption (BTUs)	78.89	23.92
Air emission (pounds weight)	0.860	0.093
Water pollution (pounds weight)	0.117	0.012
Solid waste (pounds weight)	0.24	22.18

(Source: Ottman 1993)

The table shows that, on most factors, disposables have far less environmental impact than cloth nappies. The only factors on which cloth nappies win out are on raw material consumption and solid waste (which are, of course, closely linked).

The incremental method and the life cycle method are clearly very different, and are difficult to reconcile: in most cases businesses will prefer the incremental approach because it is less costly and contains no nasty surprises. Environmentalists prefer the life cycle inventory approach, because it provides a more complete picture. Only occasionally will the life cycle inventory reveal that a company's products are actually more environmentally friendly than had previously been assumed – which is probably the case for Procter & Gamble's study of disposable nappies.

MONITORING THE ENVIRONMENT

In order to monitor the environment, managers need to do the following:

1. Identify which forces are the most important, and why.
2. Forecast how these forces might change in future.
3. Incorporate these factors into planning, preferably involving all the organization's managers in the process so that responses can be co-ordinated as far as possible.
4. Be honest when assessing the organization's strengths and weaknesses.

Monitoring the environmental factors, in practice, will mean setting up a continuous information feed: this is a management information system. The role of a management information system is to match the information needs of managers to the availability of information, to ensure that information is collected in a cost-effective and efficient manner, and to ensure that information is disseminated to those who will benefit most from it. Common complaints from managers about information systems are these:

1. Available information is often irrelevant to the decision-making process.
2. Information overload: the amount of information generated means that relevant information is hard to extract and use effectively.
3. Information is scattered throughout the organization and is not effectively collated.
4. Information is not received in a timely manner, or is destroyed before it can be used.
5. Some managers become secretive, or possessive about information, so that it is withheld from other managers.
6. Reliability and accuracy of information is hard to verify, or is problematical.

Much of the information needed for a management information system already exists within the firm: it is contained in managers' files, in computer systems, and in the minds of employees. The problem is to ensure that the information can be collected and collated in an effective manner. Sources of internal information are as shown in Table 2.3.

Table 2.3: Internal sources of environment information

Source	Explanation and Examples
Accounting system	The internal accounting system contains information on customer purchasing trends, credit trends, and raw-material cost trends. Credit trends may provide advance warning of trouble in the macro-economy, for example: a tendency for customers to pay late may be an indication that the economy is slowing down.
Sales force	Although sales people are often unreliable as sources of information (Gordon et al. 1997), they may well have information about customer attitudes, competitor activities and initiatives, and future developments which may affect customers' ability or willingness to buy. For example, sales people from rival companies occasionally have the opportunity to talk to each other, and do not necessarily do so in an atmosphere of confidentiality: in other words, they often pump each other for information, and are willing to exchange information.
Documentation centres	Some organizations have staff whose role is to scan professional or trade journals, newspapers, competitors' annual reports, and even consumer magazines in search of stories which might have an impact on the organization.
Casual information collected by managers	Most managers (and indeed other employees) read journals or periodicals which contain stories about the industry. Often they will only apply such stories to their own department, but it should be feasible to encourage managers to share information which they might pick up which is relevant to other departments.
Syndicated data	Most larger firms subscribe to information services which also supply information to competitors. In most cases, this involves the firm in disclosing information about its own markets and activities in exchange for information about the industry as a whole.
Formal marketing research systems	Marketing research is usually used to answer specific questions about specific topics – in other words it operates as a series of discrete studies rather than a continuous data-gathering system. However, systems such as consumer panels or user focus groups can provide regular information (perhaps monthly) on current problems and behaviour.

ASSESSING STRATEGIC OPTIONS

There is rarely a single right strategy (though there may be several wrong ones), at least not in the sense that an absolute set of rules can be laid down. In fact, strategies should (in an ideal world) be different for each firm in a given market – only in this way can companies offer the range of services and products which modern consumers need. Although companies often take good ideas from each other (this is the basis of benchmarking) they should not be following the same strategy: doing so would reduce competitive advantage rather than increase it.

Having said that, techniques do exist for examining strategic options and assessing which general approach might be most appropriate for a given firm. Strategy assessment falls into three main aspects: the appropriateness of the strategy, the desirability of the strategy, and the feasibility of the strategy. In practice these three aspects overlap considerably.

Table 2.4 shows the factors which fall under the appropriateness aspect.

The desirability of the strategy is the degree to which it will satisfy the objectives of the organization. If the overall strategy is going to contribute strongly to the organization's objectives, it becomes highly desirable. The aspects of desirability are shown in Table 2.5.

Table 2.4: Assessing the appropriateness of strategic options

Factors	Explanations and examples
SWOT	Analysis of strengths, weaknesses, opportunities and threats is a basic tool of environmental analysis. It is not, however, the only tool.
Effect on strategic perspective	Will the strategy have potential for improving the strategic perspective and competitive position of the firm? Can the company respond to changes in its environment?
Skills and resources	What skills are available within the firm, and what skills might be needed? The same applies for other resources: if the proposed strategy requires skills or resources which are scarce or non-existent, that is clearly a negative. Equally, if the company has skills or resources which are unavailable to competitors, that would be a positive factor.
Mission and objectives	Does the proposed strategy fit the longer-term mission and objectives of the organization?
Culture	Is the strategy consistent with the shared beliefs and values of the organization? Is there an ethical problem with the proposed strategy?
EVR congruence	Is there a meeting-point between the environment, the values and the resources? This congruence summarises the above factors – in other words, do they fit together to form a cohesive whole?

Table 2.5: Desirability of strategic options

Factors	Explanation and examples
Risk	Risk can come from factors which were overlooked, or factors which are unpredictable. All changes of direction carry risks with them: on the other hand, risk is inherent in business, and the only certainty is that businesses which fail to change will stagnate and disappear eventually. Risk comes from the likely effect on competition (and subsequent retaliation), from production changes which sometimes develop technical glitches, from overstretching resources to exploit new markets, and from market risks associated with the acceptability of the new products.
Stakeholders' needs and preferences	The organization's stakeholders may well have an opinion as to which strategies are desirable and which are not. It would not be unknown for shareholders to sell shares, or for employees to resign (or worse, become demotivated and disaffected) when the organization carries out actions of which they disapprove.
Synergy	Synergy is the degree to which the proposed strategy will enhance the organization's existing activities. Synergy is defined as the effect by which the whole is greater than the sum of its parts. For example, the launch of a new product might help sales of existing products as well as generate sales on its own account. In some cases synergy works negatively: bad publicity surrounding the Virgin Trains brand is thought to have damaged the overall Virgin brand image.
Levels of expected return	The level of return is affected by synergy and by risk. The impact of any strategy on other activities within the organization needs to be taken into account whenever a new policy is embarked on. Risk can be quantified in many cases: if there is a 10% risk of losing £4m, this can be calculated as £400K of risk. If an alternative strategy gives a 20% risk of losing £3m, the risk would be valued at £600K, so the first option is actually less risky. This type of calculation helps to distinguish between differing options.
The planning gap	The degree to which the new strategy will help close any gaps in planning is also a consideration. Short-term and long-term needs should be addressed. If most of the firm's strategies are long-term, it may be useful to include some short-term strategies, and vice-versa in order to balance the firm's activities overall.

The feasibility of the strategy will always affect its implementation. Determining the feasibility of a given course of action requires a considerable degree of honesty and self-reflection on the part of planners: it is easy to get carried away by the desirability of a strategic option and ignore the fact that the company's resources or environment render the strategy impossible to achieve.

Table 2.6: Feasibility of strategic options

Factors	Explanation and examples
Demands created by change	Any change will involve a commitment of resources, in time or money, and a commitment on the part of those who have to implement the change. The degree to which the organization would have to change its working practices or attitudes is the key determining factor in the feasibility of a strategic alternative.
Resource availability	Planners need to be realistic in their estimates of the resources needed to carry out a particular strategic change. These resources may be financial, material, or human. Unfortunately, there is a tendency to be over-optimistic about estimating resources, and many strategies fail because the organizations involved run out of resources before the strategy has time to start working.
Ability to meet key success factors	Key success factors such as quality, price level and consumer demand obviously have to be met if the strategy is to stand a chance of succeeding.
Competitive advantage	A strategy is not feasible if it will provoke such a strong response from competitors that it will negate the objective of the strategy. This seems obvious, but often firms do not take sufficient account of competitive responses: a firm which threatens the major players might find itself on the receiving end of a counter-attack strong enough to bankrupt it.
Timing	Timing relates to opportunity, but also to risk and vulnerability. Seizing an opportunity at the right moment may mean fighting it out with competitors who also saw the same opportunity. Sometimes firms who arrive later in the market can come in better prepared to avoid pitfalls that earlier firms fell foul of. In other words, the early bird gets the worm – which shows that the worm should have stayed in bed.

Table 2.6 shows the relevant aspects which can be used to assess feasibility.

Managers need to have enough time to consider the alternatives and reflect on the risks and opportunities – this time is almost always in short supply or is non-existent. Three contextual aspects have an impact on the decision (Vickers 1965):

1. Personal factors. The decision-makers' skills and values together with aspects of their personalities.
2. Structural factors. Their authority and accountability within the organization.
3. Environmental factors. The accuracy or otherwise of their understanding and awareness of the situation.

Vickers also suggests that there are three types of judgement:

1. Reality judgements. Strategic awareness of the organization and its environment, based on interpretation and meaning systems.
2. Action judgements. What to do about perceived strategic issues.
3. Value judgements. Expected and desired results, and assessments of the outcomes from each decision.

Generally speaking, judgement comes from experience rather than from textbook or classroom learning. Having said that, the analytic and synthetic skills which go to creating a good judge can be developed through study and practice: which is, at least in theory, what universities do.

CASE STUDY: PLACE YOUR BETS!

www.williamhill.co.uk
www.ladbrokes.com
www.victorchandler.com

The UK gambling industry faced a major upheaval during 1999 when several leading bookmakers threatened to move their operations offshore. The purpose of the exercise was, of course, tax avoidance, but not the usual avoidance of corporation tax or income tax. The target this time was the UK's 9 per cent betting tax, which punters pay on their winnings. This tax was worth £450 m in 1998, so the Government (in the form of Customs and Excise) would naturally be reluctant to see gambling move overseas. Some industry estimates suggest that up to half of all gambling could move offshore by 2005 – a substantial loss to the exchequer.

The industry is dominated by the Big Three bookies: William Hill, Ladbrokes and Coral. Their fears were aroused by the announcement that one of the largest of the other bookies in the industry, Victor Chandler, was moving its entire operations to Gibraltar. 'You can bet on any sport from the UK', director Ian Plumb was reported as saying. 'If someone in the UK buys a service outside the country where there is no tax levied then he or she does not have to pay any tax. So there is nothing to stop a UK resident betting tax free.'

Since telephone betting accounts for almost 20 per cent of profits for the Big Three, this is understandably worrying. After all, a punter can just as easily dial a number in Gibraltar, and most of Victor Chandler's customers already have the number. The Big Three have responded by lobbying government departments, especially the Treasury and Customs and Excise, in an attempt to combine forces and defeat the competitive menace. Customs and Excise have already reassured them that any offshore gambling operation will not be allowed to advertise its services within the UK, but Victor Chandler dismisses this threat with a cynical shrug – its Gibraltar telephone number is already well-known, and in any case it expects a substantial amount of its business to come from the Internet, which the Government has no control over anyway.

To strengthen its negotiating position with the Government, William Hill and Ladbrokes are both able to point out that they already have offshore operations based in Gibraltar. Although these currently only cater for international 'high rollers' – the well-heeled multi-millionaire gamblers from the US and Hong Kong – both companies have hinted that their operations could be substantially increased to encompass small punters if need be.

In fact, Merrill Lynch analyst Bruce Jones suggests that, although there will be a substantial increase in Internet gambling over the next five to ten years, most gambling will still take place in betting shops. Currently, more than 80 per cent of UK betting is carried out in this way (not including National Lottery participation), so it will take a long time for telephone betting to change the structure of the industry. In the meantime, the Big Three are keeping a careful watch on the progress of international tax-free betting.

CASE STUDY QUESTIONS

1. If the Government stands to lose so much revenue if bookies set up offshore, why might it not try to prevent bookies from going?
2. What restrictions might prevent British punters from placing bets in Gibraltar?
3. How else might the Big Three prevent Victor Chandler from stealing their customers?
4. Since the Government stands to be a loser from the overseas defection of Victor Chandler, why is it necessary for the Big Three to lobby government departments?

▶

▶ **5.** How might the Big Three counter the threat from Internet gambling?

SUMMARY

Government, competition, demographic and technological change interact to create the firm's external environment. The environment is dynamic (i.e. in a constant state of change), and is difficult to control: having said that, the firm's activities also form part of the external environment for other firms, so some influence is possible. For large firms this influence can be considerable.

For the majority of firms, however, it is much easier to adapt the firm's activities to meet environmental change rather than try to adapt the environment to the firm's needs: in other words, firms should live in the world as it is, rather than as they wish it were.

The key points from this chapter are as follows:

■ The external environment is difficult to control, but can be influenced.

■ Monitoring of the environment enables the firm to make informed decisions.

■ Governments exercise some control over the business environment, but they do this largely through influencing competitive practices.

■ Technological change is rapid, and is not confined solely to electronic communications.

■ Demographic shifts in Europe and the west are taking us towards an ageing population: this will affect the availability of workers as well as affect marketing strategies.

CHAPTER QUESTIONS

1. How might companies cope with currency fluctuations in today's world?

2. The Euro was introduced to make trade easier within the European Union. Why did some member states, notably the UK and Denmark, show such reluctance to join it?

3. How might the socio-cultural environment be affected by current changes in technology?

4. The European Union has been growing steadily more integrated for the last 20 years or so. Which industries are likely to have gained from this, and which have lost out?

5. To what extent is it possible to separate out the effects of each element of the external environment?

REFERENCES

Ambler, T. and Barwise, P. (1998): 'The trouble with brand valuation', *The Journal of Brand Management* vol. 5, no. 5, pp. 367–377.

Ambler, T. and Kokkinaki, F. (1997): 'Marketing Performance Measurement: Which Way is Up?' in A.D. Neely and D.B. Waggoner, eds, *Performance Measurement – Theory and Practice* vol. 1, pp. 31–38. (Cambridge UK: Centre for Business Performance, Cambridge University).

Arend, Richard J. (1999): 'Emergence of entrepreneurs following exogenous technological change', *Strategic Management Journal* 20: pp. 31–47.

Deephouse, David L. (1999): 'To be different, or to be the same? It's a question (and theory) of strategic balance', *Strategic Management Journal* 20: pp. 147–166.

DeJouvenal, H. (1989): *Europe's ageing population: trends and challenges to 2025* (London, Butterworth).

Gordon, G.L., Schoenbachler, D.D., Kaminski, P.F., Brouchous, K.A. (1997): 'New Product Development; Using the Salesforce to Identify Opportunities', *Journal of Business and Industrial Marketing* vol. 12 no. 1 pp. 33–50.

Hennart, J.F., Roehl, T. and Zietlow, D.S. (1999): 'Trojan horse or workhorse? The evolution of US-Japanese joint ventures in the United States', *Strategic Management Journal* 20: pp. 15–29.

Ottman, J.A. (1993): *Green marketing: challenges and opportunities for the new marketing age* (Lincolnwood II: NTC Business Books).

Porter, M.E. (1985): *Competitive Advantage* (New York: Free Press).

Porter, M.E. (1990): 'How competitive forces shape strategy', *Harvard Business Review*, 57(2) pp. 137–45.

Roberts, Peter W. (1999): 'Product innovation, product-market competition, and persistent profitability in the US pharmaceutical industry', *Strategic Management Journal* 20: pp. 655–670.

Vickers (1965): *The Art of Judgement: A Study of Policy Making* (London: Chapman Hall).

Wyner, Gordon A. (1996): 'Customer valuation: linking behaviour and economics', *Marketing Research* vol. 8, no. 2, pp. 36–38.

Chapter Three

The Internal Environment

INTRODUCTION

The internal environment comprises those factors which make up the organization itself: its staff, its culture, its structure (both informal and formal), its management style, its information systems, and so forth. The internal environment is what makes the organization what it is, and it derives from the people who are its members.

After reading this chapter, you should be able to:

- Explain the role of organizational culture.
- Describe ways of managing change.
- Explain how information systems can be constructed.
- Show how information systems can be used to encourage customer loyalty.
- Describe ways of monitoring and auditing strategy.

INTERNAL AUDITS

Internal audits fall into five main categories:

1. The marketing strategy audit.
2. The marketing organization audit.
3. The marketing systems audit.
4. The marketing productivity audit.
5. The marketing functions audit. This aspect will be covered in more detail in Chapter Four.

The purpose of an internal audit is much the same as that of a financial audit: it provides a 'snapshot' of the current state of affairs within the organization. In some ways, the internal audit is the easiest to do because all the information is (or should be) readily available from staff working in the firm. The problem is that staff will often feel that the audit is intrusive, or is perhaps an attempt on the part of management to find fault with their work. In order to reduce the risk of this happening, the following policies might be adopted:

1. Avoid using anything uncovered in the audit as a means to criticize staff.
2. Ensure that the audit process is transparent, in other words make it clear exactly what the information is to be used for, and make it available to staff whenever possible.
3. If possible, use outside consultants to carry out the audit. This will reduce the tendency for people to give politically-motivated responses.

Since the audit relies heavily on honesty and openness, it could be distorted by wishful thinking, or even by deliberate attempts to pervert the outcome by individuals with a political agenda. This is less likely to happen if the process is seen as supportive rather than punitive. Outside consultants are extremely useful in carrying out audits: because they have no political ambitions within the firm they are seen as impartial, and are often able to help by asking the right questions. A good consultant (in this context) is not someone who gives answers, but rather one who asks the right questions and causes the directors and managers of the organization to examine what they are doing in an objective manner.

MARKETING STRATEGY AUDIT

The marketing strategy audit will begin by looking at the business mission. The issue here is whether the mission statement is clearly stated and whether it is attainable. The mission must also have a clear focus: some mission statements contain little more than platitudes which are unhelpful when it comes to the day-to-day running of the organization.

The marketing strategy should have clear objectives and goals. This means that the corporate and marketing objectives should be clearly stated, and the objectives should be appropriate in terms of meeting overall corporate objectives. The theory behind management by objectives is that only that which is measured will be achieved. This means that a failure to set objectives will lead to a failure to achieve anything worthwhile.

The strategy audit should examine the core marketing strategy, the budgeting of resources, and the allocation of resources. Budgeting resources is possibly one of the most contentious areas for the firm, since it is the area where each manager will want to maximize his or her budget in order to maximize the resources available for the department's tasks.

Carrying out the audit is usually a matter for the directors of the company, or the senior marketing managers. In some cases, 'think tanks' of individuals from different departments are used as a task force to examine the organization's objectives and strategy: this has the advantage of keeping ownership of the process within the organization, while maintaining some objectivity. Done this way, the audit is less likely to be seen as the domain of any one department.

However it is accomplished, the strategy evaluation should provide answers to these questions:

1. Are the objectives appropriate?
2. Are the major policies and plans appropriate?
3. Do the results obtained so far confirm the critical assumptions on which the strategy has been based?

The issues which complicate evaluation surround the uniqueness of each strategy (in other words comparisons are difficult), the evaluation of goals and objectives (which are easier to set and even achieve than they are to evaluate), and the perceived threat to managers inherent in any kind of review of their activities.

It is impossible to say that a particular strategy is absolutely correct: circumstances change too often to allow this. However, it is possible to say that a strategy is flawed. For a strategy to be considered viable, it must fit within the criteria shown in Table 3.1.

Table 3.1: Criteria for successful strategy

Criterion	Explanation and examples
Consistency	Many strategies have not been specifically formulated, but have simply grown up as a result of adoption of a set of tactical actions. This means that 'the way we do things round here' can achieve the status of a strategy without ever having been examined. Indicators that the strategy is inconsistent are: Problems in co-ordination and planning, especially if these are issue-based rather than staff-based. Secondly, if success for one department is interpreted as failure for another. Thirdly, if operating problems are being constantly referred to senior managers for resolution. All these difficulties indicate that the strategy is not performing its co-ordinating function effectively.
Consonance	The business must match and be adapted to its environment, and at the same time compete with other firms which are also trying to match to the environment. The first aspect of strategy therefore deals with the basic mission of the business, the second aspect deals with the firm's special competitive position or 'edge'. The difficulty in evaluating consonance is that most of the threats to a business come from outside and threaten the entire industry, whereas managements are more usually preoccupied with their firm's competitive position relative to other firms within the industry. The key to evaluating consonance is to understand the underlying reasons for the firm's (and the industry's) existence. Understanding the basic social and economic reasons for the firm's existence enables managers to decide which types of change are most crucial.
Advantage	Generic strategy focuses on the common missions of an industry. Competitive strategy focuses on the differences between firms rather than their similarities. For example, supermarkets have almost entirely replaced traditional grocery shops where assistants would weigh goods out and collect goods from the stockroom for customers. As a generic strategy, the supermarket concept has been wildly successful, but an individual firm in the supermarket business needs to go further than this and differentiate itself from other supermarkets if it is to compete successfully. The three main forms of competitive advantage are superior resources, superior skills, or superior position.
Feasibility	Financial resources are usually the easiest to quantify, and in some ways are also the easiest to control, but feasibility of strategies also depends on human resources and physical resources. To assess feasibility, the organization needs to be assured that it has firstly the necessary problem-solving and special competences for the strategy, secondly that it has sufficient co-ordinative and integrative skill, and thirdly that the strategy can challenge and motivate key personnel and is acceptable to them.

Strategy evaluation is not a purely intellectual task: the issues are too important and there are likely to be too many political ramifications involved for the evaluation to take place in an 'ivory tower'. This means that auditing the strategy is likely to be an organizational process, probably undertaken as part of the normal planning, reporting, control and reward systems of the organization.

MARKETING ORGANIZATION AUDIT

Organizations have both a formal and an informal structure, each of which affects the organization's performance. The formal structure is the one which appears on organization charts: in the case of a hierarchical, bureaucratic structure there will be fixed lines of communications and clear distinctions regarding roles and responsibilities. The informal structure does not exist as an organizational chart, because it comprises the myriad personal relationships which build up over time as people work in close proximity with one another. For example, the organizational chart might make it perfectly clear that the correct way to obtain information on the company's sales figures is to send a memo to the sales manager: in practice, it might be quicker and easier for all concerned to talk to the sales manager's secretary or personal assistant. The informal structure is important because it is the repository of the corporate culture: the set of beliefs and attitudes which grow up around the organization. This culture is reinforced by conversations at the photocopier, or over coffee in the canteen, or at people's homes when they invite work colleagues round for dinner.

Talking Point

Informal communications at the photocopier or the coffee machine seem to be very effective in cementing the corporate culture. They also seem to be pretty good for passing on hard information – and, of course, unfounded rumours and gossip.

So if the informal system is so effective, why do we bother having a formal system at all? Everyone knows that most memos are only written in order to protect the rear end of the person writing the memo – the real work gets done on the golf course anyway. Maybe the formal structure gives us a way of recording and validating what was said: but equally, it may be simply a way of controlling the flow of information in a way that suits senior management. Can we stop the gossip and rumour and just keep the true information? Can we perhaps encourage staff to record their informal talks? If not, maybe we should look at banning such conversations altogether?

Attempts have been made by some managers (particularly adherents to the scientific management school of thought) to stamp out the informal structure. Currently, some managements are trying to restrict the use of office e-mail to prevent personal use of the system for exchanging jokes, arranging private parties, or simply chatting to friends at work and elsewhere. This type of restriction is likely to prove counter-productive, since staff will always want to swap jokes and interact with colleagues on a personal level – using the local network for this is probably a time-saver over the traditional photocopier or coffee machine meetings. In September 2000 the Tower Hamlets local authority in London (**www.towerhamlets.gov.uk**) compelled smokers to work an extra half an hour a day to make up for time spent on cigarette breaks: smokers retaliated by pointing out that some non-smoking colleagues spent working time eating, drinking coffee, chatting, or otherwise not working. Even non-smokers joined in the protests, and in the end enforcement of the policy was left to individual managers – which meant that enforcement was only sporadic.

Wiser managements will try to incorporate the informal structure into the organization by encouraging interaction between staff members. Organized staff social events, staff social clubs, and a laissez-faire attitude towards workplace gossip help to smooth communications and improve staff loyalty.

FORMAL STRUCTURES

Organizations all differ in their structure, but there are two main types of structure which represent the extremes of the continuum. The first is the hierarchical structure, also known as the bureaucratic or mechanistic structure. This is shown in Fig 3.1.

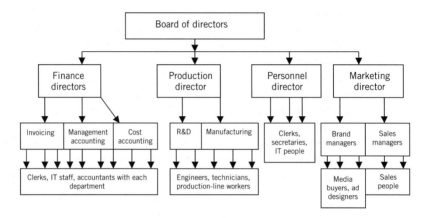

Figure 3.1: Example of a hierarchical structure

Purely hierarchical organizations are somewhat rare nowadays, and are mostly confined to government departments and traditional industries which are not subject to much change. The characteristics of a hierarchical organization are as follows:

1. Members are appointed by reason of their formal qualifications and experience.
2. Communication is assumed to travel up the hierarchy, and instructions come down.
3. The people at the top of the hierarchy are assumed to have full knowledge of everything that happens further down.
4. Roles within the organization are clearly defined, and are generally fixed unless the individual is promoted.
5. Changes in the organization are made through consultation, and on instructions from the top.

Hierarchical organizations are extremely efficient provided the industry or the environment is slow to change. The efficiency comes from division of labour and specialization: each individual becomes expert at his or her own part of the job. Little time is wasted on communication because the channels are clearly defined: communication is also smooth, provided nothing unusual happens. The problem with hierarchies is that they tend to be very slow to adapt to changing circumstances: because each person's job is strictly-defined, there is resentment at any attempt to change. Communication is slow, because it has to go up through the layers of the hierarchy (with the risk of distortion at each stage) and then instructions have to come back down the hierarchy.

At the other extreme is the organismic organization, as shown in Fig 3.2.

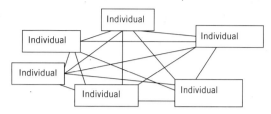

Figure 3.2: An Example of an organismic organization

In the purely organismic organization, communication flows between all the members in a completely open way. No one member is in overall charge: the task of leadership will change according to the task faced by the organization. This type of structure is again rare in its pure form, but might be typical of some consultancy firms, research groups, or small professional partnerships.

In an organismic organization, the formal qualifications of members are not necessarily the only aspect of the person that is taken into account. Because such organizations operate best in rapidly-changing environments, all the skills and experience of the members are likely to be brought into play at one time or another.

In practice, most organizations will occupy a position on a continuum somewhere between the hierarchical and the organismic. In the future it seems likely that organismic structures will be better able to survive, because of their ability to adapt swiftly to changes.

FUNCTIONAL EFFICIENCY AUDIT

The functional efficiency of the organization will depend on its communication systems, its product management systems, and its training systems.

Communication systems which follow a formal, hierarchical approach tend to be slow and can suffer from distortion: on the other hand, such systems tend to minimize the time spent in communicating, and maximize the time spent on tasks. The current thrust in communication is to use electronic methods, in particular e-mail, to speed up communication and make all the members of an organization easily accessible to each other. The drawback with e-mail is that it is too easy to send messages to a global address list: which means there is a proliferation of messages, and members of the organization have to spend inordinate amounts of time ploughing through e-mails that are of little or no relevance. Inevitably this distracts them from the tasks in hand; moreover, those who are technophobic, or computer illiterate, or even slow typists will find the system virtually unworkable and will retaliate against it by ignoring it or by using the telephone instead.

If the formal communication system does not meet the needs of the employees, they will fall back on the informal system, which will result in the most useful organizational business being conducted over the photocopier or coffee machine.

For the purposes of the marketing organization audit, managers will need to address the following questions:

1. Is the current structural type correct for the organization's environment and objectives? Should it be more hierarchical, or more organismic?

2. Do marketing managers occupy the right level in the structure? Should marketers be placed in more strategic roles? Are their responsibilities correctly allocated?

3. If the organization is essentially hierarchical, are people clear about what their roles and responsibilities might entail?

Even if the organization is essentially hierarchical in nature, the negative effects of such a structure can be offset considerably by empowering employees to take decisions without referring them to more senior managers. Empowerment of employees is covered in more detail in Chapter 12.

INFORMATION SYSTEMS

Marketing information systems are often set up to provide an automatic flow of data into the firm, with systems for regular analysis of the data. These systems used to be held on paper, with consequent emphasis on form-filling by salespeople, shipping departments, finance staff, and others. In recent years, the increased use of computers (particularly desktop PCs) has allowed far more efficient systems to be put in place, and has reduced the amount of time spent on gathering information (Proctor 2000). There is always a trade-off involved between the value of information and the cost in time, effort and money of obtaining it; by reducing the cost element, computers have increased the possibilities for obtaining useful data and converting it into useable information. Computer-based systems such as these are called **decision support systems**; an example is the electronic point-of-sale (EPOS) systems used by large retailers. These record every purchase made in the store so that the retailer can re-order stock in the correct amounts, can automatically analyse trends, and can even (with the use of loyalty cards) track an individual customer's purchases over a period of time (Evans 1994).

Decision support systems need to be user-friendly so that managers without training in data analysis can use them; this is the main reason for their popularity over paper-based information systems (Sprague and Watson 1986, Bessen 1994). As an example the ways in which sales management information systems help sales managers are shown in Table 3.2.

Table 3.2: Sales management information systems

Functional Area	Explanation
Sales reporting and analysis	Collecting and analysing call reports, levels of actual sales compared with budgeted sales, analysis of sales by market segment, and profit dimensions of sales performance. These figures can be calculated according to individual salespeople, teams or the entire salesforce.
Sales planning	Identifying leads, classifying prospects (segmenting the market), and building up customer profiles. These can be assessed across a variety of criteria including organization type, buying pattern, creditworthiness, and size of average order.
Future options and projections	Computer modelling enables the manager to try different options and predict possible future scenarios. Although this is unlikely to provide the definitive answer to problems, it can often help in rejecting some alternatives and in clarifying the manager's thinking.

As with any other management tool, there are problems attached to the use of sales management information systems. Firstly, there is the problem of information overload; sometimes so much information is generated it becomes impossible to wade through it all and arrive at a coherent decision. Secondly, computers sometimes give spurious credibility to results which have been obtained from inaccurate input data – what computer experts call GIGO (garbage in, garbage out).

Thirdly, developing the systems usually means that managers have to come into contact with IT experts. Since neither of them know enough about the other's specialism to be able to comment or make suggestions, it may take some time for them to work out an optimum system. The exigencies of making the system compatible with the rest of the firm's systems may compel the IT expert to make inappropriate compromises.

Fourthly, management requirements change rapidly. Changes in the market, the type of products being sold, the size of the firm, or the management structure may mean that the information requirements change frequently and the system needs to change with it.

Fifthly, there is the problem of technophobia. Some staff (and even managers) do not trust the computer and are almost hoping that the system will fail. This can become a self-fulfilling prophecy as the people concerned fail to provide the appropriate information at the right time.

Assessing the costs and benefits of using IT can also be problematical, since the costs are easily identified but the benefits often are not.

Information systems can also be set up in such a way that they encourage customer loyalty. For example, the Edistrict (**www.edistrict.com**) interactive advertising company operates the Leisure District entertainment service, accessed via interactive TV and the Dreamcast console. Edistrict keeps the data which it collects at registration and uses it to target customers, but the innovative part of the exercise is that Edistrict encourages customers to give more information about themselves by telling them that more information will reduce the number of irrelevant adverts they are sent. In this way the information system itself is seen to be beneficial to the customers as well as to the firm.

Customer information systems can be structured as databases to maximize the opportunities for developing customer loyalty. Database management is potentially a complex issue: Table 3.3 explains some of the current terminology and features of databases.

Table 3.3: Database terminology

Flat database	This is a database in which all the information about a given customer is stored. Management of such databases is easy, since information is easily added or edited, but the possibilities for using the database to drive strategic decision-making is limited.
Relational database	This type of database allows information about an individual customer to be accessed under several different categories. For example, a relational database containing details of doctors might be able to list them by location, by medical specialism, by purchasing frequency, by age, or by size of practice.
Data warehouse	This is an electronic storage facility which holds very large amounts of information. The information can be cross-checked against other pieces of information to clean it, and can be manipulated in various ways to generate information for decision-making.
Data mining	The process of generating information by the use of advanced statistical processes. Data mining enables organizations to find significant relationships between customers or chunks of customer information. This information provides almost instant market research, enabling firms to develop rapid responses to market trends.
Extranet	Extranets allow companies to share some information, while still retaining their own trade secrets. Driven through the Internet, extranets open some of the company's files to authorized outsiders. Trading information in this way can help markedly in ensuring industry survival.

Here is a checklist for ensuring that the customer information system is functioning correctly:

1. Has the system been designed to be state-of-the-art? Beware of setting a technical horizon based on the user's technical knowledge. Often managers will design the system based on their own knowledge of what is possible, rather than on what a technician would regard as possible.

2. What business needs should the CIS serve? What types of analysis should it be able to handle? Determine the objectives of the system, and put these in writing.

3. Involve the major users. They are closest to the system, and can identify its strengths and weaknesses better than anyone.

4. Is the system simple, both in terms of collecting information, and in terms of providing it?

5. Check that the CIS can sort information in a variety of ways: by customer purchase frequency, by order size, by geographical location, and so forth.

6. Is the system cleaned regularly to ensure that data is still current?

7. Is the system suitably backed up in the event of a computer crash?

8. Is the system secure – but at the same time is it easily accessible for authorized users?

For many firms, the information systems have become the core activity of the business. More and more firms are becoming database-driven, using a single database to inform all decisions within the firm.

The role of the database develops strategically within the firm, as shown in Table 3.4. The process described below is not necessarily a tidy one, and firms may skip stages, but it does illustrate a hierarchy of commitment to the use of the database as the driving force in the company's marketing communications activities.

Table 3.4: Strategic position of the database

Phase of Development	Explanation
Phase 1: Mystery Lists	The firm regards the database as an adjunct to its main business, as a stand-alone operation next to its main marketing activities.
Phase 2: Buyer databases	There may be several databases in use, each carrying different information. For example, the salesforce may use one database for special customers, the distribution department may have a separate one containing delivery details and scheduling, credit control may have yet another one. The Phase 2 focus is on broadening the databases, defining target markets, improving list quality, segmentation, credit scoring, response handling, testing, and management systems for campaign planning.
Phase 3: Co-ordinated customer communication	Databases are amalgamated so that one database drives all customer communication. The database is used to identify prospects within the broader market, review past performance, and segment the market.
Phase 4: Integrated marketing	Most functions automate within closed loops, but need each other's information for the plan-execute-monitor-report cycle. Each functional subsystem gets its information from every other subsystem within the context of the main database. Common IT architecture ensures maximum automatic feedback, combining lifetime management of customers with the management of campaigns for particular brands.

Integrating all the firm's activities around a single database increases the coherence of marketing communications and the possibilities for establishing relationship marketing. A single database puts the company in the position of the small corner shop; the company knows all its regular customers, and can therefore anticipate and satisfy their needs much more effectively both in terms of product and in terms of communications.

PRODUCTIVITY AUDIT

The marketing productivity audit is concerned with two areas: profitability analysis, and cost-effectiveness analysis.

Profitability can be assessed for each product, each market, each territory or each distribution channel. Most firms tend to assess profitability in terms of the profit made from each brand or product, because this is relatively easy to calculate. Conceptually this is a flawed approach, at least for marketers, because it is not market-orientated. The most customer-orientated approach is to assess profitability in terms of market segments: this may be expressed in geographical terms (so that territory is the issue), in terms of types of retail outlet (so that distribution channels are the key), or in demographics (so that the consumers are the key). In fact, any form of segmentation method can be the basis for a profitability analysis.

The profitability analysis will affect strategic planning since it allows planners to decide whether a segment is worth entering, or conversely whether a segment should be abandoned. Not all customers are worth having: sometimes resources are better allocated to other segments.

Another approach, and one which may allow for triangulation to determine the most profitable activities, is to calculate the costs and benefits of various marketing activities. For example, the return on using a telesales operation rather than a direct-mail exercise to generate leads might be calculated. The main problem with this type of calculation is that it tends to consider marketing activities in terms of short-term cash returns rather than long-term benefits. It is extremely easy to run a lead-generating exercise which produces a quick result, but which at the same time causes future problems.

For example, it is surprisingly common for firms to run exhibition stands which generate large numbers of potential sales leads and useful contacts. Often these leads are not followed up, and the contacts are left uncontacted, which not only wastes the effort that went into their collection but also antagonizes potential customers for the future (Blythe 2000). Equally, salespeople might obtain sales quickly by using high-pressure techniques at the expense of building longer-term (and hence more valuable) relationships with customers.

RESOURCE AND COMPETENCY AUDITS

Competency to achieve a given strategic objective is derived from the way resources are combined and utilized. Efficiency in the use of resources is the key to effectiveness in strategic success (usually expressed as competitive advantage). If resources are to be adequately utilized, managers must know what resources are available; and in order to ensure that those resources are being used effectively, competency auditing is also essential. Having said that, there are problems in translating theory into practice.

There has been considerable research into the importance of resources for the firm (Penrose 1959, Wernerfelt 1984, Barney 1991). There is a problem of definition here, however: some authors prefer not to use the term 'resources' when writing of the range of means at the disposal of the planners and managers, but instead refer to 'assets'. This means there is currently no generally-agreed classification of resources (or assets) within the strategic management field.

However, there are certainly some major distinctions which can be made. Firstly, resources may be tangible or intangible. Tangible resources are those assets such as machinery, buildings, vehicles, stocks of raw materials, work in progress and so forth which can be touched and handled. Intangible resources are intellectual property such as patents or software, brand equity, goodwill, and the intellectual resources of the employees. Of the two, it is the tangible assets which are the easiest to identify, value, buy and sell. Intangible assets are more fragile (in that they can easily be lost) and are harder to value (since future income streams can be hard to predict). On the other hand intangible assets often represent the major part of a firm's stock market valuation.

The second classification which can be made is to divide intangible resources into relational resources and competences. Relational resources are all of the means available to the firm derived from its relationship with its environment (Lowendahl 1997). These might include special relationships with customers, distributors, and consumers, and also the firm's reputation and brand equity.

Competence refers to the firm's fitness to perform in a given field, and is based on the effective use of resources. Durand (1996) has drawn a distinction between knowledge, capability and attitude. These are shown in Table 3.5.

Table 3.5: Knowledge, capability and attitude

Knowledge	The set of rules (know-how, know-what, know-where and know-when) and insights (know-why) that are used to make sense of information (Dretske 1981). This knowledge is contained in the heads of the employees for the most part, but is collective: examples are marketing insights, knowledge of competitors, technological expertise, and understanding of political issues.
Capability	This is the organization's potential for carrying out specific activities. Capability bases might include rapid response to market changes, or specific abilities to create new products (Stalk et al. 1992).
Attitude	This is the shared tendency to respond in a particular way to outside stimuli. Some firms are known for an aggressive attitude, or a litigious attitude, or even a caring and sharing attitude - Body Shop (**www.the-body-shop.com**) being an example of the latter. This attitude is shared by the employees, at least during working hours. Such attitudes, when seated firmly within the organizational culture, can represent substantial assets (Barney 1986).

There is some confusion between the terms 'competences' and 'capabilities'. Durand's view is that a competence in a certain area will arise when the firm's knowledge, capabilities and attitudes are aligned in such a way that synergies are created. For example, Virgin Airways' (**www.virgin.net**) service competence is a combination of knowledge of customers, the capability to adapt, and a customer-orientated attitude.

From the viewpoint of auditing resources and competences, there are considerable conceptual difficulties. As far as tangible assets go, accountants have evolved some straightforward techniques for arriving at a value: however, these values are only valid in particular circumstances. For example, a fixed asset such as a piece of machinery might be valued in one of three separate ways. Firstly, its value in terms of what it can produce, or the income stream that might be expected from it. This is also a function of the business environment, since the value of the production might vary or the demand for the product may shift dramatically. For example, a mould which produces plastic components is only valuable as long as the demand for those components continues – as soon as the demand is removed, the value of the mould drops to zero.

Secondly, tangible assets might be valued in terms of their purchase price and expected life. Thus a vehicle might depreciate by a calculable amount over a given period: the firm's accountants are usually able to calculate the value of, for example, the salesforce's company cars in this way.

Thirdly, tangible assets can be valued according to their resale value. This can be higher than the original purchase price (for example, buildings or office premises) or lower than the original purchase price (for example, vehicles or machinery), or in some cases might be virtually zero (for example, some of the tunnelling machinery used to build the Eurotunnel (**www.eurotunnel.co.uk**)).

Each of these valuation methods will arrive at a different answer. Clearly the difficulties inherent in auditing intangible assets are likely to be greater, particularly if there is pressure to audit in financial terms. Therefore few organizations do this: this is one of the problems faced by marketers when trying to justify expenditure on (for example) brand-building.

Auditing knowledge is likely to be judgement-based, since knowledge has a high rate of decay in a changing environment. A linked audit might be to consider the firm's ability and disposition towards maintaining its knowledge base. This is a function of the training of staff, of staff development initiatives, and of the firm's propensity to spend money on research and development. This audit can be assessed qualitatively by making benchmarking comparisons with other firms in the same industry.

Auditing capability is likewise a judgement-based activity, though there may be some objective elements involved. Capability might be judged by events in the recent past (for example, an exceptionally effective new-product development and launch) or it might be judged by assessing the individual capabilities of the firm and aggregating them to give an overall view of capability (i.e. what we should be able to accomplish). This latter method has the advantage of being more up-to-date, but has the major drawback of not taking account of possible synergies or unforeseen weaknesses.

Corporate attitude is probably subject to more instances of self-delusion on the part of senior managers than any other element in the competences framework. Often the attitude of senior management is not reflected further down the hierarchy, and (worse) employees may be at some pains to conceal their real attitudes for fear of appearing to be out of step with the management. This is likely to have a severely damaging effect on the co-ordinating function of the strategy, since employees are likely to act in one way while trying to convince senior management that they are in fact acting in a different way. For this reason corporate attitudes need to be monitored at grass-roots level: attitudes are difficult to measure at best, because behaviour is not a good guide and self-reports may conceal political agendas

Relational resources are even harder to pin down: with whom does the organization have a relationship, and what is the value and status of that relationship? Relationships often break down, in business as in real life. What is the value of the firm's reputation? This can sometimes be arrived at in general terms by looking at the difference between the firm's balance-sheet asset value and its stock-market valuation, but this is a somewhat nebulous measure, relying as much on factors such as the general state of the economy, the general state of the industry, and the state of competing investments, as on the current state of the firm.

Valuing a brand is not as straightforward as might at first appear, either. A well-established brand tends to have a less elastic demand curve: in other words, they are less price-sensitive (Hamilton et al. 1997). This means that a price increase on a strong brand will have less effect than a price increase on a weak brand. This implies that a strong brand will have a much better chance of weathering a recession, for example, than a weak brand: this is in itself a valuable characteristic, and is one that is well worth investing in.

Carrying out a resource and competency audit is, notwithstanding the conceptual and practical difficulties, an essential activity for any organization attempting to plan strategy.

The resource audit will cover the areas shown in Table 3.6.

The resource audit should include all the resources the firm can tap into, even when these are not actually owned by the firm: intangible resources and financial resources which can be called upon if needed fall into this category. Particular weight should be given to unique resources – those resources which competitors are unable to duplicate, for example patented products or other intellectual property.

Competence analysis cannot be measured in absolute terms: it always has to be measured against competitors' provision and customers' expectations. In particular it is important to identify the organization's core competences – the particular competences that ensure that the organization can outperform its competition in some respects. Competences can be understood and analysed in two steps: value chain analysis, and competence bases.

Value chain analysis examines the ways organizations add value to products as they pass along the chain. This involves analysing both what happens within the organization itself, and also what happens in the supplier and distributor parts of the chain. Value chain analysis recognizes

Table 3.6: Elements in the resource audit

Element	Examples and explanation
Physical resources	A list of the fixed assets of the organization, for example machinery, buildings and equipment. The audit needs to include the age and condition of the assets, their location, and their capability as well as their financial value (which is often calculated in an arbitrary manner in any case). This is to determine their usefulness in achieving strategic advantages.
Human resources	This can be a problematical area, since much of the value of staff depends on their motivation and commitment rather than on their paper qualifications and the numbers of them within the organization.
Financial resources	This should include the sources of money (whether equity or loan), the liabilities the organization has, and the possible availability of capital or loans should it become necessary to acquire more funding – this is essentially the firm's credit rating.
Intangibles	From a marketer's point of view, intangible assets such as brands, patents, reputation and relationships with customers (goodwill) are at least as important as any of the firm's other assets, since these are the capital from which marketers derive competence.

that each organization and process in the chain adds value to the product, otherwise there would be no point in their becoming involved in the process. Each increment of value should be greater than the costs attaching to its production, otherwise that part of the chain is not operating efficiently and should be changed or removed. Much of the efficiency gained by effective firms lies in their ability to manage the linkages between the activities of other organizations.

Within the value chain, there exist categories of activity which are shown in Table 3.7.

Very few companies undertake all the value activities from raw material through to final product: the oil industry is a notable exception. Specialization of role is therefore the norm, with each organization adding only part of the value to the product. For example, in the food industry a basic product such as tuna might pass through eight or more organizations on its way from the fishermen to the consumer's larder, each organization adding something to the product (canning, shipping, delivering, displaying, advertising, and so forth).

Talking Point

Most products pass through several organizations from producer to consumer, and each organization adds value. Or so we are told. But isn't it also true that each organization adds its profit? Isn't that why 'cutting out the middle man' is a well-known way of buying goods cheaper?

The factory-gate price for a consumer product such as a stereo system is often less than one-third of the price in the shop. So who's getting cheated? Why don't we all just buy from the factory – often we live near enough to one to be able to do it easily.

Or perhaps the manufacturers find it too much trouble to fiddle about with odd sales of one or two stereos when they could sell several hundred in one hit? And how is it that reverse auction websites such as letsbuyit.com have not made more inroads into the retail market? Shouldn't we all be buying from them?

Perhaps there is more to distribution than just piling goods onto shelves.

Identifying core competences will vary from one industry to another. Threshold competences are those which any business in the industry would need to have in order to survive: any car manufacturer needs a threshold competence in engineering and in design, but some car

Table 3.7: Primary and support activities

	Activity	Explanation and examples
Primary activities	Inbound logistics	All the activities concerned with receiving, storing and distributing raw materials or other inputs. Warehousing, inbound shipping, and materials handling systems are examples.
	Operations	The processes which transform the incoming raw materials into the organization's finished product. This may, of course, become raw materials or components for another firm, for example when an electronics manufacturer makes car radios for a car manufacturer.
	Outbound logistics	Collection, storage and delivery to customers. Much of this activity might be undertaken by a distributor or shipping company.
	Marketing communications	Here we are looking at the functional aspects of marketing, in which customers are made aware of the products and fine-tuning of the product offering is made to suit the needs of individual customers.
	Before-sales and After-sales service	All those activities which enhance or maintain the product value. For example, installation of equipment, repair of faulty equipment, training, and so forth.
Support activities	Procurement	The processes involved in obtaining the resource inputs needed for the primary activities. This would include raw materials purchase, equipment purchase, and acquiring suitable spaces (factory, shop or office).
	Technology development	Technological advances may reside in the product (through research and development or through product design), with the processes (more efficient production or delivery methods) or with resource improvements (for example making use of a previously-ignored raw material).
	Human resource management	The activities involved in shaping an effective workforce. This may involve hiring suitable people, offering appropriate training, ensuring suitable motivation and reward structures are in place, and (when unavoidable) firing unsuitable employees.
	Infrastructure	The systems of planning, finance, quality control, information management, communication, and so forth. The routines and structures of the organization often determine the level of flexibility the organization has: greater flexibility means greater ability to cope with change.

manufacturers have developed core competences which single them out from the competition. For example, Ferrari (**www.ferrari.it**) has core competence in stylish design, Volkswagen has a core competence in reliability, and Ford (**www.ford.com**) has a core competence in low running costs. Core competences only have relevance when compared with competitors, and with market segments.

Core competences might also be linked to critical success factors. The critical success factor in an industry is the basic elements that have to be right if the firm is to succeed, rather than merely survive. For example, Internet-based firms need a threshold competency in information technology, but the critical success factor is likely to be the design of the web page. A well-designed page will encourage business, whereas a poorly-designed one is frustrating to visit. Examples of poor design abound: the ill-fated Boo.com had a state-of-the-art animated website which was able to show all the firm's clothes in three dimensions. Unfortunately, prospective customers needed a state-of-the-art computer to download the images in anything like a reasonable amount of time. Most simply got bored and went elsewhere, or found that the connection timed out before they were able to make a purchase. Some airline websites do not give the times of the flights, but require prospective passengers to enter the time of the flight in order to check availability. Wrong guesses mean wasted time where the system says 'There is no flight at that time'. Some cheap flight websites will not offer flights that do not exactly fit the customer's specification: this means a customer may end up paying more than necessary, simply because the site is not able to mention that a much cheaper flight is available the day before. Such websites lose out to those who develop a core competence in website design, such as EasyJet (**www.easyjet.com**) or Amazon (**www.amazon.com**).

Talking Point

We are always being told that we need to be different, to develop core competences which make us stand out from the crowd. But if everybody stands out from the crowd and adds value to the core generic product, who will make the commodity products?

Maybe there's still a market out there for the basic, cheap, simple product. Maybe not everybody WANTS the extra bells and whistles! Although this might be a marketing heresy, could the production of the 'commodity' version actually be a core competence in itself?

AUDIT ANALYSIS

Finally, the audit process itself should be examined and decisions taken as to whether it is appropriate, feasible, and effective. Here is a checklist for determining whether the audit has been correctly carried out:

1. Were the right people involved? Did they have the relevant knowledge, and the necessary objectivity, to carry out the task?

2. Were the right questions asked? Did the questions elicit reliable and relevant answers?

3. Has the process been non-threatening for the people concerned? Might anybody have felt constrained to provide a particular answer in order to avoid losing face or admitting to a problem?

CASE STUDY: ORGANIZING HONDA

www.honda.co.uk

Honda's annual report for 1997 contains the following statement:'By following a corporate policy that stresses originality, innovation, and efficiency in every facet of its operation – from product development and manufacturing to marketing – Honda has striven to attain its goal of satisfying its customers.'

Nowhere is this emphasis on originality and innovation more apparent than in Honda's internal management systems. For most managers in most companies, management problems appear as a series of trade-offs: individualism versus group needs, quality versus cheapness, cost savings versus differentiation, and so forth. Japanese business practices have tended to reject these trade-offs and replace them with something wholly new – getting the quality right first time, for example, actually saves money in wasted materials and time over the previous system of testing at the end of the production line.

Honda has applied this type of thinking to the conflicts inherent in organizational structure and management. To this end, Honda has virtually done away with the hierarchical management ▶

structure. Although there are still clear vertical lines of control, the company regularly cuts past these. Senior executives often meet with shop-floor supervisors, for example, and manufacturing managers share viewpoints with sales personnel. The career paths of individuals do not necessarily follow a hierarchical path either: it is quite feasible for technical staff to be promoted several times without ever having to manage people. Staff are often promoted diagonally: in the late 1980s one of Honda's senior marketing people was promoted to oversee the expansion of one of its American factories.

Furthermore, Honda is a company which places an emphasis on praising individuals in the firm. Quality circles operate company-wide: individuals are rewarded for innovation, and remain closely associated with the products and processes for which they have become responsible. However, individualism is not stressed above co-operation – each has its place in the organization.

Honda's decision-making process is characterized by collectivism, for example. The company's top executives do not have separate offices, but instead share one large, open-plan office in which there are spaces for them to sit together and talk, as well as their individual desks. Executives are allowed to have individual offices if they so wish: most do not do so, preferring the collective system and easy communication of the open-plan room.

Honda has undergone some fairly dramatic changes of direction in the past 25 years. Again, these are seen as positive by the management: each change of tack moves the company a little further forward, building on the progress made in previous years. No doubt the firm will change direction again many times in the next 25 years, but for Honda this is just part of being a flexible and responsive company.

CASE STUDY QUESTIONS

1. What problems might arise for Honda in carrying out an internal audit, given the fluidity of its structures?
2. How might Honda's senior management reconcile the problem of creating career paths for the staff?
3. What type of organization structure does Honda appear to tend towards?
4. What would be the problems for Honda in setting up a decision-support system?
5. How might Honda respond to a technological breakthrough, for example a new type of motive power for cars?

SUMMARY

The internal environment is at the root of corporate strengths. The people who work within the firm, and the firm's physical assets, are the basis of its capabilities for dealing with the external environment. In strategic terms, they are the equivalent of the army's soldiers and weapons.

Some of these assets are difficult to assess: to contrive the military analogy, the soldiers need to be tested under fire before the generals can be sure of their mettle.

The key points from this chapter are as follows:

- Internal audits provide a 'snapshot': they do not provide a permanent view of what is happening.
- Audits should not be used to discipline staff.

▶

- Introspection, honesty and integrity are paramount: sometimes it is better to use external consultants or interdepartmental groups in order to minimize political agendas.
- Hierarchical organizations are efficient, but extremely slow to change.
- Organismic organizations are flexible, but require more time spent in communication.
- Information support systems must be user-friendly, or they will be unused or, worse, corrupted.
- Systems should be designed around corporate need, not perceived technical capability. Technicians can usually rise to the challenge.
- Resources are harder to define and to quantify than might at first be expected.
- The audit process itself should be audited.

CHAPTER QUESTIONS

1. How might an organization in the public sector, for example a local authority, carry out an internal audit?
2. How might an internal audit differ in an organismic organization from that in a hierarchical organization?
3. How might a database be used for audit purposes?
4. How might a firm decide the frequency of auditing activities?
5. If an audit is a snapshot, and a decision support system provides a constant stream of information, how can one be reconciled with the other?

REFERENCES

Barney, J.B. (1986): 'Organizational culture: can it be a source of sustained competitive advantage?' *Academy of Management Review* vol. 11, pp. 656–65.

Barney, J.B. (1991): 'Firm resources and sustained competitive advantage', *Journal of Management* vol. 17, no. 1, pp. 99–120.

Bessen, Jim (1994): 'Riding the marketing information wave', *Harvard Business Review* Sept.–Oct. pp. 150–60.

Blythe, J. (2000): 'Objectives and measures at UK trade exhibitions', *Journal of Marketing Management* vol. 16, no. 1.

Dretske, F. (1981): *Knowledge and the flow of information* (Cambridge MA: MIT Press).

Durand, T. (1996): 'Revisiting key dimensions of competence'. Paper presented to the SMS Conference, Phoenix, Arizona.

Evans, M.J. (1994): 'Domesday Marketing?' *Journal of Marketing Management* vol. 10, no. 5, pp. 409–31.

Hamilton, W., East, R. and Kalafatis, S. (1997): 'The measurement and utility of brand price elasticities', *Journal of Marketing Management* vol. 13, no. 4, pp. 285–298.

Lowendahl, B.R. (1997): *Strategic management of professional business service firms* (Copenhagen: Copenhagen Business School Press).

Penrose, E.T. (1959): *The theory of the growth of the firm* (New York: Wiley).

Proctor, Tony (2000): *Essentials of Marketing Research* 2nd edition (Harlow: Financial Times Prentice Hall).

Sprague, Ralph H. and Watson, Hugh J. (1986): *Decision support systems: putting theory into practice* (Englewood Cliffs NJ: Prentice Hall).

Stalk, G., Evans, P. and Shulman, L. (1992): 'Competing on capabilities', *Harvard Business Review* March/April.

Wernerfelt, B. (1984): 'A resource-based view of the firm', *Strategic Management Journal* April/June, pp. 171–80.

4

The Marketing Interface

INTRODUCTION

This chapter is concerned with auditing the marketing functions themselves. The chapter will follow the Booms and Bitner (1981) 7-P model, looking at auditing products, prices, place (distribution), promotion, people, process, and physical evidence. Although this appears to suggest that each of these elements of the marketing mix are discrete, they should not be regarded as independent entities. Each works on the other, and changes in one element will almost certainly require changes in the others. For the strategist, this creates problems: the situation is a complex one.

After reading this chapter, you should be able to:

- Explain how to audit the marketing functions.
- Describe what is meant by product portfolio analysis.
- Explain the importance of analysis.
- Show how the elements of the marketing mix relate to each other.

PRODUCT PORTFOLIO ANALYSIS

The Product Life Cycle (PLC) is a useful concept to describe how products progress from introduction through to obsolescence. The theory is that products, like living things, have a natural life cycle beginning with introduction, going through a growth phase, reaching maturity, then going into decline, and finally becoming obsolete. Fig 4.1 illustrates this in graph form.

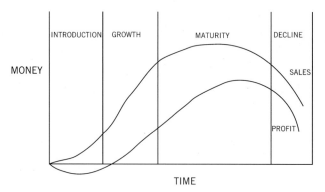

Figure 4.1: Product Life Cycle

In the introduction phase, the product's sales grow slowly, and the profit will be small or negative due to heavy promotion costs and production inefficiencies. If the product is very new, there will also be the need to persuade retailers and others to stock the product.

In the growth stage, there will be a rapid increase in sales as the product becomes better-known. At this stage profits begin to grow, but competition will also be entering the market so the producer may now need to think about adapting the product to meet the competitive threat.

In the maturity phase the product is well-known and well-established; at this point the promotional spend eases off and production economies of scale become established. By this time competitors will almost certainly have entered the market, so the firm will need to develop a new version of the product.

In the decline phase, the product is rapidly losing market share and profitability. At this stage the marketer must decide whether it is worthwhile supporting the product for a little longer, or whether it should be allowed to disappear. Supporting a product for which there is little natural demand is very unprofitable, but sometimes products can be revived and relaunched, perhaps in a different market.

The assumption is that all products exhibit this lifecycle, but the timescale will vary from one product to the next. Some products, for example computer games, may go through the entire life cycle in a matter of months. Others, like pitta bread, have a life cycle measured in thousands of years, and may never become obsolete.

The product life cycle concept is a useful way of looking at product development, but like many simple theories it has a number of flaws.

1. The theory assumes that changes in consumer preference only go one way, and that there is no swing back to an earlier preference. Some clothing fashions return after a few years, and some styles of music enjoy periodic revivals, but also some traditional products can suddenly become popular again, often following advertising campaigns based on nostalgia.

2. The model assumes that nobody does anything to revive the product when it begins to decline or be superseded by other products. Most marketers would look at their declining products and decide whether a revival is possible, or worthwhile.

3. Equally, a marketing manager might decide that a particular product no longer contributes towards the organization's overall strategic aims, and should be discontinued even though it is still making profits for the firm.

4. The model looks at only one product, whereas most marketing managers are having to balance the demands of many differing products, and decide which ones are most likely to yield the best return on investment. Again, it may be a more effective use of resources to kill off one product and divert attention to another.

To answer some of these criticisms, Enis, Lagarce and Prell re-designed the product life cycle as shown in Fig 4.2.

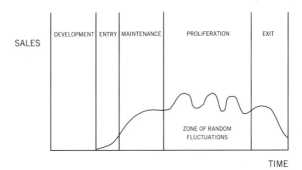

Figure 4.2: Revised Product Life Cycle
(Enis, Lagarce & Prell, 'Extending the Product Life Cycle', *Business Horizons*, June 1977)

In this more detailed model, the maturity phase now includes a section of maintenance, and one of proliferation. Maintenance is where the marketing manager is using various tactics to keep the product in the public eye and maintain sales, and proliferation is where the firm introduces variations on the original product in order to extend the life cycle. Sometimes these maintenance tactics will keep the product alive and successful for many years, but eventually the PLC theory implies that the product will be superseded and go into decline.

Note here that the Product Life Cycle concept is useful to describe what is happening, but is not much use for predicting what is going to happen, since it is virtually impossible to tell how long the maturity phase will continue. This makes it difficult to use as a strategic decision-making device; marketers are not easily able to tell which part of the product life cycle the product currently occupies. A temporary fall-off in sales might be caused by extraneous factors such as recessions or new competitive activity, without actually heralding the beginning of the decline phase. From a strategic planning perspective, therefore, the model is too simplistic because it does not take sufficient account of external environmental issues.

Most firms produce several different products at the same time, and it is possible to superimpose the PLC diagrams for each product onto the graph to give a composite view of what is happening to the firm's product portfolio. This will give a long-term overview, but the problems of prediction still remain; for many managers, a 'snapshot' of what is happening now is more useful, and this is the basis of product portfolio auditing. The Boston Consulting Group developed a matrix for decision making in these circumstances, as shown in Fig 4.3.

Figure 4.3: Boston Consulting Group Matrix

Stars are products with rapid growth and a dominant share of the market. Usually, the costs of fighting off the competition and maintaining growth mean the product is actually absorbing more money than it is generating, the problem lies in judging whether the market is going to continue to grow, or whether it will go down as quickly as it went up. The most prominent examples of Stars at present are the dot.com companies such as Amazon and Lastminute.com, which have shown astronomical growth in a rapidly-expanding market, but which have not yet shown a profit.

Cash Cows are the former Stars. They have a dominant share of the market, but are now in the maturity phase of the life cycle and consequently have low growth. A Cash Cow is generating cash, and can be 'milked' of it to finance the Stars. These are the products that have steady year-in year-out sales and are generating much of the firm's profits; examples might be the Big Mac hamburger, the Oxo cube, and Guinness (**www.guinness.ie**) stout.

Dogs have a low market share and low growth prospects. The argument here is not whether the product is profitable; it almost always is. The argument is about whether the firm could use its production facilities to make something that would be more profitable, and this is also almost always the case.

The **Problem Child** has a small share of a growth market, and causes the marketer the most headaches since it is necessary to work out a way of building market share so as to turn the product into a Star. This means finding out why the share is so low, and developing strategies to increase market share rapidly. The Problem Child (or question mark) could be backed with an even bigger promotion campaign, or it could possibly be adapted in some way to fit the market better. Market research plays a crucial role in making these decisions. Finding out how to adapt a product is a difficult area of research, but the potential rewards are huge and adapting the product to meet people's needs better is almost always cheaper than increasing the advertising spend.

The strategic policy decisions that arise from this view of the firm's product portfolio lie in the following areas:

- Which products should be dropped from the range entirely? This question not only hinges on how profitable the product itself is; sales of one product often indirectly generate sales of another more profitable product.

- Which products should be backed with promotion campaigns? Backing the wrong product can be extremely expensive; advertising campaigns have no second-hand value, so if the campaign fails the money is lost.

■ Which products could be adapted to fit the market better, and in what ways? This very much hinges on market research findings, and on customer feedback.

■ Which new products could be introduced, and at what cost?

Like the product life cycle, the BCG Matrix is a simple model which helps marketers to approach strategic product decisions; and like the PLC, it has a number of flaws. It is based on the following assumptions:

1. Market share can be gained by investment in marketing. This is not always the case. Some products will have lost their markets altogether (perhaps through environmental changes) and cannot be revived, no matter how much is invested.

2. Market share gains will always generate cash surpluses. Again, if market share is gained by drastic price cutting or even by large investments in marketing activities, cashflow may be negative. In other words, far from creating a cash surplus, the market share gain might create a cash deficit.

3. Cash surpluses will be generated when the product is in the maturity stage of the life-cycle. Not necessarily so: mature products may well be operating on such small margins due to competitive pressure that the profit generated is low.

4. The best opportunity to build a dominant market position is during the growth phase. In most cases this would be true, but this does not take account of competition. A competitor's product might be growing even faster.

Barksdale and Harris (1982) proposed two additions to the BCG Matrix -- see Fig 4.4. **War Horses** have high market share, but the market has negative growth. The problem for management is to decide whether the product is in irreversible decline, or whether it can be revived, perhaps by repositioning into another market. **Dodos** have a low share of a negative growth market, and are probably best discontinued.

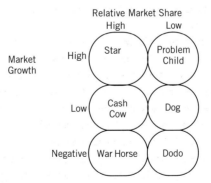

Figure 4.4: Expanded Boston Consulting Group Matrix

The BCG Matrix has proved a useful tool for analysing product portfolio decisions, but is really only a snapshot of the current position with the products it describes. It has little or no predictive value, since (like the PLC) it does not take sufficient account of environmental factors. Since most markets are, to a greater or lesser extent, dynamic the Matrix should be used with a certain degree of caution.

The size of the product portfolio and the complexity of the products within it can have further effects on the firm's management. For example it has been shown that manufacturing a wide range of products with many options makes it difficult for the firm to use just-in-time purchasing techniques, and complicates the firm's supply activities (Benwell 1996).

With all its faults, the BCG matrix is still widely used. This is because it provides a structure for planning which enables strategists to balance the portfolio, or at least identify the issues which need to be addressed. Most companies will have products scattered across all four categories: the one-product company is extremely rare.

Strategic decisions that flow from the BCG matrix are as follows:

1. Cash from Cash Cows should first be used to support Stars, then used selectively to fund Problem Children in order to increase market share and possibly reposition them as Stars.
2. Inadequate funding of Stars will lead to a fall in market share, repositioning the Star as a Problem Child.
3. As markets mature (i.e. stop growing) Stars will become Cash Cows and Problem Children will become Dogs.
4. Problem Children which cannot be funded to become Stars should be dropped.
5. Dogs can be milked for cash, but are probably better dropped.

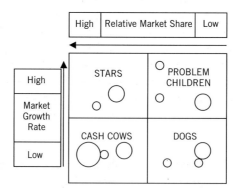

Figure 4.5: Balanced portfolio

Figure 4.5 shows a balanced portfolio: the area of the circles indicates the cash sales volume for each product, so that comparisons can be made.

This portfolio shows three Cash Cows, one of which is very substantial and has a high share of its market. One of the Stars is doing well, but is edging close to the Problem Child box: on the other hand, two of the Problem Children are small enough for the Cash Cows to support them, are already edging closer to the Star box and could probably be supported to make the transition. Two of the three Dogs are very small and unlikely to cause a great many problems if they are dropped from the portfolio: the third one has a small share of what is evidently a large (though stable) market, but is generating substantial income and might therefore be treated in the same way as a Cash Cow.

The Directional Policy Matrix (also called the McKinsey GE Matrix) offers a way of balancing the company's competitive capabilities within any given market with the prospects for the business sector as a whole. This may be helpful in enabling the company to decide which products should be retained if the firm is involved in different business sectors. The matrix is shown in Fig 4.6.

Figure 4.6: Directional policy matrix

		Business sector prospects		
		Unattractive	Average	Attractive
Company's competitive capabilities	**Weak**	Disinvest	Phased withdrawal Proceed with care	Double or quit
	Average	Phased withdrawal	Proceed with care	Try
	Strong	Cash generator	Growth leader	Leader

(McKinsey 1971)

The strategic plan which arises from each position is relatively self-explanatory. A firm whose product has a strong competitive position in an unattractive market can use the product as a cash generator: a firm weak competitive advantage in a highly-attractive market should 'double or quit', in other words either increase investment for the product in order to improve its competitive position, or leave the market altogether.

Most portfolio approaches are retrospective: market attractiveness is not necessarily easily assessed by looking into the past (Gluck 1985). Also, the portfolio approach tends to ignore the business environment: for example, in times of recession a firm might find that most or all of its products are in slow-growing or shrinking markets. Clearly they cannot all be classified as Dogs and dropped (Hambrick and MacMillan 1982). Some authors go so far as to say that decisions based on portfolio matrices are actually damaging to firms (Armstrong and Brodie 1994).

Overall, portfolio analysis is a useful way of looking at the firm's situation, but should not be relied upon as the only tool for making decisions.

PRICING AUDITS

Determining price is not simply a matter of calculating what it costs to make a product and then adding on a profit margin. Price is a useful strategic tool for marketers, which can be used in any of the following ways:

1. As a signal of quality (high or low).

2. As a competitive tool.

3. As a way of controlling demand in order to match with production capacity.

4. As a way of controlling profit margins: this is not necessarily the same as seeking to maximize profits, since there may be tax advantages in pricing in a particular way.

5. As a way of penetrating new markets.

The pricing audit needs to look at prices across the board: since few firms sell only one product, the pricing of products within the portfolio will have an effect on sales of other products in the portfolio. For example, Mercedes Benz (**www.mercedes-benz.com**) has enjoyed a reputation for producing very high quality cars, at prices to match. The cars have filled a market niche which has been perhaps one step down from Rolls-Royce (**www.rolls-royceandbentley.co.uk**) or Cadillac (**www.cadillac.com/homesite.htm**), but certainly at the upper end of the market. When the firm decided to enter the mass-market vehicle business with the A-series, this damaged the image of the larger, more luxurious cars which were the backbone of the firm's success. Selling cheap is not necessarily a good idea, it would seem.

The first stage in auditing the pricing strategy is to examine whether the pricing objectives are appropriate. Pricing policies can achieve short or long-term objectives: for example, penetration pricing (pricing low to gain a large share of a new market) reduces profits dramatically in the short term, but may be successful in keeping competitors out of the market, so that it becomes a useful long-term strategy. Note that penetration pricing is a short-term tactic to achieve a long-term strategy: the prices will have to rise once the firm's objectives have been achieved.

The second stage is to assess the impact of individual brand prices on other products in the range. For example, UK supermarket chain Tesco's (**www.tesco.com**) has a range of low-price own-brand products which sell under the collective Value brand. Sales of these products have had an impact on the firm's original own-brand products, but Tesco's has found it worthwhile to introduce yet a third range of high-price, high-quality own-brands which sell under the collective brand of Tesco's Finest. This means that, in some product categories, there are three separate own-brands on offer, in addition to manufacturers' proprietary brands, presumably all cannibalizing each other's sales. Most firms offering a range of products will have similar situations.

The third stage is to examine the impact of the pricing strategy on consumer perceptions of the brand. Reducing the price (even on a temporary basis as part of a sales promotion) may signal a reduction in quality, or a weakness in the company. This applies most to premium (high price, high quality) products. The pricing strategy therefore needs to reflect the positioning strategy: this will in turn be reflected in the promotional strategy. For example, Stella Artois beer (**www.stella-artois.be**) has been positioned in the UK as a premium-brand lager, using the strap line 'Reassuringly expensive'. In its native Belgium, the beer is a standard-price, medium-range beer: the pricing strategy is different for the different target groups of consumer.

Finally, the fourth stage is to consider price promotions and the discount structure. Are these appropriate in meeting strategic objectives? For example, if the overall strategy is to favour large customers who will place large orders, the discount structure needs to reflect this. If, on the other hand, the firm prefers to encourage a large number of small customers, the discount structure might be less generous for quantity, but more generous for regularly-placed orders. For example, a firm manufacturing hairdressing products for use by professional hair salons is faced with a market dominated by small firms. Quantity discounts are unlikely to generate much extra business, since such firms lack the necessary resources to purchase in bulk. For this reason, most such firms will offer a discount if the salon owner is prepared to use the manufacturer's products exclusively, and allow the manufacturer's sales representative to take over the stock control function. This saves salesforce time and effort, and ensures a steady market, in a situation where bulk orders are unlikely to happen.

Talking Point

Although price is a strategic tool for positioning products, fighting competition, and so forth, it is also the exchange customers give for the product. If a firm is customer-orientated, how can it justify manipulating such a basic element of the exchange in order to change perceptions, or respond to competitors?

Why should firms not merely use cost-plus pricing to set prices, in other words? Wouldn't this be fairer?

Or perhaps there is more to perception. Perhaps people sometimes prefer to pay more for something than they need – or perhaps the situation is even more complex than it at first appears.

PLACE AUDITS

The distribution audit is about ensuring that the products are available in the most effective manner. Distribution falls into two categories for the purposes of strategic auditing. The first category is the channels of distribution, which refers to the routes by which the product moves from producer to consumer; the second category is the physical distribution, which is concerned with transportation methods.

Channels of distribution include wholesalers, retailers, agents and other intermediaries. Intermediaries perform essential functions within the overall distribution strategy: it is usually more efficient for a specialist intermediary to act rather than try to do everything in-house. The cost savings made by specialist intermediaries more than cover their profit margins: if this were not so, other members of the distribution network would simply bypass them. In practice this means that 'cutting out the middle man' is more likely to raise costs (and prices) overall rather than reduce them.

Table 4.1 shows the functions of some of the members of a channel of distribution.

Table 4.1: Categories of channel members

Channel member	Function
Agents	Agents act as a sales arm for manufacturers, without taking title to the goods; agency sales representatives call on major retailers and on wholesalers on behalf of a number of manufacturers, and take orders and arrange delivery. This saves small manufacturers the cost of operating a large salesforce.
Wholesalers	Actually buy the goods from the manufacturers, often through an agent, then sell the goods on to the retailers or sometimes the final consumers.
Retailers	A retailer is any organization which offers goods directly to consumers. This includes mail order companies, door-to-door salespeople, and e-commerce organizations selling over the Internet.

For example, a wholesaler carries out the following functions:

1. Negotiates with suppliers.
2. Some promotional activities: advertising, sales promotion, publicity, providing a sales force.
3. Warehousing, storage and product handling.

4. Transport of local and sometimes long-distance shipments.

5. Inventory control.

6. Credit checking and credit control.

7. Pricing and collection of pricing information, particularly about competitors.

8. Channel of information up and down the distribution network, again particularly with regard to competitors' activities.

9. Breaks down bulk deliveries and aggregates small quantities for onward delivery.

All of these functions would have to be carried out by each manufacturer individually if the wholesaler did not exist. By carrying them out on behalf of many manufacturers, the wholesaler achieves economies of scale which more than cover the profit taken. The wholesaler also provides services to the retailers, as follows:

1. Information gathering and dissemination.

2. One-stop shopping for a wide range of products from a wide range of manufacturers.

3. Facilities for buying relatively small quantities.

4. Fast deliveries – often cash-and-carry.

5. Flexible ordering – can vary amounts as demand fluctuates.

Again, from the retailer's viewpoint it is much more convenient and cheaper to use a wholesaler. Only if the retailer is big enough to order economic quantities direct from the manufacturer will it be worthwhile to do so. For example, few hairdressers are big enough to order everything direct from the manufacturers, so a large part of a salon's stock-in-trade is bought from wholesalers.

The audit therefore needs to ask the following questions:

1. What functions do the current distributors carry out?

2. Could these be carried out more efficiently by someone else, or even in-house?

3. Are there other functions that the distributors could carry out for us, but currently do not?

4. If so, is it possible for us to agree a change in the relationship so that these functions can be carried out?

5. Are these distributors the most effective ones to meet the needs of our consumers?

6. What are the power relationships between channel members?

Producers need to ensure that the distributors of their products are of the right type. The image of a retailer can damage (or enhance) the image of the products sold (and vice-versa). Producers need not necessarily sell through the most prestigious retailer, and in fact this would be counter-productive for many cheap, everyday items. Likewise a prestigious product should not be sold through a down-market retail outlet.

Channels can be led by any of the channel members, whether they are producers, wholesalers, or retailers, provided the member concerned has **channel power**. This power comes from seven sources (Bitner 1992), as shown in Table 4.2.

Since each member relies on every other member for the free exchange of goods down the channel, channel co-operation is an essential part of the effective functioning of channels. It is in the members' interests to look after each other to some extent. Channel co-operation can be improved by agreeing on the overall targeting strategy, and by defining tasks within the channel in order to avoid duplication of effort.

Table 4.2: Sources of channel power

Economic sources of power	Non-economic sources of power	Other factors
Control of resources. The degree to which the channel member has the power to direct goods, services or finance within the channel.	Reward power. The ability to provide financial benefits, or otherwise favour channel members.	Level of power. This derives from the economic and non-economic sources of power.
Size of company. The bigger the firm compared with other channel members, the greater the overall economic power.	Expert power. This arises when the leader has special expertise which the other channel members need.	Dependency of other channel members.
Referent power emerges when channel members try to emulate the leader.		Willingness to lead. Clearly some firms with potential for channel leadership prefer not to have the responsibility, or are unable to exercise the potential for other reasons.
Legitimate power arises from a superior – subordinate relationship. For example, if a retailer holds a substantial shareholding in a wholesaler, it has legitimate power over the wholesaler.		
Coercive power exists when one channel member has the power to punish another.		

Channel conflict arises because one or other member seeks to maximize its own profits or power in the short term. In the longer run, conflict of this type is counter-productive because retaliation by other channel members means that the channel becomes less efficient, which reduces profits for everybody. Reduction of conflict can be achieved by co-operation and negotiation, often at the behest of the strongest member. It can also be carried out by using coercion, perhaps by using some of the methods outlined as follows:

- Refusal to deal. One member refuses to supply another (or refuses to buy from another) unless the other member is prepared to accede to the first member's demands.
- Tying contracts. The supplier requires that the channel member carries a full range of the firm's products. This is common in franchise agreements and dealership agreements.
- Exclusive dealing. The supplier prevents a dealer from carrying competitors' products, or an intermediary demands exclusive rights to a product.
- Restricted sales territories. Dealers are prevented from selling the products outside their immediate territory (which may be geographical, industrial, customer-based or divided in any other way).

Some of these methods might be regarded as unfair trading practices. Most attempts to control distribution by the use of power are looked on unfavourably by the courts and even by monopoly regulators in some cases, but of course channel members are unlikely to resort to legal action unless the abuse of power was extreme.

Sometimes the simplest way to control a distribution channel is to buy out the channel members. Horizontal integration means buying out members across a given level (for example, a wholesaler buying out other wholesalers in order to build a national network); vertical integration means buying out members above or below in the distribution chain. An extreme example of vertical integration is the major oil companies, which extract crude oil, refine it, ship it, and retail it through petrol stations. Again, this type of integration may attract the attention of monopoly regulation agencies, since the integration may cause a restriction of competition. The audit might therefore look at the degree and type of integration present for the firm itself, and in the industry.

Strategic distribution decisions are concerned with the location where the product should be available in order to achieve corporate objectives; physical distribution is concerned with getting the physical product to those locations. Logistics takes a wider, more strategic view of the process. Originally based on military terminology, logistics is concerned with the process of moving raw materials through the production and distribution processes to the point at which the finished product is needed. This involves strategic decision-making about warehouse location, materials management, stock levels, and information systems. Logistics is where purchasing and marketing overlap.

The purpose of any physical distribution method is to get the product from its point of production to the consumer in as efficient and effective a way as possible. The product must arrive in good condition, at the right time and in the right quantities, and in an economical manner. Transportation methods vary according to speed, cost, and ability to handle the type of product concerned. As a general rule, the quicker the method the more expensive it is, but in some cases it may be cheaper to use a faster method because the firm's capital is tied up for less time. For perishable goods such as fruit, standby airfreight can be as cheap as sea transport, when the lower incidence of wastage is taken into account.

The transportation method chosen for a particular product will depend on the factors listed in Table 4.3.

Table 4.3: Choosing a transportation method

Factor	Explanation and examples
The physical characteristics of the product	Fragile products such as chinaware need short distribution channels with minimal handling. Perishable goods (e.g. fruit) may be shipped more cheaply via standby airfreight: although the initial cost is higher, there will be less spoilage.
The methods used by the competition	It is possible to gain a significant competitive edge by using an unusual method. For example, significant advantage has been gained by some music distributors by sending digital recordings through the Internet rather than physically distributing CDs to record shops.
The costs of the various channels available	The cheapest channel is not always the best; for example, computer chips are light, but costly and therefore it is cheaper to use airfreight than to tie up the company's capital in lengthy surface transportation.
The reliability of the channel	Emergency medical supplies must have 100% reliable transportation, as must cash deliveries.
The transit time	Transit time needs to be balanced against perishability, and capital tied up.
Security	Highly-valuable items may not be easily distributed through retailers. Direct delivery may work much better.
Traceability	The ease with which a shipment can be located or redirected. For example, oil tankers can be diverted to deliver to different refineries at relatively short notice. This allows the oil companies to meet demand in different countries.
The level of customer service required	Customers may need the product to be delivered in exact timings (for example, in just-in-time manufacturing). Some document deliveries (legal documents, for example) are extremely time-sensitive.

(Adapted from Coyle, Bardi & Langley, *The Management of Business Logistics*, West 1988)

In all the above cases, there will be trade-offs involved. Greater customer service will almost always be more expensive; greater reliability may increase transit time, as will greater traceability because in most cases the product will need to be checked on and off the transport method chosen. As with any other aspect of marketing activity, the customers' overall needs must be taken into account, and the relative importance of those needs must be judged with some accuracy if the firm is to remain competitive.

The physical distribution audit will therefore need to answer the following questions:

1. Does the present system ensure that goods arrive in the right place, at the right time, and in the right condition?
2. Is the system integrated in the most effective way?
3. Would alternative systems of distribution meet our consumers' needs better?
4. Do alternative transportation methods exist which would better serve our product?
5. Could the product or its packaging be adapted in some way to make physical distribution easier or cheaper?

THE PROMOTIONAL AUDIT

The promotional audit is concerned with the full range of the promotional mix, which includes advertising, personal selling, sales promotion and public relations. Of these, PR and personal selling are often regarded as being separate from marketing: sometimes PR is seen as a completely separate issue, sometimes it is seen as encompassing marketing completely. Equally, personal selling can be seen as a completely separate activity, or as an adjunct of marketing, or even as marketing on a one-to-one basis. Resolving these conceptual difficulties is also part of the audit: managers should be aware of what the corporate attitude is, and also what the attitude of the professionals concerned is towards these classifications. For example, evidence exists that salespeople often regard marketers as being there to provide support services for the 'real' job of selling, whereas marketers typically regard the salesforce as being one of the tools of promotion, available for whatever purpose they are needed (Yandle and Blythe 2000).

Objectives need to be realistic, as always, but planners often miss the point that a marketing communications strategy can only be expected to achieve marketing communications objectives. Many firms tend to measure the effectiveness of their promotional campaigns in terms of business generated, which means that in most cases they are unable to filter out other effects caused by environmental issues such as changes in competitive activities, shifts in demand caused by economic swings, or simple seasonality. Measuring by communications outcomes means that the firm is able to make a much more accurate judgement of the effectiveness of the campaign – although this may not satisfy the accountants.

Since advertising is a high-profile activity and often a very expensive one, much attention has been given to measuring its effectiveness. Four elements appear to be important in the effectiveness of advertising: awareness, liking, interest and enjoyment. There is a high correlation between brand loyalty and brand awareness (Stapel 1990); likeability appears to be the single best predictor of sales effectiveness since likeability scales predict 97 per cent of sales successes (Biel 1989); interest clearly relates to likeability (Stapel 1991), and enjoyment appears to be a good indicator in advertising pretests (Brown 1991).

For many years effectiveness was measured in terms of sales results, the assumption being that the purpose of advertising is to generate sales. Since sales can result from many other activities (personal selling, increased efforts by distributors, increased prosperity and so forth), it is difficult to assess the overall contribution of advertising in the outcomes. A more recent view has been that the role of advertising is to communicate – to change awareness and attitudes. This view crystallized as the DAGMAR model (Defining Advertising Goals, Measuring Advertising Results) (Colley 1961). DAGMAR implies that concrete and measurable communication objectives such as awareness, brand recognition, recall of content and so forth, should be set for advertising, rather than sales turnover goals.

DAGMAR has been criticised on the grounds that it tends to lead planners to find out what can be measured easily, then set that as a goal (Broadbent 1989). The simple objectives which can be measured do not tell the whole story of major-brand success; advertising does other things which are hard to measure, such as encouraging brand loyalty or increasing word-of-mouth communication between consumers themselves.

Talking Point

Ultimately, marketing is about ensuring that sales come in. Marketers achieve this (ostensibly) by matching the organization's activities to the needs of the customers. So why should advertising be different? Why shouldn't advertising be intended directly to create sales, and therefore why should it not be judged on those criteria?

If advertising is only about communicating, what use is it? Shouldn't the communication be designed to achieve an objective? And, if the firm is to survive, shouldn't that objective be more customers, more business, and more sales?

In order to ensure that measurement of effectiveness is both valid and reliable, a set of principles called PACT (Positioning Advertising Copy Testing) have been established (*Marketing News* 1982). A good advertising testing system should:

1. Provide measurements that are relevant to the objectives of the advertising.
2. Require agreement about how the results will be used in advance of each specific test.
3. Provide multiple measurements because single measurements are generally inadequate to assess the advert's performance.
4. Be based on a model of human response to communication – the reception of a stimulus, the comprehension of the stimulus, and the response to the stimulus.
5. Allow for consideration of whether the advertising stimulus should be exposed more than once.
6. Recognise that the more finished a piece of copy is the more soundly it can be evaluated. It should also require as a minimum that alternative executions be tested to the same degree of finish.
7. Provide controls to avoid the biasing effects of the exposure content.
8. Take into account basic considerations of sample definition.
9. Demonstrate reliability and validity empirically.

Advertisements can be tested on two dimensions: those factors related to the advertisement itself, and those related to its contents. Since these two issues are sometimes difficult for the consumer to separate there is no real certainty as to which is actually being tested.

The budgeting method should also be audited to ensure that it is the most effective for the purpose. The most common methods are as follows:

1. Objective and Task. The budget is set according to the objectives and tasks to be achieved. This is probably the most strategically-orientated method, but there are considerable

difficulties inherent in calculating how much money will be needed to achieve the objective.

2. **Percent of Sales.** A fixed percentage of the company's sales allocated to promotion. This is the least market-orientated approach, but is logical and easy to calculate. The main drawback is that it creates a vicious circle, where as sales drop, expenditure drops, which further harms sales.

3. **Comparative Parity.** Here the firm matches competitors' expenditure. This has the major drawback of taking no account of changes in the market, and (perhaps worse) means that competitors are setting the firm's promotional budget.

4. **Marginal approach.** Spending continues up to the point of diminishing returns. This is very much a sales-led approach, and is also extremely difficult to calculate.

5. **All-you-can-afford.** The company spends as much as can be spared from other activities. This approach pays no attention to market conditions, and also means that the marketers are continually fighting for a share of the firm's budgets.

In the real world, marketers usually adopt a combination strategy, using several of the above methods. Even an objective-and-task approach might begin by looking at what the competition is spending (comparative parity approach) if only to determine what the likely spend would have to be to overcome clutter. Likewise, a marketer may be part-way through a campaign and be told by the finance department that no more money is available (or perhaps be told that more than anticipated is available) and will switch to an all-you-can-spend policy.

PEOPLE AUDIT

People are an integral part of the product, particularly in services markets. The waiter in a restaurant, the receptionist in an hotel, the hairstylist in a hairdressing salon are all obviously part of the service offering. Even in other contexts, though, the firm's staff is integral to the image the firm has. Delivery drivers, telephonists, progress chasers, salespeople, and even credit controllers all impact on the customer's experience.

From the employee's perspective, the firm needs to supply answers to these questions (D'Apris 1987):

1. What is my job?
2. How am I doing?
3. Does anybody give a damn?

Once the organization has answered these questions, the employee will want answers to these:

4. How are we doing?
5. How do we fit in to the whole?
6. How can I help?

The final question is, of course, the one the management of the firm is most ready to answer.

From the viewpoint of auditing the people situation, the firm needs to find answers to the following questions:

1. Who are the front-line staff, in other words which staff have regular direct contact with customers or consumers?
2. What is the person specification for those people, and does it include statements to the effect that someone with good interpersonal skills should be appointed?

CASE STUDY: TOURISM IN BRITAIN

www.visitbritain.com

Tourism accounts for around a third of Britain's invisible exports, and about four per cent of the UK's gross domestic product. Not large by the standards of Greece or Spain, but still a substantial contribution to the UK economy, and a provider of 1.5 m jobs – if part-timers are included, tourism accounts for more than ten per cent of the working population. In fact, because the UK economy is so large in the first place, Britain ranks fifth in world earners from tourism – no small contender.

The British Tourist Authority is a government-funded organization with the responsibility for co-ordinating the industry within the UK. The stated mission of the BTA is 'to strengthen the performance of Britain's tourist industry in international markets by encouraging people to visit Britain and encouraging the improvement and provision of tourist amenities and facilities'. The idea is to generate a single, coherent message about Britain – a somewhat difficult task in view of the disparate cultures within the four countries that comprise the United Kingdom.

BTA has identified three main needs if tourism is to be expanded: firstly, more airport capacity in the south-east of England, because most foreign tourists want to visit London. Secondly, there is a need for more low-cost accommodation in London: hotel accommodation is extremely expensive there. Thirdly, a more tourist-friendly attitude in the retail industry.

One of the problems BTA faces is the government attitude to tourism, which is favourable but is also directed at strategic aims of government. For example, there has been a certain emphasis on attracting tourists from countries which the government would like to influence, or from which the government would like to redress a trade imbalance. Japan was a favourite target country for a while, but as government policy shifts, the target shifts: this can upset BTA's own strategic plans, which may take years to come to fruition, but can be swept away by a change of government.

BTA has been specifically concerned with added value, or the extra value that it adds to the UK economy. This is a measure which is of paramount importance when applying for further government funding. If it can demonstrate that its campaigns are money well spent, this will affect government attitudes when setting the following year's budget. This does mean that BTA sometimes needs to demonstrate a short term gain, when in fact its objectives tend to be long-term, but this is part of the process which most organizations need to go through. BTA has some notable successes to report: an assessment carried out in New York showed that BTA generated £35 worth of revenue for every £1 spent in the budget. In Japan, one campaign which only cost BTA £10,000 generated £250,000 in tourist revenue. BTA has been creative in attracting sponsorship and assistance from companies in the tourist trade – the New York operation was helped by United Airlines, Hertz car rental, and Mount Charlotte Thistle hotels. The Japanese promotion was backed by KNT Tours, a Japanese tour operator.

BTA does not have everything its own way, however. A survey of foreign tourists revealed the following perceptions of Britain as a holiday destination:

1. Britain is not viewed as offering value for money, except when sterling is weak against other currencies.
2. Hotels are regarded as expensive, poor value for money, and not living up to expectation.
3. The failure of British people to speak foreign languages caused dissatisfaction among continental visitors, especially the French and Italians.

Overall, BTA's role in campaigning for improved facilities and attitudes towards tourism is working well: its promotion of the UK as a tourist destination is also going well, and although there has been

▶

some fall-back in recent years due to health scares (the 2001 foot-and-mouth outbreak, for example) and also the strength of the pound during 2000 and 2001, tourism has recovered and remains healthy.

CASE STUDY QUESTIONS

1. How might BTA go about auditing its 'product', the UK?
2. What do you think might be the outcome of a pricing audit?
3. Tourism is delivered through a number of channels – airlines, hotels, and so forth. How could BTA audit these channels? What problems are already apparent?
4. How might the BCG matrix be applied to BTA's problem?
5. Do countries have a product life cycle?

SUMMARY

The marketing function audits should not be seen as discrete operations, any more than the marketing functions themselves operate independently. There is considerable overlap between (for example) physical evidence and promotions, and since the corporate strategy should be a linking factor, there should be commonality in the strategy at the business level.

Here are the key points from this chapter:

- Most products go through a process of decline sooner or later: the audit will indicate which should be dropped and which continued.
- Price is about more than meeting financial objectives. It is a key factor in positioning as well.
- Distribution strategy concerns the power relationships in the supply chain as well as the convenience of the consumer.
- Promotion is potentially where a poor strategy can be the most expensive in terms of costs and benefits: communications strategies can only achieve communications objectives.
- People who have contact with customers are strategically extremely important within the organization. Loyal, empowered and committed staff are basic to providing good customer service.
- The process by which the product's benefits are delivered is part of the product.
- Physical evidence is often a trigger for word-of-mouth communication, and can be used to increase loyalty and repeat purchase.

CHAPTER QUESTIONS

1. Price is a single attribute which has many strategic implications. How might the conflicts in the pricing audit be resolved?
2. Sometimes products which are not in themselves profitable lead to the sales of other products which are. How does this relate to the BCG matrix?
3. How might an advertising effectiveness study help in controlling promotional budgets?

4. Why is 'cutting out the middle man' likely to lead to reduced efficiency?

5. Why is 'cutting out the middle man' often used as a promotional message by out-of-town discount retailers?

REFERENCES

'21 Ad Agencies Endorse Copy Testing Principles', *Marketing News* 19 February 1982.

D'Apris, R. (1987): Quoted in Arnott, M. 'Effective Employee Communication' in Hart, N. (ed) *Effective Corporate Relations* (London: McGraw-Hill).

Armstrong, J.J. and Brodie, R.J. (1984): 'Effects of Portfolio Planning Methods on Decision Making: Experimental Results', *International Journal of Research in Marketing* vol. 11, pp. 73–84

Barksdale, H.C. and Harris, C.E. (1982): 'Portfolio analysis and the PLC', *Long Range Planning* 15 (6) pp. 74–83.

Benwell, M. (1996): 'Scheduling stocks and storage space in a volatile market', *Logistics Information Management* 9 (4) pp. 18–23.

Biel, A: 'Love the Advertisement, Buy the Product?' *ADMAP* Oct. 1989.

Bitner, M.J. (1992): 'Servicescapes: the impact of physical surroundings on customers and employees', *Journal of Marketing* April, pp. 57–71.

Booms, B.H. and Bitner, M.J. (1981): 'Marketing strategies and organization structures for service firms'. In *Marketing of Services* J. Donnelly and W.R. George, eds. (Chicago Il: American Marketing Association).

Broadbent, Simon: *The Advertising Budget* (Institute of Practitioners in Advertising & NTC Publications Ltd., 1989).

Brown, G. (1991): 'Modelling Advertising Awareness', *ADMAP* April 1991.

Colley, Russell H.: *Defining Advertising Goals* (New York: Association of National Advertisers, 1961).

Gluck, F. (1985): 'A Fresh Look at Strategic Management', *Journal of Business Strategy* Fall, p. 23.

Hambrick, D. and MacMillan, I. (1982): 'The Product Portfolio and Man's Best Friend', *California Management Review* Fall, pp. 16–23.

Murphy, J.A. (2001): *The Lifebelt* (Chichester: John Wiley).

Stapel, J (1990): 'Monitoring Advertising Performance', *ADMAP* July/August.

Stapel, J. (1991): 'Like the Advertisement but Does it Interest Me?', *ADMAP* April.

Yandle, J. and Blythe, J. (2000): 'Intra-Departmental Conflict between Sales and Marketing: An Exploratory Study', *Journal of Selling and Major Account Management* vol. 2 no. 3.

Where do we want to be?

Having found out what the organization's present position is, planners are able to decide where improvements need to be made – in other words, decide where we want to be. Deciding where we want to be is partly a process of identifying a desirable position, and partly a process of identifying what is feasible within the context of the company.

Sometimes the drive for a particular objective comes from the firm's founder (a visionary entrepreneur, perhaps) or it may come from a vision of the future which has been carefully calculated by a team of planners. Either way, planning for the future is a key role of senior management in any organization.

The following three chapters cover where we want to be, looking at missions and objectives, and at the desirability (and feasibility) of approaching customers and markets.

Chapter Five

Missions and Objectives

INTRODUCTION

Mission statements and objective-setting are about where the company wants to be in future. They give the direction to the business, and are the foundation of the company's strategic planning.

After reading this chapter, you should be able to:

- Define what is meant by vision, mission, and strategic intent.
- Explain how a mission statement should be drawn up.
- Describe the typical content of a mission statement.
- Explain some of the drawbacks of mission statements.
- Explain how to turn aims into objectives.
- Explain how to determine the practicality of objectives.

MISSION, VISION AND STRATEGIC INTENT

Two broad definitions of mission are current (Campbell, Devine and Yeung 1990). On the one hand, mission is often regarded as an intellectual discipline, and a strategic tool which is fundamental to strategic management. It addresses two questions: firstly, what business are we in, and secondly what business should we be in? On the other hand, mission can be regarded as the basis of the corporate culture, in effect the 'glue' which enables the members of the organization to function together in a united way. Campbell et al. define mission as being about both culture and strategy, defining mission as follows:

'A mission exists when strategy and culture are mutually supportive. An organization has a mission when its culture fits with its strategy.'

In this model, the mission is the organization's character, identity and reason for existence. The mission divides into four parts, as shown in Table 5.1.

Table 5.1: Elements of the mission

Element	Description
Purpose	Why the company exists. Companies do not necessarily exist purely to make a profit. For most founders of companies, and indeed for most Boards of Directors, companies exist to achieve something which the senior management feel is really worth doing. Profit is what enables such companies to stay in the game. In many cases, companies exist to maximize shareholder value – which is not necessarily synonymous with making a profit in the short term.
Strategy	The company's competitive position, and distinctive competence. This is the statement of how the company expects to distinguish itself from companies offering similar benefits to customers.
Behaviour standards	Norms and rules: 'The way we do things round here'. Behaviour standards will include the way customers are dealt with, and the way staff are treated.
Values	These are the moral principles and beliefs that underpin behaviour standards. Normally these values will have first been put in place by the founders, or by the directors, but sometimes they have grown up empirically over the life of the firm.

Vision is the view taken by the founder of a firm, and concerns the ultimate achievement of an ideal. Vision can often be confused with mission, and there is a degree of overlap between the two. In general, mission is about the organization's present situation, whereas vision is more concerned with the future, and refers to a goal which can be achieved. For example, a founder of a firm might have a vision of becoming the world's largest supplier of a given product, or of bringing the benefits of a luxury product within the reach of the masses. Examples might be Fernand Porsche's vision of creating a 'people's car' which would bring motoring within the reach of ordinary working people. This vision resulted in the design and production of the Volkswagen (**www.volkswagen.de**).

A vision and a mission can be identical (Campbell et al. 1990), but if the original vision is attained it will need to be reformulated. Visions are associated with goals, whereas missions are more concerned with ways of behaving.

The third concept which overlays the concepts of vision and mission is that of strategic intent (Hamel and Prahalad 1989). Strategic intent envisions a desired leadership position and establishes the criterion the organization will use to chart its progress. Often the strategic intent will be expressed in terms which relate the firm to its competitors: for example, Komatsu (www.komatsu.com) sought to 'encircle Caterpillar' (www.caterpillar.com) and Canon aimed to 'beat Xerox' (www.xerox.com).

The concept also includes a management process which focuses the organization's attitude on winning, and motivates people by communicating the value of the target. The concept of strategic intent implies that there is a general view of where the company ought to be going, rather than a definitive statement of what the outcomes will definitely be. This means there is plenty of flexibility within the concept for individual action, team contributions, and adaptation to changing circumstances. Strategic intent suffers from the same problem of vision, in that it might be achieved, and thus the organization will lose momentum.

The mission is, in effect, timeless. Like an amoeba, it may grow and reproduce and even adapt to change, but barring accidents it is immortal. In practice, of course, circumstances will render missions obsolete in time. Vision and strategic intent can (at least in theory) be achieved, and therefore can be considered as temporary expedients. Changes in the mission should only be undertaken in the most extreme circumstances, because the mission includes within it the corporate culture. This should have become entrenched in the minds of the employees of the organization, and will be difficult to change: it requires considerable investment in human resource development, and also considerable patience to remove existing beliefs and replace them with new ones.

Vision and strategic intent are the basic character of the organization which attracts and retains both staff and customers. These two concepts define the type of organization. The mission is really a statement of intended action, the best attempt the organization can make to achieve its objectives over time.

Talking Point

Visionary entrepreneurs seem to appear with some degree of regularity. Richard Branson, Alan Sugar, Akio Morita and Anita Roddick are examples of people who have invented a business almost single-handed and made it grow through having a very clear vision of what the world needs.

Which is of course the point. These individuals have, in general, decided (from some deep well of knowledge that the rest of us do not possess) what the world really ought to buy. Each of them at one time or another has criticized formal market research approaches to finding out what customers need – in fact, some of them have been downright scathing about it. Yet they have built world-class businesses. So who's right? The marketers or the visionaries?

Maybe faith really can move mountains, and vision, determination, hard work and so forth really can persuade the world. Or maybe the bankruptcy courts are littered with equally visionary, determined, hard-working entrepreneurs who were simply wrong about what people wanted.

THE MISSION STATEMENT

Research has shown that managers tend to take two separate views of the purpose of mission statements (Klemm et al. 1991). The first view is that mission statements are primarily for external public relations purposes; the second view is that the mission statement is intended to motivate employees. There is, of course, no reason why the mission statement should not be able to achieve both these objectives, but the company should be aware of which is the primary reason, and should also be aware of what the staff perception of the mission statement is. If the management believe the mission statement is a means of co-ordinating staff activities and motivating them to achieve, but the staff believe it is merely a paper exercise intended to put a gloss on the firm's activities, then no useful business will result.

The mission statement exists to define the organization's distinctive competence (Selznick 1957). Drucker (1974) later focused on the need for the business to define its purpose, and to reflect the culture and value systems of the firm's philosophy. Klemm et al (1991) found that there is no single definition of a business statement: companies use several different terms to describe the basic concept. These are as follows:

1. Mission statement.
2. Corporate statement.
3. Aims and values.
4. Purpose.
5. Principles.
6. Objectives.
7. Goals.
8. Responsibilities and obligations.

Obviously there are difficulties of semantics involved here, since it is difficult or impossible to say with any certainty whether or not a statement of 'duties and responsibilities' actually equates to a mission statement. It appears that the elements of a mission statement are often ordered into a hierarchy, as follows (Klemm et al 1991):

Statement 1: The mission. This is a statement of the long-term purpose of the organization, reflecting deeply-held corporate views.

Statement 2: Strategic objectives. A statement of long-term strategic objectives outlining desired direction and outcomes, in broad terms.

Statement 3: Quantified planning targets. Objectives expressed in numbers, and specified over a particular timescale.

Statement 4: The business definition. This statement outlines the scope and activity of the company in terms of industry and geographical spread.

Around two-thirds of Klemm et al's respondents had both a mission statement and a strategic objectives statement. Many of these had only recently been written: it appears that the idea of formalizing a mission statement is relatively recent, and many firms begin their existences without having any formal statement. Presumably at this stage the founder's vision is sufficient to carry the firm's strategic intent, and it is only later that the organization needs to formalise the mission into a published statement in order to ensure that all staff and other stakeholders are informed of its content.

A useful blueprint for devizing a mission statement came from Bart (1997). Bart identified 25 components for the mission statement, listed as follows:

1. Organizational purpose.
2. Statement of values, beliefs and philosophy.
3. The distinctive competence or strength of the organization.
4. The desired competitive position.
5. The competitive strategy.
6. Identification of the relevant stakeholders.

7. Specific behaviour standards, and corporate policies.
8. A statement of the general corporate goals or aims.
9. One clear and compelling goal.
10. Specific financial targets and objectives.
11. Specific non-financial targets and objectives.
12. Definition of the business (what business we are in).
13. Specific customers and markets served.
14. Specific products or services offered.
15. A statement of identity or self-concept.
16. Statement of desired public image.
17. Identification of the business location.
18. Definition of technology.
19. Concern for the future, and the firm's long-term survival.
20. Concern for satisfying customers.
21. Concern for employees and their welfare.
22. Concern for suppliers.
23. Concern for society at large.
24. Concern for shareholders.
25. A statement of the corporate vision.

Not all firms will use all of these types of statement within their mission statements: most are likely to use only ten or eleven. Bart concluded that the benefits from mission statements are emotional and psychic: this means that mission statements are more likely to be of use internally than externally, and are more likely to be published to the staff. This makes sense if the purpose of the mission statement is to motivate and direct staff rather than to put a gloss on the firm's external image.

AIMS AND OBJECTIVES

There is often considerable confusion between what is meant by an aim and what is meant by an objective. An aim is a general direction in which the organization wants to go; an objective implies a quantifiable outcome. For example, a company might aim to increase the public's awareness of one of its brands. This is an aim. If the managers go on to say that they intend to raise awareness from its current level of five per cent of the population to 20 per cent of the population, that is an objective. Objectives need to be quantified if they are to be met for two reasons: firstly, there is no way of knowing whether the objective has been achieved if it is not quantified; secondly, it seems to be a truism in management that only that which is measured is achieved.

Objective-setting is widely acknowledged to be an important first step in strategic planning, but few authors go on to say how objectives should be set. McKay (1972) suggests that there are two categories of issues to be considered when setting objectives: the general, which have an application to all organizations, and the specific, which apply to individual business units.

General categories of objective include those shown in Table 5.2. It should be noted that these are headings under which objectives can be categorised rather than objectives in themselves.

The above categories of objective will apply to all industries and firms. Some types of objective will only apply in specific industries, or to the specific departments within firms.

The specific categories of objective are as shown in Table 5.3.

Table 5.2: General objectives

Objective	Explanation and examples
Business scope	What business should we be in? The difficulty with this type of objective lies in quantifying it, or in defining when it can be considered to have been achieved. For example, a company currently in the cinema business might decide that it should be in the leisure business (implying a broader range of activities). At what point can the managers say that the objective has been achieved? Is it when the company buys its first pub? Or is it when it has established chains of pubs, restaurants, hotels, sports centres, cinemas, theatres, coffee-bars and travel companies?
Business orientation	The orientation which is best suited to the business scope and the purposes of survival, growth and profit. Again, this is difficult to quantify. For example, a university might decide that it needs to become more research-orientated in order to meet its business scope objectives of becoming a centre of excellence in knowledge generation. The objective might be said to be achieved when 60% of its academic staff have published research within the last year.
Business organization	This relates to the structure of the organization and its appropriateness for achieving the other objectives. For example, an organization might decide to aim for a flatter organizational structure: the measure of achievement could be when there are only a maximum of two layers of management between any employee and the managing director.
Public responsibility	To what extent do choices of business opportunity take account of the social and economic needs of the public? For example, a firm with a record of creating pollution might aim to halve its output of toxic substances within a year.
Performance evaluation	Does the appraisal system mesh properly with the planning system? A quantifiable outcome might be for the firm to reduce the reporting time between events and appraisal.

Table 5.3: Specific categories of objective

Category	Explanation and examples
Customer classes	Objectives regarding customer classes are likely to be set at the functional level, or at least at the business level. Examples of quantifiable outcomes might be the percentage penetration into a new market.
Competitors	Objectives regarding customers might be set at corporate level (for example the strategic intent examples given earlier) or they might be set at functional level. Examples might be a firm setting the objective of winning more market share than a specific competitor within a given time frame.
Markets and distribution	These objectives are almost always set at the functional level.
Technology and products	Unless there is a major shift in technology, these decisions are taken at functional level. An example might be the replacement of all mechanical timers in washing machines with electronic programmers.
Production capability	Objectives to increase (or reduce) production capability are likely to result from other strategic objectives. For example, a firm which decides to enter an export market is likely to need to increase capacity to cope with the extra demand. Equally, an excess of production might encourage a firm to seek markets overseas – although this may not be the optimum approach to internationalisation.
Finance	Financial objectives are probably the easiest to quantify. Such objectives are likely to be set at the business level rather than the function level.
Environment	Objectives for dealing with the firm's environment might be put in place at any level and are probably difficult to quantify. An example might be a decision to lobby MPs in order to obtain a change in the law.

In setting objectives, one should move from the general to the particular, from the broad to the narrow, and from the long-term to the short-term (McDonald 1984). This means that the objectives become more focused, and therefore more attainable.

MARKETING OBJECTIVES

According to McKay (1972) there are only three basic marketing objectives: to enlarge the market, to increase market share, and to improve profitability. This somewhat simplistic view is then explained more fully in terms of generic strategies for achieving those objectives.

Figure 5.1 shows how the basic objectives fit with the generic strategies that flow from them.

Some of the terminology used might cause disquiet among marketers. For example, some of the objectives might seem sales-orientated, and the idea of advertising being a strong persuasive force might seem a little odd in some quarters. Having said that, the general principle is the same: the basic core objectives need to be broken down into intermediate objectives, and those objectives broken down into initial objectives.

Of course, all objectives should follow the SMART acronym: they should be Specific, Measurable, Achievable, Relevant, and Timed.

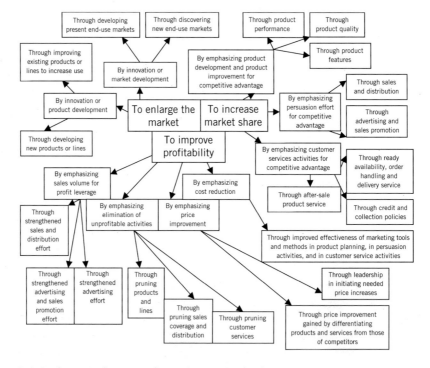

Figure 5.1: Basic marketing strategies and related objectives

COMPLEXITY AND OBJECTIVE SETTING

One of the problems of objective setting is that every problem impinges on every other problem. For example, Mason and Mitroff (1981) use the example of world problems to illustrate this principle. Figure 5.2 shows a matrix of world problems: try placing a tick in each box where you think the problems impinge on each other, in other words where the solution to one problem is related to the solution to the other problem.

Figure 5.2: World problem matrix

	Peace	Energy	Starvation	Civil rights	Population	Balance of payments
Peace	❏	❏	❏	❏	❏	❏
Energy	❏	❏	❏	❏	❏	❏
Starvation	❏	❏	❏	❏	❏	❏
Civil rights	❏	❏	❏	❏	❏	❏
Population	❏	❏	❏	❏	❏	❏
Balance of payments	❏	❏	❏	❏	❏	❏

When you have done this, you will probably find very few, if any, blanks. The same exercise works equally well if the columns and rows are headed with business problems. This essential complexity and interrelatedness of problems means that managements often feel as if they are merely clearing-houses for pressures. There are three main characteristics of complexity:

1. Any policy-making situation comprises many problems and issues.
2. These problems and issues tend to be highly interrelated, so that the solution to one problem creates other problems elsewhere, or at least requires a more global solution.
3. Few if any problems can be isolated effectively for separate treatment.

Organization is usually considered to be the route towards solving a complex problem, but in complex situations the organization can provide a barrier: what tends to happen is that each part of the problem becomes separated off, so that co-ordination is lost and the solutions are less than optimal. Most problem-solving tools work best on simple problems: often such problems have a one-dimensional value system or goal structure which guides the solution.

Complex problems cannot be solved by simple means, but when there are enough variables and the variables are relatively disconnected, the problem-solvers may be able to find a statistical solution. For example, predicting when and how an individual person will die is an extremely complex problem, because there are far too many variables which impinge on the problem. On the other hand, estimating how many individuals from a population will die, and how, and when, is a straightforward problem in statistics which is performed regularly by insurance companies.

The problem with systems of organized complexity is that variations in one element of the system cause reverberations throughout the system. Many corporate problems display this characteristic of organized complexity. Pricing problems frequently feature this characteristic, because a change in price affects profitability, customer perception of the brand, distributor margins, demand for the product, and many other aspects of the overall brand management problem.

Problems of organized complexity cannot be solved in the same way as other problems. Rittel (1972) calls such problems 'wicked' problems, not because they have evil connotations but because they tend to multiply, developing more problems as the direct result of attempts to solve them.

Wicked problems have the properties shown in Table 5.4.

The characteristics of wicked problems make them difficult to address, because the manager concerned can never be sure that the problem has gone away, and in a sense it never really does.

Table 5.4: Properties of wicked problems

Property	Explanation and examples
Ability to formulate the problem	Tame problems can be formulated and written down. Wicked problems have no definitive formulation. For example, the problem of buying a house can be formulated in terms of writing down price range, location, and size. Desirable (but not essential) features such as a south-facing garden might be added. This is a tame problem. On the other hand, planning to buy a house to retire to in 30 years' time is a wicked problem because of the huge number of variables that will affect the individual, and the property market.
Relationship between problem and solution	Tame problems can be formulated separately from any implied solution. The formulation of wicked problems cannot be separated from statements of the solution, in other words understanding the problem in itself creates the solution.
Testability	Solutions to tame problems can be tested, and judged either correct or false. There is no single way to tell whether the solution to a wicked problem is correct or false, because solutions can only be good or bad relative to each other.
Finality	Tame problems have a closing point, at which they can be deemed to have been solved: in other words the stopping-point can be tested. Wicked problems, on the other hand, have no end: there is always room for improvement, and each solution generates more problems.
Tractability	There is a large range of possible solutions for a tame problem, and these can be listed. For a wicked problem, there is no exhaustive, numerable list of possibilities.
Explanatory characteristics	A tame problem can be stated as a gap between what is, and what ought to be, and there is a clear explanation for every gap. Wicked problems have many possible explanations for the same discrepancy.
Level of analysis	Tame problems have identifiable, natural form: there is no argument about the level of the problem. The proper level of generality can be found for bounding the problem and identifying its root cause. Wicked problems are symptoms of another problem, and have no identifiable root causes. Would-be problem solvers cannot be sure that they are not attacking the symptoms rather than the root causes of the problem.
Reproducibility	A tame problem can be abstracted and modelled, and attempts to solve it can be tried out until one is found that appears to fit. Wicked problems are all one-shot propositions: there is no trial and error.
Replicability	Tame problems tend to repeat themselves in different organizations or at different times. Wicked problems are essentially unique.
Responsibility	No-one can be blamed for failing to solve a tame problem, but people are often praised. Would-be solvers of wicked problems are often blamed for causing other problems, but are unlikely to be praised because wicked problems are rarely solved in any final sense.

From the viewpoint of objective-setting, the existence of wicked problems means that objectives cannot be set in isolation. Implicitly, all objectives are interlinked within the firm, and therefore need to be considered as a complete package, not in isolation. There are two major implications for objective setting:

1. There must be a broad participation from all those affected by the decisions which are to be made.
2. Policy making must be based on a wide spectrum of information gathered from many sources.

Running organizations is becoming increasingly democratic, partly because it is sensible to use the intellectual capabilities and experience of an educated workforce, and partly because people are becoming more independently-minded and are not prepared to accept an autocratic management style. Individuals faced with being given orders which they feel are inappropriate or which affect their sense of professional responsibility, will simply not obey them. This means that setting objectives is largely a political process – a matter of achieving consensus among the interested parties. Even this approach is problematical, since each party involved in the problem is likely to have a clear idea of what ought to be done, but since each of them sees the problem from a different angle, the solutions on offer will be different.

Wicked problem-solving might be expected to use these criteria (Mason and Mitroff 1998):

1. Participative. Since both the knowledge of the problem and the resources to solve it are scattered among many individuals, the problem-solving must include as many as possible of these individuals.

2. Adversarial. The best judgement of the assumptions in a complex problem will be obtained as a result of scepticism and doubt, which leads to the concept of opposition.

3. Integrative. A unified set of assumptions and a coherent plan of action, will be needed to guide the problem-solving.

4. Managerial mind supporting. Decision support systems are likely to be inadequate for solving wicked problems. Achieving insight into the nature of the complexity of the problem requires systems that support the policymaker's thinking process.

Talking Point

There is a story about an agricultural adviser who is sent to a remote African farm, where he finds the farmer asleep under a tree. The adviser introduces himself and explains that he has been sent by a charity to help the farmer improve his methods and grow more food.

'So what do you think I should do?' the farmer asks.

'Well, if you plough that land down there you could grow a cash crop of peanuts.'

'And what would I do with the money?'

'You could buy fertilizers, and improve the yield of the land and sell the surplus in the market.'

'And what would I do with that money?'

'You could buy some more land, and grow even more.'

'And make more money', said the farmer.

'That's right! And with the extra money you could hire some men to work the land, and then you'd be able to relax more.'

'I see', said the farmer, settling back down under his tree. 'But I can relax all I want to now.' And so saying, he went back to sleep.

Should we be always looking to solve problems? Or are some problems better left unsolved? Are we too eager to be the western agricultural adviser, when maybe we should be the African farmer? Who is really the wiser of the two?

TURNAROUND MANAGEMENT

No set of problems will be more complex than that thrown up by dealing with a turnaround situation. Organizations which find themselves on an inappropriate or unsustainable course need to make radical changes very quickly in order to turn the situation round, and this type of change is likely to cause problems for some or even all of the stakeholders.

Change might be discontinuous or continuous. A discontinuous change is one which is carried out suddenly and radically, making all the necessary changes within a short period of time. A continuous change is one which is carried out piecemeal, over a lengthy period.

Advocates of discontinuous change argue that organizations do not develop gradually, moving smoothly from one state of affairs to another. Rather, organizational change is met with resistance from vested interests among stakeholders, and this is not unreasonable since a period of stability enables people to 'get on with the job'. Organizational structure can solidify, standard operating procedures can be agreed, key competence areas can be identified, corporate culture will become established and power structures will become validated. According to Mintzberg (1991), the organization will stabilize if all these elements form a consistent, cohesive configuration. Some stability is necessary if people are to be able to work effectively without continually wondering whether their jobs are going to disappear, or the work they have been doing towards an objective might be in vain (March and Simon 1958; Thompson 1967).

The downside of stability is inertia – the organization becomes set in its ways, staff become entrenched in their jobs and their attitudes, long-term commitments are put in place, people make high investments in projects which may no longer be needed after the changes, and change becomes more difficult. If change is needed in these circumstances, a series of nudges will not be sufficient, only a radical intervention will generate the necessary movement.

In some cases, radical change is forced on organizations by changes in the environment. Companies might be faced with competition from new technology, or public-sector organizations might be faced with changes brought about by government reorganization. For a company which is one step away from bankruptcy, discontinuous change is the only way forward: company turnaround consultants often acquire the reputation for being 'hatchet men' as they ruthlessly cut expenditure, fire staff, and change working practices almost overnight.

Those who favour continuous change argue that revolutionary changes need to be carried out on a regular basis: the world is changing rapidly, so it is impossible to operate on the basis that one radical, discontinuous change will last for any length of time. The damage caused to employee relations (and often to other stakeholder relations) can be very great, and will take some time to heal. For supporters of continuous change, a preference for revolution usually means a short-term perspective. Although incremental change takes time, the end result can still be dramatic: three characteristics are necessary for this to happen.

1. All employees should be committed to continuous improvement. Everyone should be committed to constructive dissatisfaction with the status quo (Stacey 1993).
2. Everyone must be committed to continuing professional development, or lifelong learning (Argyris 1990). This learning includes challenging the accepted wisdom within the organization.
3. Everyone must be committed to continuous adaptation. This presupposes that there will be flexibility in the structures and systems (probably an organismic approach) and an open and tolerant working culture.

These three characteristics are what define an evolutionary organization. In such an organization, everyone is involved in the development of change. This makes it far less likely that the changes will be resented, since everyone has had a chance to input into the process.

Table 5.5 shows a comparison between discontinuous change and continuous change.

Several models exist to examine the different components, both practical and conceptual, that go to make up an organization. The question that is hardest to answer is whether all the components of the organization should be changed at once, or whether they can be changed individually. In fact, it seems likely that, since the components of the organization all impinge on each other, and since the components of any complex problem impinge on each other, the organization will almost certainly find itself changing everything to a greater or lesser extent

Table 5.5: Continuous versus discontinuous change

	Discontinuous Change Perspective	Continuous Change Perspective
Emphasis on	Revolution over evolution	Evolution over revolution
Strategic change as	Disruptive innovation/turnaround	Uninterrupted improvement
Strategic change process	Creative destruction	Organic adaptation
Magnitude of change	Radical, comprehensive and dramatic	Moderate, piecemeal, and undramatic
Pace of change	Abrupt, unsteady, and intermittent	Gradual, steady, and constant
Fundamental change requires	Sudden break with status quo	Permanent learning and flexibility
Reaction to environmental jolts	Shock therapy	Continuous adjustment
View of organizational crises	Under pressure things become fluid	In the cold everything freezes
Long-term change dynamics	Stable and unstable states alternate	Persistent transient state
Long-term change pattern	Punctuated equilibrium	Gradual development

(Source: deWit and Meyer, *Strategy: Process, Content, Context* Thomson 1998)

whenever any substantial change is required. For adherents to the continuous change approach this will not present too great a problem, because those responsible for each component will make the changes naturally in the course of improving their own working practices. For adherents to the discontinuous change model, it will be considerably harder to make the changes since they will need to consider all the ramifications of the changes at once. This has all the hallmarks of a wicked problem, of course.

In a crisis situation, for example when the firm is on the brink of bankruptcy, the following courses of action may be necessary.

1. Find out who is absolutely necessary to the firm, whether these are individual creditors, staff, or customers.
2. Ensure that these people are safe, and feel safe.
3. Fire or otherwise divest the firm of everybody else. This may mean that some creditors will have to wait a long time for their money, or some customers will not be supplied, or some members of staff will be dismissed through no fault of their own. The alternative is for everybody to lose.
4. Stop spending money. Companies get into trouble for two reasons: too high a propensity to spend money, and too low a propensity to earn it.
5. Be prepared to be ruthless. Most managements in this situation become paralysed by fear and stop making hard decisions, living instead from day to day in the hope that something will turn up. What turns up is usually the bailiff.

Company turnround of near-insolvent or insolvent companies is a specialist area. Individuals and consultancies who specialize in this area are usually highly trained people with a very good knowledge of company law as well as an entrepreneurial approach. Most firms which find themselves in need of such help could quite easily have solved the problems much earlier and less painfully: unfortunately, the natural optimism which marks out the true entrepreneur is a two-edged sword.

RESOURCE ALLOCATION

Campbell and Goold (1988) identified two basic styles of management which relate to resource allocation: the Strategic Planning style, and the Financial Control style.

The Strategic Planning style emphasizes a long-term approach, setting objectives which may take years or even decades to come to fruition. At the corporate level, resource allocation goes hand-in-hand with objective setting. A major problem with resource allocation is that any corporate strategic objectives are likely to be framed over long time-periods, whereas the capital markets tend to take a short-term view, wanting to see a return on their money over a six-month or one-year period. Strategic Planning strategists therefore stand between the capital markets and the working managers, buffering them against the pressures to achieve instant results.

The main advantage of this style is that it allows for long-term growth, and ambitious projects which might well be the main differentiators between a firm and its competitors. The major disadvantage is that it can lead to complacency among managers, and a lack of urgency about getting the job done. Many managers would move on before they have to live with the consequences of the policies they introduced, and the managers following on would not necessarily have the commitment to the project that its initiators had: also, they have a convenient scapegoat if things go wrong.

The Financial Control style stresses multiple, separate profit centres, each with independent responsibilities. For most practical purposes, these profit centres operate as separate businesses in their own right: at the extreme, the centre does not try to co-ordinate activities between them. Resource allocation is therefore the responsibility of the profit centres themselves, but tends to adopt objectives and criteria which reflect those of the capital market. Funds from the centre flow to those profit centres which have proposals which meet capital-market criteria, and where the profit centre's past history indicates that it should be able to deliver on its promises. Usually the standards applied by the centre are rather tougher than those applied by the capital markets.

The main advantage of the Financial Control style is that it does not require the centre to have a detailed understanding of the running of the businesses it owns. This style is therefore particularly useful for holding companies, where the range of businesses might be very diverse. The main disadvantage is that it stifles long-term investment: most projects requiring a long period of time for their development would not pass the tests applied by the capital markets, even though investors like firms with a history of steady growth.

It appears that the Financial Control style of resource allocation is more prevalent in western Europe and the United States, while the Strategic Planning style is more prevalent in Japan (Campbell, Goold and Alexander 1994). This may reflect the different role of capital markets in Japan rather than a different cultural attitude to management, however.

CASE STUDY: RICHER SOUNDS

www.richersounds.com

When Julian Richer founded Richer Sounds in 1978, he was aged just 19. At that time, his main objective for the business was to repay the £20,000 loan he had taken out to get started – and he achieved this in just nine months. Over the next few years, Julian Richer developed the management style and vision that has made his hi-fi retailing chain something of a maverick among brown-goods retailers.

The company has grown steadily since 1978, at the rate of around two new shops a year. Richer believes in putting his staff at the centre of the business. By encouraging and motivating them to participate in the running of the stores, he expects that they will offer a better service to customers as well as feel more involved with the fortunes of the company. So far, this view seems to be justified – shrinkage (or pilfering) is less than half the industry average, and absenteeism is running at only

▶

one or two per cent. Staff turnover is extremely low. Staff are paid for suggestions, and have even been asked to justify working a longer-than-average week. The spin-off in terms of customer service has been remarkable: the chain's London Bridge outlet was in the Guinness Book of Records for six years running with the highest sales per square foot of any UK retailer.

Richer's approach is based on a ten-point plan which he recommends to any management of any business.

1. Talk to your staff and managers. Change is always greeted with suspicion, even cynicism. Tell everyone you are seeking improvement and why, so everyone is infected with enthusiasm.
2. Examine your mission statement. If you do not have one, form a working party to draw one up.
3. Organize an attitude survey. Find out what employees really think to set a baseline.
4. Think about fun. How can you liven up the workplace and create a happier atmosphere? Look at reward structures.
5. Revise the rule book. Get rid of outdated regulations and meaningless traditions.
6. Set up a strategic customer service group. Examine your customer service and how it can be improved.
7. Ask your customers what they think. Find ways of inviting their comments at each point of contact.
8. Launch a suggestion scheme. Get the backing of the top person in the organization and allow ideas from everyone.
9. Review your recruitment. What happens on the first day in the job? Does motivation and communication start from day one?
10. Review the values you deliver. Are you happy with the value for money of your service or product? Could the quality be improved or the price lowered?

(Richer 1997)

Richer makes a point of personally answering every customer complaint, and of personally meeting every new recruit. Given that he has time to act as a consultant for other firms as well as handle the day-to-day running of Richer Sounds and its associated companies, this in itself shows that customer complaints are very few indeed, and very few staff leave to be replaced by new recruits. Much of the recruitment is based on recommendations from existing staff members, and Richer tries to avoid hiring from rivals in the hi-fi retailing industry. Richer believes that it is easy to teach people about hi-fi, but hard to change their view of the corporate culture.

In recent years as Julian Richer has become more involved in other activities, much of the day-to-day running of the firm has been taken over by the group managing director, David Robinson. Robinson shares the vision – he began working for Julian Richer on the shop floor of the second store ever opened. The two men have remained close friends and colleagues ever since. However, as the business appears to be reaching saturation point, new opportunities will need to be explored – and the transferability of the Richer vision will be put to the test.

CASE STUDY QUESTIONS

1. Is the Richer Way truly transferable to any kind of business?
2. What problems might arise from the transfer of responsibilities from Richer to Robinson? How might these be minimized?

► 3. How does the Richer Way reconcile itself with customer orientation?

4. Why shouldn't Richer recruit from other electronics retailers such as Comet or Dixon's?

5. Why might recruitment through staff recommendation be more effective than advertising and thus attracting a wider choice of candidate?

SUMMARY

Missions, objectives, strategic intent and visions are the building-blocks of strategy. Although a sense of mission might grow up incrementally, as the organization culture often does, it is helpful to new recruits and indeed to existing staff for the statement to be made in a formal manner so that everyone is clear about the direction in which the organization is going.

The key points from this chapter are as follows:

■ The mission is the organization's character, as well as its strategic tool and compass.

■ Visions and strategic intent can be achieved, and need to be replaced. Missions usually cannot be superseded, but continue indefinitely.

■ There are three basic objectives in marketing: enlarge the market, enlarge the market share, or improve profitability.

■ Complex problems cannot be solved simply, because each solution generates more problems.

■ Organizations stabilize if competences are identified, culture is established, and power is validated. This is a good thing if the environment remains stable, but leads to inertia and reluctance to change.

■ The Financial Control style leads to short-termism but is good for controlling companies about which the planner knows little.

CHAPTER QUESTIONS

1. If a vision can be achieved, how is it to be replaced?

2. Many visionary founders of companies have lived long lives, and seen their original company grow large. What happens after the founder dies?

3. If each solution throws up three more problems, might it not be better to live with problems rather than try to solve them?

4. How might you change an organization which has achieved stability?

5. What are the main drawbacks of using a mission statement?

REFERENCES

Argyris, C. (1990): *Overcoming organizational defences: facilitating organizational learning* (Boston: Prentice-Hall).

Bart, C.K. (1997): 'Industrial firms and the power of mission', *Industrial Marketing Management* 26: pp. 371–83.

Campbell, A. and Goold, M. (1988): 'Adding value from corporate headquarters', *London Business School Journal* Summer, pp. 219–240.

Campbell, A., Devine, M. and Yeung, D. (1990): *A Sense of Mission* (London: Hutchinson Business Books).

Campbell, A., Goold, M. and Alexander, M. (1994): *Corporate-level strategy: creating value in the multibusiness company* (New York: John Wiley and Sons).

Drucker, P.F. (1974): *Management Task, Responsibilities, and Practice* (New York: Harper and Row).

Hamel, G. and Prahalad, C.K. (1989): 'Strategic Intent', *Harvard Business Review*, 67(3) pp. 63–76.

Klemm, M., Sanderson, S. and Luffman, G. (1991): 'Selling corporate values to employees', *Long Range Planning* June.

March, J.G. and Simon, H.A. (1958): *Organisations* (New York: Wiley).

Mason, R. and Mitroff, I. (1981): *Challenging Strategic Planning Assumptions* (New York: Wiley).

McDonald, M.H.B. (1984): *Marketing Plans* (London: Heinemann).

McKay, E.S. (1972): *The Marketing Mystique* (New York: American Management Association).

Mintzberg, H. (1991): 'The Effective Organization: forces and forms', *Sloan Management Review* winter pp. 54–67.

Richer, J. (1997): *The Richer Way* (EMAP Business Communications).

Rittel, H. (1972): 'On the planning crisis: systems analysis of the first and second generations'. *Bedriftsokonomen* no. 8, pp. 390–6.

Selznick, P. (1957): *Conclusion, in Leadership in Administration* (New York: Harper and Row).

Stacey, R.D. (1993): 'Strategy as order emerging from chaos', *Long Range Planning* vol. 26 no. 1 pp. 10–17.

Thompson, J.D. (1967): *Organisations in action* (New York: McGraw-Hill).

Chapter Six

Approaches to Customers

INTRODUCTION

Customers are at the heart of marketing: the marketing orientation presupposes that customers and consumers should be the starting-point for any organization's activities. This is true of strategic planning. From a strategic viewpoint, planning decisions revolve around deciding which individuals are likely to become loyal customers, what kind of approaches will be likely to meet with their approval, and what needs these customers have in common.

After reading this chapter, you should be able to:

- Explain the principles behind branding strategy.
- Explain how segmentation strategy works.
- Describe ways of developing a global strategy.
- Describe ways of evaluating alternative strategies.

SEGMENTATION

Segmentation is the process of dividing the market into groups of customers or consumers with similar needs. The more closely the needs match up, the smaller the segment tends to be, but the higher the premium customers are likely to be prepared to pay in order to have a product that more exactly meets their needs.

The advantages of segmentation are as follows:

1. Customer analysis. If the firm segments the market appropriately, it can develop a closer understanding of customer needs.
2. Competitor analysis. Once the segment has been identified in terms of its needs, it is much easier to identify organizations which are aiming to meet the same needs.
3. Effective resource allocation. Segmentation allows the firm to concentrate on those customers who are likely to prove the most beneficial in terms of meeting the firm's overall objectives, rather than wasting resources on customers who are unlikely to contribute to the long-term benefit of the firm.
4. Strategic marketing planning. Planning becomes easier once the firm understands which are the best customers to target.

The strategy will, to an extent, be dictated by the segmentation method chosen. Bases for segmentation are numerous, but tend to group broadly as follows:

1. Geographic segmentation. This relates to where people live, and can be subdivided in terms of climate, urbanization, remoteness, or even salesforce territories.
2. Psychographic segmentation. This is based on personality types. For example, a sports car manufacturer might aim for middle-aged men who wish to regain their youth, or for young professionals aiming to make an impression.
3. Behavioural segmentation. This could be based on the benefits of the product, the usage situation, the extent of use, and the loyalty factors. For example, a football club might base its segmentation on the fans' propensity to buy season tickets, or replica strip, or their propensity to pay to see matches on TV. Each of these segments will have differing needs.
4. Demographic segmentation is concerned with the structure of the population. This might be based on age, life stage, occupations, or economic factors.

For a segment to be successfully exploited, it needs to fulfil the following requirements:

- It must be measurable, or definable. If there is no way of knowing who the members of the segment are, the segment is indefinable.
- It must be accessible. This means there must be some way of contacting the members of the segment.
- It must be substantial. Too small a segment will not be worth targeting.
- It must be congruent. The needs of the members must be reasonably close to each other.
- It must be stable. The nature of the members, and their membership of the group, must stay constant long enough for marketing efforts to pay off.

The bottom line is that there are no markets for products that everybody likes a little, only for products that somebody likes a lot (Cutler 1989).

Segmentation strategy is decided at the business level or sometimes at the functional level. The strategic decision is based on the type of segmentation to be undertaken: naturally, this is subject to debate or change in the light of experience. The second area of strategy concerned with segmentation is the evaluation of market segments.

EVALUATING MARKET SEGMENTS

Each segment should be identifiable and fairly discrete. This means that it should be perfectly possible to calculate the current sales value of the segment, the projected growth of the segment, and the expected profit margins for each segment. Although many companies would want to target high-growth, high-margin segments, some companies may prefer slow-growth or even low-margin segments, either because they lack the necessary skills to enter the more dynamic markets, or because they lack the necessary resources to service those markets once they have entered them. Table 6.1 shows the factors which relate to segment attractiveness (Porter 1985).

Table 6.1: Segment attractiveness

Factor	Explanation
Current and potential competitors	Obviously a segment which is already targeted by a number of competitors, or which has strong competitors in it, is less attractive.
Substitute products	This factor is particularly relevant if the company is proposing to enter the market with a new product. The existence of close substitutes will render the segment less attractive, because substitutes limit the potential prices and profits from segments.
Power of buyers	If the buyers in a segment possess string bargaining power, entering the segment may be problematical as the buyers act to force prices (and profits) down, or extract better quality or service.
Power of suppliers	Powerful suppliers will also tend to take control, if the particular segment being targeted requires the use of specific suppliers.

Even if the segment appears attractive despite the problems identified above, managers will still need to take account of the business's strengths and weaknesses. For example, many firms have gone into e-commerce without having the capacity to handle the level of responses received. Although e-business appears very attractive, offering access to a wealthy, global, educated audience, this audience is also quite demanding, and expects more or less instant results: many small companies have found themselves quite unable to cope with demand or (perhaps more significantly) with the large number of contacts they receive which do not turn into business.

Business strengths and weaknesses may result in discarding some promising segments on the basis that they do not fit the company's long-term objectives. In other words, the segment itself may seem attractive, but the long-term costs of being seduced away from the optimum path for the firm would outweigh the short-term gains to be made.

Before moving into a new segment, the firm needs to consider its current position in the overall market. A low market share indicates a weakness: a growing market share suggests strength, and obviously a declining market share is symptomatic of a serious problem. Unique products and a valued reputation will certainly help, and non-marketing dimensions such as low costs, under-utilized capacity, technological strengths, general marketing strengths, and synergy with the firm's other activities are all positive factors.

General Electric Corporation developed a strategic business planning grid which relates industry attractiveness to business strengths. The basic grid is shown in Fig 6.1.

The grid has three zones: the three squares in the top left-hand corner represent areas where the business strengths and the industry attractiveness coincide to the extent that the segment

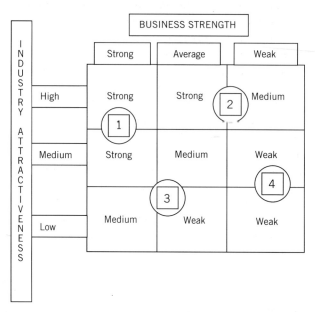

Figure 6.1: The General Electric Strategic Business Planning Grid

becomes a good one to enter or to continue with. The three squares running diagonally represent borderline cases, where the industry and the business have some synergies, but where either the business strengths are low or the segment is not very attractive. Finally, the three squares in the bottom right-hand corner are areas which should be avoided, either because the industry is unattractive or because the business is not the right one to exploit the opportunities.

The numbered circles represent corporate involvement (or projected involvement) in the areas. The analysis is as follows:

1. This circle represents a strong business in a medium to highly attractive segment. This is clearly a case for investment in the segment, or for building up an existing commitment to the segment.

2. This is a highly-attractive segment, but the business has only weak to medium strengths for this segment. Planners should really consider pulling out: unless they can build up the business's strengths here, they are unlikely to make as good a success of the segment as they would if they invested the resources elsewhere, effectively playing to their strengths.

3. This is an unattractive segment, but the firm has medium to strong capabilities in it. Here the firm has two choices: it can seek to build up the segment to make it more attractive in some way (perhaps by looking for ways to win a bigger share of customers' overall expenditure) or it can seek a more attractive segment. In many cases, the former approach might represent the better option, because the firm will still have a bulwark against competition. For example, the UK's Saga holiday firm (**www.saga.co.uk**) specializes in holidays for senior citizens, a traditionally unattractive market segment. The firm has successfully used its strengths in this segment to sell a wide range of other services, including insurance and other financial services.

4. This circle represents a business with weak capabilities in an unattractive segment. This is a clear case for pulling out and re-investing elsewhere.

Grid analyses such as this one (and the Boston Group Matrix discussed earlier) provide a useful tool for thinking about the problem. The major difficulty with any matrix analysis is that of knowing which segments or business strengths belong in which boxes. It is easy to define a segment as unattractive, for example, without seeing that there are future possibilities for the segment: the history of marketing is littered with examples of market segments which were written off as unattractive until someone found a need to fill.

A second problem with matrix planning is that it often leads companies into placing too much emphasis on growth, either through growing the firm's share of an existing market or through entering new markets which show higher growth rates. This can easily lead firms into entering markets about which they know very little, and to abandoning or milking dry the stable, core markets which are their survival insurance. In other words, going for high growth is likely to be a high-risk strategy, but is one which is likely to please the capital markets and is thus often seen as a good way to go.

Having said that, most companies still use some kind of strategic planning model, and it is often of a matrix type. This enables the firm to simplify the problem so that it can be handled more easily.

Talking Point

In many grid-type models, the axes are labelled 'high', 'low', 'attractive', 'unattractive' and so forth. Yet there do not seem to be any criteria for deciding whether a market is, for example, high or low growth. In other words, what constitutes high growth? What constitutes low growth? What growth rate does a medium-growth market have?

In practice, of course, executives make those judgements and decide whether a growth rate of, say, five per cent per annum is high or low growth. If that is the case, what value does the model have? If the basic assumptions are just arbitrary decisions by executives, why should the outcomes not also be just as arbitrary?

SEGMENTATION EFFECTIVENESS

Correct identification of segments means that the marketer can meet the needs of the segment members much more effectively than the competition can. The firm will be able to provide specialist products that are more nearly right for the consumers in the segment, and will be able to communicate better with them. Customers are usually prepared to pay an extra premium for this. Rather than accepting a product that only meets some of the customer's needs, he or she will probably pay a little more for something that more closely approaches the ideal.

The segment will be profitable as long as the premium the consumer will pay is greater than the cost to the manufacturer of making the modifications. There is therefore a trade-off between having a close match to a small segment and on the other hand having a larger market. The smaller the segment, the greater the premium the target consumers will be prepared to pay. This is illustrated in Fig 6.2.

As the segmentation becomes narrower, there will be a lower number of units sold, so the number of items sold per head of population will drop. This is partly offset by higher prices, but the profitability of the segment will only begin where the premium line and the cost line diverge. If the costs of adapting the product are higher than the premium the customers will pay, it is not worthwhile to make the adaptations. Where the premium is higher than the cost, it may be worthwhile provided the overall sales do not fall too much.

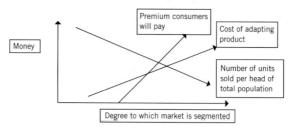

Figure 6.2: Segmentation trade-offs

TARGETING

Having divided the market into segments, managers must decide which segment to target in order to reach the firm's overall objectives. Managers do not necessarily choose the most profitable segment: a firm may decide to aim for a particular segment of the market which is currently neglected, perhaps because it has high growth potential or low competitive pressures. The process of selecting a segment to aim for is called targeting. There are three basic strategic options open to marketers.

1. **Concentrated** marketing (single segment). This is also known as **niche marketing**; Richer Sounds (**www.richersounds.com**), lastminute.com (**www.lastminute.com**) and Tie Rack (**www.tie-rack.com**) follow this approach. The niche marketer concentrates on satisfying all the needs of a single narrow segment.

2. **Differentiated** marketing (multi-segmented) means to concentrate on two or more segments, offering a differentiated marketing mix for each. Most major international airlines offer different marketing approaches to business class passengers and to economy passengers.

3. **Undifferentiated** marketers offer a basic product that would be used by almost all age groups and lifestyles. For example, the market for salt is largely undifferentiated. Although salt manufacturers might differentiate their products by offering low-sodium alternatives or flavoured versions, the use of salt is much the same for everybody, and there would not appear to be much relationship between segmentation variables and salt purchase. It would be difficult to imagine any real adaptation to the product that would meet people's needs sufficiently well to merit a premium price. Such examples of undifferentiated products are increasingly rare; even the producers of such basic commodities as petrol and flour have made great strides forward in differentiating their products (i.e. meeting consumers' needs better).

The choice of strategy to adopt will rest on the following three factors: the company's resources and competences, the product features and benefits, and the characteristics of the segment(s). If resources are limited, a concentrated marketing approach is likely to prove attractive. This is the approach taken by the UK firm High and Mighty, a menswear retailer which specializes in clothing for exceptionally tall and exceptionally large men. The market niche (men over 6' 4' [1.9 metres] tall, or over 25 stone [160 kg] in weight) is actually very small in absolute terms, but the firm is successful nonetheless because men of this size are not catered for at all by the big chain retailers. The only other alternative open to these men is to have everything tailor-made. High and Mighty (**www.highandmighty.co.uk**) is able to produce in sufficient quantities to keep prices reasonable (though considerably higher than chain store prices) while still catering for its segment.

If the firm is well-resourced and intends to approach a range of segments, managers will adopt a differentiated approach. A simple one-size-fits-all type of product, aimed at a very broad range of possible customers, will lead managers to adopt an undifferentiated approach. Table 6.2 shows this in action.

Table 6.2: Resourcing and degree of differentiation

High-resource company

Type of product	High differentiation consumers	Low differentiation consumers
Mass market	Differentiated	Undifferentiated
Specialist market	Differentiated	Concentrated

Low-resource company

Type of product	High differentiation consumers	Low differentiation consumers
Mass market	Concentrated	Differentiated (perhaps geographically)
Specialist market	Concentrated	Concentrated

Companies with a small resource base are often unable to make their voices heard in mass markets simply because they cannot afford the level of promotional spend. They therefore need to segment, perhaps by starting out in a small area of the country (geographical segmentation) and gradually spreading nationwide as resources become available.

Table 6.3 shows the decision matrix for choosing a segment to target.

Table 6.3: Targeting decisions

Segment size	Profit per unit sold	Number of competitors	Strategic decision rationale
Large	Large	Large	A large market with large profits is attractive to competitors, so a price war is likely as firms seek to maximize their market share. This will eventually lead to a drop in profits for everyone.
Large	Small	Large	This is a mature market. Such markets are difficult to enter unless the entrant has something very new to offer.
Small	Large	Large	A small segment with a high profit per unit and many competitors can often be captured in its entirety by using a penetration pricing strategy. Such strategies invite retaliation in kind, however.
Large	Large	Small	If the segment is both large and profitable competitors will certainly enter the market. Price skimming might be most appropriate for this market: as competitors enter, prices can be reduced in order to shut out competition.
Large	Small	Small	This is a mature market, but is relatively low-risk; the lack of competition makes it easy to capture a share, and the low profit margin will discourage others from entering. On the other hand, the profits to be made may be too low to make the segment attractive.
Small	Small	Large	This is a dying market. Unless there is a strategic reason for doing so, for example establishing links with potentially attractive customers, this segment is probably not worth entering at all.
Small	Large	Small	This is a niche market. It may well be possible to capture all of the segment with a tight targeting strategy.
Small	Small	Small	This is clearly not an attractive segment. Unless the firm has something very new to bring to the segment, it is probably not worth targeting.

The marketing strategy obviously needs to be built around the segment. This means that each of the seven Ps needs to be tailored to meet the needs of the segment. Accurate targeting cannot be achieved without a detailed understanding of the needs and wants of the segment. Without this, the organization is unable to decide what to offer the target audience in order to differentiate the firm from its competitors in the customers' minds. Note that three factors are being taken into account here: firstly, what do the customers in the target segment need? Secondly, what is already available to them? Thirdly, what can the firm offer that would be better than what is currently available?

Talking Point

Segmenting a market correctly is the basis of all good marketing strategy, so we are informed. Yet it takes a great deal of time and effort, not to mention nail-biting stress, to decide who are the most appropriate recipients of the firm's product offerings.

So why not offer the products to everyone, and see who buys them? Are we really so arrogant as to think that we should only offer the product to a select few? Is segmentation merely another word for elitism? Or perhaps we have no choice – perhaps the products can only be offered to a select few, with everyone else left out in the cold.

The five basic strategies of market coverage were outlined by Derek F. Abell in 1980. They are shown in Table 6.4.

Table 6.4: Market coverage strategies

Strategy	Explanation	Example
Product/market concentration	Niche marketing; the company takes over one small part of the market.	Tie Rack, Sock Shop.
Product specialization	Firm produces a full line of a specific product type.	Campbell's Soup (**www.campbellsoup.com**)
Market specialization	Firm produces everything that a specific group of consumers needs.	Titleist (**www.titleist.com**) golf clubs, golf balls, tees, caddies.
Selective specialization	Firm enters selective niches that are not closely related, but are profitable.	British Telecom (**www.bt.com**) sells telephone services to consumers and industry, but also owns satellite time which it sells to TV broadcasters and others.
Full coverage	Firm enters every possible segment of its potential market.	Renault (**www.renault.com**), which manufactures every type of vehicle from compact cars through to giant articulated lorries.

Choosing the right market and then approaching it with the right marketing mix are probably the most important activities a marketer carries out. Choosing the wrong segment to target, or still worse not attempting to segment the market at all, leads to lost opportunities and wasted resources.

Accessing the target market is an issue which is likely to affect the viability of the segment. For a segment to be viable, it must be possible to communicate effectively with the people in it, usually through some readily-identifiable communications medium. The segment may even be defined by the medium: some segments comprise people who read a particular magazine or watch a particular TV station. For example, *Loaded* (**www.uploaded.com**) readers represent a group of 'laddish' men, usually with high disposable incomes, and interests which involve expensive cars, gadgets, dating-game products, and sport. These men represent a valuable market segment in their own right, but can probably only be easily identified as a group because they read *Loaded*.

POSITIONING

Positioning refers to the place the product occupies in the individual customer's perceptual map of the market. In other words, each customer has a view of where the product stands in relation to its competitors: it may be seen as a high-quality item, or as a reliable one, or perhaps as the cheap version. The brand is positioned in the perceptual map alongside similar offerings; this is a result of the process of categorization and chunking (i.e. the mental process of grouping items of information which are perceived as being linked).

This mapping process is not rigid – each customer and each consumer will have a view of the brand based on hearsay, direct experience, advertising, or any one of many different inputs. Not all customers will put the product in the same position: a few minutes spent asking people what their opinion is of a particular brand will produce many different responses, although there may be an overall consensus on some aspects of the brand.

Consumers build up a position for a product based on what they expect and believe to be the most pertinent features of the product class. Marketers therefore first need to find out what the pertinent features of the products are in the target consumers' minds. The marketer can then adjust the mix of features and benefits, and the communications mix, to give the product its most effective position relative to the other brands in the market. Sometimes the positioning process is led by the consumers, sometimes by the marketers.

There are six basic approaches to positioning (Jain 2000):

1. Positioning by attribute. This involves associating the brand with a particular desirable attribute, such as reliability or smart design.
2. Positioning by price and quality. This involves being outstanding at either the highest price or the lowest price in the market, and making this aspect of the product the key differentiator.
3. Positioning with respect to use or application. For example, establishing a cleaning product as '*the* bathroom cleanser'.
4. Positioning by product user. For example, positioning the brand as 'the professional's choice'.
5. Positioning with respect to a product class. This means associating the brand with a class of product to which it does not (objectively) belong. For example, a soap brand might be associated with top-class perfume brands.
6. Positioning with respect to a competitor. The best-known example of this is Avis's (**www.avis.com**) 'We're number two, so we try harder'. This refers to the company's size relative to Hertz (**www.hertz.com**), which is the world's largest car rental company.

A company may have only one brand, but it is far more common for a firm to seek to position several brands at once. Motor manufacturers provide many examples of this, positioning different models in different market segments but (less obviously) having separate branding for some models. For example, Ford Motor Company (**www.ford.com**) produces family vehicles like the Focus and Mondeo, commercial vehicles such as the Transit, and sports models such as the Puma and Cougar. However, the firm also produces luxury cars under the Jaguar brand (**www.jaguar.com**), and trucks under the Iveco (**www.iveco.com**) brand which is shared with other european manufacturers such as Renault.

If a company is positioning a single brand, it should try to associate itself with a core segment in a market where it can show a clear competitive advantage. Alternatively, the company might adopt an undifferentiated approach, seeking to cover the whole of the potential market. However, this approach is difficult to implement, and almost impossible to maintain in the long run.

Positioning a single brand against a market leader is likely to be risky, but is potentially a high-return route if the incoming brand can dislodge the leader. The single brand might be able to position itself in a secondary position, in other words not threaten the market leader sufficiently to provoke damaging retaliation, but a direct assault might very well be feasible. The incoming brand may have an advantage if the leading brand in the market is part of the portfolio of a multi-brand firm, since the incoming firm has only one brand to consider. Introducing multiple brands has the advantage of spreading the risk to the firm, but it also means the firm is able to target several segments at once, each with separate needs.

Essentially, a single brand should be positioned so that it can withstand competition, and its unique position must be maintained by strong differentiation, usually as an exclusive product.

In the case of multiple brands, the firm has the additional problem of avoiding cannibalizing its own brands while at the same time competing effectively with other firms. Cannibalism is almost inevitable: at least some of the customers for a new product would have bought the firm's existing products, and for some industries the cannibalism rate has been calculated as high as 50 per cent, in other words around half the customers for the new product have been recruited from the ranks of existing customers. However, since those customers were evidently open to the idea of switching to a new product, they might equally have been lured away had a competitor introduced a similar new brand into what was (presumably) an empty market niche. Therefore the true cannibalism rate is much lower than 50 per cent. Some firms regard cannibalism as perfectly acceptable and an inevitable concomitant of a multiple-brand strategy. Brand managers in such firms are encouraged to compete with each other, on the theory that such competition will make the brands even more successful at shutting out competitors and at strengthening the brands themselves.

Products in a multiple-brand environment might be positioned to compete head-on with the market leaders, or might be positioned to be complementary to the existing brands (in other words, to fill market niches without threatening the leaders).

Positioning is actually something which happens in the minds of customers, and may have little to do with the firm's view of its products. For example, the firm's-eye view of the brand may be that it is a high-quality, reliable product; customers may think the brand is old-fashioned and expensive. Repositioning a product in customers' minds may be a matter of re-educating the customers to perceive the brand in a different way.

Talking Point

Repositioning a product involves shifting the consumers' perception of the product in some way. Yet presumably these people have some experience of the product, either directly or by hearsay, which has caused them to think of the product in a particular way relative to its competitors.

So is repositioning merely a matter of informing consumers more fully about the product and what it is really like? Or is it a form of the brainwashing that marketers are always being accused of? Should we be messing with people's minds in this way – or is this just a normal part of human communication?

Perhaps we need some new definitions here!

For example, Skoda cars (**www.skoda-auto.com**) had to fight hard to throw off the negative connotations of the vehicle's eastern european origins. Not wishing to be classed with Ladas (**www.lada.co.uk**), Yugos (**www.yugo.co.uk**) and Polski Fiats (**www.autohistories.com/pzinz/ PolskiFiat.html**) and thus share the perception of poor workmanship and unreliability, Skoda made great efforts to emphasize Volkswagen's (**www.volkswagen.co.uk**) takeover of the company and to position the car next to VW in the consumer's mind.

Skoda has pointed out that, under VW ownership, the company's quality control and engineering procedures have been brought up to at least the same standard as VW. Even before the VW takeover, Skoda was the leading eastern european car manufacture: in fact, before the Second World War Skoda had an unrivalled reputation for quality and reliability, and was regarded as the BMW of its day. This means that the company already had good (if unimaginative) engineering credentials to build on – the problem was more in the minds of the consumers than in the actual quality of the cars.

For repositioning to be effective, the firm needs to know how the brand is currently perceived. Although each brand is positioned differently in each consumer's mind, the segment as a whole should be approximately in agreement about where individual brands are positioned. If this is not the case, it may be that the segment has been wrongly identified. In order to determine the product's position within the segment, research is carried out with the target group of consumers and a perceptual map such as the one in Fig 6.3 will be produced.

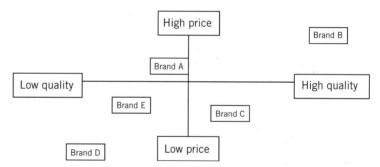

Figure 6.3: Perceptual mapping

In this perceptual map, Brand B is considered to be both high price and high quality; this is probably the Rolls-Royce of the products. Brand D is perceived as being low price, but low quality; Brand D is evidently the cheap, everyday brand. The brand manager of Brand A has a problem; the brand is deemed to be higher-priced, but below-average quality. Consumers therefore do not perceive this brand as good value and would probably only buy when there is no other choice available. Brand C, on the other hand, enjoys a low price and good quality, so is probably the top-selling brand because it clearly provides good value for money. It should be noted here that quality is very much a subjective concept: different consumers will have different views on what constitutes good quality in a brand, and will have different criteria for judging quality.

It should also be noted that these positions are based on average responses from consumers in the target groups. They are not objective, nor are they based on the firm's view of the quality of its products. For this reason, they can sometimes be changed by promotional efforts, for example advertising campaigns, but more commonly the firm will need to change the product or its price to reposition the brand.

In Fig. 6.3, the products have been mapped against only two dimensions, but in fact consumers use many dimensions to decide how a product is positioned against others. In the case of complex products, the positioning process can be a source of endless debate among aficionados: hi-fi enthusiasts might spend hours debating the differences between brands of stereo equipment for example.

Positioning maps can be used to identify gaps in the market. Using Fig. 6.3 as an example, there is a gap next to Brand A and below Brand B for a medium-to-high quality product at a medium to high price. Currently this market seems to be dominated by lower-priced brands; there is almost certainly a suitable gap for a product which offers medium-to-high quality at a price to match. Obviously other factors might have to be taken into account in practice.

GLOBAL SEGMENTATION

Although cultural variance (and differences in consumer behaviour) are still major issues for international marketers (Hofstede 1994), it is possible to identify segments which cross national boundaries. The main bases for global segmentation are:

1. By country. This means grouping countries with similar cultural characteristics (for example Canada and the US, or Latin American countries).
2. Individual characteristics of consumers (which works in much the same way as segmentation within a single country).

Countries can be used as a broad segmentation basis according to economic development criteria, by cultural variables, or by a combination of factors such as economic, political and R&D factors (Lee 1990). For example, agricultural equipment manufacturers developed the 'mechanical donkey' for use in Third World countries. There are several versions of the product, but essentially it consists of a small internal combustion engine which can drive wheels for towing a plough, or run a winch, or drive a pump. The machine is far less powerful than a tractor, but is affordable for poor farmers, is versatile, and can be maintained easily.

One of the best-known studies of country characteristics is that of Hofstede (1980) in which countries were classified according to power distance (the degree to which power is centralized), individualism (the degree to which people act independently of others), uncertainty avoidance (the degree to which people are prepared to take risks) and masculinity (the degree of male domination). Such studies should be approached with great caution since they tend to lead to stereotyping: the differences between individuals within a country are so great as to swamp any differences between the 'average' natives of the countries concerned. Also, world travel and widespread migration has led to considerable erosion of the differences between populations even since Hofstede's work was first published. Since the work was based on research carried out some ten years earlier, the results must now be seen as seriously dated.

Transnational consumer segmentation seeks market segments which transcend national boundaries. The segmentation variables are the same as would be used within a national boundary: lifestyles, behaviour, and situation-specific behaviour. An example of lifestyle segmentation is the transnational teenage market; there is also evidence of an 'elite' market (Hassan and Katsanis 1991). Within an individual country, such an 'elite' market of wealthier members of society may not be large enough to be worth targeting, but globally the segment is much larger. Also, it is the wealthy people who can travel abroad and become exposed to ideas from other cultures. An example of situation-specific segmentation is attitudes to gift-giving, which seem to be common to many cultures (Beatty et al. 1991).

Culture can be an extremely useful segmentation variable. Cultural differences encompass religion, language, institutions, beliefs and behaviours which are shared by the members of a society. Countries or groups of people who share a culture may have specific needs, an obvious example of which is religious observance. However, even a manufacture of canned food would need to segment the market according to language, if only for labelling purposes. Marketers need to take the advice of natives of the countries in which they hope to do business, since other people's cultural differences are not always obvious.

Brand names which do not cross national boundaries are a fertile source of humour, and are frequently used as such on TV programmes. For example, the Spanish potato crisp brand 'Bum!' is unlikely to do well in the UK. The Rolls Royce Silver Mist car (**www.rolls-royce.com**) had to be re-named for the German market since 'mist' means 'excrement' in German. Many cultural problems are more subtle, and have to do with the way things are said rather than the actual words used. In Japanese, 'yes' can mean 'yes, I understand' but not necessarily 'yes, I agree'. Portuguese has a total of 7 different words for 'you', depending on the status and number of people being addressed.

Gestures are also subject to changes in meaning when they cross borders. The American sign for 'OK', with the thumb and forefinger making a circle, is a rude gesture in Brazil (equivalent to sticking up the index and middle finger in Britain, or the extended middle finger in the US and most of Europe). Showing the soles of the feet is considered insulting in Thailand, and while Americans are usually very happy to hear about an individual's personal wealth and success, Australians are less likely to take kindly to somebody acting like a 'tall poppy' in this way.

Marketers and other managers need to be wary of ethnocentrism, which is the tendency to believe that one's own culture is the 'right' one and that everybody else's is at best a poor imitation (Shimp et al. 1987). For this reason, many firms will target countries where there is some **psychological proximity**. These are countries with cultural aspects in common with the firm's home country. Often this proximity comes from a shared language. English-speaking countries have a degree of common feeling for each other, as does Spain with most of Latin America. Sometimes the closeness comes from a shared history, as in the case of the former communist countries of eastern Europe. Within countries with large migrant populations there may be sub-cultures which give insights into overseas markets. Australia is well-placed to take advantage of far eastern markets and Greek markets as well as other English-speaking markets, and Brazil has good links with Germany (due to substantial immigration) as well as with Portugal, Angola and Mozambique (due to shared language and colonial history). In an interesting reversal, Ireland also has psychological proximity to many countries due to the mass emigration from Ireland of the last 200 years.

In most West African countries tribal loyalties cross national borders, so that people from the same tribe might inhabit different countries. In a sense, this is paralleled in the Basque country which straddles the border between France and Spain, and in Belgium, where half the country speaks a dialect of Dutch and the other half speaks a dialect of French.

From a marketer's viewpoint, cultural differences are probably reducing as consumers become more globally-minded. Foreign travel, the widespread globalization of the entertainment media, and existing availability of foreign products in most economies have all served to erode the world's cultural differences (Ohmae 1989). Increasingly, marketers are able to identify distinct subcultures that transcend national boundaries, for example the world youth culture fuelled by media such as MTV (**www.mtv.com**) (Steen 1995).

The basic problem for companies which seek to internationalize is that nothing can be taken for granted in a foreign country. This places a heavy premium on forward planning. Overall, a firm's internationalization strategy decisions will depend on the following factors:

1. The size of the firm in its domestic market. The bigger the firm, the lower the risk of entering a foreign market.
2. The firm's strengths compared with overseas competitors. This can be difficult to ascertain, but is obviously crucial to the firm's chances of succeeding.
3. Management experience of dealing in other countries. This may include language training, and direct experience of living and working in another country.
4. The firm's objectives for long-term growth. Growth prospects may be limited in the firm's domestic market due to saturation of the market or powerful competition. Such limitations may not exist in overseas markets.

There is more on international market entry strategies in Chapter 7, where the overall approach to foreign markets is discussed.

RELATIONSHIP VERSUS TRANSACTIONAL MARKETING

Traditionally, marketing has focused on single exchanges between organizations and their customers. The emphasis has always been on producing products that will satisfy customer needs, and the focus has tended to be on the single transaction. Little attention has been paid to issues such as repeat purchase. The assumption has been that satisfied customers will come back, and dissatisfied ones will not, so there has been an over-emphasis on acquiring new customers at the expense of ensuring that the firm keeps its old ones. Since most transactions with consumers are undertaken anonymously, the customer is reduced from being an individual person, with needs and wants and problems, to being a member of a market segment.

Relationship marketing, on the other hand, focuses on establishing and maintaining a long-term arrangement between supplier and customer. The customer is treated as an individual as far as possible, and the marketer focuses on establishing a relationship. Relationship marketing is concerned with the lifetime value of the customer. For example, over the course of a lifetime, a motorist might own 30 or more cars. This represents a total expenditure of perhaps hundreds of thousands of pounds on cars, yet car manufacturers and dealers rarely keep in touch with their customers in any organized way. The focus is on the single transaction, that of buying one (and only one) car at a time. A relationship marketing approach would seek to look at the customer in terms of his or her total value to the company over (potentially) 30 or 40 years. The difference between the orientations at first seems small, but consideration of the strategic implications shows that the potential effects are great.

Firstly, relationship marketers seek to keep in contact with customers after the sale, whereas transactional marketers will only do so if there is a complaint, or if there is a specific opportunity to make a new sale. From a practical viewpoint, this has implications for staffing and corporate communications. From a strategic viewpoint, the corporate mission is likely to change in nature; it is likely to shift away from objectives such as growth and towards objectives such as customer satisfaction.

Secondly, the service element of the product provision becomes more important, particularly after-sales service. Strategically, this means an emphasis on process and people. Firms with strong competencies in service issues will benefit from adopting a relationship marketing approach.

Thirdly, product quality is crucial as a tool for building long-term loyalty to the brand. This orientation values the small but loyal customer above the one-off big spender, and gives the firm more chance of maintaining its customer base in the long run. Recruitment of new customers should not be neglected altogether, of course, otherwise the firm will have an ageing customer base. This may be one of the drivers which has led to the success of relationship marketing in the business-to-business world, since businesses do not age as fast as human beings.

The key to relationship marketing is understanding that the bundle of benefits customers are buying includes such factors as product reliability and a pleasant service from the company they are dealing with. 21st century customers expect suppliers to value their custom; 19th century customers would expect the shopkeepers to know them by name, to be respectful and polite, to anticipate their needs, and to arrange delivery or otherwise show that they regarded the customer as important to the firm. During the 20th century, as firms have grown bigger, this level of personal attention has largely disappeared. Economic forces removed the old systems from grocery shops, so that customers are expected to find the goods themselves, carry them to the checkout, pay for them, and carry them home, sometimes without exchanging any conversation with the store staff.

This impersonal and functional view of marketing came about because of the high cost of labour. Relationship marketing seeks to address this issue by encouraging firms to treat customers as individuals with individual needs and aspirations. The use of computer technology enables firms to carry out many of the functions of the 19th century grocer without unduly raising labour costs. For example, supermarket EPOS systems capture data on the individual's buying habits, enabling the supermarket to tailor special offers to the individual. This process is almost entirely automated, but remains effective.

Table 6.5 shows the comparison between traditional, or **transaction** marketing and relationship marketing.

Table 6.5: Transaction versus relationship marketing

Transaction marketing	Relationship marketing
Focus on single sale	Focus on customer retention
Orientation on product features	Orientation on product benefits
Short time-scale	Long time-scale
Little emphasis on customer service	High emphasis on customer service
Limited customer commitment	High customer commitment
Moderate customer contact	High customer contact
Quality is the concern of the production department	Quality is the concern of all

Note: (Source: Christopher, Ballantyne & Payne; *Relationship Marketing*, Oxford, Butterworth-Heinemann 1991)

Although many firms are committed to adopting a relationship marketing philosophy, most firms still follow a traditional marketing strategy. This tends to lead to the following bad practices:

- Reactive approach to customer complaints rather than a proactive approach which prevents complaints arising.

- Failure to recognize the needs of long-term customers because of a concentration on short-term big spenders.

- Greater expenditure on promotion than is necessary, due to the emphasis on acquiring new customers. This is embodied in Ehrenberg's Leaky Bucket theory, which states that most firms treat their customer base like a leaky bucket, from which customers are continually lost and have to be replaced by heavy promotional expenditure.

- Inner conflict within departments as production people expect marketers to sell the goods, and marketers expect production people to handle quality issues.

As customer expectations rise, and more particularly as customers become longer-lived, there is likely to be an increasing emphasis on establishing relationships. This is because the value to the firm of the customer's continued custom is greater, and the customer knows this and expects better treatment in return. A possible danger is that some customers (particularly older people) may find themselves marginalized as younger customers are regarded as more valuable.

Talking Point

Courtship and marriage have often been used as an analogy for the relationship marketing approach. This makes some sense as there is definitely a strong feeling of being wooed in some companies' approach to their customers – and relationship marketers do sometimes act as if they were the vile seducers of Victorian melodramas.

But do customers really want this type of relationship? Do people really want to go on a date with their car dealer, buy a home together with their computer supplier, or marry their bank? Maybe most people simply want the products and services to work for them, at a reasonable price, without causing a lot of long-term problems. And if that's the case, and the customer is always right, shouldn't we be accommodating that viewpoint better?

In fact, despite all the hype about relationship marketing being the way forward for fast-moving consumer goods companies, the philosophy has been most successful in business-to-business markets. Most consumers do not particularly want an intimate relationship with their bank or their dry-cleaning shop, whereas the benefits of establishing closer relationships between suppliers and their business customers are tremendous. From a purchaser's viewpoint, knowing the quality of the supplier and the ways in which he works means that less time is spent in negotiating deals or checking that goods are up to standard. For the supplier, having a regular customer with known needs means less spent on sales reps and more security of income.

From the strategic viewpoint, adopting a relationship marketing approach is much more than a matter of keeping a better customer database and hiring some nice PR people. Relationship marketing implies establishing a value chain in which the customer becomes an integral part: in some ways the customers become an asset of the company, and can therefore become part of the firm's competitive advantage.

In business-to-business markets relationships may become close enough to dictate the strategy of one or other firm in the relationship. If a customer is large enough and close enough, the firm may switch its strategic positioning from (for example) product specialization to market specialization.

THE EXPANDED MARKETING MIX

The traditional marketing mix consists of the four Ps: price, product, place and promotion. Relationship marketers expand on this to include the process by which the goods are supplied, the people involved in that process, and the physical evidence of the transaction (Booms and Bitner 1981). These additional three Ps were originally introduced as a way of explaining how services marketing differs from marketing physical products.

In fact, very few services do not involve a physical product, and likewise very few physical products do not have some service element attached to them. Companies with a high service content (such as restaurants) are usually more people-orientated than providers of physical products, because more of the company personnel are in constant proximity to the customers than would be the case for a manufacturer, for whom perhaps only the salespeople make regular contact with customers. One of the objectives of relationship marketing is to make it possible for manufacturers to become as close to their customers as are service providers.

V.C. Judd (1987) developed a categorization scheme for staff based on the degree of frequency of contact with customers, and the extent to which the staff are engaged in conventional marketing activities.

Contactors are the front-liners, the people who have the most frequent contact with customers. They are salespeople, service engineers, and installation people. They need to be very familiar with the company's overall marketing strategy, and should be empowered to respond to customer needs as they arise.

Modifiers have frequent contact with customers, but have no traditional marketing role. Telephonists, receptionists and credit controllers fall into this category. They need high levels of interpersonal skills, particularly in the case of credit controllers who need to remain tactful and responsive without losing sight of their main role, which is to persuade late payers to settle their bills.

Influencers have little or no direct contact with customers. This does not mean they have no role to play in developing the company's relationship with the customers. They are the shipping department people, the market research people, the engineering research and development people. These individuals still need a customer-orientated approach; their aim should be not just to please the customers, but to delight them.

Isolateds are the people who have no contact with customers, and no traditional marketing role. They are the secretaries, filing clerks, factory-floor workers, and data processing staff. Their role lies in supporting other staff in meeting customer needs more effectively. Because such staff are important to the firm in providing the products the customer buys, but at the same time may have little sense of the reality of customer needs, it is useful to remember that the internal marketing of the firm is as important as the external marketing.

People do not do business with companies: people cannot establish a relationship with a company. A company is a legal fiction; it has no real existence. People do business with other people, so the relationship needs to start with the other people.

PEOPLE WITH WHOM BUSINESS IS DONE

Transaction marketers focus on the customer. Relationship marketers broaden the view to include other players in other markets.

Customer markets remain much the same as they are under a transaction paradigm, except there is more emphasis on keeping existing customers. For example, the growth of the use of loyalty cards in supermarkets worldwide moved rapidly into a second phase in which the loyalty cards are accepted at some other retailers, thus trapping the customer's money within the system (Mitchell 1996). This followed on from the trend for airlines to aggregate their frequent-flyer programmes so that passengers could earn and redeem points with a range of international and regional airlines, thus ensuring that virtually any destination could be reached via one or other of the partner airlines. Unfortunately, many consumers carry more than one loyalty card, thus obviating the need to remain loyal to any one store or group.

Some retailers have membership fees (the UK's MVC video and music store being one example). Customers pay the initial fee, which entitles them to buy goods at a discount. This is, in effect, a two-part pricing system which ensures loyalty at least until the initial investment is recouped (Dick 1995).

Referral markets consist of the people who might be expected to recommend the product or the company to others. These may or may not be existing customers: in many cases they are professional recommenders. For example, a building materials manufacturer needs to be aware of the needs of builders, but also needs to look after the architects who specify particular building materials in their designs. In service industries such as the holiday industry this is common; in physical product manufacturing industries it is less so.

Supplier markets are those people who provide raw materials and components for the company. In recent years suppliers have become part of the overall value-delivery team, and the traditional somewhat adversarial relationship is being replaced by the **logistics** paradigm of co-operation towards a common goal. Previously the buyer's emphasis has been on negotiating the lowest possible price from suppliers, but the emphasis has now shifted towards strategy-orientated goals such as reliability of delivery, zero-fault quality control procedures, and co-operation in design and production.

Employee markets are also part of the internal market. Recruiting appropriately-talented staff and motivating them is essential: there is an acute shortage of enthusiastic and skilled people to work in industry. Even when suitable employees have been found, firms need to ensure that they are market-orientated and understand the company's aims and objectives.

Influence markets comprise those individuals who might have influence on the firm's activities. They include the government and its many departments, financial institutions such as banks and venture capitalists, pressure groups such as Greenpeace and so forth. Traditional marketing thinking places these groups in the domain of PR activities, but relationship marketing goes further than this. While PR concentrates on building a favourable image of the company by providing information, relationship marketing examines ways of meeting the needs of those institutions and individuals and helping them achieve their own aims. In practice, this would mean consulting with a pressure group before undertaking any new activities: under the PR paradigm, the company might issue counter-publicity to nullify the pressure group rather than seeking to build bridges between the group and the firm.

Internal marketing is concerned with ensuring that everybody inside the firm is not only aware of the company's policies, but is also enthusiastic and supportive of them. Staff should feel that their own needs are being met, beyond the salary cheque at the end of the month: work is not solely about economics. For example, train crews in Australia are given considerable autonomy about how they do the job – even down to participating in the planning of train schedules on freight services. Although this may sound anarchic, the crews in fact act extremely responsibly about the way the trains operate, and in general feel much more a part of the process than do their counterparts in other parts of the world.

Internal marketing should not be a separate activity, it should be built into quality programmes, customer service programmes, and ad hoc activities throughout the normal working lives of employees.

DEVELOPING A RELATIONSHIP MARKETING APPROACH

To develop a relationship approach the firm needs to be empathetic. This means, in the first instance, developing a clear view of what the customer is buying. Levitt (1986) has suggested the following hierarchy of levels:

1. **Core** or **generic**. This is the basic physical product, or the minimum features which the customer would expect to have. For example, a car would be expected to carry the driver, some passengers and their luggage from one place to another. All cars do this: if they do not, they are no longer cars.

2. **Expected**. This is the generic product plus some extra features the customer would reasonably expect to see. In the car example, the customer would expect there to be an owner's manual, a guarantee, and some kind of servicing network in case of breakdowns.

3. **Augmented**. These are the factors that differentiate the product. For the car, this could be a stylish design, or air conditioning fitted as standard, or particular performance specifications such as rapid acceleration or high fuel efficiency. These are the features that make the customer buy one brand rather than another.

4. **Potential**. This is all the possible features and benefits that could be wanted by customers. It would be foolish for a manufacturer to try to provide all these features in one product because the cost would be too high, and consumers would not be prepared to pay for features they do not need, but it is still useful to be aware of the list so that new features can be introduced quickly in the event of competitive attacks. Also, when new models are introduced the producer should be in a position to inform the appropriate customers of the new features and benefits which are available. The idea behind this is to encourage the customer to remain loyal to the original manufacturer.

QUALITY

Quality is a somewhat nebulous concept because it relies heavily on the individual customer's perceptions. Quality might be defined as the relationship between what customers expect, and what they get. If a customer's expectations of a product are disappointed, his or her perception will be that the product is poor quality. If, on the other hand, the product exceeds expectations, the perception will be that the product is high quality.

Much of the customers' perception of quality is bound up in what they perceive as value for money. The aim of the relationship marketer is to delight the customer, not simply to satisfy or even to please the customer.

Quality is therefore not an absolute. It is only relevant to the individual customer. What is good quality to one person may not be to another, because both are beginning with different expectations. Service support is therefore critical to relationship marketing because it is during the pre-sale and after-sale support that customers are approached as individuals. It is at this time that the customer's perception of quality can be addressed, either by ensuring that the expectations of the product are realistic (pre-sale) or by correcting any faults or errors after-sale.

The strategic viewpoint that the company need only produce the highest quality product on the market in order to be successful is called the product concept. This view is seriously flawed: even Rolls Royce has gone through bankruptcy by following this precept. The product concept leads to quality being the province of the engineering department, and therefore a tendency to move the product away from the customers and more towards the company. Under a relationship marketing ethos, quality has become the integrating concept between production orientation and marketing orientation. (Gummeson 1988).

Under this paradigm, service quality is defined as the ability of the organization to meet or exceed customer expectations. Relationship marketers monitor the quality of the firm's output against two criteria: the customer's expectations, and the firm's actual output. Parasuraman, Zeithaml and Berry (1985) have developed a model of service quality which is reproduced in Fig 6.4.

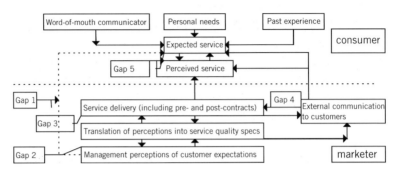

Figure 6.4: Service quality model

(Source; Parasuraman, A., Zeithaml, V.A. and Berry, L.L. (1985) 'A conceptual model of service quality and its implications for future research'. *Journal of Marketing*, 49, Fall)

The model shows various gaps in the understanding of service quality. These are as follows:

Gap 1: Difference between actual customer expectations and management perceptions of customer expectations.

Gap 2: Difference between management perceptions of customer expectations and service quality specifications.

Gap 3: Difference between service quality specifications and the service actually delivered.

Gap 4: Difference between service delivery and what is communicated about the service to customers.

Gap 5: Difference between customer expectations and perceptions of what is actually received. This gap is influenced by the other four.

In order to close these gaps, relationship marketers adopt a range of quality control procedures, as shown in Table 6.6.

Table 6.6: Quality control systems

Procedure	Explanation
Total quality management (TQM)	The firm does the rights things at every stage of the production process to ensure a high-quality outcome at the end. This approach does not take account of the customer's expectations and perceptions, but instead relies on the management's preconceptions of what constitutes good manufacturing practice. There is also some difficulty in judging the level at which the quality of the product should be pitched. Probably the main contribution that TQM has made is in reducing defects (the zero-defects target) which will, by reducing wastage, reduce costs.
Benchmarking	This is the process of comparing each department in the firm with the most successful equivalent department in the firm's competitors. If each department in the company operates on a level equivalent to the best department among competitors, this will result (one assumes) in a company which is the best of the best. The drawback is that some firms do not like the idea of having their quality control systems dictated by the competition; also the system, if adopted by everybody, would stifle innovation.
Service quality benchmarking	Service quality benchmarking extends this concept to the service area, comparing both competitors and non-competitors.

Christopher, Payne and Ballantyne (op. cit.) have drawn up the five-stage approach to service benchmarking shown in Table 6.7.

Table 6.7: Five stages for service benchmarking

Step 1	Define the competitive arena, that is, with whom are we compared by customers and with whom do we want to be compared?
Step 2	Identify the key components of customer service as seen by customers themselves.
Step 3	Establish the relative importance of those service components to customers.
Step 4	Identify customer position on the key service components relative to competition.
Step 5	Analyse the data to see if service performance matches customers' service needs.

Defining the competitive arena is not as simple as it at first appears. As we have seen in earlier chapters, companies frequently define the competition in narrow terms. The main problem for the supplier is to decide who the customer compares the firm with. For example, a cinemagoer may well compare the service with other forms of entertainment. Are the sales staff on the confectionery counter as pleasant as the bar staff at the pub? Is the film on offer as entertaining as the band playing at the club? The key issue is that the customer's assessment of the service level takes place not against other firms in the same business, but against other services the customer buys. This is another example of the failure of many firms to take a customer's eye view of the relationship.

The same thinking applies in the case of physical products. A customer who finds that the supplier is difficult about offering to replace faulty components will compare this with the fleet leasing firm who offered replacement vehicles while the firm's delivery vans are being serviced, or the computer supplier who provided free technical support when a virus hit the firm's computers. Having had a good service from the leasing company or computer supplier tends to reduce the risk of buying, and therefore increases the chances of a repeat purchase from the same company.

The key components of customer service are too often left to executive judgement without reference to the customers. For example, a computer purchaser may regard on-site maintenance as being far more important than on-line assistance. A car owner whose car is in for servicing may regard the availability of a lift to the train station as being more important than the speed of the servicing of the car.

Having established the key components of customer service, relationship marketers need to establish the relative importance of each component in the consumers' minds. Because it is impossible, in a world with limited resources, to provide every customer with everything he or she wants, the firm needs to concentrate on providing the most important aspects first.

This process relates to the positioning process, in which the firm needs to know where it is currently positioned in the consumer's perceptions and then needs to decide whether this position is appropriate relative to the desired competitive position.

This leaves the firm in a position to compare its service provision with the service priorities of its customers.

MANAGING THE RELATIONSHIP

Ultimately, the purpose of the relationship marketing philosophy is to build customer loyalty. Here are some examples of managing the relationship.

1. Supermarket loyalty cards. Loyalty cards are used worldwide to encourage customers to return to the same store for all their groceries. The next stage of the procedure is to use the EPOS (electronic point-of-sale) equipment to track the customer's spending patterns.

For example, it is theoretically possible with current technology to be able to advise a shopper that he or she has forgotten some regularly-purchased item, because the system knows how often this customer buys the product, and what brand and pack size the customer prefers. Currently supermarkets do not do this, because many consumers would regard it as an unwarranted invasion of privacy: however, others might regard it as a wonderful service (Evans 1994).

2. The UK's Nationwide Building Society has declared that it will not become a bank (as have most other building societies), since this would mean paying dividends to shareholders rather than offering benefits to customers. The intention is to retain existing customers as customers rather than encouraging them to become shareholders in a new institution.

3. Frequent Flyer programmes on airlines offer the regular users of the airlines the opportunity to have free flights or major discounts on travel. Such programmes are usually extended to partner airlines. For example, United Airlines of the US has formed the Star Alliance with Thai Air, Lufthansa, Aloha Airlines in Hawaii, British Midland in the UK, and a large number of other airlines throughout the world. Frequent Flyer points can be earned by travelling with any of these airlines, and can be exchanged with any of them. Unfortunately, most people who fly frequently (and especially those who fly long-haul) have hit on the idea of joining all the frequent flyer programmes. Given that the programmes often involve many other airlines, a frequent flyer who joins two or three programmes will almost certainly cover most of the world's airlines.

4. Museum or theatre season tickets. Mailings to season-ticket holders regarding forth-coming events are much more cost-effective than the 'scattergun' approach of advertising in the newspapers. An example is the Sydney Symphony Orchestra's Friends of the SSO scheme; members are entitled to attend selected rehearsals, buy tickets at a discount, and be invited to special events.

5. Direct marketing. This is a rapidly-growing area in marketing, as computer technology is becoming more refined. The growth in computer-based files on customers (databases) has allowed firms to develop extremely accurate information about their customers' buying habits. The capacity for exchanging databases between firms means that even more accurate profiles of each individual in the country can be developed, subject to legal restrictions such as the Data Protection Act. Martin Evans (1994) has dubbed this 'Domesday marketing' – the potential for the cataloguing of every customer in the country on a giant database.

In practice, this is still some way off – largely due to the difficulty of winning public acceptance – but in the meantime the detailed information which is available enables companies, and in particular database brokers, to carry out extremely accurate segmentation of markets. Because most of the relevant information about the customers concerned is on file, mailing list brokers are able to offer very specific mailings to companies. The positive benefit of this is that, in future, customers will no longer receive junk mail – they will instead only be sent information that is of direct, immediate interest. This represents major savings for the companies sending out the mailings as well as a reduction in irritation for the recipients of the mail.

Database marketing has become inextricably linked with relationship marketing because databases provide an unrivalled opportunity for cataloguing each customer's tastes and preferences, and for knowing what to approach each individual with, and when. This means that companies are coming much nearer to reproducing the level of service of the 19th century shopkeeper, who knew his regular customers personally; for a modern supermarket to do this a computer is required.

Many of the techniques used to generate loyalty are expensive and require considerable commitment, but in the longer term the result for the firm is a more stable and secure market, but relationship marketing is not necessarily a cheap option.

Talking Point

Junk mail is almost universally disliked. Study after study has shown that it is the most unpopular of all marketing communications devices, and yet firms persist in sending it out. Why?

Well, maybe it's because other studies have shown that it is extremely cost-effective if carried out correctly. People actually respond to it – even though every response simply provokes a further flood of mail as more marketers jump on the bandwagon. So why is there this apparent split personality among consumers?

Maybe it's to do with how well the mailings are targeted. Maybe a well-targeted mailing is interesting and useful – and a poorly-targeted one is just so much landfill!

THE SEVEN-S FRAMEWORK

Research by McKinsey & Co., reported in 'In Search of Excellence', the Peters and Waterman bestseller (Waterman 1986), revealed that the most successful companies shared a set of seven elements which they used for planning organizational change. The framework is shown in Fig 6.5.

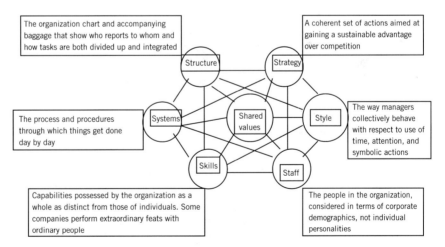

Figure 6.5: The 7-S framework

The shared values in the diagram are the ideas held in common by members of the organization. These shared values become typical of the organization, and are often its defining characteristics from the viewpoint of the customers.

The theory says that organizations which are able to integrate the 7-S framework, and who can instil in staff a set of shared values which relate to the customer, will ultimately be more successful in the marketplace. In fact, many of the companies originally studied by Peters and Waterman have since run into serious trouble, and even bankruptcy. It seems that the theory, while it undoubtedly has much to commend it, does not provide a foolproof formula for success.

CASE STUDY: IKEA – MAKING SHOPPING EASY

www.ikea.com

IKEA has been a major success story in furniture retailing throughout the 1980s and 90s and into the new century. The firm sells flat-pack furniture from outlets the size of football pitches. Quality is good, designs are simple and attractive, and the costs are kept low by the out-of-town location and the minimalist approach to staffing.

IKEA stores operate like supermarkets. Customers self-select the furniture item, pay for it, and wheel it out to their cars. The self-assembly nature of the products reduces costs partly because it removes some of the labour costs from the manufacturing process, but also because the goods can be shipped and stored much more easily. Customers are more than happy to be on the receiving end of a major discount, but this strength of IKEA's is also its major weakness.

The difficulty with flat-pack furniture is twofold: firstly, it is easy to make a mistake and pick up the wrong box (the three-drawer version instead of the four-drawer, for example). Secondly, it is often hard to read the assembly instructions, and easy to make a mistake. This is a particular problem for IKEA because this part of the process happens away from the store, where it has little control.

As for most companies, the part that IKEA can control (the store environment, staffing, production of the goods and instruction sheets, etc.) is only a small part of the customer's experience of the product. The part that happens outside IKEA's control (the assembly and use of the furniture, perhaps for many years) is actually the major part of the experience for the customers. Therefore IKEA has decided to take as much care as possible over the part of the experience it does control.

IKEA makes extensive use of 'mystery shoppers' to test the process. Someone pretending to be an ordinary customer will visit each store and assess the system, from point-of-sale signage to wait times for the first approach from a staff member. The check-out process, the queuing times, the availability of products are all checked in this way.

Secondly, IKEA has a high number of staff in each outlet whose job is solely to assist customers in finding the appropriate furniture item. These staff (whom IKEA call co-workers) are trained in sales and stock operations so they can solve almost any customer problem immediately. They are also trained to seek out and identify customers who appear confused or frustrated, and approach them before the customer finds it necessary to seek help. These co-workers are also empowered to provide solutions to problems and complaints – they are given discretion to offer free delivery, money back or discounts, or even free meals in the IKEA cafeteria.

Thirdly, IKEA goes to considerable trouble to ensure that signs, instruction leaflets, and assembly processes are as smooth and user-friendly as possible. The point of the exercise is to make it as easy as possible for customers to buy from IKEA and enjoy the products. It is an easy assumption that this will result in people buying from IKEA again.

CASE STUDY QUESTIONS

1. What market segments do you think IKEA might be targeting?
2. How do the co-workers encourage a relationship marketing outcome?

▶

3. If people are prepared to pay more for better quality, why is IKEA cheap?
4. What other market segments might IKEA realistically consider targeting?
5. How might IKEA grow even closer to its customers?

SUMMARY

Approaching customers means knowing in advance who the customers are likely to be, and what their common needs are. The marketing concept places customers at the centre of everything the firm does, so approaching customers is of central importance to the firm.

The key points from this chapter are as follows:

■ There are few, if any, mass markets left untouched.

■ Segments must be measurable, accessible, substantial, stable and congruent.

■ It is not a good idea to target a segment simply because it is attractive: company competences need to be considered also.

■ The narrower the segment, the fewer the customers, but the more they are willing to pay.

■ Some segments are defined by the media used to target them.

■ Culture affects more than just communication issues.

■ Segmentation is more difficult in an international context, but can be carried out in the same way as for a home market.

■ Relationship marketing suggests that suppliers of physical products should try to be as close to customers as service producers are.

■ Quality is the relationship between expectations and results.

CHAPTER QUESTIONS

1. How might a firm judge the quality of its offerings?
2. Relationship marketing has often been compared to marriage. Under what circumstances might a firm consider divorcing some of its customers?
3. Why might a firm not target an attractive segment?
4. What cultural problems might exist in the global beer market?
5. What is the difference between 'good value' and 'low prices'?

REFERENCES

Abell, Derek F. (1980): *Defining the Business; The Starting Point of Strategic Planning* (Englewood Cliffs NJ: Prentice-Hall 1980).

Beatty, S.E., Kahle, L. and Homer, P. (1991): 'Personal Values and Gift-Giving Behaviours; A Study Across Cultures' *Journal of Business Research* 22 pp. 149–157.

Booms, B.H. and Bitner, M.J. (1981): 'Marketing strategies and organization structures for service firms'. In *Marketing of Services* J. Donnelly and W.R. George, eds. (Chicago II: American Marketing Association).

Cutler, 1989: 'Stars of the 1980s cast their light' *Fortune* 3 July p. 76.

Dick, A.S. (1995): 'Using Membership Fees to Increase Customer Loyalty' *Journal of Product and Brand Management* vol. 4 no. 5 1995 pp. 65–68.

Evans, M.J. (1994): 'Domesday Marketing?' *Journal of Marketing Management* 10 (5).

Gummesson, E. (1988): 'Service Quality and Product Quality Combined' *Review of Business* 9, 3, winter.

Hassan, S.S. and Katsanis, L.P. (1991): 'Identification of Global Consumer Segments; A Behavioural Framework' *Journal of International Consumer Marketing*, 3(2) 1991 pp. 11–28.

Hofstede, G. (1980): *Culture's Consequences; International Differences in Work-Related Values* (Beverly Hills: Sage, 1980).

Hofstede, G. (1994): 'Management Scientists are Human' *Management Science* vol. 40(1) 1994 pp. 4–13.

Jain, Subhash J. (2000): *Marketing planning and strategy* (Cincinnatti: Southwestern College Publishing).

Judd, V.C. 1987: 'Differentiate with the 5th P, People' *Industrial Marketing Management* 16 pp. 241–247.

Lee, C. (1990): 'Determinants of National Innovativeness and International Market Segmentation' *International Marketing Review* 7 (5) pp. 39–49.

Levitt, T. (1986): *The Marketing Imagination* (New York: The Free Press).

Mitchell, A. (1996): 'How Will the Loyalty Card Evolve Now?' *Marketing Week* 30 August 1996, pp. 20–21.

Ohmae, K. (1989): 'Managing in a Borderless World' *Harvard Business Review* May-June 1989, pp. 152–161.

Parasuraman, A., Zeithaml, V.A. and Berry, L.L. (1985): 'A conceptual model of service quality and its implications for future research' *Journal of Marketing* 49, Fall.

Porter, M.E. (1985): *Competitive Advantage* (New York: The Free Press).

Shimp, T. and Sharma, S. (1987): 'Consumer Ethnocentrism; Construction and Validation of CETSCALE' *Journal of Marketing Research* Aug. 1987, pp. 280–289.

Steen, J. (1995): 'Now They're Using Suicide to Sell Jeans' *Sunday Express* 26 March 1995.

Wind, Yoram (1984): 'Going to Market. New Twists for some Old Tricks' *Wharton Magazine* 4, 1984.

Chapter Seven

Approaches to Markets

INTRODUCTION

The strategic approach to a market differs from the approach to a customer (or group of customers) because of the presence of competitors in the market. A market is all the possible buyers for a product category, plus all the other suppliers of that product category, plus regulators and others with an interest in the product category.

After reading this chapter, you should be able to:

- Explain the advantages and disadvantages of niche marketing.
- Describe the differences between being a market leader, and being a market follower.
- Describe ways of achieving a sustainable competitive advantage.
- Explain how to achieve corporate growth in declining markets.
- Describe approaches to diversification.

TYPES OF MARKET STRATEGY

Market-scope strategies deal with coverage of the market. The three main alternatives within the market scope strategies are as shown in Table 7.1.

Table 7.1: Market scope strategies

Strategy alternative	Explanation and examples
Single-market strategy	The firm devotes all its efforts to one market segment. This may be an appropriate strategy for a small firm, or one which is unable to attack the major players in the market. This means seeking out a market segment that the large firms think is too small, or too risky, or too unprofitable - in other words, niches which are probably not very attractive. Having said that, small firms can sometimes use their greater responsiveness and flexibility to good effect in such markets: also, some segments do not provide the economies of scale that large firms require.
Multi-market strategy	Here the firm opts to serve several segments. For example, a glass bottle manufacturer may serve the food industry, the brewing industry, and the soft drinks industry. Each has differing requirements, and each one is approached with a different tactical package.
Total-market strategy	Companies seeking a total-market strategy seek to serve every segment of their chosen markets. Only the very largest firms can do this effectively, since the resource implications prevent small firms from competing in this many segments.

Market scope can change as the market changes, so (like any other marketing strategy) the firm may need to adapt the market scope strategy occasionally as circumstances dictate. A firm pursuing a single-market strategy may become aware of opportunities which make a multi-market strategy more appealing: a small firm may grow, and need to conquer new segments. Equally, a company pursuing a multi-market strategy may fall on hard times and decide to concentrate on its core business.

Market-geography strategy takes geographic segmentation into the strategy area by concentrating the firm's resources into a key geographical area or type of geographical area. Local-market strategy is usually the province of the small business, particularly the small service business, but some manufacturers and even some large businesses operate within a small geographical area. For example, firms manufacturing souvenirs (such as the Grogg Factory (**www.groggs.co.uk**) in South Wales) often have few, if any, sales outside their own region. Another example is the London Underground (**www.thetube.com**), which is a very large business carrying some three million passengers daily over 253 miles of railway track, and operating 257 stations. The Underground uses capital investment counted in the billions, but it only operates within a small geographical area.

Regional-market strategy means that the firm operates within distinct geographical boundaries which go further than the merely local. Examples might be the rail companies in the UK, which operate within distinct regions but cannot really be said to be local. Another example is the brewing industry: local brewers may only sell within their own region (for example SA Brain (**www.sabrain.co.uk**) in the South-East Wales region) or may have strong local ties even though the product sells nationally (Scottish and Newcastle Breweries (**www.scottish-newcastle.com**), for example). The advantage of regional-market strategy is that it is easier to handle cultural differences within a region – SA Brain's advertising might well be incomprehensible to someone from outside the region, for example.

National-market strategy is commonly adopted as a firm exhausts the possibilities within its own region. Going national is a straightforward proposition in a small country such as Belgium, but rather a different proposition in a relatively large country such as Germany. The cultural differences between regions will be greater, for example: residents of Munich have more in common with their Austrian neighbours in Salzburg than they do with fellow Germans in Kiel or Rostock. Secondly, the resources needed for a national marketing strategy are considerably greater than those for a local or regional strategy. On the other hand, production economies of scale can be very much greater when spread across the national market.

International-market strategies may involve exporting, overseas manufacture, or even a global approach to marketing. There is more on internationalization later in the chapter.

Market-entry strategy is about the timing of market entry. There are three basic market entry strategies, as shown in Table 7.2.

Table 7.2: Market-entry strategies

Strategy	Explanation and examples
First-in strategy	Being first into a new market gives the advantage of creating a lead which others have to follow: it also carries the greatest risk in terms of possible failure in the market. The possibility of gaining an unassailable lead must be offset against the dangers of making a fatal mistake in the early days of an unknown market. Examples of the latter include Philips of Holland (**www.research.philips.com**), which introduced the videodisc in the 1980s, long before the market was ready for it: the launch of DVDs at the beginning of the 21st century has been a runaway success, building on Philips' original technology. First-in companies must stay ahead of the competition throughout, or risk paving the way for their competitors to beat them later.
Early-entry strategy	Early entrants have usually been working along the same lines as the first-in strategists, but are slightly behind. In some cases this is a deliberate decision, so that the first-in marketer tests the market, allowing the early entrant the chance to produce a me-too product which fits the market better. In other cases early-entry is an accidental strategy born of slower development. Early entry works well if the company has a superior marketing strategy and enough resources to fight the first-in company. Weaker early entrants may find themselves continually following the leader, however.
Laggard-entry strategy	Laggard entrants enter the market towards the end of the growth phase of the product life cycle, or when the market is mature. Imitators entering the market have the advantage of being able to copy the leader without having the R&D expenditures of a leader: research shows that this can be an extremely effective strategy (Calentone and Cooper 1981). Conversely, an initiator can enter a mature market with a new slant on an existing product and make considerable inroads – the Internet has provided opportunities for Amazon.com (**www.amazon.com**) and lastminute.com (**www.lastminute.com**) to establish large businesses in what were well-established markets.

Timing of entry can be crucial to the success or failure of a strategy. In general, risk reduces the later the firm enters. On the other hand, potential profit reduces equally quickly.

Market-commitment strategy is about the degree of involvement the firm has with a given market. In the same way as consumers have greater or lesser involvement with a product category, firms can have greater or lesser involvement with a market.

For example, a firm with a strong commitment to a market will probably devote much greater resources to that market than they would to other segments to which they do not feel a strong commitment. Most managers are aware that the bulk of the firm's sales come from a relatively few customers, and a strong-commitment strategy means that the firm devotes most of its attention to those customers.

Average-commitment strategy is open to firms which lack the resources to become fully committed to a given market. This may mean that the firm's attention is committed elsewhere, and the market does not warrant a very strong commitment. Such firms can make mistakes in the average-commitment market because any losses can be compensated for elsewhere, so in some ways the average-commitment firm may feel more able to take risks. Conversely, the average-commitment firm is likely to meet with very strong opposition from the high-commitment firm, as has been the case in the UK with the Direct Line insurance company (**www.directline.com**). Direct Line is the premier telephone insurance brokers. The firm is highly-committed to telephone insurance, does not maintain branch offices, and has extremely effective systems for on-line and telephone insurance sales. The success of the firm has been legendary, to the extent that many other insurers have tried to jump on the bandwagon with their own direct insurance systems. Direct Line has fought back vigorously with strong advertising campaigns, new products, and better service all round. This is because the direct insurance business is the firm's entire raison d'etre: for the other firms it is merely a sideline.

Light-commitment strategies come about when a firm has only a passing interest in a given market. Such firms operate passively and do not make new moves: they will almost always be market followers, and may not expect to make much profit from the markets they enter. In some cases the firm is only in the market in order to shut out competition, or because executives feel the firm 'ought' to be there, or for historical reasons. Provided the firm is not actually losing money by being in the market, there is no real reason not to remain in it.

Market-dilution strategies originally became acceptable during the recession of the mid-1970s, when firms found that some markets were simply not worth remaining in. The first strategy in this category is demarketing, in which the firm deliberately discourages certain groups of customers in order to reduce the costs of servicing unprofitable segments. Firms may decide to fill orders for 'key' customers ahead of the less important customers, or they may ration supplies, or they may recommend a competitor's product if the customer is really not worth keeping, or even refuse to supply a particular customer. Demarketing can be directed towards maintaining the goodwill of key customers at a time when demands cannot be met, for example during a supply crisis.

Pruning of marginal markets is another market dilution strategy. Here the firm divests itself of markets which are unprofitable or which do not meet the company's strategic objectives. A firm may withdraw from low-commitment markets in order to concentrate on the core business, or may decide to divert resources away from poorly-performing segments.

Key-markets strategy is the corollary of pruning strategy in that the firm makes a conscious decision to concentrate on key markets at the expense of its marginal markets. A key-markets strategy requires strong focus, a reputation for quality, and a strong position within the market, which may be based on quality or price or a combination of both.

Harvesting strategy is one in which the company deliberately cuts investment in a given market (or for a given product) and allows the sales to slide downwards, grabbing the profit from it without further investment in the market. This is a common strategy when a product is reaching the end of its life cycle, and is also common if the market is disappearing.

Harvesting is not always possible due to the existence of exit barriers. These barriers may exist due to heavy capital investment with little resale value, or customer goodwill issues, or even the reluctance of senior managers to let go of a brand with some historical significance. An example of this is the tobacco companies' approach to pipe tobacco. Pipe tobacco was originally sold in solid compressed chunks which had to be rubbed between the hands in order to separate the leaves. When ready-rubbed tobacco was introduced, sales of the original 'twist' tobacco plummeted, but the tobacco companies still made sales to traditional pipe smokers, mainly very elderly men. Eventually these old men would die off, but in the meantime the tobacco companies continue to supply them as a goodwill gesture, and for the historical significance of the twist tobacco: there was clearly no point in continuing to promote the product to new generations, since the ready-rubbed tobaccos were clearly far more convenient. It is unlikely that any market now remains for twist tobacco.

Companies are supposedly in business to make profits for the shareholders, or at the very least to meet the strategic objectives of the directors. Yet they often act out of apparent sentiment – preserving the company's original headquarters, keeping archive documents which have no commercial value whatsoever, even continuing to supply customers with spare parts and obsolete products when all reasonable business thinking would indicate that this is a serious waste of time and effort.

Why should any company resort to this behaviour? How can this be justified, in the light of all the research and business thinking that has gone on over the past 300 years? Are these managers mad?

Or are they perhaps merely being human? Perhaps people are more than just a collection of economic behaviours – perhaps they live by ideas rather than by money. Are tobacco companies really this sentimental? Or is it just the managers?

COMPETITIVE POSITIONS

Porter (1985) suggests four basic competitive positioning strategies, of which three are winning strategies and one is a losing strategy:

1. Overall cost leadership. A company which succeeds in minimizing its production and distribution costs is able to offer a price advantage over its competitors without sacrificing profits. To this end, many companies have moved their manufacturing operations to low-wage economies in the Third World, and many more have streamlined their distribution operations or combined them to create an integrated logistics system.

2. Differentiation. Companies which can show customers that their products are significantly different from others on the market are able to charge premium prices (provided different equates to better in the eyes of some customers). Differentiation comes from two sources: firstly, real differences in the features and benefits the product offers, and secondly strong promotional efforts to make these differences apparent to prospective customers. Both these sources cost money to implement, so the firm needs to be confident that the premium which customers are prepared to pay for the differentiated product will more than cover the extra costs.

3. Focus. Here the company concentrates on a few market segments rather than trying to compete in the whole market. Often these will be exclusive markets: the market for luxury yachts falls into this category. In business-to-business markets, some firms specialize in providing for a specific product type: Novo Nordisk of Denmark specializes in producing industrial enzymes, and has become highly profitable by being the best in its chosen specialization.

The failing strategy is to seek to achieve more than one of the above, and thus fail to achieve any of them. Combining low cost with differentiation is impossible, because a differentiation strategy requires higher expenditures on R&D and promotion if it is to work. Combining low cost with focus is also unlikely to work, because low cost requires high volumes in order to attract economies of scale. Focus and differentiation combine well, but there are cost implications. The essence of the problem is to pursue a clear strategy which customers can identify with: if they are unable to recognize whether the firm is cheap, or best at serving its market segment, or offering the highest perceived value, the firm's products will not stand out and will thus be relegated to a lower status in the decision-making framework.

Firms occasionally attempt to carry out more than one strategic approach at a time because of disagreements among top managers. Consensus among managers improves performance at the strategic business unit (SBU) level, especially for differentiation strategies (Homburg et al. 1999) but appears unnecessary if the firm is pursuing a low-cost strategy, perhaps because this is an easy strategy to understand and relate to, even if disagreements occur elsewhere.

Talking Point

We are told that it takes all sorts to make a world. We ask people what their view is about things, and often it's the people who disagree with us who are the most thought-provoking – good-natured argument is stimulating and results in creative solutions.

So how is it that directors who agree all the time about everything seem to improve corporate performance? Shouldn't we instead be looking for directors who are contentious, opinionated, and argumentative? Wouldn't this produce the most creative solutions?

Or would it simply be a recipe for continuous boardroom wrangling, with no decisions being made?

An alternative way of looking at competitive strategies is that proposed by Treacy and Wiersema (1993). This identifies three strategies or value disciplines aimed at increasing customer value. These are:

1. Operational excellence. Here the company provides better value for its customers by leading the industry in price and convenience. Similar to the cost leadership approach, the firm tries to reduce costs and create an effective and efficient delivery system.

2. Customer intimacy. Here the company creates value by precise segmentation, meeting the needs of its chosen customers very precisely. This strategy is likely to be based on developing close relationships with customers, which in turn means empowering staff to make decisions close to the customers, and in developing very detailed knowledge of customers' needs. Such companies attract customers who are prepared to pay substantial premiums to get exactly what they want, and who are prepared to be loyal to companies which deliver.

3. Product leadership. Companies pursuing this strategy offer leading-edge, state-of-the-art products and services, aiming to make the competitors' products (and indeed their own) obsolete. Such companies have large R&D expenditures, staff innovation programmes, and systems for getting new products to market quickly. Examples are 3M (**www.3m.com**) and Sony (**www.sony.com**), both of which have vigorous new product development programmes: Sony works on product lifecycles of three months or less, for example.

Unlike Porter's strategy categorizations, the Treacy and Wiersema categories are not mutually exclusive. It is possible to pursue operational excellence and customer intimacy for example (as EasyJet (**www.easyjet.com**) does), or customer intimacy and product leadership (as Virgin (**www.virgin.net**) does).

COMPETITIVE MOVES

Retaining, or carving out a new position in the marketplace, requires firms to attack competitors or defend themselves against attacks by other competitors. The moves that each firm makes will vary with the position each firm has in the marketplace.

Market leaders have the largest market share and consequently may be subject to scrutiny by government monopoly regulators: on the other hand, they have the power to control the market to a substantial extent. Market leaders therefore have two basic strategies: firstly, they can try to continue to win greater market share, and secondly they can try to expand the total market.

Expanding the total market may well prove to be a viable proposition for a market leader, for two reasons. Firstly, it may be easier to attract more customers into the market or get existing customers to spend more than it would be to wrest business from competitors, who are likely to defend their positions fiercely. Secondly, expanding the total market will not attract the attention of monopoly regulators since the overall market share is likely to remain much the same. Obviously, expanding the total market is likely to benefit the firm's competitors as well, but this is a small price to pay: after all, the intention is to run a successful business, not merely to bankrupt one's competitors. Expanding the total market can be achieved by finding new users, by finding new uses, or by encouraging more usage.

Expanding market share is usually done at the expense of the smaller companies. This has the advantage that the smaller companies will become weaker, and therefore less likely to pose a threat at some time in the future. At the extreme, of course, government monopoly regulators are likely to step in to prevent abuse of a leadership position, but for most market leaders this problem is a considerable way off. The basic routes to expanding market share are to win customers, to buy out competitors, or to increase the loyalty of existing customers.

Market leaders can also improve productivity, squeezing more profits out of the same sales volume. This is a strategy more easily carried out by market leaders because their size advantage enables them to bargain better with suppliers and distributors.

Market leaders also need to defend their positions against market challengers: Table 7.3 shows the basic defence strategies open to a market leader.

Table 7.3: Defence strategies

Defence Strategy	Explanation
Position defence	A position defence involves building barriers which prevent, or restrict, competitors from entering the market. This may mean, for example, incorporating features into the product which require a large capital investment (and consequently a large production run) to make them economically viable.
Flanking defence	Market leaders can sometimes ignore parts of the market which offer an opening to competitors. For example, Japanese car manufacturers were extremely successful in entering the US small car market, which had been left almost untouched by the American giants such as General Motors (**www.gm.com**) and Ford (**www.ford.com**).
Pre-emptive defence	Here the market leader begins by attacking the other companies before they can move against the leader. A threat of entry might be pre-empted by a large price cut, for example.
Counter-offensive defence	When attacked, the market leader launches an instant counter-attack. This can take the form of a promotion campaign, a price war, or a new product development exercise to produce an improved version of the competitor's offering.
Mobile defence	The company is proactive in defending its current market position, by expanding into new markets ahead of the competition.
Contraction defence	If the company can no longer defend all its markets, it might decide to withdraw from some or all of those markets. In military terms, this is called a strategic withdrawal: however, the next phrase used by the Army is 'to previously-prepared positions'. Sadly, some companies have managed the withdrawal part easily enough, but have not consolidated the positions which they can hold, and consequently have simply continued to retreat until there is nowhere left to go.

Market leaders need to be constantly vigilant: for other companies in the market, the most effective strategy is likely to be that of taking away the largest firm's market share. Once this process starts, it is all too easy for the market leader to end up continuing to lose share until it ceases to be market leader, or even goes under altogether.

MARKET CHALLENGER STRATEGIES

Market challengers are firms which seek to increase their share of the market, usually by aggressive competitive tactics. Market challengers are in a different position from market leaders in that they have two choices of competitor to attack: they can attack the market leader (a high-risk but potentially high-gain strategy) or they can try to pick off the smaller competitors, either by out-competing them or by taking them over. Attacking the market leader probably means that the firm will be up against a larger firm than itself. The market leader probably has the resources and the experience to mount a vigorous defence, whereas the smaller firms may not be so able to withstand a determined assault. On the other hand, beating the market leader would mean becoming market leader oneself – which has quite obvious advantages.

In order to attack the market leader, the challenger must have a clear competitive advantage: a cost advantage, or the ability to provide better value for money by offering a better product. Attacking smaller competitors may only require an aggressive promotional campaign, a short price war, or a takeover policy. The strategies open to a market challenger are shown in Table 7.4.

Table 7.4: Market challenger strategies

Strategy	Explanation
Frontal attack	The challenger matches the competitor's marketing efforts across the board. It attacks the competitor's strengths, not its weaknesses, and in effect enters into a war of attrition. The company with the greater resources usually wins in these circumstances.
Flanking attack	Here the challenger concentrates on the competitor's weaknesses rather than its strengths. The challenger tries to find some portion of the competitor's business which is being poorly served or which it feels able to serve better, and attacks that. Sometimes the competitor will withdraw without much of a fight; a lot depends on the relative resources of the two firms.
Encirclement attack	This strategy involves attacking from several directions at once. This approach works best when the attacker has more resources than the defender.
Bypass attack	Here the challenger bypasses the market leader completely and targets new markets. This might involve entering new geographic markets, or using new technology to tap into new groups of customers. This has the advantage of not offering a direct threat to the competitor, thus minimizing the risk of retaliation.
Guerrilla attack	The challenger makes occasional attacks on the larger competitor, using different tactics each time in order to demoralize and confuse the market leader. For example, a challenger might run a cut-price offer for one month only, followed the next month by a sales promotion, followed the next month by a promotional campaign. This constant switching of tactics does not allow the market leader time to organize a retaliatory strike, and instead forces the leader to become a follower, retaliating only after the challenger has moved on to the next tactic.

Guerrilla actions work best for small firms which are able to respond quickly and have the flexibility to move on as soon as their larger, perhaps more bureaucratic competitors try to retaliate.

MARKET FOLLOWER STRATEGIES

Most firms operate with the view that competitors are 'the enemy' and will therefore try to attack their competitors to seize market share. However, challenging the market leader, or indeed competing aggressively at all, is not necessarily the best way forward. The primary task of any organization is to survive, and retaliation from a more powerful company might well make this difficult.

Market followers allow the market leader to make most of the investment in developing new products and markets, then follow on to pick up on any spare segments which might have been bypassed by the leader. The follower gains in terms of reduced costs and reduced risk, and although followers will never become market leaders they are often as profitable as leaders (Haines et al. 1989).

Market followers fall into three types, as shown in Table 7.5.

Table 7.5: Market follower categories

Category	Explanation
Cloner	These firms make almost exact copies of the leader's products, distribution, promotion, and other marketing strategies. They can often do this at much lower cost because they do not have the development costs or risks of the market leaders. Firms making exact copies of products are relatively rare due to patenting and other intellectual property defences, but in some markets (particularly agricultural markets) cloning is perfectly feasible.
Imitator	Here the follower copies most of the leader's strategies, but retains some differentiation. This approach is more common than cloning because it often avoids direct competition with the market leader, and can even help the leader to avoid charges of monopolistic behaviour. Typical imitator strategies would be supermarkets selling own brands which look like the market leader brands, or burger restaurants which imitate the McDonald's (**www.mcdonalds.com**) high-speed service system.
Adapter	Adapters go one step further than the market leader, producing improved versions of products or marketing programmes. Adapters can become industry leaders, and are really only one step short of being challengers.

Being the leader always carries risks: the vast majority of new products fail when they reach the market, and the successful products have to pay for all the unsuccessful ones. Followers are able to be much more confident that their products will succeed, since they can copy only those products which are already successful. The same applies to promotional activities and distribution strategies: even though the bulk of the market is likely to go to the innovators, the costs of doing this are great, and the profits often go to the followers.

MARKET NICHER STRATEGIES

Market nichers are firms which concentrate on small segments of the market, seeking to meet the needs of those customers as closely as possible. Nichers operate on a low-volume, high-margin basis, so this is often a suitable strategic position for medium-sized companies (Clifford and Cavanagh 1985).

Competitors are closed out of the niche because the niche company develops an intimate knowledge of customer needs which would be difficult for a new entrant to acquire: also, the niche is often too small to support more than one company. The key to success in niche marketing is to specialise. Table 7.6 shows some of the ways niche marketers can specialise.

Niche marketers run the risk of their chosen market declining or disappearing. He also has all his eggs in one basket, which is fine as long as he follows Mark Twain's advice and watches that basket, but even so there is a strong chance of problems arising. For this reason some niche marketers concentrate on more than one niche, and so hedge their bets.

COLLABORATING WITH COMPETITORS

Hamel, Doz and Prahalad (1989) propose collaboration with competitors as a way forward in securing markets. Strategic alliances generated through joint ventures, product licensing, or co-operative research strengthen firms against competitors from outside the partnership by

Table 7.6: Niche rôles

Role	Explanation
End-use specialist	The firm specializes in meeting all the needs of one type of end user. For example, Radio Shack (www.radioshack.com) aims to supply all the needs of amateur electronics hobbyists.
Vertical-level specialist	The firm specializes in one level of the production-distribution cycle. For example, Pickford's (www.pickfordsrm.com) specialize in moving heavy equipment and abnormal loads.
Customer-size specialist	Here the firm concentrates on marketing to firms of a particular size. Often smaller firms are neglected by the industry majors, allowing a foot in the door for nichers.
Specific-customer specialist	The firm specializes in supplying one or two very large firms. This is typical of small engineering firms: they offer specialist manufacturing expertise to larger firms who find it cheaper to outsource than to manufacture in-house. Weber carburettors (www.webcon.co.uk) are an example: the firm supplies high-quality carburettors to most car manufacturers for their high-performance cars.
Geographical specialist	Here the firm stays within a small geographical area. For example, Welsh-language book publishers do not operate outside Wales and Argentina, where the Welsh language is spoken.
Product or feature specialist	The firm specializes in producing a particular product, or one with unique features. This type of specialization is often based on a patented system or process.
Quality-price specialist	The firm operates within a niche at the top or bottom of the market. For example, the market for executive jet planes is dominated by Lear (www.learjet.com) and Cessna (www.cessna.com).
Service specialist	The firm offers a service which is unavailable elsewhere. Only NASA (www.nasa.gov) offers a recovery and repair service for satellites, and only the Russian space agency offers space tourist flights (albeit at an extremely high price).

increasing the market coverage, reducing costs, generating greater efficiency, and raising the profile of both companies. It can be a low-cost way for firms to access new markets, and many Japanese firms have used this approach to enter European Union markets, where they would otherwise have to pay substantial tariffs to import directly from Japan.

Hamel et al.'s research shows that collaboration between Japanese firms and western partners often leaves the western partner worse off in the long run. This they attribute to poor negotiating skills, poor fit between strategic goals, and poor protection of sensitive information. On the other hand, more recent research from Hennart et al. (1999) shows that, provided the partnership is well-managed, the benefits of collaboration outweigh the risks. Firms which benefit most from competitive collaboration tend to follow the principles outlined in Table 7.7.

Table 7.7: Principles for successful collaboration

Principle	Explanation
Collaboration is competition in a different form	Successful collaborators remember that their partner may well try to take over the whole market later on, and become a major competitor. The collaboration may not last forever!
Harmony is not the most important measure of success	Occasional conflict may well lead to creative solutions for problems: like a marriage, if the partnership is a sincere commitment, arguments will happen now and then. Harmony usually only prevails where neither party really cares about the outcome, or indeed about the relationship.
Co-operation has limits	Strategic alliances often result in substantial transfers of information, perhaps well beyond that originally envisaged by senior management when they hammered out the deal. Successful collaborators will ensure that employees are well aware of what information can and cannot be passed on.
Learning from partners is paramount	Successful collaborators ensure that the new knowledge gained from the partner is diffused throughout their own organization. This knowledge will remain even if the partnership dissolves.

Western companies often enter alliances in order to avoid making investments, either in entering new markets or in developing new products. Unfortunately this often plays into the hands of the partner firm, who now have the capability to control the situation to their own advantage. Mutual gain is, however, possible if the partners conform to the following conditions:

- The partners' strategic goals converge while their competitive goals diverge. Each partner must allow the other to prosper in the shared venture, but should avoid competing directly.
- The size and power of both partners is modest compared to the industry leaders. The partners should also be of similar size compared with each other. These conditions ensure that neither partner develops a controlling influence, and also ensures that it is in both partners' interests to continue the alliance in order to avoid clashing with the industry leader.
- Each partner can learn from the other, while restricting access to sensitive information.

Collaboration offers a way forward for many smaller companies, and indeed some larger ones as well. Some highly-successful collaborations include Iveco (**www.iveco.com**), the joint venture between European truck manufacturers aimed at sharing design work, and P&O Stena Ferries (**www.posl.com**), the joint venture to run Dover-Calais ferries in competition with the Eurotunnel.

GROWTH STRATEGIES

As a general rule, most firms want to grow. Growth increases the firm's security in the market, it increases the power and influence of managers (not to mention their salaries), and it reduces costs. There are four generic routes to growth, as shown in Table 7.8 (Ansoff 1968).

Table 7.8: Growth strategies

Strategy	Explanation
Market penetration	This is the most common method of growing the business. The firm expands sales of its existing products in its existing markets, usually by taking business away from competitors.
Product development	Here the firm introduces new products within the existing market, either selling extra products to existing customers, or offering a slightly different product to people who are not entirely satisfied with the existing products.
Market development	If a firm has saturated its existing markets, growth is still possible by introducing the existing products into new markets. This is a common reason for exporting.
Diversification	Taking new products into new markets appears to be a risky growth strategy, but firms sometimes do this because the new product has production synergies. A safer route would be to expand through acquisition, buying out a firm in the target market.

Growth in growing markets is likely to happen in any case, even without any formal strategic attempts to encourage it. The key to success here lies in measuring whether the company is growing faster than the market, slower than the market, or at the same pace as the market. Often firms which couch their growth objectives in financial terms fail to notice that they are growing more slowly than the market and are thus (in effect) losing ground to competitors. Couching growth targets in terms of market share will avoid this pitfall, although obviously a reliable measure of the overall size of the market needs to be available.

During recessions most markets shrink and a common response to this is for firms to retrench, put their expansion plans on hold, and wait for the economic climate to improve. In fact, for the astute firm a recession provides tremendous opportunities for growth, provided the company is prepared in advance. Growth in declining markets is likely to happen through acquisition of ailing competitors, and this is never easier than during a recession. Here is a list of strategies for riding a recession, and coming out of it in better shape than when the recession started.

- Cash is king. During a recession credit becomes tighter, so companies with cash reserves are able to force down prices from suppliers or buy out competitors much more easily.

- Debtors default much more often. Giving credit to customers is a bad idea during a recession: payment dates stretch out, and the debtor firm may well go bankrupt leaving the debt unpaid. Debtors can be a useful source of expansion by takeover: some firms have achieved enviable vertical integration in this way.

- Deals can be struck with liquidators. If a competitor, supplier or distributor does go bankrupt, it is often possible to buy the firm from the liquidators for a fraction of its going-concern value. In fact, some firms even strike very lucrative deals with directors before the company goes under, in order to avoid the stigma of bankruptcy or even to save the directors from the scrutiny of regulators.

- Markets shrink for suppliers as well. A firm which has been a good customer in the past and shows signs of being a good payer is a valuable asset to a supplier, and one to which it is worth offering concessions.

- Good staff often become unexpectedly available. As firms go bankrupt, some highly-skilled people enter the jobs market, often for salaries below what they might have commanded in their previous jobs.

- Most financial managers insist on promotional budget cuts when times are hard. This means that share of voice is easier to achieve since competitors promote less, but it also means that advertising rates are likely to be cut as media struggle to sell space.

- Raw material prices drop. Many firms destock during recessions: towards the end of a recession, and indeed when dealing with liquidators, it is often possible to stock up with raw materials or components at very favourable prices.

Overall, recessions can be seen as an opportunity rather than a threat. The key to success in a recession is to ensure that the firm goes in with low financial gearing, and preferably with a cash 'war chest' in order to snap up bargains. Recessions normally only last a few months and are replaced within a year or two by boom conditions, during which it might be advisable to shed some assets while prices are high – in order to have cash on hand for the next recession.

Talking Point

If recessions are so good for firms, why do most firms fear them? Why is it that talk of a recession causes an almost ostrich-like rush to bury the corporate head in the sand?

Since recessions happen so regularly, surely managers should not be taken by surprise. Or perhaps the very act of preparing for a recession – firms tightening up on credit, banks cutting overdraft facilities, suppliers being cautious about whom they supply – is what triggers the recession in the first place. Should we therefore avoid preparing for it – and hope it never happens?

INTERNATIONAL MARKET ENTRY STRATEGIES

There are five basic strategies for entering foreign markets, as shown in Table 7.9.

Two basic models of internationalization are thought to be operating. The first is the stages of development model, in which firms move through a series of stages as shown in Table 7.10.

Table 7.9: International market entry strategies

Strategy	Explanation
Keep product and promotion the same worldwide	The advantage of this is that it minimizes entry costs. Coca Cola (**www.coca-cola.com**) often uses this approach, using basically the same advertising worldwide but translating any voiceovers into the local language. The major drawback of the approach is that it takes no account of local customs and attitudes, and tends to lead to a 'lowest common denominator' advertisement which can be understood by everybody and offends nobody.
Adapt promotion only	The product remains the same, but the promotion is adapted to local cultural norms. This is a fairly common approach since it enables the marketing communications to reach the consumers more effectively while at the same time avoiding a redesign of the product itself.
Adapt product only	This is less common, but has been done by some detergent manufacturers to allow for differences in local water supplies and washing-machines. Likewise, the supposedly 'global' Ford Escort is substantially modified for different markets in order to meet local emission standards and road-safety laws.
Adapt both product and promotion	Sometimes it is necessary to adapt both the product and the promotion, as in the case of Cheer washing-powder, a Procter and Gamble (**www.pg.com**) product marketed in Japan. Cheer was reformulated to allow for the extra fabric softeners the Japanese use, and the promotion emphasized that the powder worked well in cold water (since most Japanese wash clothes in cold water).
Invent new products	If the existing products cannot meet the conditions in the new market, a new product must be invented. For example, the clockwork radio was invented for use in countries where there is no mains power supply and batteries are difficult to obtain.

Table 7.10: Stages of development model

Stage	Explanation
Exporting	This implies the smallest commitment to the foreign market. The exporter produces the goods in the firm's home country, and ships them overseas to be sold through agents or distributors. In the early stages of export the firm might even be using a reactive strategy, only fulfilling orders if a foreign distributor actually seeks them out, rather than making any deliberate approach to the foreign market.
Establish a sales office in the foreign market	The firm is now committed to the market, but could withdraw if necessary. Manufacture and decision-making still takes place in the home country, but some tactical marketing has been transferred into the target country.
Overseas physical distribution	This would involve establishing a warehousing and distribution system in the target country, implying an even greater commitment to the market. At this stage much of the marketing strategy is devolved to the organization in the target country, bringing the decision-making closer to the customers.
Overseas manufacture	Manufacturing the product in the overseas market means the company can shorten the lines of supply and be more responsive to customers' needs.
Multinational marketing	The company makes and sells the products in whichever countries are most advantageous. Components might be supplied from several countries for assembly in several others, for onward export to still more countries.
Global marketing	Global marketing means standardizing products for perceived global segments. This is the approach taken by major computer manufacturers and other firms where economies of scale are available from very large-scale manufacture. National boundaries almost cease to exist for such firms, and their size ensures that their activities transcend national governments.

In practice, most firms use a customized approach to markets. Even firms pursuing a globalization strategy rarely use an entirely standardized approach across all the target countries (Harris 1996). Of 38 multinational companies surveyed by Harris, 26 claimed to standardize their advertising, but in fact only four used completely standardized advertisements.

An alternative view of internationalization strategy is offered by Dunning (1993), who proposes the eclectic theory of internationalizing. According to Dunning, firms determine their specific competitive advantage over firms both at home and overseas, and plan their market entry strategies accordingly. This means that a firm will examine its own strengths and weaknesses in relation to the overseas competitors, and instead of beginning by exporting and gradually making a greater commitment to the market, will enter the market by playing to its strengths. For example, IKEA (**www.ikea.com**) has strengths in managing retail stores at minimum cost while also minimizing customer error in purchasing flat-pack furniture. IKEA therefore entered the UK market with full-blown retail stores, rather than operating concessions within other stores or simply exporting the furniture to other retailers.

Likewise, Pilkington Glass (**www.pilkington.com**) had a competitive edge over foreign glass manufacturers due to its intellectual property position. Licensing the float-glass technique has made Pilkington's more money than it could ever have made by setting up factories overseas, and vastly more than could have been made by exporting glass.

INTERNATIONAL MARKETING BY INTERNET

The major problem about writing about the Internet is that the situation is changing extremely rapidly. This section should therefore be taken as only being relevant at the time of writing.

Many small firms lack the resources to internationalize: the psychological and organizational barriers seem too great for the firm to cope with despite government advice and assistance. Small firms are often unaware that help is available, or do not see it as applicable to their own situations.

Research by Hamill and Gregory (1997) indicates that the Internet can help small firms overcome these problems. Table 7.11 shows the barriers to internationalization that the research identified, and the Internet's role in overcoming them.

Table 7.11: International Internet marketing

Type of Barrier	Internet solution
Psychological barriers	
Ethnocentric rather than geocentric orientation. Short-term perspective. Lack of commitment to exporting. Exporting seen as 'not for us'; 'too risky'.	Increase in international awareness, confidence and commitment. Enquiries and feedback to WWW site from potential global customers. Participation in global network communities makes the world seem smaller and less daunting.
Operational barriers	
Export documentation and management of export operations, language problems, delays in receiving payment and financial risk.	Simplified export documentation through electronic data transfers. Electronic payments; on-line export assistance.
Organizational barriers	
Limited resources, both financial and managerial. Lack of knowledge of foreign markets. Lack of internationally-experienced personnel. Lack of education/training in export marketing. Problems in finding overseas representatives.	Access to low-cost export market research resources. Improved knowledge of international markets and culture. Reduced dependence on agents due to direct marketing. Establishment of virtual network of partners.
Product/Market barriers	
Products may not be suitable for foreign markets. Foreign market differences. Problems in identifying suitable foreign markets. Tariff and non-tariff barriers. Profitability.	Country/market selection made easier by on-line export market research. Consumer/market orientation easier through customer/agent feedback. Adoption of global niche rather than country-centred strategy.

More recent research conducted among UK website owners showed that significant barriers still exist. These barriers are in essence very similar to those which exist under traditional international marketing theory (Bennett 1998). The barriers identified were as follows:

1. Psychic distance. The cultural distance between the countries involved. This includes lack of ability to speak or understand foreign languages.
2. Practical export problems. These include shipping goods, handling paperwork, and lack of experience in dealing with overseas customers.
3. Resource constraints. Examples are lack of finance to offer credit, lack of suitable transportation, and lack of executive time to travel to the target countries.
4. Trade restrictions. Some countries impose restrictions on imports which can limit trade, in particular tariff barriers.
5. Market risk. The credit risks associated with dealing with customers in other countries, and difficulties of dealing with foreign exchange fluctuations.

The increasing use of the Internet in international business appears to lend support to the eclectic paradigm of internationalization rather than the stages-of-development theory (Dunning 1993).

GLOBALIZATION

Firms which globalize treat the entire planet as their marketplace and source of supply. The truly global firm ignores national boundaries when identifying competitors, suppliers, customers, employees, threats and opportunities. Such firms sometimes see themselves as being above national boundaries, even though all of them have started operations within the borders of one country at some time in the past.

In some quarters, globalization is seen as a threat. Riots and demonstrations against globalization took place during 2000 and 2001 at international trade talks in Seattle and Genoa: the riots were serious enough that some people were killed. Some governments have tried to limit the power of globalized firms, some of which are larger than some national governments, in the interests of protecting their own domestic industries. In fact, two factors militate against the protectionist approach; firstly, the advantages of international trade are too great (in the long run) to be set aside in favour of a short-term advantage, and secondly globalized firms are often so large and powerful that national governments which oppose them are likely to end up the losers.

Talking Point

Globalization seems to be a mixed blessing. On the one hand, the firms involved seem to generate economies of scale, and seem able to satisfy the needs of large numbers of customers throughout the world: on the other hand, such firms have become so monstrous they can dictate to elected governments.

But is this such a bad thing? After all, the only reason those firms grew large is because they care about their customers – otherwise why would we have given them our hard-earned cash? We only get to vote for politicians every four or five years – but we vote for McDonald's on a daily basis just by buying their hamburgers. So what IS wrong with globalization?

The main drivers for globalization are as follows:

1. Increasing economies of scale and scope for firms in the market.
2. Convergence of consumer tastes and preferences.

3. Rapidly improving communications, in terms of both telecommunications and transport systems.
4. Increased political acceptance of global trading, albeit often reluctantly.
5. The continuing growth of large firms, coupled with limits imposed by national monopoly regulators on domestic growth.

Following on from the stages of development theory and the eclectic theory, it appears that firms which are already international but are now going global move through three stages: ethnocentrism, polycentrism, and geocentrism. These stages are shown in Table 7.12.

Table 7.12: Stages in globalization

Stage	Explanation
Ethnocentrism	Home-country orientation. Ethnocentric firms see the foreign market as a place to dispose of excess production. Ethnocentric managers assume that the foreign market is basically the same as the domestic market, so marketing strategies are only adapted superficially for the overseas market.
Polycentrism	Polycentric firms only identify the differences in each market. The firm treats each market as unique, and marketing strategies are created separately for each one. Tactical decisions are made locally.
Geocentrism	The firm sees the world as a single market containing segments within that market. Tactics are uniform for the segments which have been identified whichever country the actual customers live in, so that promotions and products are similar across the globe.

Obviously it is not always possible to take a completely global view. Even firms such as Nestlé (**www.nestle.com**) have to adapt their products somewhat for local markets. For example, in India, Nestlé needs to use additives to prevent the chocolate melting in the heat. In Pakistan the company sells bottled water which is processed in China from tap water because spring water is often contaminated.

Globalization is important for all firms, even those whose markets are entirely contained within one country. These firms are obviously affected directly or indirectly by foreign competition, but they are also affected by the growing strength of domestic competitors who have themselves expanded overseas.

CASE STUDY: LEGO BUILDS A BRAND

www.lego.com
Fifty years ago the children's toy market was invaded by a little plastic brick with eight studs on it. The studs enabled the bricks to stick together, and soon millions of children were playing with Lego – the old wooden building bricks children had played with for centuries were doomed to remain at the bottom of the toy cupboard.

Lego has moved on from strength to strength – the Legoland theme park in Denmark was followed by another one in the UK, at Windsor to the west of London. Lego's brand was extending beyond its core business – and the man in charge of licensing the Lego brand, Karl Kalcher, had even bigger ideas in store.

In 1999 Kalcher opened the first Lego store in Britain, at the Bluewater shopping complex in Kent, not far from the Channel Tunnel. Kalcher is a champion of innovative thinking in marketing, something which has led to his becoming a Fellow of the UK's Chartered Institute of Marketing. He is famous for saying 'There's no such thing as children. It doesn't mean anything.'.

►

▶

This statement sounds a little odd from a man whose company targets the 0–16 age group, but in fact what he says makes perfect sense. There is a vast difference between a three-year-old and a twelve-year-old, and even between a three-year-old and a five-year-old. Kalcher says that there are only consumers – each with a separate personality and separate needs.

Lego Licensing licences watches, clothing, the Lego Island CD-ROM, and of course the Legoland theme parks. The Lego group plans to become the leading brand among families and children, which means doing a lot more than moulding eight-stud plastic bricks. The Lego store is set to help in this bold ambition. The store is designed to be as user-friendly as possible for its diminutive customers – the store adheres to the 'Lego values' and these were referred to throughout the design and construction of the store.

Beginning with the store front, Lego decided that the company's heritage lay in design and construction – so the store front is designed around the colours and proportions of the Lego bricks. Lego is a toy, so the interior of the store is a high-touch environment – customers are actively encouraged to touch things and play with things, but since Lego is also an educational toy, much of what happens in the store is also educational. For example, there is a 'rocket-race' game in which children have to memorize a number in order to make the rocket fly. Many of the displays are at children's eye level, so that children can use the store without adult intervention (until it comes time to pay, of course).

Finally, the Lego store has impressive, giant Lego models in the window area which, according to Lego's retail boss Paul Denham, creates the 'wow' factor. Kalcher believes that in creating the store he is setting a standard of innovation that retailers alone would be unable to aspire to. He believes it is up to the brand owners to invest time and trouble in extending the brand into new areas such as retailing: traditional retailers are, in effect, unable to achieve these standards.

Not unnaturally, retailers in the area objected strongly to the establishment of the Lego store. As long-term Lego stockists they felt their loyalty had been betrayed, and they feared that Lego would also undercut them on price. In fact, these fears proved groundless: Kalcher explains why. 'The Lego store is essentially about creating a superior standard for our brand, in the eyes of the consumer. This will promote the esteem of our products for all retail customers.' Kalcher could be confident in making this statement – sales were actually boosted in retailers near Lego's Minneapolis store, and near Legoland Windsor. And as regards price cutting, the Lego stores are stand-alone franchised outlets – they operate under the same constraints as any other retailer, so they have to show a profit, which means no price-cutting.

Lego has come a long way in 50 years, but they have a reputation for quality and for getting it right – so much so that even before there was any hint of Lego opening a store at Bluewater, the developers had used Legoland Windsor as a benchmark for designing the entire shopping centre. Lego now have 80 per cent of the world's construction toy market, and expect to build even further successes around the other elements of the brand.

CASE STUDY QUESTIONS

1. What market scope strategy is Lego following?
2. What market commitment strategy does Lego appear to be following?
3. As market leader in construction toys, which defence strategy might be best for Lego?
4. What growth strategy is available for Lego?
5. To what extent is Lego globalizing the brand?

SUMMARY

Approaching markets requires a wide-angled approach. The cautious strategist will consider the competitive environment, the cultural environment, and the structure of the market before committing resources to a new enterprise within it.

The key points from this chapter are:

■ Most firms adapt their approach to meet local conditions in international marketing.

■ The Internet appears to offer cheap and easy access to global markets, but has some drawbacks which may prove fatal to the unwary company.

■ Competitive strategies come from cost leadership, or differentiation, or focus: attempts to combine these strategies almost always lead to failure.

■ It is not always necessary to challenge the market leader: followers often do as well or better in terms of profitability.

CHAPTER QUESTIONS

1. Why is it not considered possible to be a cost leader and a differentiator?

2. What is the difference between a challenger and an adapter?

3. What might be the specific problems which would arise from internationalizing a service industry?

4. If a company is not itself planning to sell abroad, what is the relevance of globalization?

5. Why might a company following a focus strategy not become market leader?

REFERENCES

Anderson, C. (1996): 'Computer as Audience: Mediated Interactive Messages in Interactive Marketing' in Forrest, E. and Hizerski, R. (eds) *The Future Present* ch. 11 (Chicago: AMA).

Ansoff, H.I. (1968): *Corporate Strategy* (Harmondsworth: Penguin).

Bennett, R. (1998): 'Using the World Wide Web for International Marketing: Internet use and perception of export barriers among German and British businesses'. *Journal of Marketing Communications* 4, pp. 27–43.

Clifford, D.K. and Cavanagh, R. E. (1985): *The winning performance: how America's high- and mid-size growth companies succeed* (New York: Bantam).

Dunning, John H. (1993): *The Globalisation of Business* (London: Routledge).

Haines, D.W., Chandran, R. and Parkhe, A. (1989): 'Winning by being first to market. . . . Or last?' *Journal of Consumer Marketing* winter pp. 63–69.

Hamel, G., Doz, Y. and Prahalad, C.K. (1989): 'Collaborate with your competitors – and win'. *Harvard Business Review* Jan/Feb.

Harris, Greg (1996): 'International Advertising; Developmental and Implementational Issues' *Journal of Marketing Management* 12, 1996 pp. 551–560.

Hennart, J.F., Roehl, T. and Zietlow, D.S. (1999): 'Trojan horse or workhorse? The evolution of US–Japanese joint ventures in the United States', *Strategic Management Journal* 20: pp. 15–29.

Hamill, J. and Gregory, K. (1997): 'Internet Marketing in the Internationalization of UK SMEs', *Journal of Marketing Management*, special edition on Internationalization, Hamill, J. (ed.) vol. 13. nos. 1–3.

Porter, M.E. (1985): *Competitive Advantage* (New York: The Free Press).

Treacy, M. and Wiersema, F. (1993): 'Customer intimacy and other value disciplines'. *Harvard Business Review* Jan-Feb, pp. 84–93.

4

How do we get there?

Creating functional-level strategies

Once the overall corporate strategy has been created it becomes the task of functional-level managers to develop strategies at the functional level. For these managers, the task is to ensure that the organization reaches its objectives, or in some cases is set on the right course.

In most large organizations, the functional marketing managers will develop their own strategies to achieve their own part of the task. The media buyers, brand managers, product designers, sales managers and so forth will each have their own strategies for achieving their own objectives, with the corporate vision acting as the co-ordinating factor.

Chapter Eight

Strategy and Products

INTRODUCTION

Products comprise the benefits that customers buy and as such form a crucial element in the exchange process. A product is not necessarily physical: benefits accrue from intangible or service products, in fact very few products are wholly tangible or wholly intangible. Competitive advantage can often be derived from adjusting the balance between the service element of a product and the physical element – this is particularly the case with commodity products such as petrol.

After reading this chapter, you should be able to:

- Explain the principles of new product development for existing markets and for new markets.
- Explain how the correct product strategy produces competitive advantage.
- Describe the relationship between quality and price.
- Describe the diffusion of innovation, and identify ways of improving the take-up of new products.
- Describe approaches to product portfolio management.

PRODUCT PORTFOLIO MANAGEMENT

The product life cycle implies that all products will eventually become obsolete and be replaced by newer versions. Although considerable doubt has been cast on this theory in recent years, the fact remains that products do become obsolete and consumer tastes do shift, so that products and markets go their separate ways, to the detriment of the firm.

Portfolio management tools such as the Boston Consulting Group Matrix were discussed in Chapter 4. These provide a brief 'snapshot' of the company's current position, and can offer a way of deciding which products to keep and which to drop.

Talking Point

The Boston Group Matrix is an interesting snapshot, rather like the balance sheet of a company. And, like the balance sheet, it tells us what the situation was like a few weeks ago when the calculations were made.

How realistic is it that we should use this type of snapshot approach to our strategic planning? Should we instead be using something more dynamic, more able to predict the future rather than dwell on the past?

Or is that an impossible dream? Maybe we are not meant to know the future except as a projection of the past.

The size of the product portfolio and the complexity of the products within it can have further effects on the firm's management. For example, it has been shown that manufacturing a wide range of products with many options makes it difficult for the firm to use just-in-time purchasing techniques and complicates the firm's supply activities (Benwell 1996).

NEW PRODUCT DEVELOPMENT

Managing a portfolio may be the starting-point for strategic decisions about products, but new product development is at the heart of the firm's future. New products need to be developed to meet competitive pressures resulting from their innovation, but also new versions of existing products are necessary if existing markets are to be retained.

Firms are often advised to avoid producing 'commodity' products. A commodity product is one which offers the basic core benefits of the product category, without having any other differentiating benefits. Commodity products have to compete on price, almost without exception, and this in turn means that profit margins are squeezed. This means that it is sensible for firms to differentiate the product, adding value for the customer without putting costs up too much. Provided the cost of adding the value is less than the extra premium the customer is prepared to pay to receive the benefits, the product will be more profitable.

However, this advice should be tempered with an element of caution. Producing commodity products means that the firm has virtually zero research and development costs, considerably reduced promotional costs, and virtually zero re-tooling costs. Commodity producers often sell to other businesses which then take on the risk and expense of branding the goods and marketing them. An example is the salmon canneries on the Canadian Pacific coast, which can salmon for literally hundreds of different firms. These firms then apply their own labels to the cans, and carry out the subsequent marketing activities. Even if one of these firms was to go bankrupt, the effect on the canneries would be minimal.

Innovation is not the same as invention. Invention is about the product's features: an invention is a new product. Innovation is about new benefits for the consumer. An innovation is therefore defined as the original implementation of a discovery, concept or invention.

For strategic purposes, innovations need to fulfil the following criteria (Doyle 1998):

- Important. The innovation must offer benefits which consumers will regard as important. For example, although Concorde (**www.concordesst.com**) offered much faster air transportation, this was not seen as sufficiently important for consumers to pay the high premium involved in flying in it.

- Unique. If the new benefits are not perceived as being materially different from those offered by competitors, there is really no point in consumers buying the product.

- Sustainable. From the firm's viewpoint, the innovation should not be susceptible to being copied by competitors. In practice this is difficult to achieve, unless the innovation is so radical that it can be patented, or unless it can be protected by retaining secrecy over the process involved, as is the case with Coca-Cola (**www.coca-cola.com**).

- Marketable. The company must have the capability of bringing the product to market. Apart from the obvious need to promote and distribute effectively, the company also needs the capability to manufacture to an acceptable price, and provide a product of the right quality in terms of reliability and effectiveness.

There are six broad types of innovation strategy, as shown in Table 8.1.

Table 8.1: Innovation strategies

Strategy type	Explanation
Offensive strategy	Here the company takes pride in being the first to market, and spends substantial sums on research and development. This is very much the strategy of firms like Sony and 3M (**www.3m.com**), which maintain their competitive position through constant innovation.
Defensive	Defensive companies produce 'me-too' products which are copies of other companies' products, but with some improvements. The advantage of this strategy is that other firms take the risks of failure, and also bear most of the research and development costs. The disadvantage is that the company loses the first-to-market advantage and may have considerable difficulty later in establishing a substantial market share. Also, innovative companies often operate a skimming strategy (see Chapter 9) which effectively shuts out followers and creams off the profits early in the product life cycle.
Imitative	The strategy is to produce straight copies of other companies' products. This strategy can usually only be carried out in the event of the new product being a commodity, since there is likely to be intellectual property protection (patents, etc.) in place for any other type of innovation. Circumstances where an exact copy would be permissible are relatively few, and are likely to be confined to products where the basic technology is in the public domain.
Dependent	The firm is led by bigger companies, perhaps customers or suppliers. For example, a firm producing components for major car companies will only innovate if the car company's designers require a modification.
Traditional	These firms are not really innovative at all; the firm is merely resurrecting old-fashioned designs. Examples might include the Victorian potato-baking ovens which became popular in the 1990s, or reproduction furniture.
Opportunist	This is the selling and marketing of inventions. Because it is a product-focused approach, it may run into difficulties with consumers: what seems to be a great idea to the inventor is not necessarily what customers want. On the other hand, there are several well-known examples of products which started out as radical, even lunatic, ideas and went on to make the inventor a fortune. Inventions sometimes provide a quantum leap, whereas most new product development systems produce incremental advances.

New product development is, of course, risky. No matter how carefully the firm conducts market research, new products fail with depressing regularity. The degree of risk depends on the following factors:

1. Market risk. This is the degree of originality and complexity of the product, which will in turn determine the level of switching cost for the prospective user. Switching cost is the set of costs which apply to changing from the existing solution to a new solution. The lower the switching cost, the lower the risk.

2. Technology risk. This is the risk that the new technology will either prove ineffective, or will be rapidly superseded by even newer technology. The more effective and original the technology, the lower the risk.

3. Strategy risk. This relates to the degree of familiarity which the firm has with the market and the technology. The greater the degree of familiarity, the lower the risk.

Great effort has been expended on trying to find better ways of forecasting a product's prospects in the market, with only limited results. First of all though, it is necessary to define what a new product is, and the researchers Calentone and Cooper (1981) have identified nine categories of new product, as shown in Table 8.2. The clusters were identified according to whether the product was new to the firm or new to the world, and whether there was a production or marketing **synergy** with the firm's existing products.

Table 8.2: New product clusters

Clusters	Description	Success rate
Cluster 1: The Better Mousetrap with No Synergy	This is a product which, while being an improvement over existing offerings, does not fit in with the firm's existing product lines.	36%
Cluster 2: The Innovative Mousetrap that Really Wasn't Better	This might be a product which, while being technically excellent, has no real advantage for the consumer over existing products.	0%
Cluster 3: The Close to Home Me-Too Product	A copy of a competitor's offering. Not likely to be perceived as new by consumers.	56%
Cluster 4: The Innovative High-Tech Product	A truly new-to-the-world product.	64%
Cluster 5: The Me-Too Product with No Technical/Production Synergy	A copy of a competitor's product, but with no real connection with existing product lines.	14%
Cluster 6: The Old But Simple Money-Saver	Not a new product at all, except to the firm producing it.	70%
Cluster 7: The Synergistic Product that was New to the Firm	A product that fits the product line, but is new.	67%
Cluster 8: The Innovative Superior Product with No Synergy	A product that does not fit the existing product line, but is new.	70%
Cluster 9: The Synergistic Close-to-Home Product	A product line extension; perhaps a minor improvement over the firm's existing products.	72%

From the above categories it seems obvious that the safest strategy is likely to be to produce synergistic, close-to-home products, innovative superior products with no synergy, or old but simple money-savers. The worst strategy would be to produce the innovative mousetrap that really was not better, since the research did not find a single instance of success in this case.

The problem here is threefold: firstly, it is difficult to tell in advance whether the firm's latest product is a superior product or not – until the consumers have been offered it, the company is unlikely to be sure whether they have an 'innovative mousetrap' or an 'innovative superior product' since these categories would look identical at the outset.

Secondly, the researchers did not define the successes in terms of degree of success. A product which recoups its development costs and turns in a small profit might be counted successful, alongside another product which goes on to become a world leader and make millions for the firm.

Thirdly, each product's success or failure is calculated in isolation, and is calculated in financial terms. A product might be a success in terms of shutting out competition or in aiding sales of another product, while in itself showing a loss (Hart 1993).

Talking Point

If the safest strategy is to produce products that really aren't new at all, why do we bother? In India, manufacturers are still producing and selling the Ambassador saloon car and the Royal Enfield (**www.royalenfield.com**) motorbike, both of which are built to British designs from the late 1940s. The cars and bikes were being made in India when the British left, and so they are still made in India. Indians don't see any need to innovate – so why should we? (**www.automeet.com/hindustanmotorsproducts.html**)

Perhaps the rush for 'something new' is basic to human beings. Or perhaps it is something that marketers have instilled in us! Whichever is the case, the Royal Enfield is now a very desirable motorbike – for reasons of nostalgia alone.

Four possible typologies of innovation can be identified, as follows (Lambin 2000):

1. The degree of newness to the company.
2. The intrinsic nature of the innovation concept.
3. The innovation's origin.
4. The behavioural change implied for the user of the innovation.

The degree of newness to the company is a function of the newness of the product (which implies manufacturing and technological weaknesses or strengths) and the newness of the market (which implies marketing weaknesses and strengths). These dimensions were incorporated into a grid by Booz et al. in 1982.

Fig. 8.1: Newness assessment grid

Newness of the product for the firm	Newness of the market for the firm	
	Low	High
High	New products for the firm. Present customers. New product line.	New products for the firm. New customer groups. Diversification strategy.
Low	Reformulated products. Present customers. Next generation – improved products.	Extension of existing products. New customer groups. Addition to existing product lines.

According to Booz et al. (1982) only 10 per cent of new products are in fact new to the world. The majority of innovations involve line extensions or modifications of existing products. The reasons for this are not clear, but it is likely that firms have discovered that it is easier and cheaper to modify existing products (updating known designs) rather than continually producing wholly-new products.

The intrinsic nature of the innovation divides into the technological versus the organizational. Technological innovation is about the characteristics of the product itself or its manufacture. The physical characteristics of the product may be affected by design considerations or by the ingredients used: for example, a new model of an established car might have a modification in its appearance, or it might use a corrosion-resistant alloy for the bodywork. Either is an innovation.

Manufacturing innovations will probably impact more on the company than on the customer, but many examples exist where advances in manufacturing technique have affected customer satisfaction, even outside the service industries where such changes have obvious effects. For example, Toyota's (**www.toyota.com**) invention of techniques for rapid retooling of stamp mills meant that product modifications or rapid responses to changes in demand could be carried out in hours rather than months. This greatly increased the firm's ability to respond to customer demand. Equally, the McDonald's (**www.mcdonalds.com**) system for manufacturing hamburgers dramatically reduced the need for skilled short-order chefs (which helped the company to cut costs) but also resulted in rapid response to customer demand in the restaurants.

The origin of the innovation might be the firm or the market. Market-pull innovations require a response strategy from the firm, whereas technology-push innovations (those resulting from R&D efforts) require a creative marketing approach because such innovations are often discontinuous. This means that the needs being addressed by the innovation will not be expressly articulated by the potential adopters, and the innovation will therefore need to be promoted and explained. It transpires that a small majority of successful products have been developed in response to market demand rather than as a result of technology push (Urban et al. 1987), which appears to bear out Calentone and Cooper's research discussed above. The evidence is that successful innovation more often comes as a result of knowing the market – despite the widely-trumpeted successes of products like the Sony Walkman (**www.sony.com**), which was a technology-driven product forced through by the firm's founder over the objections of the marketing team. Such examples are the exception rather than the rule – the bulk of such products fail miserably.

Discontinuous innovation involves a change in the way its adopters behave. In consumer markets, the introduction of the Internet and e-mail has changed the way people communicate. Previous innovations such as the microwave oven and the home VCR also changed people's behaviour. In the industrial arena, increasing automation has changed the way firms operate, and has had far-reaching effects on issues such as recruitment policy. For example, car factories used to employ armies of unskilled or semi-skilled workers engaged in repetitive jobs such as bolting wheels onto the cars. These jobs are now largely carried out by robots, and the factory workers are now highly-skilled and well-qualified robotics technicians. This means that it is difficult for people with no qualifications to find work except in low-paid service industries, and at the same time there is a skills shortage in many industrial sectors.

Technological discontinuity may not change consumer behaviour: the compact disc is an example of a product which had a radical effect on manufacturing in the music industry, but had little effect on the way consumers behave. A truly discontinuous innovation is one which affects both the producer and the consumer, and can generate very considerable strategic advantage for the innovator, since it often disrupts or destroys the entire market, creating a new one in which the innovator is at the top. Examples include Microsoft's (**www.microsoft.com**) development of user-friendly software suitable for PCs which made home computing (and indeed most office computing) available to everyone. Tom Watson's famous statement made in 1948 to the effect that there would only ever be a demand for four or five computers in the entire world was neatly upset, making Bill Gates into the world's richest man.

This leaves the firm with a strategic dilemma. On one hand, the safest policy in innovation is to make only small, incremental changes to products, and to produce me-too copies of competitors' innovations. On the other hand, discontinuous innovation can result in an almost instantaneous leap from market follower to market leader. These trade-offs are illustrated in Fig 8.2 below.

Fig. 8.2: Innovation trade-offs

	High return	Low return
High risk	Discontinuous innovation.	Not a strategy worth pursuing: this is a recipe for disaster!
Low risk	The Holy Grail of innovation: unfortunately this is probably unattainable for most firms.	Me-toos, market follower strategies.

NEW PRODUCT SUCCESS RATES

New product development is notoriously risky, but the odds seem to be improving. In 1968, Booz et al. reported that out of 58 new product ideas, only one became a commercial success. By 1981 the odds had improved to one success out of seven new ideas (Booz et al. 1982). These figures were collected in the United States: similar research conducted in Europe in the early 1990s showed a worse success rate, with only 9.4 per cent of new product ideas being successful (Page 1993). The improvement over the 1960s figures might be attributed to a greater emphasis on customer orientation and much better strategic thinking. Conversely, they might also be attributable to much greater wealth in the populations of industrial nations, and the availability of much larger markets through international trade, meaning that almost any product is likely to find a market.

These figures may make depressing reading for managers. From a strategic viewpoint it is fairly obvious that a firm which has only one product is extremely likely to fail, so that portfolio management becomes a primary strategy for survival.

Cooper (1993) developed a list of key lessons for new product success, as shown in Table 8.3.

This set of rules for new product development offers a way of improving the odds for success. The next consideration should therefore be refining the process of new product development in order to remove some of the potential stumbling-blocks before too much money has been committed to the product.

THE NPD PROCESS

New products might come into being through any of the following routes:

1. Product champions. These are people who have had an idea for a new product, and pilot it through the various departments of the firm until it reaches a marketable stage. This route is common in firms such as 3M, and often runs in parallel with other, more formal approaches.

2. New product think tanks. These are groups of people drawn from various disciplines within the firm (marketing, engineering, finance and so forth) who meet periodically to develop or evaluate new product ideas.

3. Venture teams. Placed somewhere between the product champion and the think tank, a venture team is formed to develop a specific product idea and take it through to fruition. The team may then be disbanded until another idea comes along.

4. Outside consultancy. Freelance industrial designers, marketing consultancies or other outside agencies may be commissioned to come up with ideas to fill a known market gap. For example, Lyon's recently asked an outside consultancy to find a way to serve perfectly-brewed tea in catering establishments. Following on from a market research exercise, the consultants came up with the design for a revolutionary new teapot which would prevent the tea from stewing too long.

Table 8.3: Key lessons in new product success

1. The number one success factor is a unique, superior product: a differentiated product that delivers unique benefits and superior value to the customer.
2. A strong market orientation – a market-driven and customer-focused new product process – is critical to success.
3. Look to the world product: an international orientation in product design, development and target marketing provides the edge in product innovation.
4. More pre-development work – the homework – must be done before product development gets under way.
5. Sharp and early product definition is one of the key differences between winning and losing at new products.
6. A well-conceived, properly executed launch is central to new product success. And a solid marketing plan is at the heart of the launch.
7. The right organizational structure, design and climate are key factors in success.
8. Top management support does not guarantee success, but it sure helps. But many senior managers get it wrong.
9. Synergy is vital to success – 'step-out' projects tend to fail.
10. Products aimed at attractive markets do better; market attractiveness is a key project-selection criterion.
11. New product success is predictable and the profile of a winner can be used to make sharper project-selection decisions to yield better focus.
12. New product success is controllable: more emphasis is needed on completeness, consistency and quality of execution.
13. The resources must be in place.
14. Speed is everything! But not at the expense of quality of execution.
15. Companies that follow a multi-stage, disciplined new product game plan fare much better.

The advantages and disadvantages of each approach are shown in Table 8.4.

Developing the idea from its inception through to a product launch can follow one of two basic strategic routes: the sequential route or the parallel route.

The sequential route is typified by Crawford's 1991 model of the process, which runs as follows:

1. New product planning. This the strategic stage, during which the firm examines its current portfolio, opportunities and threats and determines the type of product which would best fit with the corporate strategy.
2. Idea generation. Specific ideas for the product are put forward by one or other of the groups identified above.
3. Screening and evaluation. Ideas are checked for technical feasibility, financial viability, and marketability.
4. Technical development. Engineering and production issues are resolved and a prototype built.
5. Market appraisal. Formal market research with potential customers is carried out to assess the product's market potential.

Table 8.4: Assessment of NPD routes

Route	Advantages	Disadvantages
Product champion	One person can develop enthusiasm and retain control of the project better than a group might. The vision is less likely to become diluted if one person holds it.	The individual may become blinded to problems. Product champions with strong personalities may be able to force through projects which are really not viable, whereas those with less forceful personalities might become disheartened by resistance.
New-product think tanks	The individuals concerned have the necessary skills between them to identify possible new product ideas, and to make a preliminary assessment concerning viability. By drawing these skills together, the firm can avoid wasting time on non-viable ideas and can also develop creative solutions to problems more quickly.	Think-tanks can easily degenerate into cosy talking shops. They can also become exclusive, leading to the blocking of ideas which have not come from the think tank - the 'not invented here' syndrome.
Venture teams	These teams mitigate some of the disadvantages of the product champion by encompassing a wider spread of skills and perspectives.	Venture teams can suffer from committee paralysis - a watering-down of the original idea as each member of the team modifies it or tries to encompass a pet theme.
Outside consultancy	Consultancies can be objective about NPD, because they have no political ambitions within the firm. Also, consultancies often carry more credibility with managers, since they are assumed to have skills which are not present within the organization.	Consultants have no long-term stake in the firm, and might therefore not exercise as much caution as would a manager whose career depends on the success or otherwise of the products.

6. Launch. Provided all the other factors are in place, the product goes into production and the marketing plan for it is developed and implemented.

In theory, each stage should be carried out before the next one is addressed. In practice, it seems likely that all these stages would be covered in one form or another, but not necessarily in the order given: they might also be carried out perfunctorily, or subjectively. The major drawback with a sequential approach is that it is likely to be time-consuming, giving competitors a chance to enter the market. A sequential approach might therefore increase rather than reduce the risk of failure.

The parallel approach, by contrast, uses a multi-disciplinary team to develop the product, overlapping tasks between departments. For example, while the designers are refining the product, the production engineers and marketers will have an input into the process.

The main advantages of the parallel development process is that it saves a great deal of time, which means that the finished product gets to market much quicker, and the product itself is likely to be better-designed because errors are likely to be picked up earlier. The major disadvantage is that it can result in a heavy time commitment on the part of the staff involved as each aspect of the product needs to be discussed. On balance, the advantages are likely to outweigh the disadvantages.

GENERATING NEW PRODUCT IDEAS

Idea generation can be proactive or reactive. A proactive approach means encouraging and collecting new ideas from whatever source may be available. A reactive approach means waiting for the market to innovate, then following on in order to maintain competitive position. The proactive approach is the more expensive of the two and is likely to be better suited to market leaders.

Taking a proactive approach can take the form of examining the firm's products (functional analysis) or examining customer needs (customer analysis). Functional analysis methods are shown in Table 8.5 below.

Table 8.5: Functional analysis

Approach	Explanation
Problem/ opportunity analysis	Customer use of the product is examined to see where modifications might improve function. In some cases this will involve panels of users, in other cases the analysis will take place in-house.
Attribute listing	In this case, the attributes of the product itself are examined. A list of the product's features is made, and possible recombinations are considered.
Morphological analysis	Here the most important structural dimensions of the product are examined, and the relationship between them considered in order to generate new combinations.
Reverse engineering	Competitors' products are analysed systematically by any of the above methods in order to generate ideas for me-too products.

Functional analysis will tend to lead to incremental changes in existing products rather than radical new solutions. Such creative solutions are more likely to come from brainstorming sessions, or from customer-based ideas. These are more likely to be volunteered by customers in business-to-business markets: consumers typically do not approach suppliers with requests for new products, whereas industrial buyers often do (von Hippel 1978). In a customer-active paradigm, the supplier is able to take a reactive stance: in a customer-inactive paradigm the supplier must be proactive.

In order to assess consumer needs effectively managers need to be aware of consumer responses to new products.

DIFFUSION OF INNOVATION

New products are not immediately adopted by all consumers. Some consumers are driven to buy new products almost as soon as they become available, whereas others prefer to wait until the product has been around for a while before risking their hard-earned money on it. Innovations therefore take time to filter through the population. This process is called diffusion, and is partly determined by the nature of consumers and partly by the nature of the innovation itself.

Everett M. Rogers (1962) classified consumers as follows:

- Innovators. Those who like to be first to own the latest products. These consumers predominate at the beginning of the product life cycle (PLC).
- Early adopters. Those who are open to new ideas, but like to wait a while after initial launch. These consumers predominate during the growth phase of the PLC.
- Early majority. Those who buy once the product is thoroughly tried and tested. These consumers predominate in the early part of the maturity phase of the PLC.
- Late majority. Those who are suspicious of new things, and wait until most other people already have one. These consumers predominate in the later part of the maturity phase of the PLC.
- Laggards. Those who only adopt new products when it becomes absolutely necessary to do so. These consumers predominate in the decline phase of the PLC.

The process of diffusion of innovation is carried out through reference-group influence. Three main theories concerning the mechanisms for this have been proposed: trickle-down theory, two-step flow theory, and multi-stage interaction theory.

Trickle-down theory says that the wealthy classes obtain information about new products, and the poorer classes then imitate their 'betters' (Veblen 1899). This theory may have held some truth in the 19th century when it was first proposed, but has been largely discredited in modern times because new ideas are disseminated overnight by the mass media and copied by chain stores within days.

Two-step flow theory is similar, but this time it is 'influentials' rather than wealthy people who are the start of the adoption process (Lazarsfield et al. 1948). This has considerable basis in truth, but may be less true now than it was in the 1940s when the theory was first developed. Access to TV and other information media has proliferated and information about innovation is disseminated much faster than it was 50 years ago.

The multi-stage interaction model (Engel et al. 1995) recognizes this and allows for the influence of the mass media. In this model the influentials emphasize or facilitate the information flow (perhaps by making recommendations to friends or acting as advisers).

From a strategic viewpoint, the supplier needs to understand that products will take some time to diffuse through the system. There will always be a degree of resistance to new products, and this will manifest itself in a greater or lesser speed of diffusion through the system. Consumers often need considerable persuasion to change from their old product to a new one. This is because there is always a cost of some sort. For example, somebody buying a new car will lose money on trading in the old one (a **switching cost**), or perhaps somebody buying a new computer will also have to spend money on new software, and spend time learning how to operate the new equipment (an **innovation cost**). Because of the long delays in adoption, a product might be misclassified and withdrawn too early in its life cycle. This is particularly true if a BCG matrix type assessment is being used to manage the portfolio, since the BCG matrix only offers an instant picture of the situation rather than a long-term view. For example, a new-to-the-world product in the early stages of its lifecycle might well have all the hallmarks of a Dog (low share of a slow market), but as the idea disseminates through the population the market begins to take off. The mobile telephone would have been in this position in the mid-1980s, when few people owned cellular phones and the network had serious teething problems. By Christmas 2000, mobile telephones had become the single most popular Christmas present in the UK.

On the other hand there is strong evidence that newness as such is an important factor in the consumer's decision-making process (Haines 1966). In other words, people like new things, but there is a cost attached. Provided the new product offers real additional benefits over the old one (i.e. fits the consumer's needs better than the old product) the product will be adopted.

Consumers must first become aware of the new product, then become persuaded that there is a real advantage in switching from their existing solution. A useful model of this adoption process is as follows:

- Awareness. This will often come about as a result of promotional activities by the firm.

- Trial. For a low-price item (e.g. a packet of biscuits) this may mean that the consumer will actually buy the product before trying it. For a major purchase, such as a car, the consumer will usually need to have a test-drive. Increasingly, supermarkets hold tasting sessions to allow customers to try new products.

- Adoption. This is the point at which the consumer decides to buy the product, or make it part of the weekly shopping list.

Everett Rogers (1962) identified the following perceived attributes of innovative products, by which consumers apparently judge the product during the decision-making process:

- Relative advantage. The degree to which the innovation is perceived as better than the idea it supersedes.
- Compatibility. Consistency with existing values, past experiences and needs of potential adopters.
- Complexity. Ideas that are easily understood are adopted more quickly.
- Trialability. Degree to which a product can be experimented with.
- Observability. The degree to which the results of an innovation are visible to others.

Apart from the issue of adopting a product as it stands, there is the concept of **re-invention**. Sometimes users find new ways to use the product (not envisaged by the designers) and sometimes this leads to the creation of whole new markets. For example, in the 1930s it was discovered that baking soda is good for removing stale smells from refrigerators, a fact that was quickly seized on by baking soda manufacturers. Deodorizing fridges is now a major part of the market for baking soda.

Talking Point

Manufacturers and others spend fortunes on research in attempts to develop new products which consumers will buy. Yet a casual glance at the Household Tips columns of some magazines would tell us that consumers are always thinking up good ideas for new ways to use old products.

So why pay out for research? Why not simply pay out rewards for useful ways to use the existing products? After all, if the consumers thought of it first, it has to be more acceptable than anything the company could dream up!

ASSESSING FINANCIAL RISK

There are three levels of financial success attached to the launch of a new product. Firstly, there is the simple break-even point. This is the point at which the product ceases to lose money, and begins to make money.

Secondly, there is the equilibrium break-even point. This is the point at which the money which has come in covers all the losses so far.

Thirdly, there is the capital acquisition point. This the point at which the product is sufficiently profitable to generate re-investment in new products.

The problem for the company lies in deciding whether the product will reach or surpass each of these points. The capital acquisition point should ideally be reached before the maturity phase of the PLC, or in other words the product should acquire Cash Cow status before it heads towards obsolescence. This enables the firm to put further NPD activities in place before competitors enter the market and erode profits.

Unfortunately, it is extremely difficult to predict risk in this way, because the firm has little idea of the shape of the PLC. At any time competitors may enter the market with a superior product, thus negating attempts at prediction and changing the shape of the PLC. This is, of course, part of the business risk and is also a good reason for collecting competitor intelligence.

Financial risk assessment should always be undertaken by someone who is not part of the NPD team. This is because the team will become close to the project and may well be over-optimistic about the chances for the product's success.

PRICE AND QUALITY

Quality is the relationship between what customers expect, and what they get. If a customer's expectations of a product are disappointed, his/her perception will be that the product is poor quality. If, on the other hand, the product exceeds expectations, the perception will be that the product is high quality.

Much of this is bound up in what customers perceive as value for money. The aim of the relationship marketer is not simply to satisfy or even to please the customer, but to delight the customer.

It follows from this that quality is not an absolute. It is only relevant to what the customer feels; what is good quality to one person may not be to another, simply because both are beginning with different expectations. For this reason, service support is critical to relationship marketing because it is during pre-sale and after-sale support that customers are approached as individuals. It is at this time that the customer's perception of quality can be addressed, either by ensuring that the expectations of the product are realistic (pre-sale) or by correcting any faults or errors after-sale.

In former years, quality has been seen as very much the province of the production department. This has led to the **product concept**, which holds that the company need only produce the best-quality product on the market and the customers will flock in. In fact this is not true – even Rolls Royce has gone through bankruptcy by following this precept. Under a relationship marketing ethos, quality has become the integrating concept between production orientation and marketing orientation. (Gummesson 1988).

The relationship between quality and price is therefore a delicate one, because price is often used as a surrogate for judging expected quality (see Chapter 9). The price of a product should signal its quality – whether this is the cheap-and-cheerful, generic product, or whether it is the top-of-the-range version with all the appropriate extras attached. Equally, the quality of the product should match up to the price, or preferably exceed it, if customers are to become loyal.

The basis of the **total quality management** approach is to ensure that the firm does the right things at every stage of the production process in the expectation that this will result in a high-quality outcome at the end. The problem with this approach is that it does not take account of the customer's expectations and perceptions, but instead relies on the management's preconceptions of what constitutes good manufacturing practice. There is also some difficulty in judging the level at which the quality of the product should be pitched. Probably the main contribution that TQM has made is in reducing defects (the zero-defects target) which will, by reducing wastage, reduce costs.

Benchmarking has achieved increased popularity in recent years. This is the process of comparing each department in the firm with the most successful equivalent department in the firm's competitors. If each department in the company operates on a level equivalent to the best department among competitors, this will result (one assumes) in a company which is the best of the best. The drawback is that some firms do not like the idea of having their quality control systems dictated by the competition; also the system, if adopted by everybody, would stifle innovation. It does, however, offer a useful starting-point, and certainly helps the firm to identify competitive strengths and weaknesses.

Quality is not an absolute: it is the relationship between expectation and outcome, and is therefore subjective. From a strategic perspective, marketers might be well advised to position products according to their quality: gaps in the market can be defined in quality terms as well as price terms (see Chapter 6). For most firms, this subtlety of positioning is unlikely to happen: price positioning is much more common, and indeed many firms fall into the fundamental error of trying to compete on price rather than on quality.

CASE STUDY: TRAINS, PLANES AND AUTOMOBILES

www.sabena.com, www.swissair.com, www.eurostar.com, www.thalys.com, www.buzzaway.com, www.go-fly.com, www.ryanair.com, www.raileurope.com

The european transport industry is in a state of flux. The collapse of national flag carriers Sabena and Swissair, coupled with the arrival of the Eurotunnel and low-cost airlines, has meant that travellers (and especially business travellers) are faced with some complex choices.

Because of the increased availability of high-speed trains, the difference in time between going by train and flying has been eroded or even eliminated. The destruction of the World Trade Centre on 11 September 2001 has further increased the inconvenience of flying due to longer check-in procedures. For example, Eurostar takes three hours to go from central London to central Paris: to do the same journey by air would take half as long again, when account is taken of the half-an-hour to one-hour journey to Heathrow, the one-hour check-in, one hour flight, and half-an-hour to an hour journey into Paris from Charles de Gaulle Airport. Even this does not take account of time spent waiting for baggage to be delivered, and transferring between different modes of transport. The result of this is that 60 per cent of travellers between London and Paris now use Eurostar rather than fly.

The difference over longer distances can be equally illuminating. Flights to Frankfurt by scheduled airline are considerably more expensive than the train, but low-cost airline Ryanair only flies to Hahn, a gruelling 90-minute bus ride from Frankfurt city centre.

The rail operators have not been slow to capitalize on the new opportunities. Rail travel is undergoing a renaissance on continental Europe, as national borders become less important and cross-border co-operation is actively encouraged. The Eurotunnel is an obvious example of Anglo-French co-operation, but the French, Belgian, Dutch and German rail systems have collaborated in the Thalys high-speed service, which allows travellers to buy through tickets to any destination on the network without the intervention of any border formalities. France has been a leader in these initiatives, also agreeing joint ventures with Switzerland and Spain: the overnight express from Paris to Madrid includes the sleeper berth within the ticket price, making for a rather more comfortable journey than most aircraft could provide. Taking account of the time saved by travelling overnight, not to mention the cost of a hotel room, the service has much to offer. Even within countries the train has taken over some long-distance routes previously dominated by air transport. The Stuttgart-Frankfurt route has proved so popular by train that Lufthansa no longer flies the route.

This is not to say that the rail companies are having it all their own way. Low-cost airlines such as Buzz, Go, and Ryanair offer extremely cheap flights between popular destinations. With flights between London and Barcelona coming in as low as £22 one-way, it is certainly difficult for rail operators to compete on price, let alone speed. The difference that is becoming apparent, however, is that many business travellers are opting to use these services, which means that the traditional airlines' principal Cash Cow, the business class traveller, is being lost to the major carriers. At the same time, the rail networks are offering greater comfort, facilities and service levels for those who are still prepared to pay a premium price – the Franco-Spanish Elipsos initiative is looking into offering free drinks on its services, just as scheduled airlines do.

Whatever happens, it seems as if competition is hotting up between the various transport firms. This can only be good for the travelling public, at least in the short term – but it is certainly a challenge for the traditional major airlines.

CASE STUDY QUESTIONS

1. How might the major airlines fight back against this threat?

▶

▶

2. Using Calentone and Cooper's classifications, how would you classify the Elipsos initiative?

3. Innovation in rail transport has obviously hit the airlines, but air transport is itself a relatively recent phenomenon. How does this square with the product life cycle concept?

4. When the Eurotunnel first opened, it lost money at an alarming rate. How might you account for its current successes?

5. How might a long-distance bus company seek to compete in this market?

SUMMARY

New product development is the life blood of any firm, whether it is in manufacturing or in a service industry. Without new products, the firm will eventually be left with obsolete products, so managing the product portfolio is an important route to competitive advantage.

The key points from this chapter are as follows:

- All products will eventually become obsolete.
- Developing new products is not an end in itself: if there is nothing wrong with the old products, there is little point in introducing new ones.
- Most new products fail to recoup their development costs.
- Most successful new products are not, in fact, new to the world.
- Some products which are new to the world actually do not change consumers' lives much (though they may well completely change the industries concerned).
- The number one key success factor is to have a unique product which consumers think is superior to what is already available.
- Generating, evaluating, developing and launching new products is not a tidy process.
- Innovations take time to diffuse through the population.

CHAPTER QUESTIONS

1. If all products eventually become obsolete, how is it possible to account for such recent marketing successes as the Chrysler PSV and new Volkswagen Beetle?

2. Consumers are notoriously fickle. How might a company ensure that a new product will represent a significant advantage over an old product?

3. In the case of a relaunched product (for example the yo-yo), how might Rogers' classification of consumers be relevant?

4. Considering Calentone and Cooper's findings, why would any firm try to produce truly innovative, new-to-the-world products?

5. How might the new-product development sequence change for a firm in a service industry?

REFERENCES

Benwell, M. (1996): 'Scheduling Stocks and Storage Space in a Volatile Market', *Logistics Information Management* vol. 9 no. 4 pp. 18–23.

Booz, Allen and Hamilton (1982): *New Products Management for the 1980s* (New York: Booz, Allen and Hamilton).

Calantone, Roger J. and Cooper, Robert G. (1981): 'New Product Scenarios; Prospects for Success', *American Journal of Marketing* Spring vol. 45 pp. 48–60.

Cooper, R.G. (1993): *Winning at new products* 2nd edition, (Reading MA: Addison-Wesley).

Crawford, C.M. (1991): *New Products Management* (Homewood Illinois: Irwin).

Doyle, P. (1998): *Marketing Management and Strategy* (Hemel Hempstead: Prentice-Hall).

Engel, James F., Blackwell, Roger D. and Miniard, Paul W. (1995): *Consumer Behaviour* 8th International Edition, (Fort Worth TX: Dryden Press).

Gummesson, E. (1988): 'Service quality and product quality combined', *Review of Business* 9, (3), Winter.

Haines, George H. (1966): 'A Study of Why People Purchase New Products', Proceedings of the American Marketing Association, 1966.

Hart, S. (1993): 'Dimensions of success in new product development: an exploratory investigation', *Journal of Marketing Management* vol. 9 no. 1 pp. 23–42.

von Hippel, E. (1978): 'Users and Innovators', *Technical Review*, October 1978, pp. 98–106.

Lambin, J.J. (2000): *Market-driven management: strategic and operational marketing* (London: Macmillan Business).

Lazarsfield, Paul F., Bertelson, Bernard R. and Gaudet, Hazel (1948): *The People's Choice* (New York: Columbia University Press, 1948).

Page, A.L. (1993): 'Assessing New Product Development Practices and Performance: establishing crucial norms', *Journal of Product Innovation Management* 10(4), pp. 273–90.

Rogers, Everett M. (1962): *Diffusion of Innovations* (New York: Macmillan, 1962).

Urban, G.L., Hauser, J.R. and Dholakia, N. (1987): *Essentials of new product management* (Englewood Cliffs: NJ, Prentice-Hall).

Veblen, T. (1899): *The Theory of the Leisure Class* (New York: MacMillan 1899).

Chapter Nine

Strategy and Pricing

INTRODUCTION

Pricing was, at one time, seen as a tool of the finance department. Prices were determined largely by the costs of production, and calculations based on marginal costs or on fixed plus variable costs were in common use. This meant that the use of price as a means of establishing competitive advantage was largely ignored since pricing was undertaken independently of market considerations. A simplistic view (which is still frequently adopted in many companies) was that the route to success lay in cutting costs to the bone in order to reduce prices.

Pricing can be used to achieve strategic outcomes, and in a market-orientated company this is likely to be seen as an important weapon in the firm's armoury.

After reading this chapter, you should be able to:

- Explain the strategic implications of different pricing methods.
- Calculate prices on the basis of different strategic objectives.
- Choose the correct pricing strategy to fit a firm's overall objectives.
- Explain the contribution of economic theory to the marketer's view of price and value.

ECONOMIC THEORIES OF PRICING AND VALUE

Classical economists assumed that prices would be set by the laws of **supply and demand**. Figure 9.1 shows how this works.

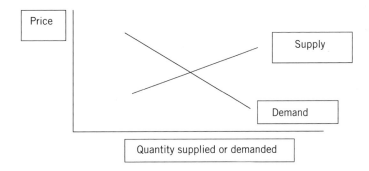

Figure 9.1: Supply and demand

As prices rise, more suppliers find it profitable to enter the market, but the demand for the product falls because fewer customers are prepared to pay the price being asked. If, on the other hand, prices fall there will be an increase in demand, but fewer suppliers will be prepared to enter or remain in the market so less is produced. Eventually a state of equilibrium is reached where the quantity produced is equal to the quantity consumed, and at that point the price will be fixed.

This model is a somewhat simplistic view of what happens in the market. It has a number of assumptions underpinning it which are not realistic, as follows:

- The model assumes that customers have perfect knowledge of the market, and know where they can buy the cheapest products.

- It assumes that all the suppliers produce identical products. This is only true in a very few markets – virtually all companies try to differentiate their products in some way.

- It assumes that price is the only factor affecting customers' decisions. This is again only true in a few (fairly limited) circumstances.

- The model assumes that customers always behave rationally. Studies of consumer behaviour show that this is not the case, and indeed it is not the case for industrial buyers either.

- The model assumes that people will always buy more of a product if it is cheaper. This is not true of products like wedding rings or wooden legs, and it is rarely true of products like stereo systems or washing machines.

- The model assumes that none of the suppliers has the power to set prices in the market. This is clearly untrue, as most markets are in monopolistic competition, in which the leading firm sets the prices and the others have no choice but to follow.

The model does, at least, take account of customers, and it was the pioneer economist Adam Smith who first said that 'the customer is king' (Smith 1776). Although the model offers an interesting way of thinking about supply and demand, its shortcomings mean that it has little practical use.

In the intervening 225 years, economists have added considerably to the theory. The concept of elasticity of demand states that different products will show different degrees of sensitivity to price change.

Figure 9.2: Price elasticity of demand

In Figure 9.2, the graph on the left shows a product where the demand is only slightly affected by a change in price. The classic example of this is salt: it is a low-cost item which everybody needs no matter what the price charged. Even if the price were to drop substantially, people would not be inclined to buy more of it. The diagram on the right shows a product where even a small difference in price leads to a substantial shift in demand. An example of this is cars: even a 10 per cent shift in the price of a particular model makes a marked difference in demand, because there are many substitutes available from other manufacturers. Although these examples show how price shifts affect demand, the same is true for the supply side. In some cases suppliers can react very quickly to changes in the quantities demanded (for example, banking), whereas in other cases the suppliers need long lead times to make changes in production levels (for instance, farming).

Price elasticity theory implies that products cannot be defined as necessities or luxuries. If a necessity is defined as something which is essential for survival, its demand curve would be entirely inelastic; whatever price is charged, people would have no alternative but to pay it. In practice, no such product exists.

Talking Point

> Despite the fact that there is no basis in economic theory for a distinction between luxuries and necessities, most people still manage to make this distinction.
>
> So is beer a necessity or a luxury? Is food a necessity or a luxury? And if food is a necessity, does that necessity extend to caviar? To bread? To ciabatta with smoked salmon and cream cheese?
>
> In other words, how DO we draw a line between necessities and luxuries?

According to economic theory, there can never be enough resources in the world to satisfy everybody's wants. This means that resources have to be rationed in some way, which will almost certainly lead to a degree of dissatisfaction. Resources used for one purpose cannot at the same time be used for another purpose; this has given rise to the concept of the **economic choice.**

For example, an engineering firm may only have a certain number of skilled welders available to work a certain number of hours. This means that it may only be possible to produce one type of product with the available resources. If the manufacturer has two orders, each for a different type of product, he will have to choose which order to supply, and disappoint the other customer.

From the customer's viewpoint, the economic choice means having to choose between having a holiday or buying a new car; there may not be the money to do both. Because of this, customers may be affected by the price of products or services other than those the prospective supplier is providing. The tour operator, for example, is unlikely to think of a car manufacturer as being competition, but a fall in the price of cars might well leave the customer with enough money over to afford a holiday. This is of considerable strategic importance, and the lesson is not lost on all manufacturers: Harley Davidson is well aware that its competition is not from other motorcycle manufacturers, but from home-improvement companies. Harley Davidson (**www.harley-davidson.com**) is selling a dream, and a lifestyle, not personal transportation.

Although the economists' view of pricing offers some interesting insights, there is little practical value in the theories offered because they take little account of the consumer decision-making process. Consumers are not always rational; marketers need to take account of this.

PRICING AND MARKET ORIENTATION

In any question of marketing, managers need to look at the problem from the customer's viewpoint. Pricing is therefore dependent on the customer's reaction to the prices set. Customers rarely buy the cheapest products; they buy those which they perceive as good value for money. If this were not so, the most popular cars in Britain would be Ladas (**www.lada.co.uk**) and Yugos (**www.yugo.co.uk**), rather than Vauxhalls (**www.vauxhall.co.uk**) and Fords (**www.ford.com**).

Typically, customers will make an assessment of what the product is and what it will do (often based on what the supplier is promising), and will measure this against the price being asked (Zeithaml 1988). The problem for the marketer lies in deciding what the customers will see as good value for money, while still allowing the company to make a profit.

Pricing methods can be categorized as either cost-based, customer-based, or competition-based. Cost-based methods are the least market-orientated of the three: two methods which are still commonly used are **cost-plus pricing** and **mark-up pricing.**

Cost-Plus pricing works by calculating the cost of manufacturing the product, including distributed overhead costs and research and development costs, then adding on a fixed percentage profit to this figure in order to arrive at the price. It is a method which is often advocated by accountants and engineers, as it is easy to calculate and is thought to ensure a known profit margin provided sales targets are reached. The main problem with cost-plus pricing is that it is entirely self-referential: the market is effectively ignored, and often firms using the system are tempted to shave the profits in order to meet competitive initiatives.

Although cost-plus pricing appears to be a safe means of establishing a price, it actually runs two strategic risks. The first is that the calculation produces a price below that which customers are prepared to pay, and thus the firm loses profits. The second is that the calculated price is above that which customers are prepared to pay, and the firm loses sales. In rare cases the price will be close to that which customers find acceptable, but this is really a matter of luck rather than judgement. Cost-plus pricing does not take account of competition or profitability, and therefore does not contribute to competitive advantage or to shareholder value, and therefore throws away a major strategic opportunity.

Some government contracts are awarded on a cost-plus basis, but experience in the United States has shown that allowing cost-plus contracts to be granted will often result in the supplier inflating the costs to make an extra profit. Cost-plus contracts also remove any pressure to increase efficiency.

Mark-up pricing is the method used by most retailers and is similar to cost-plus pricing. Typically, a retailer will buy in stock and add on a fixed percentage to the bought-in price (a mark-up) in order to arrive at the **shelf price**. The level will vary from retailer to retailer, depending on the type of product; in some cases the mark-up will be 100 per cent or more, in others it will be near zero (if the retailer feels that stocking the product will stimulate other sales). Usually there is a standard mark-up for each product category.

Retailers use this method because of the large number of different products the shop may stock. Buyers use their training and knowledge of their customer base to determine which lines to stock: if the buyer thinks the product represents good value for money, the retailer will stock it, if not, it will not be given shelf space. The method differs from the cost-plus method in two ways: firstly, retailers are in close contact with customers, and usually have a good 'feel' for what customers will be prepared to pay. Secondly, retailers have ways of disposing of unsold stock, so that mistakes need not be too costly. In some cases, this will mean discounting the stock back to cost and selling it in the January sales; in other cases, the retailer will have a sale-or-return agreement with the manufacturer, so that unsold stock can be returned for credit. In effect the retailer is test-marketing the product; if the customers do not accept the product at the price offered, the retailer can drop the price to a point that will represent value for money, or can return it to the manufacturer for credit. Manufacturers are not in this position, because a new product often represents a substantial up-front outlay which cannot be recovered by discounting, even when the initial production costs might be recoverable.

Customer-based pricing does not necessarily mean offering products at the lowest possible price, but it does mean taking account of customer needs and wants.

Customary pricing is customer-orientated in that it provides the customer with the product for the same price at which it has always been offered. An example is the price of a call from a coin-operated telephone box. Telephone companies need only reduce the time allowed for the call as costs rise. For some countries (e.g. Australia) this is problematical since local calls are allowed unlimited time, but for most european countries this is not the case.

The reason for using customary pricing is to avoid having to reset the call-boxes too often. Strategically, this can represent a cost saving but carries the risk that profits will be eroded. Ultimately, customary pricing cannot continue indefinitely: examples of very long-term customary prices are that of pepper, which for 500 years held the same price (one ounce of pepper for one ounce of gold), and bread in Soviet Russia, which for 60 years was 3 kopeks for a loaf. In the first instance, cheaper sea routes to the Indies broke the merchants' monopolies, and in the second case inflation meant that the bread was so cheap most of it was being wasted. In both cases, therefore, market forces resulted in a change of price, despite the best intentions of the price setters.

Demand pricing is the most customer-orientated method of pricing, because the starting-point is the demand for the product at different price levels. The demand is assessed by means of customer research exercises, or occasionally by examining the past records of the firm's sales and using these to construct a demand curve.

As the price rises, fewer customers will see the product as good value for money. The fall-off is not necessarily linear i.e. the number of units demanded might fall dramatically once the price goes above a particular figure. This calculation could be used to determine the stages of a skimming policy (see below), or it could be used to calculate the appropriate launch price of a product.

From a strategic viewpoint, the demand curve can be used to decide the most appropriate price for meeting different possible objectives. If the objective is to maximize profits, the next stage of the process would be to calculate the costs of producing at different levels of demand. As more product is sold, economies of scale will reduce costs, but this curve is equally unlikely to be linear: in other words, some parts of the supply curve may not be in parallel with the demand curve. This is shown in Fig 9.3.

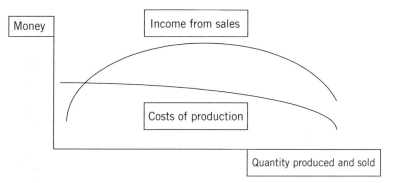

Figure 9.3: Demand pricing and manufacturing costs

Figure 9.3 shows a product where, at low quantities of production, the cost of producing far outweigh the income generated. As production increases, economies of scale reduce costs (quite dramatically at the highest levels of production). Unfortunately, as the price falls and demand increases, a point is reached where the new business generated by reducing prices actually results in less revenue despite increased demand: the product is now being sold so cheaply that increased sales are not compensating. There is therefore a point at which net revenue falls, although profit might still increase due to the reduction in manufacturing costs. The gap between the two curves represents the gross profit at each level of sales.

The tooling-up cost is the amount it will cost the company to prepare for producing the item. This will be the same whether 1,000 units are made or 30,000 units.

For a profit maximizing firm, the price can be set so that the gap between the cost line and the revenue line is at its widest. Other strategic objectives might require other approaches, however. For example, a firm seeking to maximize unit sales as a way of buying into the market might aim to price at the far right of the scale. This might result in shutting out potential competitors or in establishing the firm with key customers.

Table 9.1: Costings for demand pricing

Number of units	Unit cost (labour and materials	Tooling-up and fixed costs	Net cost per unit
30,000	£1.20	£4,000	£1.33
25,000	£1.32	£4,000	£1.48
15,000	£1.54	£4,000	£1.81
5,000	£1.97	£4,000	£2.77

Table 9.2 shows how much profit could be made at each price level.

The price at which the product is sold will depend on the firm's overall objectives; these may not necessarily be to maximize profit on this one product, since the firm may have other products in the range or other long-term objectives that preclude maximizing profits at present.

Table 9.2: Profitability at different price bands

Number of units sold	Net profit per unit	Total profit for production run	Percentage profit per unit
30,000	£2.17	£65,100	62%
25,000	£3.02	£75,500	67%
15,000	£3.61	£54,150	66%
5,000	£3.73	£18,650	57%

Based on these figures, a firm seeking to maximize profits would price at £4.50. Firms seeking the highest profit per unit would charge £6.50, but at this price the firm would only sell 5,000 units and make £18,650. The price that would generate the highest sales would be £3.50, which would therefore be an appropriate price for a firm seeking to shut out the competition.

Demand pricing is therefore a means of achieving strategic objectives by managing demand appropriately. It does not of itself take account of the effect that sales of one product might have on sales of another within the product line.

> **Talking Point**
>
> Demand pricing seems to assume a degree of rationality – the consumer thinking carefully about whether the product is worth the money or not. And this in turn implies some kind of comparison with other products at other prices.
>
> But is this really what happens? What about impulse buying? What about those times when we buy something KNOWING that it isn't good value for money, but buying anyway because we just get the urge? What about all that rationalizing afterwards, about saving time by spending more, or telling ourselves that we deserve something nice?
>
> Are we, as human beings, really all that rational?

Product-line pricing means setting prices within linked product groups. Often sales of one product will be directly linked to the sales of another, so that it is possible to capture a chunk of the market by selling one item at a low price, realizing the profit on sales of the dependent one. This is an effective strategy for new products because it overcomes the initial resistance of consumers towards buying something untried, but allows the firm to show high profits in future years.

Polaroid chose to sell its instant cameras very cheaply (almost for cost price) for the US market and to take its profit from selling the films for a much higher price. For Europe, the firm chose to sell both films and cameras for a medium level price and profit from sales of both. Eventually this led Kodak (**www.kodak.com**) to enter the market with its own instant camera, but this was withdrawn from sale in the face of lawsuits from Polaroid (**www.polaroid.com**) for patent infringement.

Skimming is the practice of starting out with a high price for a product, then reducing it progressively as sales level off. It relies on two main factors: firstly, that not all customers have the same perception of value for money, and secondly that the company has a technological lead over the opposition which can be maintained for long enough to satisfy the market.

Skimming is an appropriate strategy for firms with a technically-advanced product. Initially the firm charges a high price for the product, and at this point only those who are prepared to pay a premium price for it will buy. Overall profit may not be high, even though profit per unit is likely to be high, because the number of units sold will be low. Once the most innovative customers have bought, and competition is becoming apparent in the market, the firm can drop the price and 'skim' the next layer of the market, at which point profits will begin to rise. Eventually the product will become a commodity product, allowing the firm a minimum profit, at which point only replacement sales or sales to late adopters will be made.

The advantage of this method is that the cost of developing the product is returned fairly quickly, so that the product can later be sold near the marginal cost of production. This means that competitors have difficulty entering the market at all, since their own development costs will have to be recovered in some other way.

Skimming is commonly used in consumer electronics markets. This is because firms frequently establish a technological lead over competitors, and can sometimes even protect their products by taking out patents which take some time for competitors to overcome. An example of this was the Sony Walkman (**www.sony.com**), which cost over »70 when it was first introduced in the early 80s. Allowing for inflation, the price is now around one-tenth of what it was then. Research shows that customers are aware of skimming in the electronics markets, and are delaying purchases of new electronic devices until prices drop. This may affect the way firms view skimming in the future.

Skimming requires careful judgement of what is happening in the marketplace, both in terms of observing customer behaviour, and of observing competitive response. Market research and careful monitoring of sales to know when to cut the price again is basic to the success of a skimming policy.

Psychological pricing relies on emotional responses from the consumer. Higher prices are often used as an indicator of quality (Erickson and Johannson 1985), so some firms will use **prestige pricing.** This applies in many service industries, because consumers are often buying a promise; a service which does not have a high enough quality cannot be exchanged afterwards. Consumers' expectations of high-priced restaurants and hairdressers are clearly higher in terms of the quality of service provision; cutting prices in those industries does not necessarily lead to an increase in business. From a strategic viewpoint, prestige pricing is an alternative means of creating competitive advantage – where other firms might enter a price war and cut prices, the prestige firm increases prices. Obviously the product itself must match up to the raised expectations of the customers.

Odd-even pricing is the practice of ending prices with an odd number, for example £3.99 or $5.95 rather than £4 or $6. It appears that consumers tend to categorize these prices as "£3 and a bit" or "$5 and change" and thus perceive the price as being lower than it actually is. The effect may also be due to an association with discounted or sale prices; researchers report that '99' endings on prices increase sales by around 8% (Schindler and Kirby 1997).

Second-market discounting is common in some service industries and in international markets. The brand is sold at one price in one market, and at a lower price in another. For example, museums offer discounts to students, some restaurants offer discounts to elderly people on weeknights, and so forth. Often these discounts are offered to even out the **loading** on the firm; weeknight discounts fill the restaurant on what would otherwise be a quiet night, so making more efficient use of the premises and staff.

In international markets products might be discounted to meet local competition. For example, prices of feature films on video are much lower in the UK than in the US, due to stronger competition from video rental companies (Zikmund and D'Amico 1995).

Competitor-based pricing recognizes the influence of competition in the marketplace. Strategically, the marketer must decide how close the competition is in meeting consumers' needs; if the products are close, then prices will need to be similar to those of the competition. A

meet-the-competition strategy has the advantage of avoiding price wars and stimulating competition in other areas of marketing, thus maintaining profitability. An **undercut-the-competition** strategy is often the main plank in the firm's marketing strategy; it is particularly common among retailers, who have relatively little control over product features and benefits and often have little control over the promotion of the products they stock. Some multinational firms (particularly in electronics) have the capacity to undercut rivals since they are able to manufacture in low-wage areas of the world, or are large enough to use widespread automation. There is a danger of starting price wars when using an undercutting policy (see penetration pricing below). Undercutting (and consequent price wars) may be becoming more common (Mitchell 1996).

Firms with large market shares often have enough control over their distribution systems and production capacity within their industries to become **price leaders.** Typically, such firms can make price adjustments without starting price wars, and can raise prices without losing substantial market share (see Chapter 2 for monopolistic competition) (Rich 1982). Sometimes these price leaders become sensitive to the price and profit needs of their competitors, in effect supporting them, because they do not wish to attract the attention of monopoly regulators by destroying the competition. Deliberate price fixing (managers colluding to set industry prices) is illegal in most countries.

Penetration pricing is used when the firm wants to capture a large part of the market quickly. It relies on the assumption that a lower price will be perceived as offering better value for money (which is, of course, often the case).

For penetration pricing to work, the company must have carried out thorough research to find out what competitors are charging for the nearest similar product. The new product is then sold at a substantially lower price, even if this cuts profits below an acceptable level; the intention is to capture the market quickly before competitors can react with even lower prices. The danger with this pricing method is that some competitors might be able to sustain a price war for a long period and will eventually bankrupt the incoming firm. It is usually safer to compete on some other aspect of the offering, such as quality or delivery.

In some cases, prices are pitched below the cost of production. The purpose of this is to bankrupt the competition so that the new entrant can take over entirely; this practice is called **predatory pricing** and (at least in international markets) is illegal. Predatory pricing was successfully used by Japanese car manufacturers when entering european markets in the 1970s, and is commonly used by large firms who are entering new markets. For the strategy to be successful, it is necessary for the market to be dominated by firms who cannot sustain a long price war. It is worth doing if the company has no other competitive edge, but does have sufficient financial reserves to hold out for a long time. Naturally, this method is customer-orientated since it can only work by providing the customers with very much better value for money than they have been used to. The company will eventually raise prices again in order to recoup the lost profits once the market presence has been established, however.

Competitor-based pricing is still customer-orientated to an extent, since it takes as its starting-point the prices that customers currently pay to competitors.

SETTING PRICES

Price setting follows eight stages, as shown in Table 9.3.

Price setting can be complex if it is difficult to identify the closest competitors, but it should be borne in mind that no product is entirely without competition; there is almost always another

Table 9.3: Eight stages of price setting

Stage	Explanation
Development of pricing objectives	The pricing objectives derive from the organization's overall objectives; does the firm seek to maximize market share, or maximize profits?
Assessment of the target market's ability to purchase and evaluation of price	Buyers tend to be more sensitive to food prices in supermarkets than to drinks prices in clubs. Also, a buyer's income and availability of credit directly affect the ability to buy the product at all.
Determination of demand	For most products demand falls as price rises. This is not necessarily a straight-line relationship, nor is the line necessarily at 45 degrees. For some products even a small price rise results in a sharp fall in demand (e.g. petrol) whereas for other products (like salt) even a large price rise hardly affects demand at all.
Analysis of demand, cost, and profit relationships	The firm needs to analyse the costs of producing the item against the price that the market will bear, taking into account the profit needed. The cost calculation will include both the fixed costs and the unit costs for making a given quantity of the product. This quantity will be determined by the market, and will relate to the selling price.
Evaluation of competitors' prices	This will involve a survey of the prices currently being charged, but will also have to consider the possible entry of new competitors. Prices may be pitched higher than the competitors in order to give an impression of exclusivity or higher quality. This is common in the perfume market, and in services such as restaurants and hairdressing.
Selection of a pricing policy	The pricing policy needs to be chosen from the list given in the early part of the chapter.
Development of a pricing method	Here the producer develops a simple mechanism for determining prices in the future. The simplest method is to use cost-plus or mark-up pricing; these do not take account of customers, however, so something a little more sophisticated should be used if possible.
Determining a specific price	If the previous steps have been carried out in a thorough manner, determining the actual price should be a simple matter.

Note: Adapted from Dibb, Simkin, Pride & Ferrell: *Marketing Concepts and Strategies*, 3rd Edition. London: Houghton Mifflin 1994.

way in which customers can meet the need that the product supplies. Also, different customers have different needs and therefore will have differing views on what constitutes value for money – this is why markets need to be segmented carefully to ensure that the right price is being charged in each segment. As in any question of marketing, it is wise to begin with the customer.

PRICE AS A STRATEGIC WEAPON

Price is a major component in customers' judgement of both product and company. As a guideline to the positioning of a product it serves two purposes: it acts as a guide to quality, and it acts as an absolute indicator against competing products.

As a source of competitive advantage, prices can be set low (so as to offer better value to the customer than competitors do) or it can be high to differentiate the product by signalling higher quality. A firm adopting a cost-leadership strategy will almost certainly need to price low; a firm adopting a differentiation policy is likely to price high. Likewise, market leaders are likely to price high, whereas market followers will price low, but not so much lower that they provoke a competitive response.

In short, price has little or nothing to do with the cost of production. Price is a strategic weapon, is occasionally a tactical tool (as in sales promotions), and is frequently a source of competitive advantage. As one of the factors in turnover (the other being unit sales) it is also the main driver of shareholder value and profitability.

CASE STUDY: INTERNET AUCTIONS

The Internet has opened up many opportunities for increasing democracy, and nowhere has this been more apparent than in the proliferation of auction sites on the Net.

Sellers are able to post goods on sites, with or without reserve prices, and buyers are able to place their bids from (theoretically) anywhere in the world. The price rises as more people bid for the item, until there is only one bidder left, who pays for the product using a credit card and has the item delivered. The Internet allows the process to happen extremely quickly; not quite at the speed of light, but certainly fast enough so that interested buyers need to move quickly if they are to avoid being outbid.

Recently the process has moved a step further along the democratic line with the advent of reverse auctions. The philosophy of the reverse auction is simple; there is no point in bidding against other purchasers, and putting the price up, if you can join with other purchasers in order to force prices down. The US company Priceline pioneered the software, but UK firm adabra has its own version of the reverse auction.

Reverse auctions work by harnessing the power of bulk buying. Typically the products sold are consumer 'brown goods' such as stereos and TV sets. The price paid to the supplier will depend on the number of buyers, so adabra begins by agreeing a set of price bands with the suppliers. For example, a VCR might carry a £200 price tag in a normal retail store, but the manufacturer may be prepared to cut the price to £175 if 100 people are prepared to buy the product. If 500 people will buy, the price drops to £150, if 1,000 will buy it drops to £125. These prices are posted on the auctioneer's website for a 'sell spell', perhaps five days or so, in order to allow time for bids to be registered.

Purchasers wanting to join in the reverse auction state the price they are prepared to pay; those who bid low run the risk of not getting the product at all, because the deal will not go through if the reverse auction company does not get enough purchasers. Those who bid high might have to pay the price they offer, but if enough people offer to buy at the lower price, the high bidders will still only pay the lower price. In the example above, if 80 people are prepared to pay £175, and 450 are prepared to pay £150, while a further 300 are prepared to pay £125, the product will be sold to 530 people for £150. The remaining 300 people will not be able to buy.

The implications of this for traditional High Street retailers are potentially extremely damaging. Although they might argue that consumers will still prefer to come to a store where they are able to see and even try out the products, there is nothing to stop people doing this, then going home and joining the reverse auction. The implications for manufacturers are equally wide-reaching: although the power of retailers will be seriously curtailed, the power of consumers will become much greater. On the one hand, reverse auctions offer manufacturers a kind of instant marketing research, but on the other the process may mean the end of price skimming, psychological pricing and other tried-and-tested techniques for maximizing the profitability of innovative products.

In some cases, consumer power has gone even further by cutting out the service provider altogether. Some buyers of major capital goods, for example cars or computers, have taken to sending tenders to dealers asking them to bid for supplying the product. On a new car purchase, an astute logged-on consumer might save hundreds or even thousands of pounds in this way – a saving which more than compensates for the time taken to send the e-mails.

These changes are not all bad for manufacturers, but the overall effect is a sea-change in the way pricing is carried out. Prices are being much more directly dictated by the end consumer than they ever have been before.

▶

▶

CASE STUDY QUESTIONS

1. How might a manufacturer retain a skimming policy when dealing with a reverse auction?
2. How might a car dealer encourage a prospective customer to increase the tender price?
3. What advantages might there be for manufacturers in participating in reverse auctions?
4. How might a manufacturer calculate the appropriate price bands for a reverse auction?
5. What might retailers do to counteract the threat of reverse auctions?

SUMMARY

Value for money is a subjective concept; each person has a differing view of what represents value for money, and this means that different market segments will have differing views on whether a given price is appropriate. Marketing is about encouraging trade so that customers and manufacturers can maximize the satisfaction gained from their activities; to this end, marketers always try to make exchanges easier and pleasanter for customers.

Key points from this chapter:

- Prices, ultimately, are fixed by market forces, not by suppliers alone. Therefore suppliers would be ill-advised to ignore the customer.
- There is no objective difference between necessities and luxuries; the distinction lies only in the mind of the customer.
- Customers cannot spend the same money twice, so they are forced to make economic choices. A decision to do one thing implies a decision not to do another.
- Customers have a broad and sometimes surprising range of choices when seeking to maximize utility.
- Pricing can be cost-based, competition-based, or customer-based; ultimately, though, consumers have the last word because they can simply spend their money elsewhere.

CHAPTER QUESTIONS

1. What is the difference between margin and mark-up?
2. When should a skimming policy be used?
3. How can penetration pricing be used in international markets?
4. Why should a firm be wary of cost-plus pricing?
5. How does customary pricing benefit the supplier?

REFERENCES

Erickson, G.M. and Johannson, J.K. (1985): 'The Role of Price in Multi-Attribute Product Evaluation', *Journal of Consumer Research* vol. 12.

Mitchell, A. (1996): 'The Price is Right' *Marketing Business* May no. 50 pp. 32–34.

Rich, Stuart A. (1982): 'Price Leaders; Large, Strong, but Cautious About Conspiracy', *Marketing News*, 25 June p. 11.

Schindler, R.M. and Kirby, P.N. (1997): 'Patterns of right-most digits used in advertising prices: implications for nine-ending effects', *Journal of Consumer Research* (Sept 1997) pp. 192–201.

Smith, Adam (1776): *An Inquiry into The Wealth of Nations*.

Zeithaml, Valerie A. (1988): 'Consumer Perceptions of Price, Quality and Value', *Journal of Marketing* 52 (July 1988) pp. 2–22.

Zikmund, William G. and D'Amico, Michael (1995): *Effective Marketing: Creating and Keeping Customers* (St. Paul MN: West).

Chapter Ten

Strategy and Promotion

INTRODUCTION

Customer and consumer responses to commercial communications are possibly the most important factor in communications planning. As in any other area of marketing, the customer is the starting point for all communications: the target audience will have already been defined through the process of segmentation, targeting and positioning. The key messages that support that positioning should then be developed with the target group in mind.

In communications terms this means finding out which magazines or business journals the target audience reads, which TV stations they watch, what their leisure activities are, whether they are interested in football or opera or horse racing, and so forth. This is a substantial part of the market research that is carried out daily; customers not only consume products, they also consume communications media. Knowing which media they consume enables the astute marketer to target accurately and avoid wasting the budget on trying to communicate with people who are not paying attention and have no interest in the product.

The strategic decisions concerning communications fall initially into two parts. The first is decisions about 'message', which can be divided into content, structure and format. The second set of decisions revolves about the 'messenger', which is the route by which the message will be communicated. Although both are strongly related the key target message should be the first area developed.

Two specific areas of marketing communication have been singled out for special attention in this chapter. The reason for this is that both are characterized by their interactive nature. The first is personal selling, which involves a two-way communication between individuals; the second is the Internet, which allows one-to-many and many-to-one type communications between firms and their customers, as well as one-to-one communications.

After reading this chapter, you should be able to:

- Describe the main strategic issues involved in communications planning.
- Explain how integrated marketing communications provide marketing synergies.
- Explain the role of personal selling and its relationship to marketing strategy.
- Explain the issues surrounding major account management strategy.

ELEMENTS OF THE COMMUNICATIONS MIX

Table 10.1 lists some of the elements of the mix. This list is unlikely to be exhaustive, and there is also the problem of boundary-spanning; some elements of the mix go beyond communication and into the realms of distribution (telemarketing and home shopping channels for example) or even into new product development (as with many new websites).

The range of possible tools at the marketer's disposal is obviously large. Creating a strategic mix of communications methods is akin to following a recipe; the ingredients have to be added in the right amounts at the right time, and treated in the right way, if the recipe is to work. Also, one ingredient cannot substitute for another; personal selling cannot, on its own, replace advertising, nor can public relations exercises replace sales promotions. Figure 10.1 shows how the above elements of the mix relate to each other. For example, public relations efforts, sales promotions

Table 10.1: Elements of the communications mix

Element	Description
Advertising	A paid insertion of a message in a medium.
Ambient advertising	Messages placed on items such as bus tickets, stamp franking, till receipts, petrol pump nozzles and so forth. Any message that forms part of the environment - for example 'art installations' in city centres.
Press advertising	Any paid message that appears in a newspaper or magazine.
TV advertising	Commercial messages shown in the breaks during and between TV programmes.
Radio advertising	Sound-only advertisements broadcast on radio.
Outdoor advertising	Billboards, bus shelters, flyposters etc.
Transport advertising	Posters in stations and inside buses and trains.
Outside transport advertising	Posters on buses and taxis, and in some countries the sides of trains. British Airways (**www.british-airways.com**) has recently carried other companies' logos on the tailplanes of aircraft.
Press releases	News stories about the firm or its products.
Public relations	The planned and sustained effort to establish and maintain goodwill and mutual understanding between an organization and its publics (Institute of Public Relations 1984). (**www.ipr.org.uk**)
Sponsorship	Funding of arts events, sporting events etc. in exchange for publicity and prestige.
Sales promotions	Activities designed to give a temporary boost to sales, such as money-off coupons, free samples, two-for-the-price-of-one promotions etc.
Personal selling	Face-to-face communications between buyers and sellers designed to ascertain and meet customers' needs on a one-to-one basis.
Database marketing	Profiling customers onto a database and sending out personalized mailings or other communications to them.
Telemarketing	Inbound (helpline, telephone ordering) or outbound (telecanvassing, teleselling) telephone calls.
Internet marketing	Use of websites to promote and/or sell products.
Off-the-screen sales	Using TV adverts linked to inbound telephone operations to sell goods. Also home shopping channels such as QVC. (**www.qvc.com**)
Exhibitions and trade fairs	Companies take stands at trade fairs to display new products, meet consumers and customers, and raise the company profile with interested parties.
Corporate identity	The combination of the overall image that the company projects, the company's 'personality', and the corporate brand.
Branding	The creation of a multi-dimensional character for a specific product: the character acts as the mechanism by which marketing communications are co-ordinated.

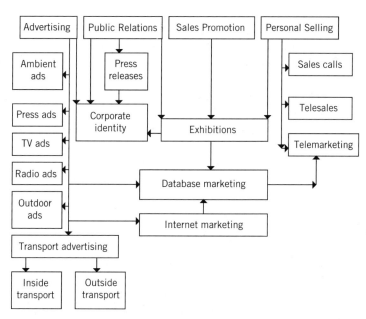

Figure 10.1: A taxonomy of marketing communications

and personal selling all feed into the creation of a successful exhibition. The exhibition, in turn, feeds into developing a corporate identity and may also contribute to development of the database.

The interconnections between the various elements shown in Fig 10.1 are only the main ones; in fact, every marketing communication impinges on every other in some way or another. The tactical methods used will depend on the firm, the product and the audience.

In terms of developing competitive advantage, marketing communications is often the only differentiating feature of the brand. For example, Saxa Salt was very successful in differentiating its product from other salt manufacturers' brands during the early part of the 20th century. This was achieved entirely by running a lengthy (and expensive) series of advertisements showing a young child chasing a bird. The advertisement played on a common myth that one could catch birds by putting salt on their tails. Many children believed this story, but of course anyone who could get close enough to the bird to salt its tail would have no trouble catching it by hand anyway. The advertisements were thus charming, emphasized the product, and also lent themselves to several puns about the salt being free-running. (**www.rhmfoodservice.co.uk**)

Another example is the Coca-Cola (**www.coca-cola.com**) versus Pepsi-Cola (**www.pepsi.com**) battle. In blind taste tests, most people prefer Pepsi, so the differentiation of the actual product is in fact in Pepsi's favour. The superior sales of Coca-Cola are achieved entirely by effective marketing communications.

STRUCTURING THE COMMUNICATIONS MIX

Structuring the communications mix will differ from one firm to another, and indeed from one promotion to another within the same firm. Developing effective marketing communications follows a six-stage process:

1. Identify the target audience. In other words, decide who the message should get to.
2. Determine the response sought. What would the marketer like the audience to do after they get the message?
3. Choose the message. Write the copy, or produce an appropriate image.
4. Choose the channel. Decide which newspaper, TV station, radio station or other medium is most appealing to the audience.
5. Select the source's attributes. Decide what it is about the product or company that needs to be communicated.
6. Collect feedback. For example carry out market research to find out how successful the message was.

Communication is often expensive; full-page advertisements in Sunday colour supplements can cost upwards of £11,000 per insertion; a 30-second TV ad at peak time can cost £30,000 per station. It is therefore worthwhile spending time and effort in ensuring that the message is comprehensible by the target audience, and is reaching the right people. Figure 10.2 shows how the communications mix operates.

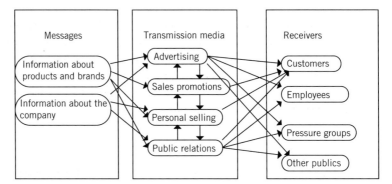

Figure 10.2: The promotional mix

In the above diagram, messages from the company about its products and itself are transmitted via the elements of the promotional mix to the consumers, employees, pressure groups, and other publics. Because each of these groups is receiving the messages via several media, the elements of the mix should also feed into each other so the messages will not conflict. The choice of method will depend upon the message, the receiver, and the desired effect.

Talking Point

The model of communication shown here implies that there is some kind of transfer of information from one brain to another. But is this always what happens? Don't people sometimes lie to each other, so that the received information is not what was in the first sender's picture of reality? And, perhaps more importantly, don't we sometimes disbelieve things we are told?

Perhaps the receiver is not quite so passive as the model suggests!

PUSH VERSUS PULL STRATEGIES

Two basic strategic alternatives exist for marketing communications, at least as far as promotional activities are concerned. **Push strategy** involves promoting heavily to the members of the distribution channel, i.e. to wholesalers, retailers and agents on the assumption that they will, in turn, promote heavily to the end consumers. In this way the products are pushed through the distribution channel. **Pull strategy** involves promoting heavily to end users and consumers to create a demand that will pull the products through the distribution channels. The ultimate pull strategy was adopted by Levi Strauss (**www.levi.com**) when it launched Levi 501s into the UK market; the firm ran a series of TV adverts before the product was actually available in the shops. This generated consumer demand, which led to the shops demanding that Levi supply the jeans as quickly as possible. An example of a push strategy is the approach taken by pharmaceutical companies when selling prescription drugs. These are promoted heavily to intermediaries (doctors) who then prescribe for patients. Patients rarely have any knowledge of the benefits (or otherwise) of the competing drugs on the market, and would be unlikely to go against the doctor's advice even if they were allowed to participate in the prescribing decision.

Push strategies tend to place the emphasis on personal selling and sales promotion, whereas pull strategies tend to place the emphasis on mass advertising. The two strategies are not mutually exclusive, but rather represent opposite ends of a spectrum; most campaigns contain elements of both.

Competitive advantage might be gained by shifting the emphasis between push and pull. If most of the firms in the industry tend towards a pull strategy, for example, a firm might make considerable gains by promoting to channel intermediaries. Successful promotion here might help shut out competitors from gaining shelf space, might encourage intermediaries to make favourable recommendations to consumers or other intermediaries, and might increase the supplier's control over the distribution channel.

PLANNING THE CAMPAIGN

Table 10.2 shows the activities which need to be carried out when planning the communications campaign.

Having decided the overall plan for the promotional campaign, the marketer needs to decide what the organization can afford. The level of noise from advertising **clutter** means that (unless the creative people are very creative indeed) companies must spend a certain minimum amount to be heard at all, so there is likely to be a minimum level below which there is no point in spending any money at all.

Formulating the most appropriate message is not easy and many organizations undertake marketing research to test understanding and response before launching extensive communications programmes. Some thought needs to be given to the fit between the individual message and those normally communicated from the organization.

Having formulated the message, the planner needs to decide on the appropriate medium (or messenger). A basic taxonomy of promotional tools is the traditional four-way division into advertising, public relations, sales promotion, and personal selling. This taxonomy is really too simplistic; each of the elements subdivides further, and there are several elements which do not readily fit into these categories. For example, T-shirt slogans are clearly communications, but they are not advertising, nor are they really public relations; yet T-shirts with brand logos on, or even adaptations of brand logos, are a common sight and can be considered as marketing communications.

Table 10.2: Communications planning activities

Planning activity	Explanation
Situation analysis	1. Demand factors. These include consumer needs and decision-making processes, cultural and social influences on demand, product category and brand attitudes, individual differences between consumers. 2. Identify the target. It is better to approach a small segment of the market than to try to use a 'scattergun' approach on everybody. 3. Assess the competition - other products, possible competitor responses, etc. 4. Legal and regulatory restrictions that might affect what we are able to do
Defining the objectives	Deciding what the communications are supposed to achieve. It is essential here to give the advertising agency, PR agency, salesforce and indeed everybody associated with the campaign a clear brief: 'We want to raise awareness of the product to 50% of the adult population' is a measurable objective. 'We want to increase sales as much as possible' is not measurable, so there is no way of knowing whether it has been achieved.
Setting the budget	This can be done in four basic ways (there is more on this in Chapter 7). 1. The **objective and task** approach, whereby objectives are set and an appropriate amount of money is set aside. This method is difficult to apply because it is difficult to assess how much will be needed to achieve the objective. 2. The **percentage of sales** approach whereby the budget is set as a percentage of sales. This is based on the false idea that sales create promotion, and usually results in less being spent on marketing communications when sales fall, thus reducing sales further. 3. The **competition matching** approach whereby the company spends the same as the competition means that the firm is allowing its budgets to be set by its enemies. 4. The **arbitrary** approach whereby a senior executive (usually a finance director) simply says how much can be allowed within the firm's overall budgets. This does not take account of how the firm is to achieve the objectives.
Managing the elements of the mix	Media planning. This is about deciding which media will carry the communications. There are two main decision areas: the **reach** (number of potential consumers the communication reaches) and the **frequency** of coverage (number of times each consumer is exposed to the communication). In advertising, the decision is frequently made on the basis of cost per thousand readers/viewers, but this does not take into account the impact of the ad or the degree to which people are able to skip past it. Briefing the sales force. Deciding whether it is to be a push or pull strategy, choosing the PR and support communications.
Creating the platform	Deciding the basic issues and selling points the communication must convey. This clarifies the agency briefings, or at least clarifies the thinking on producing the communications.

TYPES OF CAMPAIGN

Promotional campaigns can take several forms, depending on the message being conveyed and the nature of the target audience. In this context 'message' is defined broadly: a message may be a set of ideas rather than a set of facts, for example.

Image building campaigns are designed to convey a particular status for the product, and to emphasize ways in which it will complement the user's lifestyle. For example, Volvo promotes the reliability and engineering of the car rather than its appearance, thus appealing to motorists who prefer a solid, reliable vehicle. Marlboro cigarettes promotes a masculine, outdoors image.

Product differentiation campaigns aim to show how the product is better than competitors' products by emphasizing its differences. In most cases this will take the form of the **unique selling proposition** or **USP** for short. The USP is the one feature of the product that most stands out as different from the competition, and is usually a feature which conveys unique benefits to the consumer. Mature products often only differ very slightly from each other in terms of performance, so a USP can sometimes be identified in terms of the packaging or distribution, and is very commonly generated by a prestigious brand. Of course, the USP will only be effective if it means something to the consumer – otherwise it will not affect the buying decision.

Positioning strategies are concerned with the way consumers perceive the product compared with their perceptions of the competition (see Chapter 6). For example, a retailer may claim 'lower prices than other shops' or a restaurant may want to appear more up-market than its rivals. Avis car hire (**www.avis.co.uk**) said 'We're Number Two, so we try harder' thus positioning its product as number two in size (behind Hertz (**www.hertz.com**)) but emphasizing the positive aspects of this.

Direct response campaigns seek an immediate response from the consumer in terms of purchase, or request for a brochure, or a visit to the shop. For example, a retailer might run a newspaper campaign which includes a money-off coupon. The aim of the campaign is to encourage consumers to visit the shop to redeem the coupon, and the retailer can easily judge the effectiveness of the campaign by the number of coupons redeemed.

Talking Point

Direct response campaigns are often carried out using mailings, or what is popularly called junk mail. Is junk mail a popular thing for people to receive? The research says not – so why do firms continue to send it out? What response are they aiming for? Surely not the one that most of the mail gets! Or are we really so annoyed by it? Is there sometimes something that comes in that we really feel is worth having? Maybe one really useful mailshot is worth a dozen really annoying ones!

The choice of campaign becomes a strategic issue (rather than a tactical issue) if the purpose of the exercise is to reposition the company or its brand, or to respond to a competitive threat. Budgetary considerations may also apply to the choice of method.

INTEGRATION OF MARKETING COMMUNICATIONS

Recently there has been much interest in the integration of marketing communications. The assumption is that communication will work better if all the various elements which make up an organization's communications are co-ordinated, so that each is 'singing the same song'. Integration of marketing communications is often extended to include corporate communications, reducing the risk of conflicting messages being sent.

Orchestrating an integrated communications strategy is by no means simple. In practice promotional mix elements often operate independently (Duncan and Caywood 1996) with specialist agencies for PR, advertising, exhibitions, corporate identity, branding, etc. all working in isolation. There are nine types or levels of integration, as shown in Table 10.3. Note that these do not necessarily constitute a process, or represent stages of development, and indeed there may be considerable overlap between the types.

Part of the reason for separating the functions is historical; traditionally, marketing communications were divided into **above the line** and **below the line.** Above the line means advertising; below the line means everything else. This came about because of the way advertising agencies were (and to an extent still are) paid. Essentially, agencies are paid commission by the media they place adverts in (usually the rate is 15 per cent of the billing), and/or by fees paid by the client. Traditionally, any paid-for advertising attracted commission (hence above the line) and any other activities such as PR or sales promotion was paid for by fees

Table 10.3: Levels of integration

Level of Integration	Explanation
Awareness stage	Those responsible for communications realize that a fragmented approach is not the optimum one.
Planning integration	The co-ordination of activities. There are two broad approaches: functional integration, which co-ordinates separate tools to create a single message where appropriate; and instrumental integration, which combines tools in such a way that they reinforce one another (Bruhn 1995).
Integration of content	Ensuring that there are no contradictions in the basic brand or corporate messages. At a higher level, integrating the themes of communication to make the basic messages the same.
Formal integration	Using the same logo, corporate colours, graphic approach and house style for all communications.
Integration between planning periods	Basic content remains the same from one campaign to the next. Either basic content remains the same, or the same executional approach is used in different projects.
Intra-organizational integration	Integration of the activities of everyone involved in communication functions (which could mean everybody who works in the organization).
Inter-organizational integration	Integration of all the outside agencies involved in the firm's communications activities.
Geographical integration	Integration of campaigns in different countries. This is strongest in large multinationals which operate globally, e.g. the Coca-Cola Corporation (Hartley and Pickton 1997).
Integration of publics	All communications targeted to one segment of the market are integrated (horizontal integration) or all communications targeted to different segments are attuned (vertical integration).

(hence below the line). As time has gone by these distinctions have become more blurred, especially with the advent of **advertorials** (advertisements which look like editorial) which are usually written by journalists, and with ambient advertising and other new media which do not attract commission.

To an extent, strong branding will tend to lead to the integration of marketing communications since it acts as a focusing device for the firm's messages about products. For many firms, the corporation itself becomes the brand and has a brand image which transfers to all its activities and products (Virgin (**www.virgin.com**) being a prime example of this). For these firms, the integration of communications becomes a company-wide concern, not just the province of the individual brand managers as it would be in most fast-moving consumer goods (FMCG) firms.

There is increasing interest in integration of marketing communications, and this is being extended to include all corporate communications (Nowak and Phelps 1994). The need for integration is shown in the following factors (Borremans 1998):

1. Changes in the consumer market:

- The information overload caused by the ever-increasing number of commercial messages.

- Advertising in the mass media is increasingly irritating.

- Media fragmentation.

- Increasing numbers of 'me-too' products, where differences between brands are minor.

- Complexity and change in FMCG markets, with increased distances between suppliers and consumers making it harder for publics to have an image of suppliers.

- Increasing media attention to the social behaviour of companies, putting goodwill at a premium.

2. Changes in the supplier market:

- Multiple acquisitions and changes in structure in and around corporations.
- Interest of management in short-term results.
- Increased recognition of the strategic importance of communication.
- Increased interest in good internal communications with employees.

Integration offers the possibility of reducing the ambiguity of messages emanating from the firm, and also of reducing costs by reducing duplication of effort. There are barriers to integration (Petrison and Wang 1996); in some circumstances, attempts to force integration might be inappropriate or would actually detract from the effectiveness of communications since the communications themselves are tailored to specific markets or circumstances.

- **Database marketing** allows customers to be targeted with individually-tailored communications. Integrated communications are almost always mass methods which would reduce the opportunities to tailor messages to individuals.
- **Niche marketing** and **micromarketing** mean that suppliers can communicate with very small and specific audiences, using different messages for each group. This tends to militate against integration.
- Specific methods and working practices used for different communication tools will affect the message each transmits, making integration difficult.
- Corporate diversification means that messages which are appropriate for one branch of the corporation may not work elsewhere.
- Different international (and even national) cultures mean that a single message comprehensible to all is difficult to achieve.
- Existing structures within organizations mean that different departments may not be able or willing to 'sing the same song'. For example, salespeople may not agree with the public relations department's ideas on what customers should be told.
- Personal resistance to change, and managers' fear of losing responsibilities and budgets, may prevent centralization of communications. This is particularly true of firms which have adopted the brand manager system of management.

Overall, the advantages of integrating communications almost certainly overcome the drawbacks, since the cost savings and the reduction of ambiguity are clearly important objectives for most marketers. There is, however, the danger of losing the capacity to tailor messages for individuals (as happens in personal selling) or for niches in the market, and there are certainly some major creative problems attached to integrating communications on a global scale.

THE STRATEGIC ROLE OF PERSONAL SELLING

Personal selling is usually considered to be part of the promotional mix, along with sales promotion, advertising, and publicity. Each of the other elements is usually a one-way communication, but personal selling is unique in that it always offers a two-way communication with the prospective customer. This is partly what makes personal selling such a powerful instrument; the salesperson can clarify points, answer queries, and raise the profile of issues which seem to be of greatest interest to the prospect.

Salespeople will, of course, have considerable knowledge of the products in the range, and probably of the industry in general. The customer can therefore 'pick the salesperson's brains' for useful information to help in the problem-solving. The customer's knowledge of his or her unique situation combines with the salesperson's knowledge of products and industry to generate a creative solution. This is shown in Fig 10.3 below.

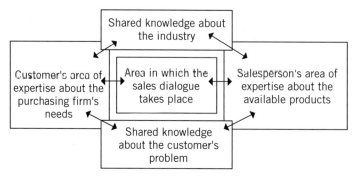

Figure 10.3: Areas of knowledge and the sales dialogue

Although some customers still regard salespeople with suspicion, the evidence is that salespeople in fact seek to develop and maintain good relationships with their customers even when this conflicts with instructions from their marketing departments (Anderson and Robertson 1995).

For the customer, the salesperson is a source of information, a source of help in problem-solving, and is an advocate back to the supplying company. Good salespeople are also adept at helping their customers through the decision-making process; often this is the hardest part of making a sale.

Talking Point

Interestingly, many people have tales to tell about how helpful a salesman was – and very few people have tales to tell about salespeople who were pushy or aggressive. So why do salespeople have such a bad reputation? Why is it that salespeople are sometimes reluctant to tell people what they do for a living?

Is it perhaps because we believe, deep down, that salespeople have the power to manipulate us? That maybe they can work some spell on us to make us part with our money – and smile while we do so? Or is it just that salespeople make convenient scapegoats for our own lack of judgement in buying inappropriate products?

Marketers have long taken the attitude that selling is somehow antithetical to marketing. Peter Drucker's famous quote that 'the aim of marketing is to make selling superfluous' has certainly hit home with marketers (Drucker 1973). Drucker says that there will always be some need for selling, but that marketing's aim is to produce products that are so ideally suited to the customer that the product 'sells itself'. This view of personal selling has coloured marketing thinking for 25 years, and it is often coupled with Levitt's statement that 'selling focuses on the needs of the seller; marketing on the needs of the buyer' (Levitt 1960). The net result is that marketers have tended to adopt a suspicious view of selling; at worst, salespeople are viewed as dinosaurs, forever wedded to the selling concept (which has little to do with the practice of selling) and at best they are viewed as a necessary evil, filling in the gaps in the communications mix. Marketers appear to be working to the model shown in Fig 10.4.

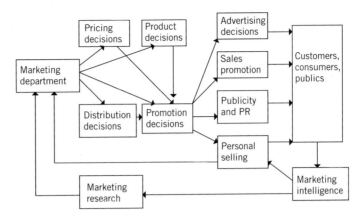

Figure 10.4: Marketer's view of the role of personal selling

Feedback for decision-making can come from two sources: marketing research, and from the salesforce. Since market researchers are paid by the hour not by the result, the information obtained from marketing research is often assumed to be unbiased, objective and untainted by a desire to maximize earnings; unlike the information from the salesforce which is often assumed to be subjective and therefore less reliable. For example, Gordon et al. (1997) found that the salesforce could not be relied upon as a source of information for new product development.

Equally, it has been claimed that the detailed information the salesforce can provide on each individual customer can be replaced by low-cost databases (Dwyer, Schurr, and Oh 1987) and combinations of databases can fill gaps in that knowledge. At first sight the marketer's view of personal selling appears to allow for replacement of selling with other (often IT-based) techniques.

Undoubtedly personal selling does have a major communications element, involving as it does a two-way dialogue between salesperson and prospect, but there is a great deal more to personal selling than this. An examination of what salespeople actually do will clarify this.

Firstly, the emphasis in selling practice is not on telling, but on asking. The salesperson's role in the sales presentation is characterized not by persuasive sales talk, but by asking appropriate questions to find out the prospect's needs, and to lead the discussion and negotiation in a particular direction. DeCormier and Jobber (1993) found a total of 13 different types of question in use by salespeople. Rackham (1991) categorized questions in four dimensions: situation, problem, implication and need-payoff. In each case the emphasis is on asking the prospect about his/her situation, with a view to finding a solution from among the salesperson's portfolio of products. Note that the needs of the buyer are paramount; the salesperson is asking questions; the marketing department's 'message' is not relevant to this core process.

For salespeople, then, the model of the relationship between marketing and sales will look more like that shown in Fig 10.5. In this model, the salesforce does the real work of finding out customers' needs and fulfilling them, and the marketing department exists mainly to provide back-up services. Marketers provide information to the salesforce, and to the production department, but the salesforce exists to solve customers' problems using products supplied by production.

For the salesperson adopting this model, the marketing department occupies a subservient role. Since the salesforce is in the 'front line', dealing directly with the customers, it is clear that every other department in the firm depends on them to bring in the business. It is, in fact, the only department which brings in money; everything else only generates costs. Sales training

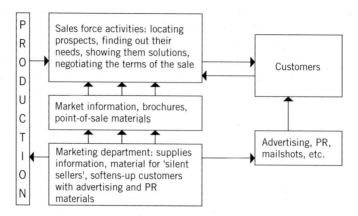

Figure 10.5: Salesperson's model of the relationship between marketing and selling

programmes sometimes emphasize this. Salespeople are told that the average salesperson supports five other jobs, they are told that 'nothing happens until somebody sells something', they are encouraged to think of themselves as the most important people in the firm. Furthermore, recent research has shown that many salespeople are defensive of their good relationships with customers even when this conflicts with instructions from the marketing department, since it is easier for salespeople to find a new company to work for than it is to find new customers (Anderson and Robertson 1995).

While there may be some justification for this, it is equally true to say that salespeople would have nothing to sell were it not for the efforts of the production department, would have no pay-packet and no invoicing without the finance department, would have no deliveries without the shipping department, and so forth. Salespeople may be given a false view of their own importance, but trainers may do this in order to counteract the often negative image and low status that selling has in the eyes of other departments.

In this model, the salesforce collects information about the customer from the marketing department's research and directly from the customer. Product, price, delivery, sales promotion and the use of advertising and PR materials (contained in the salesperson's **'silent seller'**) are all used in negotiation with the customer, with the aim of obtaining an optimum solution for both parties in terms of both information exchange and product/price exchange.

For many salespeople, the marketing department also paves the way for a sales call by providing publicity and advertising; it is obviously easier for a salesperson to make a call knowing that the prospect has already heard of the company and has some favourable impressions. For the salesperson, the marketing department performs a support function, providing a set of products to choose from, a price structure to negotiate around, a distribution system which can be tailored to suit the customer, and promotional back-up in the form of advertising and publicity. Sales promotions are used as ways of closing sales (as deal-makers) but the basic problem-solving and decision-making is done by the salespeople when they are with the customer.

In fact, it is this problem-solving and decision-making function that distinguishes the salesforce from other 'promotional tools'. The salesforce does not think of itself as being primarily a communicator; but primarily as decision-makers.

If the salespeople are correct in this view, then it would clearly be impossible to replace them with a database (at least, given the current state of the art). The computer can hold and manipulate information very effectively, but is unable to solve problems creatively or negotiate effectively, or indeed establish a long-term relationship on a human level. For these functions a human being is necessary.

Salespeople therefore occupy a strategic role in marketing rather than the tactical role which is usually assigned to them. The distinction between salespeople and marketing people is, in many companies, an artificial one. The salespeople can be viewed as field marketers, as opposed to the desk marketers who work from the office. Nowhere is this strategic role of salespeople clearer than in the management of major accounts.

MAJOR ACCOUNT MANAGEMENT

Major accounts (or key accounts as they are also known) have the following characteristics (Donaldson 1998):

■ They account for a significant proportion of existing or potential business for the firm.
■ They form part of a supply chain in which efficiency is enhanced by co-operation rather than conflict.
■ Working interdependently with these customers, rather than independently, has benefits in lower transaction costs, better quality or joint product development – perhaps all three of these benefits.
■ Supply involves not just product but other service aspects, whether technical support, just-in-time manufacturing, or market development potential.
■ There are advantages to both parties in close, open relationships rather than a focus on transaction efficiency.

Customers can be classified in terms of their relationship with the firm, as shown in Table 10.4.

As firms move through these stages, the level of involvement with the customer increases and becomes more complex, and the relationship becomes more collaborative.

Table 10.4: The relational development model (Millman and Wilson 1995)

Stage	Explanation
Pre-key account management	The preparation and identification of potential key accounts, now and in the future. The decision is based on the nature of the exchange; if it is low-value and essentially transactional, key-account management is unlikely to be necessary.
Early KAM	An initial order has been received, and the emphasis is now on building on that order to develop a longer-term and more strategic relationship. Opportunities for increasing the firm's involvement with the customer are being sought; for example, setting up training programmes, offering technical support or carrying out joint promotions.
Mid-KAM	At this stage the buyer is becoming committed to the firm, although other competitors may still be involved. The buyer will expect to be given preferential treatment, but will also be prepared to give some preferential treatment in return. Negotiation is important at this stage; the future relationship between the parties will depend largely on what is agreed at this time.
Partnership KAM	This develops from the mid-KAM stage. At this point each party is committed to the other, there is open discussion of needs and wants, and a number of joint initiatives will be undertaken.
Synergistic KAM	At this level, the companies are almost synonymous with one another, but there has not actually been a merger. The problem now becomes one of internal and external co-ordination to ensure the achievement of mutual objectives. In a sense, the salesforce is no longer involved at this stage; the staff of both firms will be involved directly or indirectly in ensuring a close fit between the firms.

Managing the process begins with salespeople, but as the firms move through the stages of KAM other staff become involved – brand managers, distribution managers, production managers and so forth until virtually all the executive specialists in each firm will have some involvement. Consequently the salespeople need to occupy a much greater strategic and planning role than they would in a transaction-based selling environment.

Managing major accounts must, in the initial stages, be left to those who have the closest contact with the customers. This means that sales management in a major account environment takes on a completely different complexion. Managers need to adopt an even more hands-off approach than is normal in sales management, and must be particularly careful not to place themselves in a position where the client company becomes dependent on them (Rackham 1991). Since major accounts are, by their nature, of strategic importance, very good communications need to be maintained with the salespeople who handle this crucial part of establishing customer relationships.

Major-account management does not necessarily imply bottom-up strategy development. It may be that the key-account salespeople are, in fact, senior decision-makers within the firm, and are accorded a high status. For a customer-orientated firm this structure would make sense – the salespeople need to be given the authority to carry through the wishes of the customers, and to make the necessary changes within the firm to cement the relationships they initiate.

STRATEGY AND THE INTERNET

Internet marketing (e-commerce) has been widely billed as the wave of the future. As a communication tool, the Internet offers the opportunity to access a valuable market segment: computer-literate, relatively wealthy individuals, often at the younger end of the age spectrum, and representative of a global market of epic proportions. Within this segment, sub-segments can be identified, and the market further divided.

At another level, the Internet offers an entirely new approach to marketing. Firms which embrace the full possibilities of the Internet are cutting out whole stages in the implementation of marketing strategies. For example, some firms distribute their products entirely over the Internet, with only the physical distribution to be taken care of, usually by subcontracting to logistics facilitators. The Net will eventually replace some marketing approaches altogether.

Internet marketing has the characteristics outlined in Table 10.5.

Current thinking is that the effect of increased use of the Net for marketing purposes will eventually lead to a new environment for marketing. The speed of information flow within firms, especially those operating globally, will mean greater possibilities for real-time negotiations between firms. The rapid growth in virtual shopping (accessing catalogues on the Internet) means that consumers can buy goods anywhere in the world and have them shipped – or, in the case of computer software, simply downloaded – which means that global competition will reach unprecedented levels. Because of the availability of colour monitors, virtual shoppers are able to access high-quality pictures of products, holiday destinations, and even pictures of restaurant food before committing to a purchase. A recent development is **webcasting:** the automatic delivery of items of interest direct to the individual's PC. Webcasting involves the subscriber in stating in advance what type of information he or she is interested in, and having this automatically delivered by the webcaster, thus avoiding the time and effort spent in searching the Net using a search engine.

Table 10.5: Characteristics of the Internet as a marketing tool

Characteristic	Explanation
Communication style	The style is interactive, and is either synchronous (happens immediately) or asynchronous (there are significant time delays between message and response).
Social presence	The feeling that the communications are taking place at a personal level. Social presence is influenced by the characteristics of the channel; a telephone is more personal than a newspaper advert, for example. Internet communications have relatively high social presence if they are synchronous, particularly as the recipient is usually within his or her home environment when the communication takes place.
Consumer control of contact	Because the consumers are able to control the time and place at which they access the information, they are more willing to participate in the process of getting information from a machine (Carson, Peck and Childers 1996).
Consumer control of content	If the consumers can control the content of the message to some extent, the communication becomes truly interactive (Anderson 1996). For example, a consumer accessing a website can use a hyperlink to move to another page, or can skip past information. An e-mail address allows customers to ask specific questions and thus tailor the communications.

Talking Point

Research shows that the most irritating form of marketing communication is junk mail. Perhaps it's the feeling that our privacy has been invaded, that the advertisers have come into our homes with their messages. Perhaps it's simply a sense of annoyance about wasting time opening the letters, only to find that it's another attempt to get our money off us.

So why is it that people seem quite happy to allow webcasting? Surely allowing marketers to invade our computers is an even greater compromise of our privacy? On the one hand we clamour for laws to protect us from unsolicited mail, but on the other hand we are quite happy to invite marketers in to share our cyberspace – and even place cookies in our PCs so that they get to know our buying habits!

Or perhaps it is the element of invitation that makes the difference? The trusted friend, rather than the doorstep salesman?

Self-selection of messages is dependant on level of involvement (Carson, Peck and Childers 1996), and since the Net represents sought communication the messages should be informative rather than persuasive. The Web is not merely a simulation of the real world, it is an alternative to it in which consumers can have the illusion of being present in a computer-mediated environment (Hoffman and Novak 1996). Consumers have a role in creating the communications themselves; bulletin boards attract users, and the success of the board attracts more users and adds credibility to the site. This means that more consumers will see the marketer's messages. Bulletin boards of newsgroups allow marketers to monitor the success of word-of-mouth campaigns, and can also be directly useful in market research; Web users' comments are often useful in assessing consumer attitudes.

Other research possibilities inherent in the Web include virtual focus groups and rapid concept testing of new products. Increased consumer control of the communication channels may even result in consumers being able to invite tenders for supplying major purchases such as cars and home improvements (Hoffman and Novak 1996), and (given the flexibility and speed of response of the Web) some firms will find this extremely advantageous. Although many of these consumers will be shopping for the lowest price, it should be possible to follow up these leads with further information as well as a quotation.

However, the following assumptions underpin the Utopian forecasts being made about the impact of the Net (Benjamin and Wigand 1995):

■ All consumers and organizations will be interconnected.

■ The connections will be at a high enough bandwidth to support multimedia transactions.

■ That access and use will be affordable.

■ The technology will provide interactive capabilities sufficient to make free market choices easy.

■ No favouritism will be designed into the systems by governments or other vested interests.

There are several mitigating factors which are likely to impede progress towards a virtual marketplace. These are as shown in Table 10.6.

Table 10.6: Factors limiting growth of the Internet

Factor	Explanation and examples
Technophobia	Substantial numbers of people have considerable resistance to the technology. Currently use of the Net requires a degree of computer literacy which is not present in the majority of the population, although voice-operated computers will reduce this problem.
Cost of connection and use	Most of the predictions of growth have been based on research in the US and to a lesser extent Australia. In the US, local telephone calls are free, so connection to the Net only costs the subscription fee paid to the Net service provider. In Australia, local calls are charged at a flat rate irrespective of the time the call takes. In most of the rest of the world, calls to the server are charged by the minute, and thus a lengthy session surfing the Net can prove very expensive for the average consumer.
Pressure on the system	The number of subscribers has increased so fast that the technology has had difficulty in keeping up. This problem is now less than it was, as the number of subscribers shows signs of topping out.
Cost of hardware	Although costs of computer equipment are dropping dramatically, and WebTV (devices for accessing the Net via an ordinary TV screen) are being developed, the cost is still high enough to deter many potential users in lower socio-economic groupings, and certainly high enough to prevent access by most of the Third World. This means that the Net is still likely to be the virtual world of the relatively rich for some considerable time to come.

A further use of the Net is to use internal networks within the firm to replace or supplement internal communications such as staff newsletters. This can have a stronger effect than paper versions, because it is rather harder to ignore; the staff member is generally more likely to read an e-mail than to open a staff newsletter, and the e-mail version is also quicker and cheaper to produce and distribute. In some organizations paper memos and newsletters have virtually disappeared (although so many people make hard copies of their e-mails that the paperless office is still some way off).

The main problem with making any predictions about the Internet is that events move extremely rapidly in the virtual world. Recent government initiatives have been announced in the UK to arrange for free access to the Internet for those in lower socio-economic groups; on the other hand, UK cable company, NTL (**www.ntl.com**), has been forced to introduce charges for Internet access for all its subscribers due to increasing financial problems. The rapidity of change makes it difficult for planners to take a strategic approach to the Internet, since strategy (by definition) is about the longer-term view of the organization's objectives and approaches.

CORPORATE BRANDING

Corporate branding is about establishing an overall image of the organization. This has strategic implications in the following ways:

- Firms with a strong corporate brand are perceived more favourably by shareholders.
- Firms with a strong corporate brand tend to ride out crises much better – their stakeholders tend to be more forgiving.
- Strong corporate branding has spin-offs in terms of recruitment and retention of both employees and customers.
- Corporate branding has a halo effect on product branding.

Corporate brand architecture carries with it three alternative approaches: a monolithic structure, an endorsed brand structure, or a hybrid structure.

The monolithic structure has the corporate brand at its centre, with all the product brands carrying the same logo and brand values, but with variations to distinguish the products. For example, Virgin operates a monolithic structure in which the Virgin logo attaches to everything from cola drinks through to airlines. The advantage of this structure is that each product transfers goodwill to the centre. The major drawback is that the reverse is also the case – a product which performs badly will cause a loss of goodwill towards the other products in the range.

An endorsed brand structure seeks to establish each product brand in its own right, but to transfer the values of the corporate brand to the product brands in order to strengthen them further and provide a cohesive whole. An endorsed brand strategy has the advantage that the transfer of goodwill is more likely to be one-way: in other words, it is relatively easy for a firm to isolate the corporate brand from a failing product brand. This approach is taken by major car manufacturers such as Ford (**www.ford.com**). Ford has several individual product brands (Ka, Focus, Mondeo) as well as discrete brands such as Jaguar which operates almost as a separate corporation. Other firms allow the product brands to stand out more, with the corporate brand being lower-key. 3M and Mars operate in this way.

Hybrid strategies have become more common in recent years with the increase in globalization. A hybrid strategy involves setting up a number of 'banner' brands which act as umbrellas for a number of product brands. This works best when a global company has well-established brand names in different countries, so that local brand values can be communicated to different products.

CORPORATE BRAND MANAGEMENT

Corporate brands need to be rounded and meaningful for all stakeholders. The most successful corporate brands of recent years are those which have projected the vision of the firm's founder: putting the corporation on a human level appears to be a strategy with which stakeholders can identify. Public relations is far and away the most important element in creating a strong corporate brand.

Sponsorship of the arts or sporting events has proved to be an effective way of raising the corporate image. Sponsorship attempts to link beliefs about the sponsoring organization or brand and connecting them to an event or organization that is highly valued by target consumers (Erdogan and Kitchen 1998).

Sponsorship will not be effective unless it is part of a broader marketing communications strategy. Two to three times the cost of sponsorship should be budgeted for advertising if the exercise is to be effective (Heffler 1994). The advertising is used to clarify the reasons for the firm's sponsorship of the event. For example, a firm which simply calls itself 'Official sponsors of the Triathlon' will not be as successful as one which says 'Our snack gives energy – and that's what every triathlete needs more than anything. That's why we sponsor the Triathlon.'. Sports enthusiasts would be quite prepared to read and absorb this explanation.

Research shows that consumers do feel at least some gratitude towards the sponsors of their favourite events; whether this is gratitude per se or whether it is affective linking is hard to say, but the difference is probably academic since the results are the same (Crimmins and Horn 1996). There are certainly spin-offs for the internal PR of the firm; most employees like to feel that they are working for a caring organization, and sponsorship money also (on occasion) leads to free tickets or price reductions for staff of the sponsoring organization.

Corporate brand management depends heavily on public relations, but corporate advertising also has a role to play.

CORPORATE IMAGE ADVERTISING

Corporate image advertising can be considered as an extension of PR. In a sense, it falls somewhere between true advertising and public relations. Instead of advertising specific brands or products, the advertising promotes the firm's image. Expenditure on corporate advertising tends to be low, because the results are intangible (and seldom directly related to market share) and this makes it difficult to justify to senior management. Corporate advertising can achieve important objectives, as follows:

1. Ensure that the company's activities are properly understood by its publics.
2. Generate new behaviour from stakeholders based on increased knowledge of the firm and its values.
3. Ensure that the company's view is communicated without the filtering (and occasionally mutating) effect of putting a press release through the editorial process.

The techniques that are used will depend on which of the firm's publics is being addressed, and what the objective of the exercise is. BOC Group (**www.boc.com**) increased its stock market valuation by several million pounds by advertising to an audience of less than 50 chemical industry analysts in the City of London (Maitland 1983). Conversely, British Telecom (BT) (**www.bt.com**) ran a corporate image campaign on TV, billboards and in the press which cost £16m and was intended (among other things) to improve the nation's perception of BT's technology (Newman 1986). The campaign worked; perception of BT's use of up-to-date technology rose by 15 per cent following the campaign.

The purpose of corporate advertising is basically the same as for press releases and other public relations exercises: to establish a positive image for the company. It is not directly about making sales (although sales often do increase, because the favourable impression of the firm tends to spill over into a belief that the products are better, more reliable or more ethical), but it is rather about making the management task easier by smoothing the path of progress.

Corporate advertising has the following characteristics:

1. It is intended for long-term image-building, not immediate sales.
2. It rarely mentions specific brands or their features and benefits.
3. It does not require any immediate response from the observer.
4. The advertisements appeal to the reader's cognition rather than to affect (although the effect may be affective).

PRODUCT PLACEMENT

Product placement (the placing of brands in films and TV shows) also contributes strongly to establishing a positive image of the firm. Film and TV producers accept a contribution towards the cost of making the show in exchange for ensuring that the firm's products are displayed prominently or are used by the actors. The advantages of this are that the product takes on the values of the film. For example, Aston Martin (**www.astonmartin.com**) paid substantially towards the cost of making the early James Bond films, in exchange for which the producers specified that James Bond would drive an Aston Martin. Unfortunately for Aston Martin, when the film *Tomorrow Never Dies* was made the cost of product placement was too high, and the contract went to BMW.

Product placement has the advantage that the audience are scarcely aware that it is happening, and therefore do not filter out the promotional message. The potential disadvantage is that if the film flops, the sponsorship money is wasted (at best) or the brand image is damaged (at worst).

CASE STUDY: LASTMINUTE.COM

www.lastminute.com

Lastminute.com floated on the UK stock market in March 2000, with a valuation of £730 m, despite having only been launched in November 1998. The company could not have existed without the Internet, because it offers a service which ordinary 'off-line' companies are unable to provide.

Lastminute.com sells services such as theatre tickets, hotel rooms, flights, restaurant bookings and even hairdressing appointments over the Internet. The essence of Lastminute.com is that customers can book the service of their choice instantly, on the date they want, right up to the last minute. For the consumer, this means that a last-minute bargain can often result, while for the service provider it means that the highly perishable goods on offer can be disposed of rather than lost forever.

Of course, airlines and hotels have traditionally offered late-booking bargains; it is better to sell an aeroplane seat for a low price than have the 'plane take off with seats unsold. The difference with Lastminute.com is that the process becomes virtually instantaneous due to the rapid communicating and processing power of computers and the Internet. For the airlines, this means they can sell tickets at the normal price much later than they could previously, knowing that they should be able to dispose of any remaining seats easily (and instantly) over the Net.

Founders Brent Hoberman and Martha Lane Fox are both young (30 and 26 respectively) and had planned the idea for the company for some years; they needed to wait for the right moment to launch the idea, and the growth of the Internet was the spur needed to get the enterprise off the ground. The company began with £600,000 of funding, but went on to raise a further £6.6 m from venture capitalists. Much of this funding was used to promote the company, mainly (paradoxically) through off-line media such as print advertising, billboard advertising, and posters on the London Underground.

The company's ethos is to 'encourage spontaneous, romantic, and sometimes adventurous behaviour by helping our users to live their dreams at unbeatable prices'. Given the pace at which most people live nowadays, Lastminute.com aims to enable people to make the most of their limited

▶

▶ free time. This has meant recruiting a large number of partner companies; the firm's suppliers include 30 airlines, 500 hotels, 75 tour operators, 60 restaurants and 120 gift suppliers. The company brings suppliers and customers together virtually instantaneously to generate benefits for both.

Part of the reason for the company's success is its care over choosing suppliers. Each company wishing to join Lastminute.com goes through a rigorous vetting procedure; Lastminute.com intends to ensure that the final consumers always have a good experience. One of the problems facing the company is that it has little control over the quality of the service the customer receives, so it needs to be particularly careful about the part of the process that is in its direct control.

Fox and Hoberman intend to extend the service further to include other service products such as taxis, childminders, laundry services, and other transport systems. The firm also aims to expand rapidly in countries where Internet access is higher than in the UK, for example in Scandinavia, Germany and France.

So far, the company has not been running long enough to generate a profit of any sort; this has made analysts all the more surprised that this small company (less than 150 employees) is worth almost as much as some long-established retailers such as WH Smith. Part of the reason for the high valuation is undoubtedly the 'dotcom fever' which gripped City investors, but there is little doubt that Lastminute.com has staked a claim to what would appear to be a very lucrative market with tremendous growth potential.

CASE STUDY QUESTIONS

1. Why might a customer contact Lastminute.com rather than simply call an airline direct?
2. What benefits does Lastminute.com offer to its suppliers?
3. What benefits does Lastminute.com offer to the consumers?
4. What branding problems might the firm encounter as it extends the service?
5. How might Lastminute.com ensure that its consumers have a good experience?

SUMMARY

Communications strategy is at the heart of good marketing practice since it is at the interface between the firm and its publics. From the viewpoint of the general public, and the firm's customers in particular, marketing communications actually are the company; messages conveyed by salespeople, advertising, product attributes and all the other components of the brand are the basis for decision-making by customers.

The key points from this chapter are as follows:

■ The traditional categorization of communications into selling, sales promotion, advertising and PR is a gross oversimplification.

■ Creating a strategic communications mix is like following a recipe; ingredients must be added at the right time, and in the right quantities.

■ Strategic competitive advantage can be gained through effective integrated communications.

■ Messages can be consistent without being identical.

■ Personal selling is a strategic element rather than a tactical one.

■ Major account management is always a strategic issue, but must be dealt with at a tactical level.

CHAPTER QUESTIONS

1. Why might a 'push' strategy be used to market life insurance?

2. How might individuals within an organization be encouraged to adopt an integrated communications strategy?

3. Why might some firms still operate under a selling concept?

4. Why should managers allow major-account salespeople to make their own judgements about how to handle the account?

5. If major account salespeople are allowed a free hand in communicating with their prospective customers, how can this be reconciled with an integrated communications policy?

REFERENCES

Anderson, Erin and Robertson, Thomas S. (1995): 'Inducing Multi-line Salespeople to Adopt House Brands', *Journal of Marketing* vol. 59 no. 2 (Apr) pp. 16–31.

Anderson, C. (1996): 'Computers as Audience: Mediated Interactive Messages in Interactive Marketing' in Forrest, E. and Hiyerski, R. (eds) *The Future Present* ch. 11 (Chicago: AMA).

Benjamin, R. and Wigand, R. (1995): 'Electronic Markets and Virtual Value Chains on the Information Superhighway', *Sloan Management Review* Winter pp. 62–72.

Booms, B.H. and Bitner, M.J. (1981): 'Marketing Strategies and Organization Structures for Service Firms', in *Marketing of Services* J. Donnelly and W.R. George, eds, American Marketing Association 1981.

Borremans, T. (1998): 'Integrated (Marketing) Communications in Practice'; Survey Among Communication, Public Relations and Advertising Agencies in Belgium. Proceedings of the 3rd Annual Conference of the Global Institute for Corporate and Marketing Communications.

Brassington, Frances and Pettitt, Stephen (1997): *Principles of Marketing* (London: Pitman Publishing).

Bruhn, M. (1995): *Intergrierte Unternehmenskommunikation: Ansatzpunkte fur eine Strategische und Operative Umseitzung Integreirter Kommunikationsarbeit.* (Stuttgart: Schaffer-Poeschel).

Carson, S., Peck, J. and Childers, T. (1996): 'Preliminary Results on the Determinants of Technology Assisted Shopping: A Model, Measure Development and Validation'. Proceedings of the AMA Winter Educators' Conference, pp. 229–39

Cooper, Simon (1997): *Selling; Principles, Practice and Management* (London: Pitman Publishing).

Copulsky, J.R. and Wolf, M.J. (1990): 'Relationship Marketing; Positioning for the Future', *Journal of Business Strategies* 11, no. 4, pp. 16–20.

Crimmins, J. and Horn, M. (1996): 'Sponsorship: From Management Ego Trip to Marketing Success', *Journal of Advertising Research* vol. 36 iss. 4 (Jul/Aug) pp. 11–21.

DeCormier, R. and Jobber, D. (1993): 'The Counsellor Selling Method; Concepts, Constructs, and Effectiveness', *Journal of Personal Selling and Sales Management*, 13(4), pp. 39–60.

Dewsnap, B. and Jobber, D. (1998): 'The Sales and Marketing Interface; Is It Working?'. Proceedings of the Academy of Marketing Conference, Sheffield.

Dibb, Simkin, Pride & Ferrell (1994) *Marketing Concepts and Strategies* second European edition (Houghton Mifflin).

Donaldson, B. (1998): *Sales Management Theory and Practice* (London: MacMillan Business).

Drucker, P.F (1973): *Management; Tasks, Responsibilities, Practices* (New York: Harper & Row).

Duncan, T. and Caywood, C. (1996): 'The Concept, Process and Evolution of Integrated Marketing Communication', pp. 13–34 in Thorson, E. and Moore, J. *Integrated Communication. Synergy of Persuasive Voices* (Mahwah: Lawrence Erlbaum).

Dwyer, R.F., Schurr, P.H. and Oh, S. (1987): 'Developing Buyer-Seller Relationships', *Journal of Marketing* 51, April, pp. 11–27.

Erdogan, B. and Kitchen, P.J. (1998): 'The Interaction between Advertising and Sponsorship: Uneasy Alliance or Strategic Symbiosis?' Proceedings of the 3rd Annual Conference of the Global Institute for Corporate and Marketing Communications, Strathclyde Graduate Business School.

Evans, M.J. (1994): 'Domesday Marketing?' *Journal of Marketing Management* vol. 10, no.5 pp. 409–31.

Gordon, G.L., Schoenbachler, D.D., Kaminski, P.F. and Brouchous, K.A. (1997): 'New Product Development; Using the Salesforce to Identify Opportunities', *Journal of Business and Industrial Marketing* vol. 12, no. 1, pp. 33–50.

Hartley, B. and Pickton, D. (1997): 'Integrated Marketing Communications – A New Language for a New Era'. Proceedings of the 2nd International Conference on Marketing and Corporate Communications, Antwerp.

Heffler, M. (1994): 'Making Sure Sponsorship Meets All the Parameters', *Brandweek*, May p.16.

Hoffman, D. and Novak, T. (1996): 'A New Marketing Paradigm for Electronic Commerce', The Information Society 13(1).

Levitt, T. (1960): 'Marketing Myopia', *Harvard Business Review* July-Aug. pp. 45–56.

Lund, Philip R. (1979): *Compelling Selling* (London: MacMillan).

Maitland, A.J. (1983): 'To see ourselves as others see us', *The BOC Group Management Magazine*.

Millman, T. and Wilson, K. (1995): 'From key account selling to key account management', *Journal of Marketing Practice* 1 (1) pp. 9–21.

Newman, K. (1986): *The Selling of British Telecom* (New York: Holt, Rinehart and Winston).

Nowak, G. and Phelps, J. (1994): 'Conceptualising the Integrated Marketing Communications Phenomenon', *Journal of Current Issues and Research in Advertising* vol. 16, 1, Spring pp. 49–66.

Peppers, D. and Rogers, M. (1995): 'A New Marketing Paradigm: Share of Customer, not Market Share', *Planning Review* 23, no. 2, pp. 14–18.

Petrison, L.A. and Wang, P. (1996): 'Integrated Marketing Communication: An Organizational Perspective', pp. 167–184 in Thorson, E., and Moore, J., *Integrated Communication. Synergy of Persuasive Voices* (Mahwah: Lawrence Erlbaum).

'Public Relations Practice – Its Roles and Parameters' (London: The Institute of Public Relations, 1984).

Rackham, N. (1991): *The Management of Major Sales* (Gower, 1991).

Zikmund, William G. and D'Amico, Michael (1995): *Marketing* (St. Paul MN: West).

Chapter Eleven

Strategy and Distribution

INTRODUCTION

Producing something that consumers would like to buy is only part of the story; people can only buy products which are available and easily obtained. In terms of the seven Ps distribution is the means by which place is determined. Marketers therefore spend considerable effort on finding the right channels of distribution, and on ensuring that the products reach consumers in the most efficient way.

After reading this chapter, you should be able to:

- Understand the role of distribution as providing an integral part of the product's benefits.
- Be able to explain the way agents, wholesalers, and retailers work in the distribution system.
- Be able to choose the best distribution channel for achieving strategic aims in a given market segment and for a given product.
- Be able to explain some of the challenges facing retailers.
- Know what to expect of different types of wholesaler.
- Understand the difference between logistics and distribution.

LOGISTICS VERSUS DISTRIBUTION

Physical distribution is concerned with the ways organizations get the physical product to a point where it is most convenient for the consumer to buy it. Physical distribution is to do with transportation methods; distribution strategy decisions are about which outlets should be used for the product. The purpose of any physical distribution method is to get the product from its point of production to the consumer in as efficient and effective a way as possible. The product must arrive in good condition, and fit the consumer's need for convenience, or cheapness, or choice, or whatever else the particular target market thinks is important. Thus, from a marketing viewpoint, the subject of distribution covers such areas as transportation methods, wholesaling, High Street retailing, direct mail marketing, and even farm-gate shops.

In some ways the physical distribution of a product is part of the bundle of benefits that make up that product. For example, a jacket bought through mail order offers convenience benefits which a chain-store jacket does not. Conversely, the chain-store purchase may include hedonic benefits (the fun of shopping around, the excitement of finding a real bargain) that the mail-order company does not supply. Even when the actual jacket is identical, the benefits derived from the distribution method are different.

Transportation methods vary according to speed, cost, and ability to handle the type of product concerned. As a general rule, the quicker the method the more expensive it is, but in some cases it may be cheaper to use a faster method because the firm's capital is tied up for less time. For perishable goods such as fruit, standby airfreight can be as cheap as sea transport, when the lower incidence of wastage is taken into account.

The transportation method chosen for a particular product will depend on the factors shown in Fig 11.1.

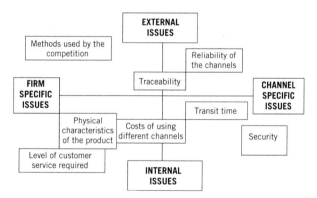

Figure 11.1: Factors in transport strategy

It is often possible to gain a significant competitive edge by using a method which is out of the ordinary. For example, most inner-city courier companies use motorbikes to deliver urgent documents, but a few use bicycles. In heavy traffic, bicycles are often quicker, and can sometimes use routes that are not open to powered vehicles, so deliveries are quicker.

In all the above cases, there will be trade-offs involved. Greater customer service will almost always be more expensive; greater reliability may increase transit time, as will greater traceability because in most cases the product will need to be checked on and off the transport method chosen. As with any other aspect of marketing activity, the customer's overall needs must be taken into account, and the relative importance of those needs must be judged with some accuracy if the firm is to remain competitive.

Table 11.2: Categories of channel members

Channel member	Function
Agents	Agents usually act purely as a sales arm for the manufacturer, without actually buying the products. The agent never takes title to the goods; agency sales representatives call on major retailers and on wholesalers on behalf of a number of manufacturers, and take orders and arrange delivery. This saves the manufacturer the cost of operating a large salesforce to carry perhaps only a small product range.
Wholesalers	Actually buy the goods from the manufacturers, often through an agent, then sell the goods on to the retailers or sometimes the final consumers.
Retailers	A retailer is any organization which offers goods directly to consumers. This includes mail order companies, door-to-door salespeople, and e-commerce organizations selling over the Internet.

These intermediaries carry out functions which would otherwise need to be carried out by the supplier. Some recent trends in retailing are likely to affect distribution strategy in future: Table 11.3 has some of the more important ones.

Table 11.3: Trends in distribution

Trend	Strategic implications
Greater car ownership	This tends to increase outshopping (shopping outside the area in which one lives). This means that geographic segmentation devices such as ACORN are becoming less relevant. (**www.upmystreet.com**)
High city-centre rents and property taxes	This has led to an increase in edge-of-town shopping estates which have a number of retail warehouses. This has implications for delivery quantities and trucking resources.
Inner-city redevelopment	Former industrial sites are being converted to retail parks, which again has implications for physical distribution.
Loyalty cards	Retailers with successful loyalty schemes may have a key role to play in relationship marketing.
E-commerce and the Internet	So far, the effects on traditional distribution channels have been patchy, but it seems likely that e-commerce will increase. This is likely to lead to large gains for delivery firms, and possibly increased road traffic. There is more on this later in the chapter.
Telemarketing	More business is being done directly over the telephone than ever before. This may lead to increased business for delivery firms.
Internet auction sites	These sites allow consumers to buy collectively at wholesale prices. This clearly cuts out several layers of intermediaries, but may involve the suppliers in extra delivery problems and administration unless the auctioneer carries this load.

Talking Point

Supermarkets, airlines, even pharmacies are all plugging their loyalty cards. The idea is to get us to shop at the same place every time – and also to provide information about how we shop so the retailer can improve the relationship between us.

But do we really want to have a relationship with a retailer? Would we go on a long walking holiday with our supermarket? Or marry an airline? Perhaps we would rather they just sold us what we want, when we want it, and leave us alone the rest of the time – which is hardly the basis for a good relationship!

MANAGING DISTRIBUTION CHANNELS

The management of distribution channels is of considerable importance for the firm's strategic implementation. Channels can be led by any of the channel members, whether they are producers, wholesalers, or retailers, provided the member concerned has **channel power.** This power comes from seven sources (Michman and Sibley 1980), as shown in Table 11.4.

Table 11.4: Sources of channel power

Economic sources of power	Non-economic sources of power	Other factors
Control of resources. The degree to which the channel member has the power to direct goods, services or finance within the channel.	Reward power. The ability to provide financial benefits, or otherwise favour channel members.	Level of power. This derives from the economic and non-economic sources of power.
Size of company. The bigger the firm compared with other channel members, the greater the overall economic power.	Expert power. This arises when the leader has special expertise which the other channel members need.	Dependency of other channel members.
Referent power emerges when channel members try to emulate the leader.		Willingness to lead. Clearly some firms with potential for channel leadership prefer not to have the responsibility, or are unable to exercise the potential for other reasons.
Legitimate power arises from a superior – subordinate relationship. For example, if a retailer holds a substantial shareholding in a wholesaler, it has legitimate power over the wholesaler.		
Coercive power exists when one channel member has the power to punish another.		

Channel co-operation is an essential part of the effective functioning of channels. Since each member relies on every other member for the free exchange of goods down the channel, it is in the members' interests to look after each other to some extent. Channel co-operation can be improved in the following ways:

1. The channel members can agree on target markets, so that each member can best direct effort towards meeting the common goal.

2. Define the tasks each member should carry out. This avoids duplication of effort, or giving the final consumer conflicting messages.

A further development is **co-marketing**, which implies a partnership between manufacturers, intermediaries and retailers. This level of co-operation involves pooling of market information and full agreement on strategic issues (Marx 1995).

Channel conflict arises because each member wants to maximize its own profits or power. Conflicts also arise because of frustrated expectations; each member expects the other members to act in particular ways, and sometimes these expectations are unfulfilled. For example, a retailer may expect a wholesaler to maintain large enough stocks to cover an unexpected rise in demand for a given product, whereas the wholesaler may expect the manufacturers to be able to increase production rapidly to cover such eventualities.

An example of channel conflict occurred when EuroDisney (now Disneyland Paris) (**www.disneylandparis.com**) first opened. The company bypassed the travel agents and tried to market directly to the public via TV commercials. Unfortunately, this did not work because european audiences were not used to the idea of booking directly (and also were not as familiar with the Disney concept as American audiences) so no bookings resulted. At the same time

Disney alienated the travel agents, and have had to expend considerable time and money in wooing them back again.

Channel management can be carried out by co-operation and negotiation (often with one member leading the discussions) or it can be carried out by the most powerful member laying down rules which weaker members have to follow. Table 11.5 shows some of the methods which can be used to control channels.

Table 11.5: Channel management techniques

Technique	Explanation	Legal position
Refusal to deal	One member refuses to do business with one or more other members. For example, hairdressing wholesalers sometimes refuse to supply mobile hairdressers, on the grounds that this is unfair competition for salons.	In most countries suppliers do not have to supply anybody they do not wish to deal with. However, grounds may exist for a lawsuit if the refusal to deal is a punishment for not going along with an anti-competitive ruling by a supplier, or is an attempt to prevent the channel member from dealing with a third party with whom the manufacturer is in dispute.
Tying contracts	The supplier (sometimes a franchiser) demands that the channel member carries other products as well as the main one. If the franchiser insists that all the products are carried, this is called **full-line forcing**.	Most of these contracts are illegal, but are accepted if the supplier alone can supply goods of a given quality, or if the purchaser is free to carry competing products as well. Sometimes they are accepted when a company has just entered the market.
Exclusive dealing	A manufacturer might prevent a wholesaler from carrying competitors' products, or a retailer might insist that no other retailer be supplied with the same products. This is often used by retailers to ensure that their 'price guarantees' can be honoured - obviously consumers will not be able to find the same product at a lower price locally if the retailer has prevented the manufacturer from supplying anybody else.	Usually these are legal provided they do not result in a monopoly position in a local area. In other words, provided the consumer has access to similar products, there will not be a problem.

Most attempts to control distribution by the use of power are likely to be looked on unfavourably by the courts, but of course the abuse of power would have to be fairly extreme before a channel member would be likely to sue.

Sometimes the simplest way to control a distribution channel is to buy out the channel members. Buying out members across a given level (for example, a wholesaler buying out other wholesalers in order to build a national network) is called **horizontal integration**. Buying out members above or below in the distribution chain (for example a retailer buying out a wholesaler) is **vertical integration.** An example of extreme vertical integration is the major oil companies, which extract crude oil, refine it, ship it, and ultimately sell it retail through petrol stations. At the extremes, this type of integration may attract the attention of government monopoly regulation agencies, since the integration may cause a restriction of competition.

Producers need to ensure that the distributors of their products are of the right type. The image of a retailer can damage (or enhance) the image of the products sold (and vice-versa). Producers need not necessarily sell through the most prestigious retailer, and in fact this would be counter-productive for many cheap, everyday items. Likewise a prestigious product should not be sold through a down-market retail outlet.

EFFICIENT CONSUMER RESPONSE

Efficient consumer response seeks to integrate the activities of manufacturers and retailers using computer technology; the expected result is a more responsive stocking system for the retailer, which in turn benefits the manufacturer. Some of the features of ECR are as follows:

1. **Continuous replenishment** under which the supplier plans production using data generated by the retailer.

2. **Cross-docking** attempts to co-ordinate the arrival of suppliers' and retailers' trucks at the distribution centres so that goods move from one truck to the other without going into stock. Although transport efficiency falls because a supermarket truck collecting (say) greengrocery might have to wait for several suppliers' trucks to arrive, the overall speed of delivery of products improves, which can be crucial when dealing with fresh foods.

3. **Roll-cage sequencing** allows storage of products by category at the warehouse. Although this adds to the labour time at the warehouse, it greatly reduces labour time at the retail store.

The main problem with ECR is that it relies on complete co-operation between supplier and retailer. In any channel of distribution where the power base is unequal, this is less likely to happen. Despite the overall savings for the channel as a whole, self-interest on the part of channel members may lead to less-than-perfect co-operation.

CASE STUDY: CHAPTERS BOOKSTORE

Founded in 1995 by Harvard Business School graduate Larry Stevenson, Chapters Bookstore chain has been a success story almost unparalleled in Canadian business history. Chapters was formed by merging SmithBooks, a struggling 176-store chain formerly owned by Britain's WH Smith, and the Coles chain, a 258-store Canadian bookstore. Stevenson closed down unprofitable stores and opened new superstores, created around his own unique formula.

Stevenson borrowed ideas from US book giants Barnes & Noble and Borders. Each Chapters store offers a combination of discounts, strong promotional campaigns, long opening hours, and a Starbucks coffee shop in every store. This encourages customers to stay longer in the store, as well as providing extra revenue. The results of this aggressive approach to bookselling have been impressive; Chapters now has around 25 per cent of the entire Canadian book market, estimated to be worth C$2 bn, and expects to grow by a further 20 per cent by the end of 2001.

Stevenson is also expanding vertically; he has formed a new book wholesaler, Pegasus, to supply his store. This has released him from the need to deal through existing Canadian wholesalers, and has given the firm a dominant position in the book market; publishers complain that they are being squeezed by Chapters, which they claim is using its power to delay payments. Chapters has also launched an on-line bookstore which is now Canada's leading Internet retail site, turning over C$3.7 m in the first quarter of 1999 alone. The firm's rapid expansion has led to substantial losses; the firm lost C$8.1 m in the third quarter of 1999 due to losses in the online business and start-up costs for Pegasus.

Chapters' rise to power has not been without challenge either; rival bookstore chain Indigo, founded by Heather Reisman, uses a similar formula to Chapters but aims at a younger audience. Reisman has hit Chapters with a C$31 m law suit alleging that Chapters is using monopoly power to prevent Indigo entering the market. The dispute was triggered by a contest for a prime Ontario

▶

▶ bookstore site, but has spilled over into charges of industrial espionage, poaching of senior staff, and pre-empting the best city-centre sites. Indigo also sells CDs and other lifestyle products, and has its own Internet retail site.

Ex-soldier Stevenson and the flamboyant Ms Reisman look set to continue the battle by any means which present themselves: in the meantime, smaller retailers find themselves squeezed out by the discounts, advertising and choice the bigger companies can offer, and publishers sit tearfully on the sidelines waiting to see which of the contenders will finally win the power in the marketplace.

CASE STUDY QUESTIONS

1. How might Indigo meet the challenge of Pegasus?
2. What might the publishers do to limit Chapters' power in the distribution channel?
3. What might the smaller independent bookstores do to improve their position?
4. If Chapters is abusing its power, as the publishers claim, why do they not refuse to supply the stores?
5. What other approaches might Heather Reisman take to establish a stronger presence in the market?

SUMMARY

This chapter has been about getting the goods to the consumer in the most efficient and effective way possible. Here are the key points from the chapter:

- Distribution forms part of the product because it has benefits attached to it.
- The faster the transport, the more expensive in up-front costs, but the greater the savings in terms of wastage and capital tied up.
- Transport methods must consider the needs of the end user of the product.
- Cutting out the middleman is likely to increase costs in the long run, not decrease them.
- Retailing includes every transaction in which the purchase is to be used by the buyer personally or for family use.
- Retailing is not necessarily confined to high-street shops.

CHAPTER QUESTIONS

1. Under what circumstances might air freight be cheaper than surface transport?
2. How might wholesalers improve the strength of their position with retailers?
3. Why might a wholesaler be prepared to accept a restricted-territory sales agreement?
4. When should a manufacturer consider dealing direct with retailers?
5. When should a manufacturer consider dealing direct with the public?

REFERENCES

Marx, W. (1995): 'The Co-Marketing Revolution', *Industry Week* 2 October 1995 pp. 77–79.
Michman, R.D. and Sibley, S.D. (1980): *Marketing Channels and Strategies*, 2nd ed. (Worthington, Ohio: Publishing Horizons Inc.).

Chapter Twelve

Strategy and People

INTRODUCTION

This chapter is about developing a customer-orientated internal culture for the organization. Ultimately, companies do not achieve anything: a company cannot hire people, cannot fire people, cannot make strategic decisions, cannot make purchases, cannot manufacture products, and cannot generate sales. A company is a legal fiction, consisting of a set of computer printouts or physical documents filed at the company registry. Only people can achieve outcomes, working on behalf of the other people within the organization.

Human resource strategies are not just about ensuring that the right people and policies are in place, although people are a part of the total package the customer buys and are therefore a legitimate concern for marketers. Human resource strategies are also about ensuring that the people within the firm make the right strategic decisions. In the current climate of employee empowerment, even the lowliest staff members will occasionally be required to make decisions or take actions which have strategic implications.

After reading this chapter, you should be able to:

- Explain the importance of internal marketing.
- Describe ways of involving staff in strategic decision-making.
- Show how staff contribute to the achievement of strategic objectives.
- Describe effective ways of managing organizational change.

HUMAN RESOURCE STRATEGY

For an organization to be successful it needs to attract, motivate, reward and retain competent employees. In the current employment climate within industrialized countries, the bulk of employees are well-educated and somewhat independently-minded. Unemployment is relatively low, and most people are no longer prepared to accept autocratic approaches to management. This means there is an increasing emphasis on co-operative management practices, and an increase in the empowerment of employees.

This creates a tension for employers: on one hand, decisions need to be centralized in order to maximize consistency and control, but on the other hand employees often wish to be empowered and therefore decisions need to be decentralized. Recent thinking on customer relationship management has been that empowering front-line employees is the most appropriate strategy for ensuring rapid response to customer needs and problems (Murphy 2001). Some writers have predicted that organizations will, in future, become increasingly decentralized: the emphasis will be on federations of profit centres rather than on centralized conglomerates, with decision-making devolved to the individual. In this scenario, many knowledge-based, professional workers will be paid fees for specific tasks rather than salaries for specific jobs, so that employment on the current pattern (regular working hours for a single specified employer) will become less common. This scenario was predicted in the early 80s (Handy 1984) and there are signs that it is, in fact, becoming a common picture of employment practice.

HRM strategy can be divided into hard and soft approaches: the differences are as shown in Table 12.1.

Table 12.1: Assumptions of hard and soft HRM

Hard HRM Assumptions	Soft HRM Assumptions
People are viewed as a resource to be used efficiently and effectively.	Workers are seen as individuals, to be informed about the company mission, strategy and success levels. In this way their increased commitment will result in increased productivity.
Deployment and development of employees is delegated to line managers, responsible for groups of people.	Workers are involved in teams which exercise collective decision-making.
Scientific management principles can be used, with caution.	Employees can be trusted to make the right decisions without constant management supervision.

The two approaches can be equally effective: some employees prefer not to be involved in decision-making, but are more than happy to leave the company's problems to the senior managers, and simply do as they are told during the working day. Such employees would prefer working for a 'hard' company. Other employees like to feel involved, and like to be consulted: they would work best for a 'soft' company. Also, some industries lend themselves better to each of the approaches: an industry employing a high proportion of highly-qualified professionals (for example a law firm or accountancy firm) will almost certainly have to adopt a soft approach, delegating decision-making to the front-line workers. A firm operating in a complex but regimented environment (for example a railway operator) is more likely to adopt a hard approach (although it is interesting to note that the Australian railway system (**www.railpage.org.au**) uses a soft approach, allowing freight train crews to make many of the decisions relating to crewing of trains, and even departure and arrival times).

For example, during 1994 United Airlines (**www.ual.com**) suffered serious financial problems, and was at one point planning to seek the protection of Chapter 11, the US bankruptcy laws. A rescue package was agreed with airline staff under which the staff would exchange a pay cut for a controlling interest in the airline. Decision-making was decentralized, and staff who had previously only been expected to make tactical decisions found themselves being encouraged to think strategically. At the time of the changes, United had a reputation for poor service, high prices, and poor reliability; now its service level has been transformed, its reliability is among the world's best, and it has even managed to compete successfully against no-frills airline SouthWest Airlines. (**www.southwest.com**)

From a customer response management viewpoint, front-line staff are much more likely to understand the types of problem which arise for customers, and will in most cases have ideas about how problems might be resolved. Proximity to the problem enables them to be clearer about the solutions.

EMPOWERING STAFF

There are three basic objectives of empowerment, as follows:

1. To make the organization more responsive to outside pressures.
2. To remove layers of management in order to reduce costs. This means that managers are expected to support and coach staff rather than direct them, which also reduces workload and often reduces stress for the managers since they do not have to concentrate on every aspect of the task at hand.
3. To create employee networks which feature teamwork, collaboration, and horizontal communications.

Empowerment implies increasing the information and knowledge of employees so they can more adequately perform the job. The basic empowerment options are as follows:

1. Employees can be encouraged to contribute ideas. This can range from the token empowerment represented by suggestion boxes, through to the substantial cash rewards paid by the Ford Motor Company (**www.ford.com**) for successful employee ideas.
2. Establishment of work teams which are allowed to share and manage their own work within guidelines and limits laid down by senior managers. This tends to increase motivation and job satisfaction, but lays a responsibility on managers to encourage team-building activities.
3. Empowerment to change strategic parameters in order to achieve an overall result. The emphasis here shifts from employees taking responsibility for their own actions to taking responsibility for the overall outcome. Evaluation of the team is based on collective outcomes, and collective accountability means that teamwork becomes a high priority, as does communication of the corporate strategic objectives.

Empowerment is a powerful motivator for most employees: otherwise staff can feel like small cogs in a large machine, especially in modern global organizations, and being part of a small, empowered team brings the workplace down to a human scale. Problems arise from the following areas:

1. When the empowerment is taken away as soon as the most important and interesting decisions have to be taken.
2. When the parameters are not clear so that employees become afraid of making wrong decisions.
3. When communication is poor.

4. When the organization's strategic objectives have not been appropriately communicated.

5. When different teams apply different solutions to the same problem: this is particularly problematical when dealing with customers, who may find that one team is more generous than another in making reparations for mistakes or service failures.

Purely from the viewpoint of how the customer will be treated (ignoring for the moment the effects on staff morale), the deciding factors in empowerment are the competitive environment, and the relative importance of close linkages with customers. Fig. 12.1 illustrates the trade-offs involved.

Fig. 12.1: Trade-offs in staff empowerment

	High customer contact	Low customer contact
Highly-structured, rigid competitive environment with little change	Limited empowerment	No empowerment
Unstructured, rapidly-changing competitive environment	High empowerment	Limited empowerment

The environment is, in general, becoming more turbulent and subject to rapid change, so it might be expected that there will be an increased emphasis on empowerment in future. The environment also affects recruitment strategies: companies seeking to move quickly to respond to new opportunities will place more emphasis on recruiting from outside (Cappelli and Crocker-Hefter 1995). Organizations which compete on flexibility are more likely to recruit from outside, presumably so they can bring in people with existing skills rather than develop those same skills in-house with existing employees. This contrasts with companies in established markets with long-standing relationships, which tend to develop staff internally so as to maintain continuity and emphasize organization-specific skills.

The problem here is that the rapidly-changing business environment will tend to emphasize hiring from outside in order to facilitate rapid change: at the same time, companies need to maintain a solid infrastructure and sound internal architecture if the necessary co-operation between employees is to be maintained. In simple terms, firms need a hard core of loyal, long-term staff to maintain the corporate culture. If promotion from within is not available, and there is a constant stream of staff arriving and leaving, the core staff are likely to become demoralized, and may well leave in turn. This is clearly less of a problem if the firm is growing rapidly, as new staff will be needed anyway and there will be enough promotion opportunities for all concerned: the difficulty arises if the market is mature, but still changing rapidly. Achieving a balance between the two extremes in order to establish a strong and cohesive culture while still retaining flexibility is a major challenge: in this context, the section on organization structures in Chapter 3 shows ways of achieving greater flexibility without changing the essential structure of the business.

As with any other strategy, empowering staff does present problems. Some people are risk-averse and are therefore often reluctant to assume the responsibility which goes with empowerment. This means that suitable support frameworks must be in place, and also suitable reward systems for those who are successful in their decisions. Most importantly, there should not be a culture of blame: middle managers or front-line staff who feel they might get into trouble if they make a wrong decision will end up making no decisions at all, which is of course the worst outcome.

When setting the parameters for empowerment, it is important that clear guidelines are given. This is difficult to do, because the whole purpose of empowerment is to enable the staff member to act when something unusual occurs – if all the possible circumstances could be outlined in advance, they could presumably be prevented before they arise and therefore empowerment would be unnecessary.

Murphy (2001) points out that empowerment does not always benefit employees. Many employees find empowerment threatening, while others simply see it as a way for management to pass the buck without paying any extra money for the extra responsibility involved. If the employee becomes alienated from the process, either because of being given too much responsibility without a commensurate pay rise or by being given too restricted a remit, he or she may behave in ways which are either detrimental to customer relations, or detrimental to the financial well-being of the organization. For example, an employee might decide to be over-generous to a favourite customer, or to neglect a customer who complains vociferously. Employees might be tempted to set traps for unpopular managers, give extra benefits to their friends, or sabotage the firm in some way.

Talking Point

Empowerment has been one of the fashionable ideas of the 90s. Employers are encouraged to hand over power to their staff, and allow them ever-increasing leeway in dealing with customers, in the hope that this will increase customer satisfaction.

But does it? Wouldn't it be better if customers knew where they were? Do people really want the level of service they get to be decided by the 16-year-old Saturday kid on the till? Or even by the receptionist on the hotel desk? What do we do when a demand to see the manager is met by the bland statement, 'I am the manager, at least for anything we're prepared to do for you'.

Maybe it was better in the good old days, when service was poorer but at least you knew where you were!

The concept of empowerment leaves something to be desired in any case, since it implies a devolvement of power from senior managers to junior managers. It might be more productive to think in terms of expecting employees to exercise their initiative. Initiative implies that the employee tries to act in ways that management will approve of: a clear understanding of what the firm is hoping to achieve will, with luck, translate into an understanding of what management would expect to see as the outcome of initiative.

If empowerment is to be effective, the following rules need to apply:

1. Employees need to be selected, trained, and nurtured with empowerment in mind.
2. Employees should be given clear guidelines, but not be hidebound by rules which cannot, in any case, cover every eventuality.
3. Empowerment works best when combined with a team approach: the support of the other members of the team offers invaluable reassurance.
4. Rewards must reflect the contribution the employee makes.
5. There should not be a culture of blame – employees should see failure as an opportunity to learn, not as a pitfall for which they will be punished.

Empowerment is not a strategy which allows managers to relax and pass the buck to subordinates: it is more likely to create extra work and problems, and require even more skilful management than the prescriptive, hierarchical approach.

MANAGEMENT SKILLS

Successful staff need the support of competent managers: under the hard HRM model, managers need to provide a suitable framework of parameters for behaviour, and a suitable supervisory system for ensuring that the parameters are adhered to. Under a soft HRM paradigm, managers need to support staff and provide the necessary advice and backing for staff to achieve their potential. In either case, it is the primary role of managers to provide the right conditions under which employees can carry out the real work of the organization.

At Cadbury Schweppes (**www.cadburyschweppes.com**), managers are appraised against a list of 50 skills and competencies, broken down into six basic groups as shown in Table 12.2.

Table 12.2: Six basic dimensions of management competence

Dimension	Explanation
Strategy	The ability to think critically and challenge accepted wisdom. Awareness of the business environment.
Drive	Self-motivation and energy.
Influence	The ability to communicate effectively, and to help staff to develop their own potential.
Analysis	The ability to reason effectively, to identify relevant information, and analyse, organize and present numerical data.
Implementation	The ability to understand the impact of decisions, especially in terms of their effect on other parts of the organization.
Personal factors	The ability to implement unpopular decisions, and the ability to present decisions to staff in a positive way.

In practice many managers will have been promoted for their competence in doing a particular task. In a hierarchical organization the assumption is that each manager knows how to do the job of the subordinates immediately below him or her in the hierarchy, and that promotion further up the hierarchy will result once the manager knows everything about the job at his or her existing level. This view is somewhat naive, for the following reasons:

1. In a changing environment (faced by virtually all organizations in the 21st century) the jobs of subordinates will have changed within a short period of time after the manager has been promoted. After two or three years away from the 'grass roots' job the manager will almost certainly be out of date.

2. The model assumes a top-down management style in which senior managers tell their subordinates what to do and the subordinates then do it. In fact, subordinates will often interpret instructions in ways which were not intended by senior managers, or will act without authority.

3. It is impossible for the person at the top to know everything. Life has become too complex.

4. Hierarchies are slow to adapt, because communications channels are too slow: this means that employees will sometimes short-circuit the system using an informal network in order to cut through the red tape.

Reducing or removing hierarchies has the unfortunate effect of reducing opportunities for promotion, however, and this can be a demotivator. Research carried out by the Roffey Park Management Centre (1995) showed that many employees remain cynical about attempts to establish teamworking, flexibility and empowerment. Some felt despondent and insecure because of reduced promotion prospects and the view that such exercises are about cost-cutting rather than about improving conditions for employees. This is perhaps not surprising in view of the fact that many authors and consultants advocate such measures on the basis that they will increase profitability.

TEAM BUILDING

Building a front-line team which is able to respond to customers' needs quickly is in itself a marketing task. Individual contributions to the overall team effort are determined by personal growth needs (Cummings 1981), so staff will need to see what advantages are available to them in becoming effective team members. A successful team needs shared objectives (preferably agreed between the members), effective internal communications, and the ability to manage both the tasks in hand and the relationships between members.

In an ideal world, the team would have a set of complementary skills and would have individual strengths and weaknesses which would cancel each other out in the team environment. Obviously in the real world this is unlikely to happen, so the team will need to be aware of their strengths and weaknesses as a team, and try to obtain outside assistance when necessary. Belbin (1981) suggests that teams should be able to perform (between them) the following tasks:

1. Create useful ideas.
2. Analyse problems effectively.
3. Get things done.
4. Communicate effectively.
5. Have leadership qualities.
6. Evaluate problems and options logically.
7. Handle the technical aspects.
8. Control their work.
9. Report back effectively either verbally or in writing.

Individual team members might contribute in one or more of these areas, but would not necessarily contribute in all areas: some team members may be good at having creative ideas, while others are better-equipped to analyse problems or handle technical aspects. Leadership of the team should be low-key: the most effective teams tend to be those with an organismic rather than hierarchical structure. This means that leadership devolves to the person best equipped to lead for the task currently facing the team. In many cases this will mean that different people take responsibility for guiding the team through different tasks which are being carried out in parallel: in other words, at any one time the team may have several leaders, each in charge of different aspects of the team's overall responsibilities.

Group support systems fall into four general types: keypad systems, soft systems modelling, workstation systems, and cognitive mapping systems. These are explained in Table 12.3.

MANAGEMENT AND LEADERSHIP

Managers have been classified in many different ways, but from the viewpoint of team leadership they can be classified as transactional leaders or transformational leaders. The differences are as shown in Table 12.4.

Table 12.3: Group support systems

Support system	Explanation and examples
Keypad systems	Each member of the group is provided with a keypad and display. For each issue under discussion the members will be asked to respond using the keypad, and the results are displayed on a computer screen. The advantage of this type of system is that group members do not have to be identified: this makes it easier for group members to dissent from the 'accepted' view, and helps create a more wide-ranging discussion.
Soft systems modelling	The first stage in modelling soft systems is to identify the individuals who have issues to discuss. The facilitator (or modeller) then works with those individuals to discover patterns, themes or features which encapsulate the problem. This may be to do with aspects that make people angry or frustrated, or produce other strong emotions. The next step is to produce theoretical systems to resolve the problem, taking account of the issues raised by the group members.
Workstation systems	A workstation system allows real-time discussion of problems using personal computers in a local area network. Such systems can operate in a similar way to a chat room, publicly displaying each group member's input to the debate.
Cognitive mapping	Here the facilitator draws up a map for each individual, based on the thought processes each has about the problem under discussion. The map will pay particular attention to the cause and effect relationships which each group member sees in the problem.

Table 12.4: Transactional versus transformational leadership styles

Characteristics of Transactional Leaders	Characteristics of Transformational Leaders
Controls team members by the use of rewards and punishments (Bryman 1992).	Controls team members by force of personality or charisma (House and Shamir 1993).
Provides a set of rules to follow (Bass 1985).	Provides a role model and a vision (Podsakoff et al. 1990).
Operates by modifying behaviour.	Operates by modifying attitudes.
Uses management by exception (Bass 1985): concentrates on improving poor performance and praising excellence.	Fosters acceptance of group goals and has high performance expectations (Podsakoff et al. 1990).

The two types of management are not, in fact, mutually exclusive: it is possible for a manager to be charismatic and attitude-changing, but also to reward good performance and be critical of poor performance. Research conducted by Mackenzie et al. (2001) showed that transformational leader behaviour augmented the impact of transactional leadership behaviour, or in other words transformational leader behaviour will influence team members to perform above the call of duty. The research was conducted among sales managers and their teams, and concluded that sales managers could improve their overall success rates in leading their teams if they paid more attention to their transformational leadership behaviour.

Handy (1989) suggests that a leader is someone who shapes and shares a vision which gives point to the work of others. According to Handy, the vision should be:

1. Different from what everybody else is doing.
2. Clear, understandable and capable of making a vivid impression.
3. Able to make sense to people, and relate to the work they do.
4. Lived by the leader, and visibly believed in by the leader.
5. Shared by the team: the leader must develop a team committed to the vision.

From a strategic viewpoint, leaders need to be developed from within the ranks of the staff. Although it is theoretically possible to recruit people with leadership potential, such potential is often difficult to assess, and leaders often emerge from the most unlikely places. Developing leaders will usually involve allowing people to take measured risks, and to use failure as a means of learning rather than as an opportunity to punish. Learning organizations have the following characteristics:

1. Systemic thinking. Decision makers are able to use the perspective of the whole organization.
2. Management development and personal growth. Effective empowerment and leadership is encouraged throughout the organization, allowing managers to respond to environmental shifts.
3. Shared vision. Changes should be consistent throughout strategic levels: the vision is the guide to ensure consistency.
4. Appropriate values and corporate culture.
5. Commitment to continuous improvement.
6. Team learning through open discussion and problem sharing.

A key issue in developing a learning organization (and indeed in developing leaders) is to avoid developing a culture of blame. If mistakes are made (and they will be as people are learning) they should be used as a basis for future learning. Progress and change can only come about by taking risks: if failure is punished, no-one will be prepared to take risks and the organization will stagnate.

KNOWLEDGE-INTENSIVE FIRMS

At the beginning of the 20th century, manufacturing was the major preoccupation of the western world. The economies of Europe, and to a lesser extent the United States, were dominated by firms who made things. These goods were exported to the other nations of the world in exchange for raw materials.

During the 20th century, the other nations of the world also industrialized, and were often able to out-compete the West due to lower wage costs and greater proximity to raw materials supplies. Thus the beginning of the 21st century sees the West with relatively little reliance on manufacturing, and much greater reliance on knowledge-based industries and service industries. Only a tiny minority of the working population (around 5 per cent in most western countries) are employed directly in manufacture – most of the process of actually making things is carried out in the far East, or South America, or even Africa. Where manufacture does exist it is heavily automated, because the cost of robots is very much less than the salaries of employees. In simple terms, we can no longer afford to pay someone to put the wheels on – even £10 an hour is uneconomic, when an Indian manual worker costs £10 a week.

This process is not likely to reverse itself. Even now, companies are realizing that most Indians speak very good English, and therefore even telephone call centres can be located in India, with substantial savings in salaries. In the west, for many firms, what we have to sell to the rest of the world is our knowledge and experience. In this environment, it may be that the ability to learn faster than one's competitors becomes the only sustainable competitive advantage (Stata 1989). Learning organizations are those which are skilled in continually seeking out knowledge deficiencies, acquiring, creating, spreading and managing knowledge, and expert at modifying their behaviour to reflect their new knowledge.

Much of the knowledge thus acquired resides in the heads of employees, but some will be contained in the organization in the form of customer records, how-to manuals, commonly-held knowledge about the company's culture and experiences, and many other forms.

Talking Point

As automation increases, the number of employees in any given organization decreases. Or so we are told. Yet there are more people employed now than ever – so what's going on?

Maybe people are spending more time learning, and less time getting on with the job. Fifty years ago, most people left school at 15 and never studied anything academic again as long as they lived. Nowadays, more than 40 per cent of school leavers go on to tertiary education – effectively leaving school at 21 or 22 with degrees, and often ending up working at jobs they could easily have done at 15. And it doesn't end there – we expect people to continue to study, to go for Master's degrees, postgraduate certificates, continuing professional development and a whole range of other qualifications.

Are we spending so much time learning to do the job that there is no time left over for actually working? Or is there more to education than simply providing cannon-fodder for employers?

In many cases, knowledge deficiencies will become apparent because of outside events. Competitors may develop a new process which is not clearly understood by the firm's technicians, or sales may fall for no discernible reason. In the first instance, the firm's technical research staff will need to spend time and effort in learning about the competitor's new process. In the second instance, the firm's marketing staff will need to discover the cause for the fall-off in business. Car manufacturers frequently buy competitors' new models and dismantle them in order to learn about any innovations.

An alternative approach is that adopted by some Japanese firms, in which the company expands knowledge by setting its staff 'impossible' tasks (Nonaki and Takeuchi 1995). This stimulates the creative process, and encourages members of the organization to create 'impossible' solutions.

Acquiring knowledge from outside the organization may be a process of taking information in to the organization for its subsequent interpretation, but it may also be a process of hiring knowledgeable people from elsewhere. The main methods of acquiring knowledge are as shown in Table 12.5.

Having acquired or developed knowledge, the organization has a role in disseminating it. Support for individual learning might involve paying for training courses or providing in-house training. The organization should also examine ways in which individual knowledge becomes converted into group knowledge. Although dissemination of knowledge appears at first sight to be risky, since staff might be poached by competitors, the downside is worse: retaining knowledge in the heads of a few key personnel means that these people become prime targets for competitive headhunting, and may leave taking the knowledge with them. Research shows that the effect of a key employee leaving can be nothing short of disastrous: a survey by KPMG Management Consulting (**www.kpmg.com**) in 1998 showed that 49 per cent of firms reported losing knowledge of best practice in a specific area as a result of a key employee leaving, and 43 per cent reported damaged relationships with key clients or suppliers. A further 14 per cent reported loss of information vital to the running of the business, and 13 per cent lost significant income (KPMG 1998).

In a knowledge-based business such as an advertising agency, the loss of a key employee will lead to such problems. A key employee might very well take clients with him or her, will probably take considerable expertise and knowledge of the subtleties of dealing with those clients who do

Table 12.5: Main ways of acquiring knowledge

Method	Explanation and examples
Access information which is in the public domain	Within the UK and indeed most of the developed world, large amounts of information are available from government sources. Most of this information is free: other sources include commercial research organizations such as Mintel (**sinatra2.mintel.com/sinatra/mintel/d/f/home**), which charges for its reports, and of course the Internet, where some information is free and some is charged for. Internet information is of variable standard, however, and is often unvalidated.
Market research and business intelligence	Market research generates knowledge about the activities of competitors and the needs and wants of customers. Increasing the firm's understanding of customers gives it an obvious competitive edge as does increased understanding of competitors.
Benchmarking	Benchmarking is the process of comparing the firm's individual operations with the individual operations of other companies. The other companies may or may not be competitors. For example, a firm may compare its reliability of delivery with one firm and its customer-care ratings with another. If each individual operation is brought up to the standard of the best firms (the theory runs) the firm will become the 'best of the best'. In practice, of course, the costs are likely to be prohibitive and there is a risk of trying to please everybody and provide everything, but the process at least leaves the firm confident of where it sits in relation to other firms.
Gathering information through relationships	Stakeholders are a rich source of information, whether they are customers, shareholders, suppliers, or distributors. In cases where the firm has a key-account relationship with another stakeholder, opportunities for exchanging information will be numerous.
Introducing diversity into an organization	Diversity and fresh viewpoints can be introduced either by recruiting new people from outside the organization, or by employing consultants. Recruiting new people has the advantage that they bring with them knowledge of how other organizations solve problems, but the downside is that it can be seen as a barrier to career progression for existing staff, who may feel that their loyalty has been misplaced. Also, their knowledge may take some time to apply, or may be worthless in a different environment from the one in which it was acquired. Consultants are usually seen as being independent and detached, without a political agenda, which means that their advice is more likely to be accepted. The downside here is that they often have a 'one size fits all' approach to organizations, offering one solution for everybody's ills rather than tailoring the solutions to the organization's specific needs.

remain, and may well leave the agency with a serious problem regarding re-establishing a good working relationship with remaining clients. For a small firm, the loss might well be fatal.

Individual learning requires the conditions shown in Table 12.6.

Knowledge management is the systematic capture and structuring of knowledge within an organization in order to improve business performance. There are two main modes for this: firstly, the codified knowledge management strategy, in which knowledge is collected and disseminated for use by others. The second mode is the personalized knowledge-sharing strategy, in which knowledge is shared through personal contact and mentoring rather than through a formalized recoding system.

Codified knowledge management systems have the advantage that procedures and techniques can quickly be accessed by all concerned: the disadvantage is that not all knowledge can be reduced to written formats. Sometimes gut feelings and personal knowledge of (for example) colleagues' personalities may not be easily transferred onto paper.

Personalized knowledge-sharing strategies enable much knowledge that might be too sensitive to commit to paper to be transferred. The drawback here is that the transfer might be incomplete or subjective, and is also subject to a risk of misunderstanding. The process is also less easily controlled by senior management: whether this is a benefit or a drawback will depend on the competence of senior management, of course.

Table 12.6: Conditions for individual learning (Finlay 2000)

Condition	Example and explanation
Provide a purpose for learning	The organization might link promotion or pay rises to the learning process, rewarding success on training courses. At a lower level, simply approving of learning (so that the employee collects 'brownie points' for it) will certainly help. The main incentive, however, will be a clear understanding of how learning will make the employee's job run more smoothly.
Provide education and training	In-house training is basic to the learning organization, but equally training can be 'farmed out' to organizations which are able to provide it more cost-effectively. Sponsoring employees to study for postgraduate qualifications at universities is an example of this.
Give time to search out information and digest it into knowledge	Employees need to be allowed to fail, so that the knowledge gained can be put to good use. The corollary to this is that the lesson does need to be learned: analysis of the failure and the possible ways similar events could be avoided in future need to be captured and disseminated to other employees. This is likely to be an embarrassing process for the person who failed, so due consideration must be given to his or her feelings.
Provide an appropriate level of autonomy	The greater the autonomy, the greater the potential to learn (Bennis and Nanus 1985). This is because someone who is constantly told exactly what to do will not need to pass the information through his or her brain, and has no particular reason to remember what is being said: after all, it is easy enough to ask again later. Most of us are familiar with the difference between being driven along a route, and driving it ourselves: in the latter case we are much more likely to remember the route for next time.
Encourage redundant information	Redundancy has two meanings in this context: firstly, information is duplicated in more than one location so that it is less likely to be lost; and secondly information which is not of immediate use is made available so that it can be accessed rapidly in case of need. The greater the redundancy, the greater the learning.

CASE STUDY: PROFESSIONAL DEVELOPMENT

Continuing professional development is proving likely to be the buzz-phrase of the early 21st century. CPD is about continuing to add to one's skills throughout one's professional life, and it is proving to be a fertile area for organizations who offer training courses and postgraduate qualifications.

Many of the professional associations such as the Chartered Institute of Marketing and the Institute of Chartered Accountants require their members to demonstrate that they have not only kept up with developments in the industry, but have gone beyond this and have demonstrated an improvement in their knowledge and skill. At the same time, employers have recognised the value of encouraging staff to improve. On one hand, the employees often have to demonstrate their competence by carrying out some task which is directly beneficial to the employer (for example preparing a market research report) and on the other hand the staff who undertake CPD often become more loyal to their existing employer.

For example, strategic marketing company Zalpha has a Learning to Grow programme under which staff are allowed to spend 15 per cent of their time on learning. The staff are also given a £1,000 budget each to pay for their courses or to go to conferences and so forth, and have an annual bonus which is contingent not only on work performance, but also on the degree to which they have taken up the training opportunity. Staff are free to study anything they think might be useful – some study languages, some are taking MBAs, others are learning to drive. The company view is that any learning will be useful in some way or another. The end result of this is a workforce which is more flexible, better equipped to achieve results, better motivated and more loyal to the firm.

▶

Leading UK CRM consultancy, Dunnhumby, has its own Internet-based 'academy', which operates on the same lines as a traditional college, with three semesters, a timetable, and taught sessions. The company invests £200,000 a year in training its 130 staff – over £1,500 per staff member. Edwina Dunn, the company's chief executive officer, sees it as part of the firm's investment in people, and more importantly as part of its recruitment and retention strategy. 'The reason people love coming here is that they know that they will grow', she says.

There is an old adage that says that companies should develop people so they are good enough to leave: this will ensure that they want to stay. This is not merely out of gratitude: employees whose companies help them to grow know that staying on can only increase their growth. Working with other people who want to grow and develop is also highly motivational: firms who are prepared to invest in their staff usually have a better working atmosphere than those who do not. And in an ever-changing world, it takes all the running most of can do just to stay in the same place.

CASE STUDY QUESTIONS

1. Why would an employer spend large sums of money on training people who might then leave to go to their competitors?
2. Would you say Edwina Dunn fits the pattern of a transactional manager, or a transformational manager?
3. If the firm develops its people by offering internal training courses, how might new knowledge enter the organization?
4. Given that people working for Zalpha are given a free hand in deciding what to study, how would you prevent someone from studying flower-arranging or ancient Latin?
5. Why might the CIM and the Chartered Accountants require members to demonstrate CPD activity?

SUMMARY

The people who work in an organization are central to its success, because business can only be conducted between human beings. The problem facing managers in the 21st century is that employees are an expensive item: automation is obviously cheaper, but then the employees who remain must be very high calibre indeed, and must also consequently be paid more. Hence the wealthy nations of western Europe and the US have unprecedented standards of living, and at the same time need huge investments in training. Competitive advantage often lies in the firm's effective recruitment, retention and management of its workforce, and this is nowhere more true than in the marketing context.

Key points from this chapter are as follows:

- Hard and soft HRM strategies are equally effective, but with different staff.
- Empowering staff makes organizations more flexible, and most staff like to be empowered, but not all staff respond positively to it.
- Hiring from outside the organization speeds change.
- Knowledge-intensive firms are likely to be the dominant business form for the 21st century.
- Training people makes them more effective, and usually makes them more loyal as well.

CHAPTER QUESTIONS

1. Why does hard HRM work for some people and not others?
2. Given the prevalence of computers, why is knowledge capture and retention problematical?
3. What are the drawbacks to hiring from outside the firm?
4. How might you reconcile a hard HRM strategy with the learning organization?
5. 'We can't all make a living opening doors for each other.' How is it possible for the western countries to stop making things and concentrate instead on knowing things?

REFERENCES

Bass, Bernard M. (1985): *Leadership and Beyond Expectations* (New York: Free Press).

Belbin, R.M. (1981): *Management Teams: Why they succeed or fail* (London: Heinemann).

Bennis, W. and Nanus, B. (1985): *Leaders: the strategies for taking charge* (London: Harper and Row).

Bryman, Alan (1992): *Charisma and Leadership in Organisations* (London: Sage).

Capelli and Crocker-Hefter (1995): 'HRM: The key to competitive advantage', *Financial Times* 'Mastering Management' series, no. 6, December.

Cummings, T.G. (1981): 'Designing effective work groups'. In *Handbook of Organisational design* eds. P.C. Nystrom and W.H. Starbuck, (Oxford University Press).

Finlay, P. (2000): *Strategic Management: an introduction to business and corporate strategy* (Harlow: Financial Times Prentice Hall).

Handy, C. (1984): *The future of work* (London: Blackwell).

Handy, C. (1989): *The age of unreason* (London: Hutchinson).

House, Robert J. and Shamir, Boas (1993): 'Toward the integration of transformational, charismatic and visionary theories'. In *Leadership Theory and Research: Perspectives and Directions* eds. Martin M. Chemers and Roya Ayman, (San Diego: Academic Press).

KPMG Management Consultancy, 'Knowledge Management' research report 1998, p. 7.

Mackenzie, Scot B., Podsakoff, Philip M. and Rich, Gregory A. (2001): 'Transformational and Transactional Leadership and Salesperson Performance', *Journal of the Academy of Marketing Science* vol. 29, no. 2, Spring.

Murphy, John A. (2001): *The Lifebelt: The Definitive Guide to Managing Customer Retention* (Chichester: John Wiley & Sons).

Nonaki, I. and Takeuchi, H. (1995): *The Knowledge-Creating Company: How Japanese Companies Create the Dynamics of Innovation* (Oxford University Press).

Podsakoff, Philip M., Mackenzie, Scott B., Moorman, Robert H. and Fetter, Richard (1990): 'Transformational leader behaviours and their effect on followers' trust in leader, satisfaction, and organisational citizenship behaviours'. *Leadership Quarterly* 1 (2): pp. 107–142.

Roffey Park Management Centre (1995): *Career development in flatter structures*. Research report.

Stata, R. (1989): 'Organisational learning – the key to management innovation', *Sloan Management Review* vol. 30, Spring, pp. 63–74.

13

Process and Physical Evidence

INTRODUCTION

Particularly in service industries, the process by which the product is delivered and the physical evidence that it has arrived are both key elements in differentiating the firm from its competitors. As routes to competitive advantage, the process and physical evidence can therefore offer key advantages at relatively low cost.

After reading this chapter, you should be able to:

- Explain how processes offer opportunities to differentiate the product.
- Describe ways of adapting processes to make them more customer-friendly.
- Show how process offers opportunities to build customer loyalty.
- Explain how physical evidence can be used to build loyalty.
- Describe ways of providing physical evidence which improves competitive advantage.
- Explain the role of physical evidence in promotion.

MARKETING OF SERVICES

Services and physical products both offer bundles of benefits to consumers. Although most writers on the subject tend to speak as though services and physical products are separate, in fact they merely represent extremes of a continuum: most physical products contain service elements, and most services contain physical products. For some academics, the conceptual difference is so small as to be unimportant, so that no real distinction needs to be made between the marketing of services and the marketing of physical products (Wickham et al. 1975, Goodfellow 1983). For these authors, more multi-dimensional classifications are needed in which the marketing strategy of the firm is a function of the characteristics of the offer it makes to its customers, characteristics of its markets, and characteristics of the process under which the exchange takes place. For other authors, the most important criterion is customers' expectations, expressed in terms of the satisfaction they obtain from the offering (Levitt 1974, Donnelly and George 1981).

While this view may well apply at the conceptual level, differences still remain at the practical level at which consumers operate. The greater the service element in the overall product, the greater the risk from the consumer's viewpoint, because the service element is intangible, is produced at the same time it is consumed and can therefore not be tested in advance, and is also likely to be more variable than a physical product. Most importantly, it cannot be returned in the event of a failure – the most the customer might hope for is reimbursement of the purchase price, although sometimes service firms will go further than this in order to make redress.

For example, a customer who is disappointed with a haircut is unable to have the cut hair restored. Likewise, a hotel guest who has had a poor night's sleep cannot be given a good night's sleep to compensate. This makes the service element a risky proposition for the purchaser, but it also makes it a risky proposition for the supplier. The dissatisfied hairdressing customer might refuse to pay, or the disgruntled hotel guest might complain to a consumer affairs programme: the hairdresser will be unable to repossess the haircut, and the hotelier will be unable to re-let the room for the previous night.

There is thus a considerable difference between physical products and services in terms of the purchasing process. When a consumer buys a physical product, the decision to buy is followed by payment, then consumption, then post-purchase evaluation. In most service purchases, the decision to buy is followed by consumption, then post-purchase evaluation, then payment. It could be argued that the degree to which payment comes after the service has been delivered is one of the distinguishing factors between mainly-physical products and mainly-service products. In fast-food restaurants or bars, where the service level is low, payment usually takes place before consumption; in high-class restaurants, hotels, and in the case of professional services such as lawyers or accountants, payment takes place after consumption.

PROCESS IN THE STRATEGIC CONTEXT

A process is a series of actions taken in order to convert inputs to something of greater value (Finlay 2000). The process therefore needs to be efficient and effective: a process which does not create greater value from the raw component inputs is dysfunctional. For example, a chef may take basic ingredients such as flour, eggs, apples, sugar and so forth and make an apple pie. A great chef will use the same ingredients to create a confection which is a work of art: a bad chef might create an inedible mess. In the business world, every process combines the following four resources:

1. Basic assets. These are the tangible and intangible assets of the business, as expressed in the financial reporting systems. Tangible assets would include plant and machinery, cash, work in progress, buildings, fixtures and fittings. Intangible assets include reputation of the firm, reputation of brands, and goodwill.

2. Explicit knowledge. This is knowledge which can be written down or otherwise recorded. Much of this would be in the public domain: the legal restrictions that companies in the industry need to work within, the technical problems associated with the industry, or the published market research which forms the basis of the tactical marketing planning. Some explicit knowledge might be in the form of customer databases or patents.

3. Tacit knowledge. This is knowledge which is difficult or impossible to codify, and usually resides in the heads of employees. For example, skilled workers or professionals within the organization may have particular abilities which cannot be written down: skilled welders, toolmakers or machinists have honed their skills over many years of practice. Likewise, a skilled buyer or corporate lawyer will develop skills (such as the ability to read another person's true intentions) which cannot be taught in college. Some tacit knowledge might be disseminated throughout the organization, for example customer-care skills.

4. Procedure. This is the mechanism by which the basic assets, explicit knowledge, and implicit knowledge are brought together.

Procedure can easily be mistaken for process, but the two differ. A good procedure which lacks the necessary staff skills to carry it out will not produce an effective process, nor will a bad procedure be compensated by (for example) an abundance of basic assets. The procedure must therefore take account of the available assets, explicit knowledge and tacit knowledge.

Procedure is the element which is most easily changed by management, and is therefore the element which most commonly changes. This is often unsettling for staff and requires a degree of re-learning and re-ordering of knowledge. From a tactical point of view, this can prove to be severely counter-productive.

When processes are linked together to deliver a set of benefits to customers they become the components of a capability. A capability should be more than the sum of the individual processes: synergies should result from the combination of the processes. This will not happen if the processes are inappropriately linked or mutually damaging in some way (Stalk et al. 1992). An organization may combine its processes in different ways in order to develop different capabilities, either at the same time or in order.

For example, a company may have developed effective processes for recruitment, for stock purchasing, for delivery, and for efficient invoicing. These processes might all arise from having combined an asset base of state-of-the-art computer equipment and the tacit knowledge of a group of IT experts within the firm. This is shown diagrammatically in Fig 13.1.

Obviously different managers might combine the same components in a different way in order to generate new processes and competences. This is a more complex management task than simply altering procedures, so is somewhat rarer and also is a valuable ability for a manager to have. An example of this is the nuclear waste reprocessing plant at Sellafield in Cumbria. Originally this was a facility which was used in conjunction with the nearby nuclear power plant, but managers realized that the firm's resources would be better spent on developing the waste reprocessing facility rather than expanding the power plant. British Nuclear Fuels (**www.bnfl.com**) now has a world reputation for reprocessing nuclear waste.

Generating new capabilities from existing components is in itself a process, involving creative thought as well as the ability to identify which components are available and which processes

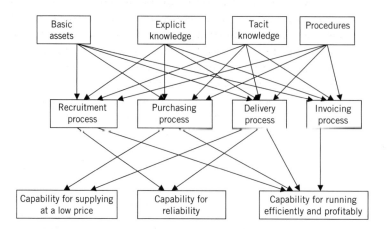

Figure 13.1: Developing resources into processes and capabilities

they can be diverted from in order to strengthen other components. From the viewpoint of the end customer, the process is a major part of the benefits of the product, and forms a large part of the perception of both company and brand. For most firms, improving the firm's competitive position will mean developing new capabilities, which in turn means either changing processes in some way or recombining processes in order to generate new capabilities.

For example, a computer software company moving into a foreign market will need to develop the capability to service that market. This may mean changing the process of recruitment to include foreign-language speakers, it may mean changing the training process to encompass training in the foreign software protocols (or at least learning the usual jargon in the foreign language). Conversely, it may mean combining an existing process for translating foreign-language documents into English with an existing capacity for writing software, so that the translation is simply carried out in reverse. In practice, it probably means a combination of all these changes, plus several more.

Talking Point

Nowadays there is great pressure on everybody to get more from the resources we have. Time management is a highly-regarded skill – yet usually it means working evenings and weekends rather than actually getting more from the working day. Cutting corners, screwing every last piece of value out of resources, pressuring everybody and everything to achieve more – is this really just a way of ignoring the details, shelving problems which are not immediate, and even building up problems for the future by thinking short-term?

Maybe rearranging resources in new ways is the equivalent of rearranging the deck chairs on the Titanic. Perhaps what we really need is to look at increasing the resources which are available!

DEVELOPING SERVICE PROCESSES

Since the process is part of the bundle of benefits that go to make up the product, the starting point for improving the process is the customers' needs. In some cases these can be presented in a hierarchy: for example, an aircraft manufacturer may not have a particularly strong need for rapid delivery of spare parts for engines, but would have a requirement for prompt delivery of the engines themselves. For the aero engine manufacturer, therefore, the process of providing spares is secondary to the process of providing engines. This means, in practice, that stocks of spare parts will be kept low, and will be 'raided' for parts to finish engines whenever necessary. This may, of course, cause problems for the airlines who operate the aircraft, since spares will be difficult to come by if the engines need to be serviced.

Service processes for customers might fall into three general categories: before-sales service processes, during-sale service processes, and after-sale service processes. The components of the three elements are as shown in Fig 13.2.

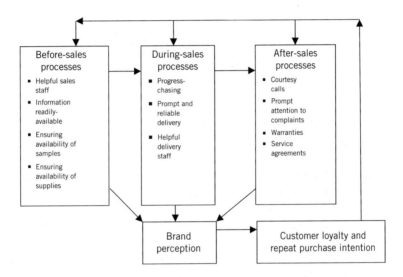

Figure 13.2: Service processes

Improvements in the service processes offer an opportunity to build loyalty because they tend to involve human interactions. Unfortunately, they are also relatively easy for competitors to copy and even exceed, so that it can be difficult to maintain a competitive edge for long simply by providing ever-improving service. There is even some evidence that firms which cut back dramatically on the service process (for example low-cost airlines) can build a competitive advantage through providing low prices rather than good service. Even here, though, the emphasis is on providing a service level that the customer is prepared to pay for: the essential elements of running an airline are that it should provide flights which go where they are supposed to go, arrive reasonably on time, and transport the passengers and their baggage in an efficient manner. Low-cost airlines do this effectively, and the more effective of them also use streamlined Internet-based booking systems which provide passengers with a rapid means of booking – this is, in fact, a service improvement over booking through travel agents even though it is also cheaper for the airline.

Competitive advantage therefore lies in setting the right kind and level of service to meet the target audience's needs, and also meet the strategic objectives of the firm. This seems obvious, but many firms still try to provide a high-grade service for a low-grade price, which can only be done by shaving profits or otherwise laying the firm open to competitive actions.

Processes can be considered as structural elements which can be used to deliver a strategic position. A process-orientated approach to strategy involves the following steps (Shostack 1987):

1. Break down the process into logical steps to facilitate its control.

2. Take the more variable processes into account: variability leads to different outcomes at different times because of variations in the judgement of the people delivering the service, or because of human error, or even customer choice.

3. Set tolerance standards which recognize that service processes do not always run perfectly, but rather function within a performance band.

Service processes can be analysed in terms of complexity and divergence. Complexity is concerned with the number of stages the process has to go through, while divergence is concerned with the variability of the stages, and consequently of the outcomes.

For example, an airline has a complex service: in order for the passengers to get where they are going, the travel agent must go through a complex process of booking a ticket for the particular airline, time and date of travel, and to the correct destination. The aircraft must be correctly serviced and fuelled. The airport at each end of the journey must provide check-in and baggage handling processes, and the air traffic controllers need to provide a highly-complex international set of processes to ensure that the route is clear for the 'plane. On board the aircraft, the pilots have a complex set of tasks to carry out, as indeed do the cabin crew, and the catering company must deliver the right number of meals and the right variations on the meals to allow for the dietary requirements of passengers. The correct amount of drinks needs to be supplied, and so on and so forth. On the other hand, the service is not very divergent. The meals are virtually identical for everyone on the flight, the flight attendants are all in uniform and are generally fairly uniform in their approaches to passengers. The aircraft take off from where they are supposed to take off from, usually within a fairly narrow band of the right time, and they arrive where they are supposed to arrive within a fairly narrow time frame. The airline industry is therefore highly-complex, but not very divergent.

On the other hand, a hairdresser might exhibit exactly the opposite characteristics. In most hair salons, the customers will only be attended by one or two of the staff, and the process does not involve anyone else. Yet the results might vary considerably – each customer is an individual, and should receive an individual hairstyle based on the client's facial characteristics, personality, self-image and so forth. On the downside, things can go wrong more often: the hairstylist might just be having a bad day, or the client asks for something which is really unsuitable, or the client's hair displays an unexpected characteristic such as being unable to take a perm.

From a strategic viewpoint, the complexity or divergence of the service can be changed to establish a competitive position. This is illustrated in Table 13.1.

Table 13.1: Complexity and divergence as strategic tools

Reduced divergence	This reduces costs, improves productivity and also makes distribution easier. This is the approach taken by fast-food restaurants as opposed to a la carte restaurants: it can lead to a perception of lack of choice, however.
Increased divergence	Greater customization, greater flexibility, and sometimes higher prices to match. This approach is more likely to found among niche marketers or small, flexible businesses.
Reduced complexity	This usually means specializing in a basic, no-frills service offering the core benefits of the product.
Increased complexity	This is a strategy which increases customer choice by offering a wider range of products or a higher level of service. For example, an airline might offer business-class passengers the use of in-flight communications or office facilities, which adds another set of complications to providing the service but which offers added value to the passengers concerned.

The matrix shown in Fig 13.3 shows the trade-offs between complexity and divergence, with examples of the type of firm that might occupy each cell of the matrix.

Figure 13.3: Complexity and divergence

	Low complexity	High complexity
High divergence	Small firms. Flexible approach.	Upmarket, expensive products with highly-empowered staff.
Low divergence	Low-cost, standardized products.	High-price, standardized products usually from large firms.

Low and high complexity may not be apparent from the viewpoint of the customer, but the level of divergence will almost always be apparent. From some customer aspects high divergence is good, because it allows for greater flexibility in service provision, but in other respects it is not good because there is less certainty about outcomes.

PHYSICAL EVIDENCE

Evidencing the provision of a service is another area in which competitive advantage is obtainable. Although virtually all services involve some kind of physical product (just as virtually all physical products encompass some form of service) there are examples of products where the main benefits are contained within the intangible service elements which attach to it.

For example, insurance policies are almost entirely intangible. In the case of life insurance, the purchaser never benefits in any material way from the policy: the proceeds go to the person's estate only on the death of the purchaser. The benefit is the intangible knowledge that one's family will be taken care of in the event of premature death. The life insurance policy therefore represents the extreme example of a service product. The physical evidence attached to a life insurance policy is the policy document, and whatever other documentation the insurance company provides.

In order to create competitive advantage the insurance policy needs to appear as solid, glossy and impressive as it can be made to look. For merely legal purposes, the policy could be written on a single sheet of paper, but for marketing purposes it should be much more substantial. Since the documentation has to be sent out anyway, there is no reason why it should not contribute to adding value as much as additions to a physical product might add value.

Talking Point

Improving the physical evidence sounds like a good idea, and certainly most firms have gone this route – but do we really care? Do we really want the hamburger restaurant to give our kids a glossy certificate when they have eaten all their dessert? And do we care about the slickness of the insurance policy?

Is this kind of thing counter-productive? Maybe a gorgeous brochure makes us suspect how much has been spent on the actual service, and how much on the brochure – and should we be paying for the sales rep's nice new suit? Not to mention putting petrol in his Mercedes!

In less extreme examples of services, the physical evidence may be much more tangible and much more part of the delivery process. For example, a hotel offers several levels of physical evidence. The building itself, the decor, and the facilities on offer are part of the experience for the guest: a swimming-pool is undoubtedly a physical thing, and is evidence for the visit. Gifts to take away, souvenirs, or vouchers against future stays are also part of the product. Another example might be car ferry services: the condition of the cabins, the condition of the public areas, and the overall standard of maintenance of the ferry are all part of the evidence for the passenger, but some companies (for example Brittany Ferries (**www.brittany-ferries.com**)) take passengers' photographs as they embark so that the passengers have a souvenir of the beginning of their holiday. This adds value to the service by providing permanent physical evidence of the trip.

There are four generic ways to add value through physical evidence:

1. Create physical evidence which increases loyalty.
2. Use physical evidence to enhance brand image.
3. Use physical evidence which has an intrinsic value of its own, for example a free gift.
4. Create physical evidence which leads to further sales.

For example, airlines use frequent-flyer points to increase loyalty. KLM's Flying Dutchman (**www.klm.com**) club has three levels: the Blue Wing, which entitles the passenger to accumulate points and eventually obtain free flights, the Silver Wing, which has all the benefits of the Blue Wing but also comes with priority luggage labels and other benefits, and the Royal Wing, which has all the benefits of the other two levels but also entitles the passenger to priority check-in procedures, use of the business-class lounge at airports, and so forth. The physical evidence of each level is the loyalty card (which has its status embossed on it) and the luggage labels, which are made of strong plastic and are a permanent fixture on the passenger's luggage. These extras make it more likely that the passenger will fly KLM in preference to other airlines, as it is the frequency of flying which determines the status level of the passenger: failure to maintain the frequency of flying will result in being downgraded.

Secondly, brand image can be enhanced by using physical evidence which evidences the brand's essential qualities. For example, insurance companies may use glossy policy documents or (if they wish to appear to be businesslike, efficient firms) they may produce documentation which explains the terms of the policy in plain English. The physical evidence need not always be upmarket: EasyJet's 'tickets' are in fact e-mailed to the recipient, so that the passenger has to print them off on ordinary paper. This is about as basic as physical evidence gets, but it enhances the essential quality of the airline, which is that it cuts every possible cost out of the equation in order to minimize fares.

Physical evidence with an intrinsic value of its own is a common ploy in financial services. Carriage clocks, pen sets, and radio-alarms are commonly given out to purchasers of pension plans, funeral insurance, or savings plans. It seems unlikely that many people would buy the insurance or pension plan simply to gain a carriage clock, but it does mean that there is some permanent reminder of the existence of the policy.

Physical evidence which leads to further sales might include a hairdresser's record card which gives the client a date to return for further treatment. Medical appointment cards fall into this category. Many firms send out reminder cards: garages send cards to remind customers that their cars need servicing, dentists send reminders when a check-up is due, computer software companies send reminders that an update is necessary. In each case the physical evidence of the previous service leads to a further sale.

Physical evidence is the customer's proof that the service has taken place and offers a permanent (or at least semi-permanent) reminder of the quality of the service. Without this the consumer would rely on memory, which is notoriously fallible.

CASE STUDY: EASYJET REBUILDS ITS PROCESSES

www.easyjet.com

EasyJet, the low-cost no-frills airline, has been the subject of many case studies and is widely-used as an example of how an innovative approach to marketing can result in remarkable successes.

However, things have not always gone smoothly for the firm. At one point it looked as if it was going to be the victim of its own success – passenger demand was growing much faster than the airline's ability to purchase new aircraft, leaving the firm with a major problem in servicing demand. The answer was either to raise fares to the point where demand would fall (which would have destroyed the airline's competitive advantage) or to find ways of making the existing fleet of aircraft work harder. EasyJet chose the latter course.

The key to the problem was seen as shortening the aircraft turnround times. The less time the aircraft spent on the ground being serviced, the more time it could spend in the air carrying passengers. A consultancy firm which specialized in developing innovative cultures was called in, and over the next three months the consultants interviewed all the people involved in turning round the aircraft. This included baggage handlers, catering firms, refuelling companies, airport staff, front-line EasyJet employees, and even the cleaning contractors. Consultants observed the process in action, spending time on the aircraft or working with the staff to see exactly what the existing processes were. Unlike the old-style time-and-motion consultants, the innovation consultants then set up the right conditions for people who actually do the job to pool their ideas.

One of the early discoveries was that the teams carrying out the various tasks involved had little or no idea of what the other teams did, and still worse did not understand how each job was reliant on every other job. For example, the ground engineer had previously waited until all the passengers had disembarked, then boarded the plane to talk to the pilots about servicing needs for the aircraft. Now the technical people wear headphones so they are able to talk to the pilots while the passengers disembark, and are thus able to go straight to work as soon as the aircraft is empty.

Ideas were disseminated by videoing the sessions and allowing staff to see what others did. Ideas are continuing to flow from the initial briefings – staff have developed an innovative culture, and who better to understand the job than those who do it all day, every day?

The net result of the activity is that turnround times are down from an average 50 minutes to an average 33 minutes. This may not seem a lot, but if an aircraft makes an average four return flights a day, this represents over an hour saved in downtime per day. Over a working year, this will total more than 60 return flights from Luton to Nice – representing additional revenue of over a million pounds per aircraft. No small amount for a firm which prides itself on cutting costs to the bone.

CASE STUDY QUESTIONS

1. To what extent did EasyJet change procedures, and to what extent did they change processes?
2. How did the processes combine to create capabilities?
3. What role did staff empowerment play in the process of creating an innovation culture?
4. Why might staff be unprepared to co-operate in such an exercise?
5. What might motivate staff to co-operate in the exercise?

SUMMARY

Process and physical evidence go beyond the realm of service products. Every bundle of benefits includes a process, and some physical evidence: these often provide a ready way for the firm to differentiate itself and create competitive advantage. From a strategic viewpoint, the key issue is to establish the correct process and physical evidence to reflect the customers' expectations: these are not necessarily the highest standards possible, as many low-cost suppliers have demonstrated.

The key points from this chapter are as follows:

- Physical products and services represent extremes on a continuum, not mutually-exclusive entities.
- The greater the service element in a product, the greater the risk for consumers and providers alike.
- Process converts inputs into outputs of greater value.
- Procedure and process are not the same.
- Generating new capabilities from existing resources is itself a process.
- Improving service processes improves loyalty.
- Physical evidence offers opportunities to increase sales and loyalty, and enhance value and brand image.

CHAPTER QUESTIONS

1. How might physical evidence be important in unsought services such as funeral directors?
2. Why do low-cost airlines virtually ignore the provision of physical evidence?
3. How might process become an issue in Internet marketing?
4. If physical evidence acts to reduce risk, why is there suspicion of glossy brochures?
5. How might an Internet service provider use physical evidence?

REFERENCES

Donnelly, J.H. Jr. and George, W.R. (eds) (1981): *Marketing of Services* (Chicago Il: American Marketing Association).

Finlay, P. (2000): *Strategic Management* (Hemel Hempstead: Financial Times Prentice Hall).

Goodfellow, J.H. (1983): 'The marketing of goods or services as a multidimensional concept', *The Quarterly Review of Marketing* Spring pp. 19–27.

Levitt, T. (1974): *Marketing for Business Growth* (New York: McGraw Hill).

Shostack, G.L. (1987): 'Service positioning through structural change', *Journal of Marketing* vol. 51, January 1987, pp. 34–43.

Stalk, G., Evans, P. and Shulman, L. (1992): 'Competing on capabilities', *Harvard Business Review* March-April.

Wickham, R.G., Fitzroy, P.T. and Mandry, G.D. (1975): 'Marketing of services: an evaluation of the theory', *European Journal of Marketing* 9 (1): pp. 59–67.

Section Five

How do we know we got there, and how do we ensure we stay there?

In this final section, we will be looking at ways of ensuring that the organization retains its competitive advantage. Managers at the top of a large, hierarchical organization can easily get out of touch – subordinates often do not give the full picture, and it may be many years since the managers themselves were at the sharp end of the business. Controls and feedback are therefore essential if the strategic plan is to stay on course.

The final chapter looks at some of the current thinking on strategic issues, and considers some of the implications for strategic management in the future.

Chapter Fourteen

Feedback and Control

INTRODUCTION

Formulating a strategy is, of course, only the beginning. The strategy itself cannot be set in stone, because circumstances change therefore managers need to monitor the implementation of the strategy to ensure that the firm remains on course. This chapter is about developing suitable feedback systems which will inform the strategic planning process, and which will also help in flagging up key issues for the staff who have the task of implementing the strategy and converting it to a set of tactical outcomes.

After reading this chapter, you should be able to:

- Describe the features of an effective monitoring system.
- Explain how monitoring helps ensure that plans are carried out.
- Describe systems for feeding back the results of monitoring.
- Explain the main features of a balanced scorecard approach.

IMPLEMENTING STRATEGY

Formulating an effective strategy is undoubtedly a wonderful thing to do, but unless the strategy is implemented effectively nothing will change. It is not unusual for strategic plans to be shelved and forgotten about: this has been called SPOTS (Strategic Plan On The Shelf) by Piercy (1997). In some cases this happens because the planners only produced a strategic plan because their bankers or shareholders required one. In other cases, attempts at implementation proved fruitless because of resistance to change within the organization. In still other cases, the plan proved so time-consuming to produce that it was obsolete by the time it was completed: the world does not stand still while the planners finalize their strategies.

Strategies therefore cannot be divorced from implementation considerations. The questions which need to be asked are as follows:

1. Is the structure of the organization capable of implementing the strategy?
2. Are resources deployed effectively – and if not, can the necessary changes be made?
3. Are managers suitably empowered to implement changes?
4. Do organizational policies support the strategies?
5. Will staff members be affected by the strategy in such a way that they might try to sabotage its implementation?

Even when planners believe they know the answers to these questions, subsequent experience can prove them wrong. Because responsibility for operations is delegated, effective monitoring and control systems need to be in place. The structure of these systems is dictated by the strategy, but the practicalities of operating the systems is itself likely to lead to changes in the interpretation of the strategy.

For example, if managers decide on a strategic objective of increasing sales to a particular group of customers, a system may be put in place to compare sales to this group with sales overall. The system may be designed to give extra rewards to salespeople who sell a higher proportion of the business to the special group of customers, but the result may be that salespeople concentrate almost exclusively on the special group, neglecting their existing customers in the process. A shift in the proportion of sales to the new group may then occur simply because sales to anybody else fall off due to this neglect. In other words, what gets measured is what gets done – what is not measured suffers as a result.

The relationship between strategy and systems structure is therefore symbiotic. Strategy dictates system, which in turn dictates strategy and so forth.

IMPLEMENTATION AND CHANGE

Any new strategy involves change for somebody. Difficulties arise because change is not always acceptable for some people: resistance to change is endemic in organizations, and in particular in hierarchical, mechanistic organizations where the individual's standing in the organization might be adversely affected by any changes.

Some of the changes brought about by strategy implementation are direct, and some are indirect. Often it is the indirect changes which are the most desirable, but the direct changes which are the easiest to dictate. Equally, the direct changes are the ones which are most likely to provoke attempts at sabotage, and the indirect changes which are least likely to be diverted. Aspects which can be changed directly are shown in Table 14.1.

When strategic plans are implemented, some changes will occur indirectly. These are as follows (Thompson 1997):

Table 14.1: Directly-changeable aspects of implementation

Aspect	Explanation and examples
Organization structure	The hierarchy of the organization can be redrawn with new posts created or old ones removed. The informal structure will remain intact, insofar as the individual staff remain employed under the new structure.
Management systems	Information systems, feedback systems and control mechanisms (for example rewards and sanctions offered to staff) will be easy to change, but will require some investment in retraining.
Policies and procedures	Procedures are often the easiest aspects to change, and therefore are often the first aspects which the less-competent manager will address.
Action plans and short-term budgets	Action plans outline the tactics to be used to achieve the strategy. Tactics are relatively easy to change: short-term budgets can also be altered with relatively little difficulty.
Management information systems	The methods by which management is fed information affect the type of information that is supplied. Managers cannot be aware of everything that is going on within the organization: therefore they are, to some extent, at the mercy of the staff below them, who supply the information on which decisions are based. Changes in the information system will inevitably impact on future strategic decision-making.

1. Communication systems. Formal information flows are affected directly by management, but a large part of the communication system within any organization is carried out informally. Any changes to this system are indirect (for example if staff are moved to a different location), and it is not usually possible for managements to make direct changes.

2. Managing and developing quality and excellence. Much of the quality and excellence in the organization's work comes from the attitude of staff and their willingness to pay attention to detail. This cannot be dictated by management, although it can be fostered by appropriate policies.

3. Manifested values and the organizational culture. The organization culture is the product of the people who work within it. Again, this cannot be directly changed by management, even though changes can be fostered: if staff are not prepared to accede to management plans to change the culture, they will not go along with it.

4. The fostering of innovation. Creativity and innovation cannot be ordered. In Edison's words, creativity is 2 per cent. inspiration and 98 per cent perspiration, and there is really no way that managers can demand that people be inventive. It is, of course, possible to reward creativity and create the right conditions under which it can flourish, but this alone will not force it to happen.

There are four problem areas associated with strategy implementation (Owen 1982):

1. Strategy and structure need to be matched so they support each other, but at the same time each product in the organization's portfolio needs to match closely with its target market. This inevitably creates conflicts.

2. Communications and feedback systems may not be adapted to the new regime, so that managers have difficulty in assessing whether the strategy is running into trouble or is proceeding smoothly.

3. Any strategic change involves risk and uncertainty. This creates problems for staff, who may therefore agree to changes when in meetings but will not implement the changes later.

4. Other management systems such as staff development schemes, pay structures, and communications systems have been developed to meet the previous strategic structure of

the company. Constant modification is difficult or impossible, so these historical schemes may stand in the way of implementing the new strategy.

Additional problems may also arise (Alexander 1985). Managers often fail to assess correctly the amount of time and the problems that implementation involves. Secondly, there are many other distractions which divert attention away from making strategic changes. Thirdly, because strategy implementation is necessarily time-consuming, the reasons for making the changes might disappear or at least change in nature in the meantime. Therefore, even if the strategy was well thought out in the first place, problems such as those outlined above will still militate against an orderly process of change.

Overcoming these problems is never likely to be 100 per cent effective, but some precautions might help. Owen (1982) suggests the following:

1. Clear responsibility should be allocated for the outcomes of strategic change.
2. The number of changes being implemented at any one time should be limited. The ability of staff to cope with change is often a key determinant of strategy.
3. Necessary actions to implement strategy should be identified and responsibilities allocated.
4. Progress measurement points should be established, so that strategy implementation can be mapped against expectations.
5. Performance measures should be established along with suitable monitoring and control mechanisms.

In the 21st century environment, change is a constant factor. It is no longer feasible in most industries to consider change as a series of discrete events, but rather as a continuous flow.

Talking Point

We hear a great deal about the rapid change that is the characteristic of 21st century business life. But is change really more rapid than it was 100 years ago? Where's the evidence?

In 1903 the Wright Brothers carried out the first powered flight: within the following decade, airmail services had been established, war aircraft had been designed and built, and the first passenger services were beginning. Within 20 years of the first flight air travel had become regular, with scheduled services between London and Paris. Within 50 years, jet transport was available, intercontinental passenger services were established, and the sound barrier had been broken – not to mention that the first space flights were well under way.

Compare with the Internet, which has its beginnings in the 1960s. Forty years later, most people in western Europe still do not have access to it, virtually no companies using it for commercial purposes have made any money at it, and it is beset by software problems from viruses to simple overload of the system. So is change really moving faster? Or is this just a perception of the stressed-out, overloaded 21st century mind?

MONITORING AND EVALUATING MARKETING PERFORMANCE

Feedback is essential for monitoring performance, and (in an ideal world) no marketing activity would be undertaken without having a monitoring and evaluation system in place beforehand.

There are two basic groups of approaches for performance analysis: sales analysis and marketing cost analysis. **Sales analysis** looks at the income generated by the firm's activities, whereas marketing analysis looks at the costs of generating the income. Table 14.2 illustrates some sales analysis measures.

Table 14.2: Methods of sales analysis

Analysis Method	Explanation
Comparison with forecast sales	The firm compares the actual sales achieved against what was forecast for the period.
Comparison with competitors' sales	Provided the information is available, the firm can estimate the extent to which marketing activities have made inroads into the competitors' business. The problem here is proving that the difference has been caused by the high quality of the firm's marketing activities, rather than by the ineptness of competitors.
Comparison with industry sales	Examination of the firm's performance in terms of market share. This is commonly used in industries where a relatively small number of firms control the market; for example, the car industry.
Cash volume sales analysis	Comparison of sales in terms of cash generated. This has the advantage that currency is common to both sales and costs; it has the disadvantage that price rises may cause the company to think it has done better than it has.
Unit sales analysis	Comparison of sales in terms of the number of units sold, or sometimes the number of sales transactions. This is a useful measure of sales force activities, but should not be taken in isolation; sometimes the figures can be distorted by increased sales of cheaper models.
Sales by geographic unit	Sales are broken down regionally so the firm can tell whether one or two regions are accounting for most of the sales, and whether some less-productive regions are not worth what they cost to service.
Sales by product group or brand	This is particularly important for judging the product portfolio (see the BCG Matrix in Chapter 6). This serves two purposes: it is possible to identify products which should be dropped from the range, and it is also possible to identify products which are moving into the decline phase of the product life cycle and should therefore be revived.
Sales by type of customer	Can reveal, for example, that most effort is being expended on a group of customers who make relatively few purchases. May reveal that the firm's customers tend to be ageing, and may therefore be a declining group in years to come.

Considerable amounts of information will be needed if the firm is to make effective use of sales analysis to monitor activities. This may involve the firm in substantial market research expenditure, since market research is the cornerstone of monitoring and evaluation.

The other part of the picture is to examine the cost of achieving the goals which have been specified. **Marketing cost analysis** is a set of techniques for breaking down the costs of the firm's activities and associating them with specific marketing objectives. Costs can be broken down (broadly) into **direct costs** such as salespersons' salaries which can be directly attributable to a given activity, **traceable common costs** such as costs of advertising which can be traced back to specific products, and **non-traceable common costs** such as the cost of PR or corporate advertising which cannot be allocated to any particular product range or brand.

The main problem with marketing cost analysis lies in organizing the firm's accounting systems in such a way as to permit analysis. For example, payroll records may not be easily broken down by job function; it may be difficult to sort out which of the administration staff spend most of their time on marketing-related tasks, or even to find out what the pay bill is for the salesforce. Likewise, defining which jobs constitute marketing jobs and which do not also presents problems. Clearly the cost of servicing customers in remote areas is a marketing cost – so should transportation costs be taken into account as well as salesforce mileage costs? Also, if a given product is not performing well, should we be looking at the costs of production?

For the dyed-in-the-wool customer-orientated firm these answers are obvious, since all the activities of the firm are regarded as marketing activities. In other firms, not all managers agree with the basic premises on which marketing is based. At the very least, many people find it difficult to translate the theory into practice and to gear the organization's activities towards a consumer orientation, as seen in Chapter 1.

A problem with all of the above approaches is that they are financially-based and predicated on the assumption that marketing is about making sales rather than about achieving strategic marketing objectives. For example, a firm may have a legitimate marketing objective to improve customer loyalty. While this may increase sales in the long run, the appropriate measure of success would be the degree to which customers make repeat purchases, which in the short term may actually lead to a reduction in sales as the firm shifts the emphasis away from recruiting new customers towards retaining existing ones.

BALANCED SCORECARDS

The balanced scorecard approach was suggested by Kaplan and Norton (1992). The authors suggest that the organization should measure performance using a limited, specific set of measures derived from the success factors which are most important to the stakeholder groups.

The measures to be used can be grouped in the following categories:

1. Financial measures. These would include return on capital employed, cash flow, growth in share value and so forth.
2. Customers. These measures would include perceived value for money (not necessarily cheapness), competitive benefits package, and so forth.
3. Internal processes. These might be enquiry response time, conversion rate from enquiry to order.
4. Growth and improvement. This would include the number of new products on offer, the extent of employee involvement and empowerment, employee attitudes to the firm, and so forth.

The balanced scorecard is an attempt to integrate all the factors which would impact on the organization's long-term success so that the strategy does not become unbalanced. To be most effective, managers need to apply some weighting to each of the factors in order to ensure that attention is paid to those areas which are most closely allied to the corporate mission or vision.

FEEDBACK SYSTEMS

When a discrepancy appears between the expected performance and the actual performance, the marketing manager will need to take action. This will usually take the following sequence:

■ Determine the reason for the discrepancy. Was the original plan reasonable? Have the firm's competitors seized the initiative in some way, so that the situation has changed? Is someone at fault?

■ Feed these findings back to the staff concerned. This can be in the form of a meeting to discuss the situation, or in the form of memos and reports.

■ Develop a plan for correcting the situation. This will probably involve the co-operation of all the staff concerned.

Feedback should be both frequent and concise, and any criticisms should be constructive; managers should never (for example) go to a sales meeting and offer only criticisms since this sends the salesforce out with negative feelings about themselves and the company.

Marketing strategy and planning is much like any other planning exercise; it relies on good information, a clear idea of where the organization is going, and regular examination of both outcomes and methods to ensure that the plan is still on target.

CONTROL SYSTEMS

The purpose of any strategic control system is to decide whether the current strategy is correct and should therefore be retained, or whether circumstances have altered in such a way that the strategy should be scrapped and a new one formulated.

Most control is reactive: it seeks out variances in performance, and applies a correction to redress the variance. Such feedback is called negative feedback, because it acts against the trend of the variance in order to reduce it. Feedback which tends to increase the variance is called positive feedback, and is generally considered to be counter-productive since it creates a situation where the system runs away with itself entirely in one direction. In some cases, a variation which is self-correcting, i.e. a temporary blip in performance, may be over-compensated for so that variance increases rather than decreases. This comes about because of time delays in the feedback systems. Figure 14.1 illustrates how this works in practice.

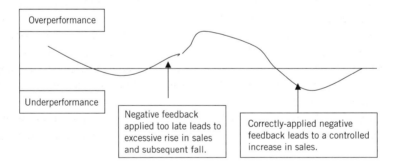

Figure 14.1: Positive and negative feedback

In Fig 14.1 the first arrow shows how feedback applied too late will send sales rocketing too high. This may seem like a good outcome, but it is likely that the feedback applied will have been a costly sales-boosting exercise such as a major sales promotion or an advertising campaign, the result of which is a fall in profits, possibly a fall in competitive position, and at worst provokes an insupportable competitive reaction. The second arrow shows a correctly-applied negative feedback, which helps the fall in sales to bottom out and return to normal.

Some fluctuation is inevitable. Minor deviations from the plan will always occur sooner or later: the difficulty for managers lies in judging the extent to which such deviations are permissible before action must be taken.

The concept of feedback and control is borrowed from engineering. The controls for a machine are intended to maintain the status quo: some controls are automatic (for example the governor on a steam engine) while others are designed for used by a machine operator (for example the accelerator on a car). In either case the machine will obey the control systems, because that is what it has been designed to do.

Human beings are not machines. The most difficult management issues concern the control of human beings, and this is the area where the feedback systems most often break down. For the purposes of feedback and control, processes can be divided into systematized processes such as repetitive clerical or assembly-line tasks, and unstructured processes, which are activities requiring judgement (Dermer 1977). Examples of the second type would include professional activities such as the law or accountancy, and within the firm they would include senior managerial tasks and one-off projects. For most 21st century firms, unstructured processes are in the majority simply because repetitive clerical work has been taken over by computers and most factory work has been automated. Since Dermer first formulated this division in 1977, the number of people working in manual jobs has more than halved: at the same time, the number of clerical tasks such as filing and typing has dramatically reduced due to the use of computers. It is unlikely that any firms nowadays have a typing pool, but in the 1970s such systems were commonplace.

DIFFICULTIES WITH CONTROL SYSTEMS

The type of thinking that applies to engineering problems is not necessarily applicable to human problems. Each has its own set of assumptions which may not hold true for the other: certainly many of the assumptions made by managers prove to be false when attempts are made to put them into practice. Finlay (2000) says there are four assumptions borrowed from engineering which do not transfer to management. These are shown in Table 14.3.

Because of these problems, firms need to use adaptive controls. While much of the control system can be automatic, managers need to use human judgement to override the system when necessary, otherwise long-term change is unlikely to happen. Hofstede (1978) uses a biological analogy to explain this in terms of a living cell, but it may be more appropriate to think of a more complex organism. Fluctuations in outside temperature can be compensated for by the body's

Table 14.3: Assumptions underlying control systems

Assumption	Problems with this view
Objectives can be devised and can be stated precisely.	Most organizations do not have clear objectives, but rather have broad goals. For example, it is almost impossible to set objectives for a personnel department or a legal department, and in many cases it is difficult to do so for a marketing department. Companies led by visionaries neither have nor need objectives – the vision is sufficient.
Achievement can be measured and a measure of variance can be calculated.	Without measurable objectives, achievement cannot be measured. Even if there is a measurable objective, the reason for the variance may be difficult to calculate – a fall in sales may be due to a great many factors, some of which are beyond the marketer's control.
Variance information can be fed back.	Unstructured activities involve judgement and are often unique, so feedback for one activity is unlikely to be directly applicable to another. Indirect feedback is about accumulating knowledge and extrapolating from it, not about applying a set, known correction.
The feedback is sufficient to maintain control.	The system will only work if the applied feedback is bigger than the environmental shift. For example, a company selling over-the-counter cold medicines might decide that a fall-off in sales should be followed by an advertising campaign to boost customer interest. This will not work if someone finds a permanent cure for the common cold.

natural homeostatic mechanisms – sweating when the temperature is too high, shivering when it is too cold – but beyond certain limits of comfort a human being will exercise judgement and either go somewhere cooler or wear something warmer, as appropriate. In a similar way, organizations need to exercise judgement when the environment behaves in a way that is beyond the control system's capacity.

Two methods of control exist: firstly, to change the organization's behaviour in some way to overcome the difficulty and reach the objective, or secondly to change objectives and aim for something that is achievable rather than something that is not. The ancient Greek philosopher Diogenes was perhaps the greatest exponent of the latter course: in order to avoid the problems of earning enough money to live in a house, he chose to live in a barrel instead. This option may not always be the optimum one.

Controls come in hierarchies, and levels of control are exercised at different levels of the organization. Three generic ways of controlling the course of events in the business are available: firstly, changing the inputs to the system; secondly, the process itself can be controlled; thirdly, the objective of the organization can be changed.

TACTICS OF CONTROL

There are three basic types of control, as shown in Table 14.4 (Johnson and Gill 1993).

Table 14.4: Types of control

Type of Control	Explanation and examples
Administrative control	Based on systems, rules and procedures, administrative control is typical in hierarchical organizations which often have large numbers of rules and regulations.
Social control	The control exercised by workmates and the organizational culture. This is common in organismic organizations and smaller organizations.
Self-control	Control exercised by individuals on themselves, based on their own interpretation of correct behaviour. This is common in organizations composed of professional people, who may be working to a professional code of ethics rather than a set of rules laid down by the employer.

Administrative control is often exercised through planning systems which control the allocation of resources and monitor the utilization of resources against the plan. Planning systems might be top-down, centralized systems in which the standardization of work procedures is paramount. Even in service industries the routinization of working practices has been achieved: McDonald's (**www.mcdonalds.com**) hamburgers are produced in a routinized way which would have been thought impossible in the restaurant businesses of 100 years ago. Such centrally-planned systems often use a formula approach, for example setting budgets as fixed percentages of turnover or allocating resources on the basis of numbers of customers dealt with. This tends to place an emphasis on bargaining within the organization to vary the formula in some way.

Within a devolved organization structure, administrative control is more likely to centre on bottom-up planning, carried out within an overall set of budget constraints. In these circumstances, each division needs to reconcile its activities with other divisions in order to ensure consistency: this becomes the main role of senior management within the organization. The risk of bottom-up planning is that key strategic issues are left out of the equation, because each division focuses on its own part of the problem without seeing the overall picture. Again, co-ordination is a function of senior management: the centre needs to establish the boundaries and reconcile the plans of the divisions, which may in turn mean that the centre should benchmark in order to establish best practice.

Control through direct supervision is common in small organizations where one person is able to control resources effectively. In large organizations it is only really possible in conditions of stability or during times of crisis (for example if the survival of the organization is threatened). Autocratic direct control by one person might be the only way the necessary changes can be forced through – although, of necessity, this is a route which is likely to lead to considerable resentment among lower-grade staff who are displaced or undermined.

Control through performance targets has become popular during the 1990s, especially as a way of controlling the newly-privatized natural monopolies of power supply, railways, telephone systems and so forth. Setting the correct performance indicators is far from easy: indicators often give only a partial view of the overall situation, and it is usually the case that activities which are measured are the ones that get done, regardless of the real-life situations faced by the staff and managers in the organization.

Responsibility for marketing is likely to be devolved to the divisions, since marketing (in a customer-orientated firm) pervades all the activities of the organization. An organization given to using financial controls is likely to establish such divisions as profit centres, which rather complicates the issue for the divisions since they will be working towards marketing-based objectives, but will be judged on a finance-based objective. Strategic planning based organizations will be more likely to use cost or revenue centres, with marketing planning being carried out at the centre.

Social and cultural control comes from the standardization of norms of behaviour within the organization. In such organizations, administrative controls have a lower priority: people behave in the way they do because it is the right way to behave, not because they have a boss applying the yardstick at every stage. In the 21st century organization, this type of control is likely to become much more prevalent: people are becoming more individualistic and more idealistic, and less inclined to obey orders blindly. Also, social controls are much more effective in organizations which are facing chaotic situations or circumstances of rapid environmental change, in which it is impossible to lay down fixed procedures for dealing with every possible eventuality.

Social controls can sometimes work the other way by hindering senior management when changes become necessary. The reason is that cultural norms are difficult to change, and people who regard themselves as professionals are likely to prove difficult if asked to do something which they feel impinges on their professional prerogatives.

In some respects, the 21st century workplace is likely to be less about controls and more about influences. Managers may not be able to impose fixed procedures on workers, partly because such procedures will be difficult to formulate, and partly because a well-educated, independent-minded workforce is unlikely to be as prepared to accept management by diktat as workers were 50 or 100 years ago. Influence can come from many sources, but the greatest influences are likely to be social ones, created by and in turn creating obligations between the staff. This implies that managers will need to be charismatic rather than autocratic, and lead rather than drive the workforce.

CASE STUDY: J.P. GETTY

When Getty was a young man of 21 he went into the oil business. He searched out oil wells, operating largely by instinct, drilling holes wherever he thought he might strike oil and living largely on hope. He bossed his tough gang of drillers himself, sometimes with the force of his personality and sometimes with tests of physical strength – he once famously raced one of his men to the top of the drilling rig, to teach the man not to turn up for work drunk. By the time he was 24 he owned a Model T Ford, three sets of overalls, and enough successful oil wells to make him a millionaire. So he retired, went to live in Hollywood, and enjoyed an endless round of wild parties and high living.

At age 26 he got bored with this and went back to work. For the rest of his life he amused himself by buying up failing companies and turning them round – with astounding success. He seemed to have the Midas touch: every company he bought went from rags to riches, and of course he continued to make money – but this was almost a by-product of what he was really doing, which was having fun solving puzzles.

His secret was to control what was going on in companies which had begun to run out of control. He had a fixed policy for all his companies: he aimed to halve the overheads, and double the sales. Controlling the overheads meant introducing strict rules: every employee was required to turn out lights when leaving rooms empty, not because this made a great saving on the electricity bill but because it got the message across that there was to be no waste. People were required to write on both sides of the paper – at a time when environmentalism had yet to be invented. Lax attitudes to company property were not tolerated – he once sent an executive a bill for $11 for scrap wood which the executive had taken home to fix his garden shed.

But it was in the area of social controls that Getty excelled. Apart from developing a parsimonious culture in his companies, he made people feel that they wanted to do better for the companies. At one company, the practice had been for the workers to start at eight a.m. and the executives to start at nine. Getty thought this was unfair and unreasonable, and certainly not what he would have done in his wildcatting days, so he required the executives to start at eight as well. At first, there was considerable resentment from the executives and some even went so far as to refuse to do it, but Getty began a regime of showing up at seven himself, and calling a breakfast meeting at eight with all the senior executives. After a while they came around to the idea – after all, if the billionaire boss was prepared to get up at five a.m. to drive 100 miles to the company headquarters in order to be there for seven, it seemed a little ridiculous not to be prepared to match this by showing up at eight.

On another occasion he found that some of his executives had made mistakes which had cost the company thousands of dollars. He instructed the pay department to deliberately make 'errors' on the executives' pay cheques of $5 each, and to refer the executives to him if they complained. On pay day, the executives came to see Getty one by one, as they had opportunity to check their salaries. In each case Getty said much the same thing. 'Last year you made mistakes which cost this company ▶

$10,000 without ever worrying about it. But when the company makes a mistake which costs you $5, you're up here to see me about it.' All but three of the executives saw the point and learned the lesson: the other three remained indignant, and eventually had to be fired.

Getty was famous for ruling with an iron fist, but at the same time having respect for the people working for him, and for never asking someone to do something that he was not prepared to do himself. As a charismatic manager, he inspired respect: as a sharp businessman, he demanded obedience: and as a stubborn and opinionated man he generated success in others.

Getty's private life was also characterized by the same unbending principles. He had a payphone installed in his house for his house guests to use – partly because his work habits were difficult to break, but also because rich men attract freeloaders. When his grandson was kidnapped he refused to pay up, saying that to do so would put the rest of his family at risk – and he stuck to his guns even when the kidnappers cut off his grandson's ear and mailed it to him. The end result was that the kidnappers realized they were not going to get the money, and the grandson was released. Getty also endowed the world's largest and richest arts foundation, which collects art works from throughout the world for the Getty Museum. Money was always just a tool for him – the real challenge in life lay in controlling things, and making them work better.

CASE STUDY QUESTIONS

1. What types of control system was Getty using?
2. As a change agent, what style did Getty adopt?
3. To what extent would Getty's management style be transferable to other managers?
4. What role did feedback play in Getty's management style?
5. What were they key drivers for Getty's management success?

SUMMARY

Feedback and control are essential if the strategy is to be kept on course, even if the company is in a changing environment. For firms in stable environments, formalized systems of feedback with clear parameters for working will be effective: in a rapidly-changing environment, the strategic vision is maintained by social and cultural controls rather than formal regulations.

The key points from this chapter are as follows:

- Creativity can be encouraged, but cannot necessarily be ordered.
- Marketing measures are usually based either on sales or on costs.
- Feedback is about identifying divergence from pre-set targets.
- Control is reactive: it responds to divergences identified by the feedback system.
- Human beings are not machines. Feedback systems based on engineering theory will need to include the possibility of being overridden by human managers.
- Administrative controls work best in stable environments, socio-cultural controls work best in conditions of change, self-controls work best in professional organizations.

CHAPTER QUESTIONS

1. A common method of obtaining feedback in service industries is the use of customer response forms. How might you ensure that every customer completes one of these forms?

2. If control is reactive, how might you ensure that managers are able to vary the responses to match actual circumstances?

3. Socio-cultural controls exist in the minds of staff. How might this affect an induction programme?

4. What are the problems associated with giving feedback in circumstances of rapid environmental change?

5. How might administrative controls be helpful in an organismic organization?

REFERENCES

Alexander, L.D. (1985): 'Successfully implementing strategic decisions', *Long Range Planning*, 18 (3).

Dermer, J. (1977): Management Planning and Control Systems: Advanced Concepts and Cases (Irwin).

Finlay, P. (2000): *Strategic Management*. (Harlow: Financial Times Prentice-Hall).

Hofstede, G. (1978): 'The poverty of management control philosophy', *Academy of Management Review*, vol. 3 no. 3, July pp. 450–61.

Johnson, P. and Gill, J. (1993): *Management Control and Organisational Behaviour*. (Paul Chapman Publishing).

Kaplan, R.S. and Norton, D.P. (1992): 'The balanced scorecard – measures that drive performance', *Harvard Business Review* Jan–Feb.

Owen, A.A. (1982): 'How to implement strategy', *Management Today*, July.

Piercy, N. (1997): *Market-led Strategic Change: Transforming the Process of Going to Market* (Oxford: Butterworth-Heinemann).

Thompson, J.L. (1997): *Strategic management: awareness and change* 3rd edition (London: International Thomson Business Press).

Chapter Fifteen

Managing the Process

INTRODUCTION

Deciding what needs to be done is only a part of the story. Managers need to ensure that the strategies decided upon are translated into tactics, and the tactics are correctly applied within the organization.

After reading this chapter, you should be able to:

■ Explain how to translate strategy into tactics.
■ Explain the effects of different organizational structures on the process.
■ Describe ways of motivating staff to carry out the desired actions.
■ Describe the main sources of conflict in organizations, and suggest ways of minimizing it or of using it to advantage.

TRANSLATING STRATEGY INTO TACTICS

The dividing line between strategy and tactics is often blurred. Network level tactics become strategies at the corporate level, and so forth down to the functional level, which for marketers is the level at which the four Ps (or seven Ps) are handled. Strategies are formulated and handed down to managers to achieve, and in turn these managers need to organize resources (including staff) to carry out the strategic plan.

One of the key identifying features of tactics (as opposed to strategy) is that tactical decisions are relatively easier to reverse. This means that tactics can more easily be changed in unstable environmental conditions.

For a strategy to be converted to tactics, the following four elements need to be put in place:

1. A specific action (what is to be done).
2. An accountability (who is to do it).
3. A deadline (when it should be done by).
4. A budget (what it will cost to do it).

Usually a set of tactics will be developed to implement the strategy, and these tactics will need to be coordinated. An example in marketing is the development of integrated marketing communications. For example, a fast-food company entering a new country might make a strategic decision that expansion to a new part of the country will only take place once a 20 per cent brand awareness has been achieved within the target area. The tactical approach to this will involve advertising, press releases, advance promotions such as discount coupons, and possibly sponsorship deals to create local interest. Thus the media buyers and creative staff at the advertising agency will need to carry out their tasks at specific times and within specific budgets, the PR staff will need to create the press releases and arrange (as far as possible) for them to appear in the Press at the right times, and the promotions people will need to time their promotions to follow on from the other publicity. If the processes do not happen at the right times, the whole campaign will be adversely affected: discount coupons coming out ahead of the advertising will mean nothing to the recipients, and newspapers are unlikely to print stories about a company they have never heard of.

Furthermore, in the example above, market research will need to be carried out in the area on a regular basis to ensure that the message has been received and understood by the population at large. Within the framework described, a failure to reach 20 per cent brand awareness within the specified time frame will result in a shift in tactics – the market research should, if it is conducted properly, reveal better ways of achieving the ultimate strategic goal. Note that the strategy remains unaltered by the tactical changes.

STRATEGY AND ORGANIZATIONAL STRUCTURE

The structure of an organization is intended to define the roles, tasks and work to be carried out, breaking it down into components which might define the boundaries of the various departments or business units which have to carry out the work.

The first question to be answered is whether strategy dictates structure, or structure dictates strategy. The former view appears more logical, since decisions about what kind of organization is necessary to carry out strategic plans appear to be basic to the process: however, the latter view also has its merits. Since strategy is the art of the possible, the organization structure will be a factor in deciding which strategies are appropriate. The lack of an appropriate structure might preclude some strategies from consideration, whereas a different kind of structure might well encourage managers to believe that a different type of competitive advantage can be obtained.

For example, a small organization with a flexible structure might be able to develop competitive advantage by being quicker to respond to customer needs. A small software house might be able to respond much more quickly to customer needs simply because it is small, and has a more organismic structure which is able to adapt to change more quickly.

Equally, a hierarchical, inflexible structure does not lend itself to rapid changes and the strategy needs to take account of this. A strategy which involves maintaining the status quo is appropriate for such organizations, and works well in firms which are large enough to have some degree of control over their environment – for example, major oil companies. A large firm such as BP has considerable control over the environments in which it operates, and can therefore operate well with a fairly hierarchical structure.

Managers need to ask the following questions:

1. Is the structure capable of implementing the ideas?
2. Are resources deployed effectively within the organization?
3. Are managers suitably empowered?

If any of the answers to these questions is No, then either the structure of the organization is wrong or the strategy is wrong. Either one can be changed, but obviously the decision will rest on which is easier (or safer) to change in order to ensure the organization's survival in the longer term.

Continual tinkering with the structure is not an optimum solution in most cases, because employees will become unsettled by the changes: it is probably better to build in the required degree of flexibility when first designing the corporate structure. The downside to changes in the structure (from the staff viewpoint) are as follows:

1. Changes in structure mean that people's career paths become unclear.
2. Effort which has been put into building relationships with colleagues can be wasted.
3. Changes often mean learning new roles. This means the benefits of the structural changes will be slow in arriving.
4. Learning new roles means that more mistakes will be made at first.
5. If change is being forced through against a staff member's wishes.
6. The people who are most able to change jobs are usually the most talented.
7. Changes in structure inevitably mean changes in status: those whose status improves might be happy about this, but those whose status is lowered will not.

These practical problems may mean that it is easier to change the strategy, and some managers will certainly take this option. On the other hand, a change in the strategy might prove fatal to the organization, and therefore the strategy which is correct for the organization might be forced through over the objections of the staff.

This is clearly problematical: if staff do not support the changes, feel threatened by them, and feel that their status or job security is threatened, they are likely to sabotage the changes. This may happen officially, through industrial action or through union representation, or it may happen covertly through non-co-operation with the changes. Managements in hierarchical organizations can easily acquire the reputation of being bullies, and it is common for firms in trouble to bring in 'hatchet men' who use force of personality to push changes through, often with little regard for casualties.

The following tactics might be useful in reducing the problems outlined above.

Table 15.1: Tactics for improving the acceptance of structural changes

Problem	Tactical alternatives
Career paths become unclear.	New career opportunities under the new regime will exist, and these should be pointed out early in the process: for example, a document which begins 'Due to our ongoing commitment to improving the organization, a restructuring will be implemented. This will mean that the following new posts will be created, and priority will be given to existing staff in making appointments to these posts.' This positive approach is more likely to be supported than an approach which says that posts will disappear.
Networks with colleagues will disappear.	Time spent in building networks is never wasted. People who are well-networked should be identified, as they are often the best drivers for the new structure since they are usually influential in the organization.
New roles take time to learn.	Before the new structure is implemented, an audit should be taken of staff to find out who already has the necessary skills for the new structure. These people should be given status, and preferably also the task of teaching others whenever this is possible. Obviously managers should be tolerant of mistakes at this early learning stage.
More mistakes will be made.	Tolerance of mistakes is of course essential, but managers also need to be extra vigilant during transition periods. Training is only partly effective: often people will do well on the training sessions, but only apply the learning correctly once they have actually started trying to do the job they have trained for.
Staff may feel that this is an opportune moment to leave.	Change is always disruptive, even when it is beneficial. Staff who can see that the change will be beneficial to themselves are more likely to accept the changes: emphasizing the career benefits and medium-term improvements that the changes will bring will certainly help. Emphasizing the ways in which the firm will benefit is likely to be counterproductive, since it signals that the management are more concerned with the shareholders than with the staff. Although this might be obvious to staff anyway, it is tactless to make it explicit.
The most talented people will find it easiest to leave.	Any strategic changes should (ideally) benefit the most talented staff most directly. These people need to be brought into the confidence of senior management: in fact, if possible everybody in the organization should be kept as fully-informed as is reasonable.
Some people will lose status.	Ideally, this should not happen but if it does then such people should either be compensated in some way, or should be offered the chance to take redundancy payments. They would almost certainly be entitled to this anyway, as a reduction in status would probably be regarded as a constructive dismissal by an industrial tribunal. Perhaps surprisingly, however, some people may be prepared to downshift in status if this also means a quieter life.

Sometimes replacement of staff is unavoidable. Some skills become obsolete, others become essential and are unavailable from within.

Strategic changes will be easier to implement if managers (and indeed staff) feel that they own the mission and corporate strategy. Suitably empowered managers and staff will be able to be more innovative, more flexible and more able to take risks in order to improve the outcomes of environmental threats and opportunities.

Failure to predict the time implementation will take and the problems which will arise, failure to take account of other problems which will divert attention and resources elsewhere, and failure to forecast correctly the bases on which the strategy was formulated will also affect the outcomes (Alexander 1985).

In fact, much can be achieved within the existing framework by changing the way people operate within it. An alternative to trying to change the structure of the organization is to use an organismic organization structure, as discussed in Chapter 5. Organismic structures have the following characteristics:

1. Communications flow evenly between all the members of the organization.
2. There is no fixed leadership: leadership devolves to the person best fitted to deal with the situation facing the organization at the time.
3. Status in the organization comes from knowledge and skill rather than from qualifications and experience.
4. The organization makes use of a broader range of skills from each individual than would be the case in a hierarchical organization.

These characteristics mean that an organismic structure is able to react quickly to external changes, and thus does not need to go through the painful readjustments that a hierarchical organization would need. Organismic organizations can react extremely quickly: of course, they also have drawbacks, as follows:

1. A great deal of time is spent in discussions, and in resolving leadership issues.
2. Career paths can be difficult to identify.
3. The bigger the organization, the more complex communications become.
4. In periods of stability, managers tend to become confirmed in their leadership roles. In other words, the organization tends to become hierarchical if conditions remain stable.

In fact, most organizations combine features of hierarchies and organisms. One method of combining both is to use a divisionalized structure, which splits the organization into separate entities which each have a large degree of autonomy within the overall structure. Each division is free to organize itself along whatever lines are most appropriate in the opinion of management. Divisions can be created along product lines, geographically, or by type of work (manufacturing, distribution and so forth). The major advantage of divisionalization is that it devolves management decision-making to a point nearer the customer. This inevitably makes the decision-making more appropriate and faster.

Like segmentation, there is no single right way of dividing up an organization. There are several wrong ways however, most of which derive from a failure to consider the effects of conflict within the organization.

Talking Point

Organismic structures are commonly cited as a way of coping with change. The rapid communications within these structures enables change to happen fast, and the fluidity of leadership means that the right person is on hand to lead for any particular task.

But all this fluidity means that there must surely be more possibilities of conflict. How do people know what they are supposed to be doing? How are leadership conflicts resolved? Wouldn't it be simpler all round if there was one boss who just told everybody what to do?

Maybe organismic organizations would need a referee to resolve conflicts. Or maybe any organismic organization simply reverts to being a hierarchy eventually, with the strongest personality at the top!

CONFLICT IN ORGANIZATIONS

Broadly speaking, conflict is a psycho-social outcome of interaction (Ruekert and Walker 1987) and can be described as a breakdown or disruption in normal activities in such a way that the individuals or groups concerned experience difficulty working together (Reitz 1977; Hellreigel and Slocum 1988; Hodge and Anthony 1991; Robbins 1991; Daft 1998; Hatch 1997). The view that one person is negatively affecting something that the other person cares about is part of the traditional view of conflict as being dysfunctional, where all conflict is seen to impact negatively on the organization (reducing productivity and decreasing morale) and should therefore be avoided at all costs. In other words, the traditional view of conflict in the workplace is that it is a bad thing, reducing the efficiency of the organization by focusing attention on the conflict rather than on the aims of the organization.

An alternative view is that conflict is inevitable where people have a diversity of background, interests and talents. The interactions or functional view of conflict is that it can be a positive force which helps effective performance and encourages creativity, and that far from diverting attention away from the aims of the organization, conflict ultimately generates more effective ways of achieving those aims.

Conflict can be interpersonal, intrapersonal, intragroup or intergroup. Interpersonal conflict (personality clash) is difficult to anticipate in a formal organizational sense, and requires sensitive handling by managers. Intrapersonal conflict – cognitive dissonance, for example (Festinger 1957) – involves the individual and is often resolved internally without management intervention. Intragroup and intergroup conflicts are probably the main causes for managerial concern, and the types of conflict which are at once the most difficult to resolve, and the most productive in terms of creative solutions.

No two groups in an organization can truly exist independently, and this provides conditions for interdependency. This in turn implies that there is something of interest between parties as one department depends on another for resources, work or information. Interdependency can be pooled, sequential or reciprocal; these are given in order of increasing chance of conflicting circumstances (Hellreigel et al. 1995; Gibson et al. 1995; Luthan 1995; Robbins and Coulter 1996). Pooled interdependency occurs when groups rely on each other only because they belong to the same parent organization, thus requiring no interaction among groups except through the total organization. The potential for conflict in these circumstances is relatively low.

Sequential interdependency means that one group relies on the prior activities of another group in order to complete its own task. Although the potential for conflict is higher, it is common for one group to exercise greater power in the relationship and therefore conflict is resolved quickly. Reciprocal interdependency means that two groups must interact repeatedly in the course of completing each others' tasks, and this maximizes the opportunities for conflict to arise. Since the groups are usually roughly equal in the power relationship, the conflicts are difficult to resolve, but are likely to lead to creative solutions.

Interdependency can be seen as an open social system (Ruekert and Walker 1987). There have been many applications of systems theory (Katz and Kahn 1978; Gillette and McCollom 1990; Tyson and Jackson 1992) and all draw upon the same analogy of organizations being like biological organisms, receiving inputs and exchanging energy in the form of new resources and transforming it into new outputs. Tyson and Jackson (1992) believe the relationship between the parts is built on feedback loops and the output from one subsystem being the input to another. The importance of linkages between subsystems (individual employees, work teams, departments and management groups) and systems is highlighted, emphasizing that a breakdown in one part may lead to a collapse of the whole system. The concept of inputs, throughputs and outputs has been used by several authors to explain interdepartmental conflict (Hutt 1995; Menon et al. 1997; Calantone et al. 1993; Clare and Sanford 1984; Crittenden et al. 1993; Menon et al. 1996; Achrol 1997; Souder 1981). The level at which departments are interconnected depend on resource dependency (the need to obtain resources from other departments in order to perform activities), and domain similarity (where different units share the same goals) (Tsui 1990).

Boundaries and barriers affect the process of interaction; observable group boundaries (physical, spatial and temporal) differentiate one group from another (Gillette and McCollom 1990). Subjective group boundaries are the psycho-social boundaries of the group's functional identity (Dutton and Jackson 1987). Turf barriers protect functional territory from invasion by others, interpretive barriers inhibit understanding of issues due to the different thought worlds of functional units, and communication barriers exist when group members misinterpret and distort information due to coding scheme errors (Hutt 1995).

Successful interactions depend on the ability to permeate these barriers; this can come via formal rules and procedures (Menon et al. 1996) or by informal influences (Ruekert and Walker 1987).

CASE STUDY: HILTON HOTELS

www.hiltonworldwide.com

The concept of process innovation follows on from business re-engineering, the favourite concept of management gurus in the early 90s. Business re-engineering means re-examining the firm's structures and finding ways of making them operate more smoothly and efficiently – unfortunately, most re-engineering delivers no measurable benefits whatever, with four out of five re-engineering exercises failing to result in any measurable improvements. The concept of process innovation seeks to overcome this problem by encouraging innovative approaches at grass-roots level. Rather than restructuring the whole business (re-engineering), process innovation examines the processes involved at each stage of delivery, and seeks innovative ways of improving them.

Hilton International took the approach of setting up an 'innovation hub' staffed by some of its most creative brains from within the organization. The innovation hub operates as a think-tank, tasked with coming up with new ideas for running the organization. Hilton recruited futurologists, designers, architects and technologists to join the hub, seeking out people who could communicate effectively and who could apply a fresh approach to the way Hilton operates. The team were given psychometric analysis and communication training, with the aim of enabling them to work better as a team: they were encouraged to identify themselves as part of the innovation hub, rather than as representatives of their departments within the organization. The intention was to create a group that would look outwards towards customers, and would work on behalf of the company as a whole rather than look inwards to their own departmental roles and their career paths within that department.

They were faced with a difficult task. Hilton had been losing ground steadily as its product ceased to be clearly differentiated from any of a dozen business-class hotel chains. Guests had moved in as individuals, so that customer loyalty was no longer working for Hilton: other hotels offered facilities which were as good or better, and Hilton was losing market share.

The innovation hub began by thinking the unthinkable. They created business hotel rooms based around lifestyles, using four themes. The themes were technology, inner calm, business effectiveness and relaxation. These concepts were tested on hotel guests and on hotel staff and managers: the new rooms allow greater flexibility in responding to guests' needs and remove the standardized, one-size-fits-all approach of the vast majority of business hotels worldwide.

The hub is looking for other processes to innovate: they are open for business, solving problems that departments send to them, or by observing competitors and adapting (not copying) good ideas ▶

from them. The hub also acts as a sounding-board for ideas from Hilton's partner organizations, assessing the merit of good ideas. This has reduced the tendency for good ideas to be lost simply because the partner organization approached the wrong people at Hilton.

The innovation hub has proved to be a fast way for the previously unchangeable Hilton empire to move forward into the 21st century. Further innovations might be expected to stream forth from the group – leaving other hotel chains to flounder in the wake of Hilton's success.

CASE STUDY QUESTIONS

1. What potential for conflict might there be in Hilton's approach?
2. Which came first for Hilton – strategy or structure?
3. What barriers to change might there be as a result of the innovation hub's existence?
4. How might process re-engineering help Hilton to develop competitive advantage?
5. How does accountability feature in the innovation hub's activities?

SUMMARY

Implementing strategy is not always easy because of the vested interests involved within most organizations. Conflict is almost inevitable, but conflict is not necessarily a bad thing. It often leads to creative solutions and, handled correctly, can be a lever for change rather than a barrier to it.

Here are the key points from this chapter.

■ Tactics need to include a specific action, accountability, deadlines, and a budget in order to be successfully implemented.

■ Strategy and structure are mutually dependent: they are like the chicken and the egg, with no way of saying which comes first.

■ Tinkering with the structure is usually not an optimum solution.

■ In hierarchical organizations, change is always unsettling and often leads to claims of bullying.

■ Organismic structures work better in unstable environments.

■ Conflict can lead to creative solutions: it is not always a bad thing.

CHAPTER QUESTIONS

1. What effect might conflict management have on the accountability issue?
2. What might be the effects of sequential dependency in an organismic organization?
3. How might conflict resolution theory be useful in re-organizing a hierarchical organization?
4. Why is it that very large organizations such as multinationals are able to operate as hierarchies, whereas smaller organizations tend to be organismic?
5. If strategy comes from structure, how can change strategies come from hierarchies?

REFERENCES

Achrol, R.S. (1997): 'Changes in the Theory of Interorganisational Relations in Marketing: Toward a Network Paradigm', *Journal of the Academy of Marketing Science* vol. 25, no. 1, pp. 56–71.

Alexander, L.D. (1985): 'Successfully implementing strategic decisions', *Long Range Planning* 18(3).

Calantone, R.J., Benedetto, C.A. and Divine, R. (1993): 'Organizational, Technical and Marketing Antecedents for Successful New Product Development', *Research and Development Management* vol. 23, no. 4, pp. 337–351.

Clare, D.A. and Sanford, D.G. (1984): 'Co-operation and Conflict Between Industrial Sales and Production', *Industrial Marketing Management* vol. 13, pp. 163–169.

Crittenden, V.L., Gardiner, L.R. and Stam, A. (1993): 'Reducing Conflict between Marketing and Manufacturing', *Industrial Marketing Management* vol. 22, pp. 299–309.

Daft, R.L. (1998): *Organisation Theory and Design* 6th edition (Ohio: South Western College Publishing).

Dutton, J.E. and Jackson, S.E. (1987): 'Categorizing strategic issues: links to organizational action', *Academy of Management Review* vol. 12, no. 1, pp. 76–90.

Festinger, L. (1957): *A Theory of Cognitive Dissonance* (Stanford CA: Stanford University Press).

Gibson, J.L., Ivancovic, J.M. and Donnelly, J.H. Jr. (1995): *Organisations; Behaviour, Structure, Processes* 8th edition (Homewood III: Richard D. Irwin).

Gillette, J. and McCollom, M. (1990): *Groups in Context: A New Perspective on Group Dynamics* (London: Addison-Wesley).

Hatch, M.J. (1997): *Organisation Theory – Modern Symbolic and Postmodern Perspectives* (Oxford: University Press).

Hellreigel, D. and Slocum, J.W. Jr. (1988): *Management* 5th edition (London: Addison-Wesley).

Hellreigel, D. and Slocum, J.W. Jr. and Woodman, R.W. (1995): *Organizational Behaviour* 6th edition. (New York: West Publishing).

Hodge, B.J. and Anthony, W.P. (1991): *Organization Theory – A Strategic Approach* 4th Edition (London: Allyn and Bacon).

Hutt, M.D. (1995): 'Cross-Functional Working Relationships in Marketing', *Journal of the Academy of Marketing Science* vol. 23, no. 4, pp. 352–357.

Katz, D. and Kahn, R.L. (1978): *The Social Psychology of Organisations* (London: John Wiley and Sons).

Luthan, F. (1995): *Organisational Behaviour* 7th edition (London: McGraw Hill).

Menon, A., Bharadway, S.G. and Howell, R. (1996): 'The Quality and Effectiveness of Marketing Strategy: Effects of Functional and Dysfunctional Conflict in Interorganizational Relationships'. *Journal of the Academy of Marketing Science* vol. 24, no. 4, pp. 299–313.

Menon, A., Jaworski, B.J. and Kohli, A.K. (1997): 'Product Quality: Impact of Interdepartmental Interactions'. *Journal of the Academy of Marketing Science* vol. 25, no. 3, pp. 187–200.

Reitz, H.J. (1977): *Behaviour in Organisations* (Homewood III: Richard D. Irwin Inc.).

Robbins, S.P. (1991): *Organisational Behaviour – Concepts, Controversies and Applications* 5th edition (London: Prentice-Hall).

Robbins, S.P. and Coulter, M. (1996): *Management* 5th edition (London: Prentice-Hall).

Ruekert, Robert W. and Walker, Orville C. Jr. (1987): 'Marketing's Interaction with Other Functional Units: A Conceptual Framework and Empirical Evidence', *Journal of Marketing* vol. 51, January pp. 1–19.

Souder, W.E. (1981): 'Disharmony between R&D and Marketing', *Industrial Marketing Management* vol. 10, pp. 67–73.

Tsui, A.S. (1990): 'Multiple-consistency model of effectiveness: An empirical examination at the human resource subunit level', *Administrative Science Quarterly*, no. 35, pp. 458–483.

Tyson, S. and Jackson, T. (1992): *The Essence of Organisational Behaviour* (London: Prentice-Hall).

Chapter Sixteen

The Future of Marketing Strategy

INTRODUCTION

For obvious reasons it is always difficult to write about the future. Firstly, predicting the future is not always easy; secondly, the future has a habit of happening while the writer is still writing.

Having said that, this chapter is intended to introduce some of the ideas which are current in marketing and corporate strategy, with an examination of some of the implications for planning.

After reading this chapter, you should be able to:

- Explain how postmodernism is affecting marketing strategy.
- Explain the four main schools of thought on corporate strategy.
- Describe the effects on national policy of adopting each of these schools of thought.
- Describe the main features of value-based strategy.
- Explain how value-based strategy affects marketing thinking.

POSTMODERNISM

Postmodernism is a school of philosophy which has aroused considerable interest in marketing circles. The philosophy is intended to replace the modernist school, which believes that the world is progressing towards something, that there are objective truths and laws which can be discovered, and that the world can be divided into convenient areas for study.

Postmodernism, on the other hand, holds that the concept of progression is not applicable to the world, that there are probably not any universal truths to be discovered, and that the distinctions between different areas of study are blurred. Postmodernism has the characteristics shown in Table 16.1.

Table 16.1: Features of postmodernism.

Feature	Explanation
Pastiche	Most human activities are composed of elements of many disciplines, and are usually made up of previously-known elements. Nothing is new: everything has already been written and we are merely recombining old ideas in different ways.
Fragmentation	There is an omnipresence of disjointed moments and experiences in life and sense of self. The world is dynamic, and therefore people cannot be permanently assigned to groups: people shift attitudes, behaviour and intentions too frequently. In other words, life is not a coherent dialogue but is rather a series of sound bites.
Hyperreality	There is a constitution of social reality through hype or simulation, and this is powerfully signified and represented. There is a confusion of the borders between reality and simulation (Baudrillard 1983).
Chronology	Time is often reversed: the latest model might be based on an old design (e.g. the Chrysler PSV), or the latest fashion in design becomes futuristic. Much depends on era: in the 50s and 60s design fashions were futuristic, whereas in the early 21st century the fashions are retro. The world is not progressing towards anything: everything happens in the 'now'.
De-differentiation	The differences between aspects of society are gradually being eroded. The distinction between chemistry and physics, between art and science, between music and the written word, are all broken down in the postmodern view. In other words, there is a blurring of boundaries.
Reversal of consumption and production	The current cultural assumption is that we define ourselves by what we consume, not by what we produce. Production is low in importance, consumption is high in importance.
Anti-foundationalism	This is also described as anti-authoritarianism. Established rules and models are seen as suitable targets for attack, lampoon and satire.
Pluralism	The acceptance of difference in styles and culture without making judgements about superiority or inferiority. This has become a feature of western societies, growing out of the hippy movement of the late 1960s and early 1970s.
Acceptance of disorder and chaos	Unlike modernists, postmodernists accept that chaos is a natural concomitant of change. It is therefore the natural order of things, the common state of existence. Modernists seek to create order out of chaos: postmodernists see this as futile.
Emphasis on form and style rather than content	Meaning is determined by the form rather than the content. An academic paper may contain the same information as a novel, but the message to the reader is different, and the values conveyed are vastly different.

Postmodernism is in part an explanation of how the world currently operates, and partly a set of recommendations for how we should behave, and therefore how the world should operate. The philosophy itself is complex, and even postmodernists disagree about its content – in fact many of them now deny being postmodernists at all, which rather complicates the picture for the rest of us. Stephen Brown (2000) regards marketing as archetypally postmodern, and recent marketing thinking seems to give credence to this.

There is, of course, plenty of evidence in favour of the postmodernists' view. Many of the most popular products available are retro – and the boundaries have certainly become blurred in the arts. Within marketing itself, the difference between promotion and product is often blurred, and even the difference between the consumer and the product.

For example, consider a nightclub. The nightclub provides a service to single people, who are able to use the venue as a meeting place. However, the venue would have no future if only a few people turned up – and could not function at all if only one gender turned up. The main purpose of going to a nightclub is not to listen to the music or dance, but to meet members of the opposite sex: in this sense the consumers also become the product. Nightclubs need to ensure at least an approximately even mix of the genders, and also a reasonable mix in terms of attractiveness: that is why the bouncers check the appearance of those coming in.

In a negative sense, boisterous or violent customers in a restaurant will adversely affect the enjoyment of the other diners: equally, a restaurant which is known to attract a famous clientele is able to charge premium prices.

Generation X has shown that consumers are becoming marketing-literate, and are not prepared to be manipulated: the 'I am not a target market' attitude is spreading. People have lives rather than lifestyles, and resist being segmented: membership of a given segment at a particular point in one's life is not likely to mean that membership of that segment will continue. This is evidence for the fragmentation described by postmodernists.

Hyperreality can almost be considered as the entire basis of marketing communications. Advertising slogans almost invariably go beyond reality – 'whiter than white' being a classic example. More recently, Rowntree's Fruit Pastilles (**www.nestle.com**) claim to 'take you beyond fruit', and the Renault Scenic (**www.renault.com**) apparently causes severe hallucinations for the driver as the car moves through impossible landscapes. However, hyperreality also appears in other areas of marketing – the virtual price war which retailers have been conducting for many years now being an example.

Chronology also becomes confused in advertising, with ads based on nostalgia appearing next to ads based on futuristic themes. In each case, the product being advertised is likely to bear no relationship to what was, or will be, consumed: Hovis (**www.rankhovis.co.uk**) bread is a prime example. Although it is advertised as being 'as good now as it's always been' the original product was baked in local bakeries using specially-provided Hovis baking tins and wheat flour supplied from the brand owner. The modern product is sliced, baked in a factory production line, and plastic-wrapped. A non-existent past is being re-invented to suit the needs of the present.

Anti-foundationalism is reflected as a lack of respect for previous thinking. Modernists believe in building on the foundations of past discoveries in order to inform the present and clarify the future. In postmodern times, old-fashioned thinking is suspect, and critique of the ideas of the past is the norm.

Pluralism and tolerance are regarded as high ideals in modern society, yet tolerance for outdated ideas is not. Also, tolerance must surely have limits – should we tolerate criminal behaviour because the criminal is able to justify it in his own eyes? Yet postmodern society often seeks to do exactly this.

Acceptance of disorder manifests itself in the belief that we live in times of constant change. This may be true, but how sure are we that the same conditions did not apply in the past? The rapid change in 19th century Britain brought about by the industrial revolution must surely have seemed as cataclysmic as the changes brought about by the information revolution of the late 20th century. It is the acceptance that disorder is the norm, and not merely some passing phase that we are able to overcome, that is the essence of postmodern thought.

Finally, the emphasis on form and style is apparent in the marketing of many products. Few teenagers care what the performance characteristics of their trainers are – their interest lies in wearing the right logo.

Postmodernists are trying to explain the problem that marketing is failing to fulfil its early promise. During the 50s and 60s, it was thought that adopting a marketing philosophy would automatically lead to business success. This has not turned out to be the case: many marketing-orientated firms have failed, while others which lack the marketing concept seem to have succeeded well. This may not mean that customer orientation is dead: it may simply mean that marketers need to rethink the problem.

Some of the implications for strategy are as shown in Table 16.2.

Table 16.2: Postmodernism and strategy

Feature of Postmodernism	Implications for Marketing Strategy
Pastiche	Postmodernists would use existing knowledge and attitudes within the organization to develop a strategy. This is, of course, what happens in most organizations, lending further support to the postmodern view of society.
Fragmentation	If society is indeed fragmenting, then segmentation strategy becomes problematical. Segmentation is predicated by mass-production drivers, but in fact it may not be feasible to segment reliably. The organization is unlikely to be able to develop long-term relationships with individuals, since the consumption behaviour exists only as a fragmentary experience. This may explain why relationship marketing has not been very successful in consumer markets.
Hyperreality	If the world is hyperreal, corporate visions may also be hyperreal. Interestingly, the most hyperreal strategies of all are those represented by the dot.com companies, some of which have been valued by shareholders at amounts well beyond the values of more substantial companies with real assets, without ever having shown a profit.
Chronology	If all that exists is the now, then the corporate strategy which seeks to build for the future is unrealistic. Postmodernism implies an adherence to the ad-hocracy familiar in some organizations. In organismic organizations, this may be a perfectly acceptable and realistic way forward – the chaos becomes the strategy.
De-differentiation	The distinction between strategy and tactics is already seriously blurred, as is the difference between planning and action – sometimes actions are undertaken then justified afterwards. Postmodernism accounts for this phenomenon effectively.
Reversal of consumption and production	If consumers define themselves by what they consume, this has implications for advertising strategy in term of modelling products. There may also be implications in staffing and motivation policies.
Anti-foundationalism	A tendency to criticise the past is probably healthy in terms of strategic planning, but care should be taken not to dismiss earlier policies simply because they represent earlier thinking.
Pluralism	Pluralism has profound implications for marketing strategy in that stereotypes are unlikely to be helpful in determining product use. As an obvious example, an assumption that only Indian people enjoy curry would be ridiculous in modern (or postmodern) Britain: one should be careful not to make similar assumptions in less obvious contexts.
Acceptance of disorder and chaos	Acceptance of disorder is a healthy attitude for organismic organizations, but is of course the death knell for hierarchies. If disorder is acceptable to staff, though, the strategy need not be rigid, and should not be overly-prescriptive.
Emphasis on form and style rather than content	This is clearly the case for many mission statements, which use flowery rhetoric with little substance behind it. In some cases, the corporate vision should be expressed in such hyperreal tones: this gives the something to aim for rather than something which is laid down as an expected outcome.

Postmodernism is a way of looking at the world, and should not be taken as proven fact. Postmodernists would hotly deny that it is possible to take anything as proven fact within a social context in any case: and the very attempt to subdivide the philosophy into a set of parameters and features is itself incurably modernist. If the postmodernists are right, and current society does exhibit a desire to experience the moment and live in the present (Firat and Schultz 1997), the implication is that strategic planning is really a total waste of time. If so, the implications are far-reaching indeed (another modernist assumption).

In fact there is considerable evidence for a postmodernist approach in the way that modern enterprises are run. Boundaries between divisions are breaking down, and senior managers are expected to have considerable expertise outside their own professional specialism. Marketers are expected to understand accountancy and financial reporting, HRM specialists are expected to take account of marketing issues, and financial experts are expected to understand engineering issues. Hierarchical organizations are giving way to flatter structures with fewer formal barriers to communication and greater cross-fertilization between departments. Strategy is no longer separate from operations, nor are tactics divorced from strategic planning.

Although postmodernism seems like a recipe for chaos, it is instead an acknowledgement that the world is inherently chaotic. The chaos is caused by the very large number of variables involved, and the implied impossibility of taking account of every factor which might impinge on the organization. In practice, of course, it is fairly easy to predict some factors in modern life. We can predict with reasonable certainty how people will respond to a given advertising campaign, we can predict fairly accurately what sales will be over the forthcoming year, and we can estimate the potential return on investment which will arise from a proposed new venture. What we cannot do is predict these things with 100 per cent accuracy.

VALUE-BASED MARKETING

Value-based marketing is the almost single-handed creation of Peter Doyle (2000). Starting from the premise that the central task of management is to maximize shareholder value, the theory goes on to look at how this affects marketing thinking and action.

Maximizing shareholder value is not the same as maximizing profits. Maximizing profits is often a short-term, tactical process involving cutting costs, reducing investment, downsizing, increasing sales volumes at the expense of long-term customer loyalty, and so forth. Shareholder value is about creating a long-term, secure, and growing investment. Increased sophistication among investors has led them to look for long-term growth prospects rather than short-term profits. The risk of speculating in firms with spectacular profits but little underlying substance has become well-known, and city analysts look more and more towards using measures such as customer loyalty, brand awareness, and investment levels in judging whether stocks are likely to increase in value in the long term. Because speculation is so dangerous, investors look for stocks which they will own for the long term.

Unfortunately for the investors, the shifting global marketplace means that companies do not survive long. The life expectancy of a firm is now less than 20 years (De Geus 1997). Maintaining a profitable competitive advantage is likely to be even more elusive: as soon as it becomes apparent that a firm has found a profitable niche, competitors enter the market and profits are rapidly eroded until they reach the point where the company is unable to maintain an adequate return on its original capital investment (Black et al. 1998).

Obviously some companies are exceptions to this general trend. Large, well-established firms seem able to maintain their shareholder value year after year, using profits to increase capital value rather than pay dividends. Such blue-chip companies are regarded as safe investments because they maintain steady growth, even if the dividends are unexciting. In fact, for some investors a small dividend is a sign that the company is re-investing profits rather than distributing them imprudently. Even such companies are not immune from environmental shifts, and often the weight of their carefully-calculated strategic plans helps to bear them down. Recent examples include the Welsh water supplier, Hyder, which (despite being in an industry which is regarded as virtually bullet-proof) managed to become unprofitable and uncompetitive. The problems faced by Swissair (**www.swissair.com**) during 2001 are another example. When an airline gets to the point where planes are grounded because of unpaid fuel bills, matters have become serious. For marketers, the idea that the company exists to increase shareholder value may seem to fly in the face of the customer-orientated, high-service approach which has been advocated by marketing academics for the past 50 years. In fact, customer orientation does not necessarily mean that the company gives the customers everything they want: it does mean that the company ensures that customers are satisfied and loyal in order to maximize the long-term survival potential of the firm.

Because marketers have focused almost exclusively on the customers, while other (often more senior) managers have focused on the shareholders, marketing thinking has not realized its early promise, and has been met with suspicion at boardroom level. In fact, marketing can and will fulfil the objective of maximizing shareholder value once marketers accept that the customers and consumers are the means to an end rather than the end in themselves.

Doyle (2000) has offered an alternative definition of marketing which encompasses this view.

'Marketing is the management process that seeks to maximize returns to shareholders by developing and implementing strategies to build relationships of trust with high-value customers and to create a sustainable differential advantage.'

This definition has the advantage of removing profitability from the equation and substituting shareholder value. It also includes an oblique reference to the relationship marketing perspective. However, it is certainly not hard to imagine successful firms which do not bother to build long-term relationships, and which do very nicely from dealing with a large number of low-value customers. The point here is that loyalty is important for building shareholder value (hence the relationship marketing focus) and low-value customers tend not to be loyal.

Relationship marketing has also not fulfilled its early promise, except in business-to-business markets. Establishing relationships of trust is easier in an environment where the benefits are obvious to all concerned: in consumer markets the benefits are often obscured. Consumers do not necessarily want to establish a relationship with the companies which supply their needs, and many people are irritated by firms' attempts to move the relationship beyond the business level. Having said that, customer loyalty is likely to be much greater when the products exceed expectations, and the customer is delighted.

Growth is essential in a shareholder-driven company, because growth in the value of the shares (rather than the dividends) is what investors seek. Therefore it is the central factor in creating shareholder value. For marketers, this means an emphasis on two possible strategies: firstly, recruiting more customers, and secondly selling more to existing customers. In the past, transactional marketing has concentrated on the former, whereas relationship marketing focuses on the latter. It seems likely that both are necessary if the firm is to achieve the levels of growth shareholders require. In these conditions, the use of existing customers as recruiters for other customers becomes a desirable tactic, and thus the emphasis again shifts to delighting customers.

This does not necessarily mean offering customers more and more for less and less – that way lies bankruptcy. EasyJet manages to delight customers by offering a no-frills service (the core benefit of a flight being transportation from one location to another) while being less basic than customers expect. The seats are comfortable, the cabin staff cheerful and helpful, and the planes are modern and well-maintained. This is often rather more than the customers expected, considering the price they are paying to fly, but most airlines would regard this as a starting-point for adding value rather than an end in itself.

Much of the value that will be added to the shareholders' assets will be through growth in the brand value. This is the key area which marketers are able to influence. Increases in brand value reveal themselves in four ways, as shown in Table 16.3.

Table 16.3: Aspects of brand value

Aspect	Examples and explanation
Obtain higher prices	A well-known brand can command higher prices because it reduces risk for the consumers. Most major brands follow this approach to deriving value from the brand: Kellogg's (**www.kelloggs.com**), Heinz (**www.heinz.com**), and IBM (**www.ibm.com**) are all more expensive than their competitors, but justify this by offering a high-quality, reliable product.
Higher volume growth	By keeping prices competitive, a brand owner can increase the amount of business done. This is the approach taken by Dell (**www.dell.com**), EasyJet (**www.easyjet.com**), and McDonald's (**www.mcdonalds.com**).
Lower costs	If a brand achieves a large market share, many of the marketing costs are amortized across a larger production run. The marketing costs for a major brand may well be lower per unit of production than the costs for a less well-known brand.
Higher asset utilization	A major brand which follows a high-volume strategy will make better use of production assets. A brand which goes for a high-price strategy will generate greater returns on assets

The difference in orientation between aiming for an increase in shareholder value and aiming for an increase in customer satisfaction is a small one. It is really a difference in focus rather than a new philosophy altogether: a key focus for marketers is the twofold problem of how to increase the brand value, and how to cash in on the increased value in the long term. Simply harvesting profits is not the way forward – re-investing profits in further building of the brand, or in other ventures, is realistic and will increase shareholder value.

Possibly the most important of the tactical decisions that spring from this difference in perspective is that of deciding which brands to keep and which to drop. Previously this decision would have been made on the basis of the BCG Matrix or some similar tool, but under a value-adding regime the decision is more likely to be made on the basis of the growth potential for each brand rather than the current profitability or sales status. This may give different answers to those obtained from a BCG analysis.

Talking Point

If most firms are seeking shareholder value, why is it that so many talk about their employees and their customers in their mission statements? Do they think that paying lip service to customers and employees will divert attention away from their true purpose?

Alan Sugar once famously said 'We just want your money!' This refreshing honesty did not seem to hurt business at all – maybe customers and employees are accepting of such naked self-interest. So why not extend this to everything else we do? Why not have advertising which tells customers that we are providing the minimum we can get away with, for the highest price we think we can charge? Where do we draw the line on honesty?

DOES STRATEGY MATTER?

Richard Whittington's 2001 text 'What is strategy – and does it m€
approach of most strategic management texts (this one included). V
generic approaches to strategy, which are outlined in Table 16.4.

Table 16.4: Generic approaches to strategy

Approach	Explanation
Classical	Relies on rational planning methods, using environmental analysis as the basis for d€_ _.-making and planning for the long term.
Evolutionary	Assumes that only the fittest will survive. Correct strategies will result from adapting to the environment, and ad-hoc solutions are used in response to environmental pressures. Evolutionary strategic thought is about accommodating to the law of the jungle: long-term planning is therefore not feasible.
Processualist	Strategy accommodates to the fallible processes of both organizations and markets. Strategy is therefore a bottom-up process, coming from the exigencies of the situations faced by the firm.
Systemic	The ends and means of strategy are linked to the cultures and powers of the local social systems in which it takes place. Companies therefore follow policies which are predicated by their local social constraints rather than by strict business considerations.

The generic perspectives on strategy can be mapped against processes and outcomes, as shown
in Fig 16.1 below.

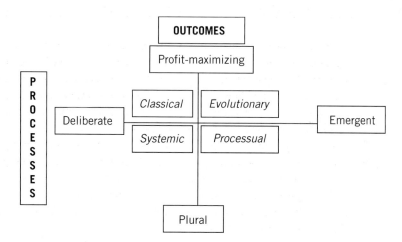

Figure 16.1: Generic perspectives on strategy

Each approach offers a different set of answers to what strategy is. Classicists say that strategy
is rational and consists of a set of deliberate calculations aimed at achieving a market position and
maintaining it in the face of opposition. It implies rationality, long-range focus, responses to
environmental shifts in a calculated manner, and so forth.

Evolutionists believe the environment is too unpredictable for long-range planning to have any
reasonable chance of success. For the evolutionists, it is the market not the managers which
makes the important choices, and firms are almost certainly unable to adapt quickly enough to
make much difference to their survival chances (Hannan and Freeman 1988, Williamson 1991).
Thus successful strategies only emerge as a result of ruthless natural selection, in which the firms

with inappropriate strategies go broke and the ones who happen to have hit on a strategy which meets the needs of the market go on to succeed.

For Processualists, the processes of organizations and markets are rarely perfect. This means that the market is not as implacable as the Evolutionists believe, nor is the firm able to plan as thoroughly as the Classicists would like. People are unable to be so precise and unvarying as to be able to carry through a detailed plan, particularly in the face of the difficulties and unforeseen circumstances which are bound to arise in an imperfect world. Therefore, firms develop strategy (or have it forced upon them) via a series of bodgings, ad-hoc decisions, compromises with reality, and learning by mistakes rather than by long-range planning and rationality (Mintzberg 1994). For the Processualist, failure to carry out the perfect marketing strategy is unlikely to prove fatal (although there may be some loss of ground).

Systemic theorists believe that people are capable of carrying out rational plans of action, and are also confident that it is possible to define strategies in the face of environmental forces. However, their view is that the objectives and practices of strategy are embedded in the social system to which they belong. This means, for example, that profit maximization is not necessarily a strong factor in strategic planning. This argument carries considerable weight in a world in which the non-profit organization and the 'fair trade' corporation are in the ascendant.

The Systemic perspective also finds support in the fact that firms within different social systems have differing strategic perspectives. German and Japanese businesses were restructured after the Second World War to engender close co-operation between banks and enterprises, and to operate within a paternalistic state structure which encouraged worker participation and universal social security. The Anglo-American business structure, meanwhile, operated in an environment of hostile takeovers, impatient lenders, adversarial labour relations and (frequently) governments committed to giving capitalism free rein.

In fact, all the generic philosophies of strategy have some facets which are evidenced in the real world. The business world is sufficiently complex to allow for a wide range of experiences and models. For example, some industries change very little over time: light-bulb manufacture has changed relatively little since the 19th century, nor has house-building, even though the technology has shifted somewhat in the meantime. This means that it is reasonable to develop long-term strategies for these industries, to take account of fairly predictable economic or environmental shifts. In other industries, such as the restaurant trade, conditions can change rapidly and unpredictably, so an Evolutionary paradigm prevails. Processualists find support for their arguments in those industries which are dominated by small firms, and in industries such as computer software where technological breakthroughs happen on an almost daily basis.

The differences between the generic strategies do matter, because they offer radically different recommendations for managers. For every manager, the strategy formulation process always begins with a decision as to which theoretical picture of the world best fits with his or her own experiences and attitudes. If the manager's view is that the world is orderly, with sufficient information and capacity to analyse, and sufficient availability of organizational control, then the Classical paradigm would be most likely to be adopted. If, on the other hand, the manager believes that the environment is cut-throat and unpredictable, the Evolutionist paradigm will prevail.

Some of the different contexts under which each strategic paradigm will succeed are shown in Fig 16.2.

The consequences for national policy are also manifold. The four generic strategies have a profound effect on national policy. For Classical strategists the national economic performance is rooted in individualism and rationalism. Evolutionary and Processual managers would be

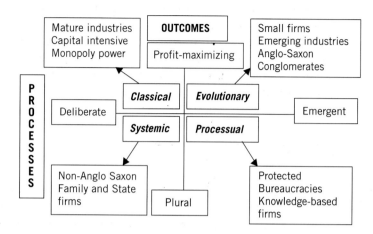

Figure 16.2: Contexts for strategy

sceptical of government intervention because the environment is viewed as being complex enough without 'artificial' interference from government. The view would be that the government might only act to spoil emergent successes. The Systemic manager's view is that government should make radical social and institutional change rather than tinker with the problem.

The Classical viewpoint is that economic success comes through becoming cleverer, and planning better: Baruch and Peiperl (1999) estimated that the UK economy needs approximately 75,000 MBA graduates per annum to replace managers who retire and to allow for some growth, compared with a total actual number of approximately 10,000 who graduate from business schools. Whittington (2001) claims that this under-investment in management education 'reinforces the characteristic shambolic and amateurish nature of British managerial elites'. Of course, other Master's programmes exist apart from MBAs: many more graduates have Master's degrees in accounting, in marketing, in human resources and so forth, but the picture still remains depressing for the Classicists.

Processualists view the situation completely differently. Mintzberg (1996) believes that top-down, deliberate programmes of change are dangerous and probably unworkable anyway, and has expressed the view that conventional MBA programmes should be shut down altogether. Processualists believe in bottom-up strategy development, with policy growing as a result of historical and cultural accident.

Evolutionary managers go further. Since they believe that markets and entrepreneurship control the outcomes of business enterprises, they tend to value the visionary high-flyer above the rational, calculating MBA graduate. Many of the risk-taking, high-earning entrepreneurs who run fast-growing and fast-changing organizations are unburdened by too much education. Not having been told that there is a right and a wrong way of doing things, they invent their own rules as they go along, often with highly-creative solutions as a result. Of course, it seems probable that most of these entrepreneurs either fail miserably or at best only ever scrape a living, but this is true of most of the animal kingdom, which vindicates the Evolutionist viewpoint.

Systemic theorists have yet another view of the route to economic growth. Since they believe that strategy develops from local social norms, they believe that the way forward is to establish clusters of firms in the same industry – examples include Silicon Valley and Hollywood, the engineering firms around Baden-Wurttemburg, and the motor-racing cluster in Oxfordshire. These clusters exist because of the reluctance of key employees to move far from home when changing jobs, so firms setting up in the same industry tend to move to where there is a suitably skilled workforce already available.

The result of this disagreement about the basic shape of the world is that there is really no clear consensus about what policy is best for national economic growth. Strategists will continue to argue about this for some time to come, and changes of government will only exacerbate the problem as policies shift towards one view or another. Ultimately, the complexity of business life is such that it is unlikely that a definitive answer will ever arise. the truth is different according to one's circumstances and perspective.

CASE STUDY: THAI UNION FROZEN PRODUCTS

Thiraphong Chansiri has reason to feel smug about his business. He inherited the tuna-canning company from his father in 1995, and now, at age 36, he finds himself presiding over one of the world's largest tuna-canning businesses. A combination of complying with the exacting requirements of foreign buyers, and going against the trend during the mid-90s, has resulted in a fortuitous mix of entrepreneurism and prudence which has proved to be a winning formula.

The first element in the company's success was its decision to cater for the niche religious markets. Its tuna products are certified kosher (a rabbi regularly inspects the plant to ensure compliance), are also certified halal (following inspections from Muslim clerics), and also meet the food hygiene regulations for the dozen or more countries in its export market. Furthermore, the tuna are certified dolphin-friendly, and the company's canned shrimp are certified turtle-friendly, thus meeting at least some of the environmental requirements of the company's First World customers.

Building on this ability to respond to the requirements of other cultures in its global market, Thai Union pulled off its greatest entrepreneurial coup in 1997, when it paid $323.5 m for a 50 per cent stake in Chicken of the Sea, the ailing US tuna company.

'The ultimate goal for everyone is to own a brand. You have a better control over your own destiny.' Thiraphong says. His belief in owning a brand was so strong that he bought out his partners in Chicken of the Sea for $38.5 m, thus establishing a 100 per cent ownership of the brand. No small achievement for a family business from the Third World – and a tribute to Thiraphong's financial prudence.

During the early 1990s capital markets in Thailand were liberated and most Thai firms rushed to borrow dollars to take advantage of low interest rates. This intemperate haste proved to be disastrous – when economic change hit Thailand in 1997, the collapse of the baht meant that companies were struggling to repay loans which had suddenly increased by 30 per cent or more. Low interest rates certainly could not compensate for this shock – and the conclusion of many Thai business people was that globalization represented a threat to Thailand. Some even saw the crisis as a foreign plot to take over the Thai economy.

However, Thai Union had resisted the urge to join the rush to borrow dollars. When the crisis hit, the company had virtually no foreign borrowings at all, and thus was well-placed to ride out the storm. Since the firm was already heavily into exporting, its revenues soared in local terms as the baht fell against the major world currencies – thus generating more cash for investment and expansion.

It has not all been plain sailing for Thai Union, however. Taking over Chicken of the Sea proved problematical, even though Thai Union knows the tuna business inside out. 'We never worked in the

▶

American environment', Thiraphong says. 'There are so many rules and regulations, so many laws. The cost of doing business there is very expensive.'

The investment has proved worthwhile, though. Market share of Chicken of the Sea has risen from 15 per cent in 1997 to 18 per cent in 2001, and Mr. Thiraphong expects to be able to increase this to 20 per cent within the next year. Costs have been cut by relocating the canning plant from California to American Samoa (in August 2001), saving $2.5 m per year. The share value rose by 49 per cent during 2001, against a general rise of 13 per cent, and in spite of the US recession.

Mr. Thiraphong is not ignoring his home market either – the company has introduced a range of canned tuna with added chilli to suit the Thai predilection for fiery foods. He is also looking to expand into China, but no firm plans have been formulated as yet. A confident, outward-looking attitude (as befits a man of 36) has resulted in a strong belief in the benefits of globalization – although he has harsh words for western countries. He is a supporter of free trade, but says that developed countries actually open up markets in which they are themselves strong – when he exports to the European Union, he faces a 24 per cent tariff barrier, whereas former european colonies in Africa and the Pacific are allowed to export to the EU duty-free. 'Developed countries only ask you to open markets where they are strong, like technology. Why don't they open for agricultural products?' he complains.

These setbacks do not seem to be affecting the company's vision, however. Mr. Thiraphong is not dismayed by the West's attitude – and it appears he is justified. After all, very few Thai companies can boast of owning an important American brand.

CASE STUDY QUESTIONS

1. To what extent does Mr. Thiraphong fit the pattern of the opportunistic entrepreneur?
2. Which of the four generic strategic approaches does Thai Union most closely resemble?
3. How is Thai Union adding value for its shareholders?
4. How might Thai Union improve its fit with the American market?
5. What were the key factors in Thai Union's successful acquisition of Chicken of the Sea? To what extent did luck play a part in the acquisition?

SUMMARY

Strategic thinking is itself a product of the social order within which it is generated. The strategic approaches of 50 or 100 years ago might carry some lessons for the present, but they are unlikely to be applicable in any wholesale, prescriptive manner. Strategy, like any other branch of thought, is in a constant state of re-examination and redevelopment. For the Modernists, this is a progression towards a perfect understanding of how the world works, for the Postmodernists it is a constant re-adaptation to a chaotic universe.

New perspectives such as the shareholder value orientation help to inform possible strategies and perhaps explain why previous strategies have been less than optimal. At the same time debate continues about what strategy is and how it should work in the real world.

The key points from this chapter are difficult to define, because of the nature of the debate. However, some of them may be as follows:

■ Postmodernism may be a better description of the world than Modernism: if so, strategic planning may be irrelevant.

▶
- Shareholder value may be a more realistic objective for firms to pursue, even if they do so via customer satisfaction.
- Classical strategic planning is not the only way forward, and may not even be the best in many industries.
- Evolutionary strategy assumes that many new enterprises will fail, with only the fittest surviving.
- Systemic strategists believe that strategy only occurs in the context of the social environment.
- Processualists believe that strategy is a bottom-up process, largely outside the control of managers, who simply react to outside forces.

CHAPTER QUESTIONS

1. How might the inherent contradictions of postmodernism be resolved in a practical marketing context?
2. What might replace classical strategic planning?
3. Evolution implies rapid mutation to cope with environmental shifts. How might firms ensure that they have the capability to mutate favourably?
4. If strategy appears as a result of employee activities, what is the role of senior management?
5. What is the role of a mission statement in a postmodern world?

REFERENCES

Baruch, Y. and Pieperl, M. (1999): 'The impact of an MBA on graduate careers', *Human Resource Management Journal* 10 (2) pp. 69–89.

Baudrillard, J. (1983): *Simulations* (New York: Semiotext(e)).

Black, Andrew, Wright, Philip, and Bachman, John E. (1998): *In Search of Shareholder Value* (London: Pitman).

Brown, S. (2000): *Postmodern Marketing* 2 (London, Thomson).

De Geus, Arie (1997): *The Living Company* (Boston MA: Harvard Business School Press).

Doyle, P. (2000): *Value-Based Marketing: Marketing Strategies for Corporate Growth and Shareholder Value* (London: Wiley).

Firat, A.F. and Schultz, C.J. (1997): 'From Segmentation to Fragmentation: Markets and Marketing Strategy in the Postmodern Era', *European Journal of Marketing* vol. 31, no. 3/4, pp. 183–207.

Hannan, M.T. and Freeman, J. (1988): *Organisational Ecology* (Cambridge MA: Harvard University Press).

Mintzberg, H. (1996): 'Learning 1, Planning 0', *California Management Review* 38 (4) pp. 92–94.

Mintzberg, H. (1994): *The Rise and Fall of Strategic Planning* (New York: Free Press).

Whittington, R. (2001): *What is strategy – and does it matter?* (London: Thomson).

Williamson, O.E. (1991): 'Strategising, economising and economic organisation', *Strategic Management Journal* 12: pp. 75–94.

Index

Education

Other Marketing Titles from McGraw-Hill Education

Principles and Practice of Marketing, 3rd Edition
Professor David Jobber, University of Bradford
ISBN: 0077096134

Principles and Practice of Marketing leads the field in European marketing texts. It presents a comprehensive, clear and contemporary introduction to the subject. Fully revised and updated with expanded coverage of Internet marketing, marketing ethics and relationship marketing, this text retains the straightforward student friendly approach that has helped to make it so successful.

Foundations of Marketing
Professor David Jobber, University of Bradford
Professor John Fahy, University of Limerick
ISBN: 0077098668

Foundations of Marketing is designed to provide a concise introduction to the fundamental principles and practices of marketing.

Ideally suited to the needs of short or one-semester marketing modules for students from all disciplines, the text begins by introducing fundamental concepts from the ground up, such as the marketing environment, customer behaviour and segmentation, and positioning. Offering a clear presentation of marketing mix decisions, the text then concludes with strategy and implementation topics.

Marketing spotlights, marketing-in-action and e-marketing boxes offer students the opportunity to consistently apply and evaluate the theories in the book. Up-to-date and interesting cases from a variety of real companies conclude each chapter, providing the framework in which to integrate and analyse key concepts in a real-world context.

The clear and straightforward style presents a solid grounding in the principle concepts of marketing. It pares down the subject to the foundation topics, whilst maintaining the rigour and authoritative insight of David Jobber's highly successful text *Principles and Practice of Marketing* 3rd Edition.

Retail Marketing, 2nd Edition
Peter McGoldrick, Professor of Retailing at Manchester School of Management, U.M.I.S.T
ISBN: 0077092503

Since its publication, the first edition of *Retail Marketing* has established itself as the leading and most authoritative textbook on the subject. This eagerly awaited major revision will confirm its reputation as the "essential" text for all courses in retail marketing.

The new edition, written for all serious students of retailing, focuses upon the basic functions and challenges of retail marketing management. The text retains the analytical and scientific approach to the strategies within retail marketing, but also emphasizes the vital role of flair and creativity. Current and emerging techniques are analysed, but no universal solutions are prescribed. The approach is to encourage students to develop their own frameworks and guidelines for the effective analysis of retailing problems.

This revised edition has been significantly expanded and restructured to assist students in their understanding of retail marketing today.

Marketing Research, 6th Edition
Peter Chisnall, Professor
ISBN: 0077097513

The new edition of this established and respected text provides a comprehensive yet concise introduction to the key concepts of marketing research. Fully revised and updated to take more of a qualitative approach in line with course trends, the statistical data has been reduced and computerized statistics packages (SPSS) have been introduced.

The rapid changes in computerized research have been taken on board, and new coverage of the Internet and email has been added to bring this edition completely up-to-date. Finally, a new 2-colour text design, new case material, and improved pedagogical features have been added to make this text more applied and student friendly.

Essentials of Marketing, 4th Edition
Geoff Lancaster, Professor in Marketing, University of North London
Lester Massingham, Chairman and Managing Director of CMC Consultants
Ruth Ashford, Lecturer, Manchester Metropolitan University and Senior CIM Examiner
ISBN: 0077098609

The new edition of *Essentials of Marketing* synthesizes contemporary marketing knowledge to present the fundamental principles that underpin any introductory marketing course, while retaining the core coverage of marketing perspectives, tools, and planning from the previous edition. This edition also meets the needs of students taking the CIM Marketing Fundamentals examination.

If you would more information about these titles, or any McGraw-Hill Education books, please contact:

Customer Services McGraw-Hill Education
Shoppenhangers Road
Maidenhead
Berkshire
SL6 2QL
UK

Tel: +44 (0) 1628 502700
Fax: +44 (0) 01628 770224

or visit our website at www.mcgraw-hill.co.uk